THE ASHGATE RESEARCH COMPANION
TO EXPERIMENTAL MUSIC

This fine collection of essays and interviews casts light on, through, and around the fabric of experimental music, woven as it is from threads first spun by John Cage in the 1950s. Whether tracing single lines or analyzing complex patterns, the authors—composers and performers, more than scholars—write with a clarity and focus that derives from decades of practical experience. Their work illuminates not only a half-century of invention but also the present and future of what has become, paradoxically, an experimental 'tradition'.

–William Brooks, University of York, UK

ASHGATE
RESEARCH
COMPANION

The *Ashgate Research Companions* are designed to offer scholars and graduate students a comprehensive and authoritative state-of-the-art review of current research in a particular area. The companion's editors bring together a team of respected and experienced experts to write chapters on the key issues in their speciality, providing a comprehensive reference to the field.

The Ashgate Research Companion to Experimental Music

Edited by

JAMES SAUNDERS

Bath Spa University, UK

ASHGATE

Published by
Ashgate Publishing Limited
Wey Court East
Union Road
Farnham
Surrey GU9 7PT
England

Ashgate Publishing Company
Suite 420
101 Cherry Street
Burlington,
VT 05401-4405
USA

www.ashgate.com

British Library Cataloguing in Publication Data
The Ashgate research companion to experimental music
   1. Avant-garde (Music)
   I. Saunders, James
   780.9'04

Library of Congress Cataloging-in-Publication Data
Saunders, James, 1972 Dec. 12–
   The Ashgate research companion to experimental music / James Saunders.
      p. cm.
   Includes bibliographical references and index.
   ISBN 978-0-7546-6282-2 (hardcover : alk. paper) 1. Music—20th century—
History and criticism. 2. Music—21st century—History and criticism.
   3. Avant-garde (Music) I. Title.

ML197.S232 2009
780.9'04—dc22

2009008714

ISBN 978-0-7546-6282-2

Reprinted 2010, 2012

Printed and bound in Great Britain by the
MPG Books Group, UK

Contents

Musical Examples

Notes on Contributors

Antoine Beuger was born in 1955 and studied composition with Ton de Leeuw in Amsterdam. In 1992, together with Burkhard Schlothauer, he founded Edition Wandelweiser, whose managing director he has been since 2004. In 1994 he started his now widely known concert series KLANGRAUM (Düsseldorf). Beuger's music has been performed worldwide and awarded several international prizes.

Laurence Crane was born in Oxford in 1961 and studied composition with Peter Nelson and Nigel Osborne at Nottingham University. His music is mainly written for the concert hall, although his list of works includes pieces written for film, radio, theatre, dance and installation. He lives and works in London.

Rhodri Davies has been engaged with improvised music for over ten years and is based in Newcastle-upon-Tyne. He plays harp, electric harp, live electronics and builds wind, water and fire harp installations. His regular groups include Branches, a duo with John Butcher, Broken Consort, Common Objects, Cranc, Portable, Apartment House, The Sealed Knot and a trio with David Toop and Lee Patterson. He also performs and researches contemporary music and has commissioned new works for the harp by Carole Finer, Catherine Kontz, Michael Parsons, Tim Parkinson, Ben Patterson, Mieko Shiomi and Yasunao Tone.

John Levack Drever is a lecturer in composition and head of the Unit for Sound Practice Research at Goldsmiths, University of London. He is a co-founder of the UK and Ireland Soundscape Community and chair of Sonic Arts Network. His work demonstrates an ongoing practice-based inquiry into environmental sound and human utterance.

Christopher Fox is a composer who also writes about new music. He studied music at Liverpool, Southampton and York universities. Since 2006 he has been Research Professor in Music at Brunel University; he lives in north London with his wife, his youngest daughter and a cat.

Bernhard Günter was born in 1957 in Irlich, Germany. In 1980 he moved to Paris to undertake auto-didactic studies of contemporary composition techniques. In 1986 he returned to Germany, and in 1987 began working on computer-based music. He released his influential first CD *Un Peu de Neige Salie* in 1993, and in 1995 founded CD-label trente oiseaux. He has since released numerous CDs and performed around the globe. He lives and works in Koblenz, Germany.

Bryn Harrison studied composition with Gavin Bryars at De Montfort University. His music has been widely performed and broadcast internationally following commissions for ensembles such as Klangforum Wien, London Sinfonietta, Ensemble Recherche and the LSO. He holds a PhD from the University of Huddersfield where he is Head of Composition.

Philip Jeck studied visual arts at Dartington College in the 1970s and has been creating sound with record players since the early 1980s. He has worked with many dance and theatre companies and played with musicians such as Jah Wobble, Gavin Bryars and Steve Lacy. He has released eight solo CDs and the about to be released *Suite* on vinyl only. His largest work, made with Lol Sargent, *Vinyl Requiem*, for 180 record players, slide projectors and 16 mm film, received The Time Out Performance Award. *Vinyl Coda I–III*, a commission from Bavarian Radio, won The Karl Sczuka Foderpries for Radio Art. He also still works as a visual artist having shown works at the Hayward Gallery, the Hamburger Bahnhof Gallery, Berlin and at the Shanghai Bienalle.

Andy Keep is a senior lecturer at Bath Spa University, UK. He is also a performer of live electronics (with a keen focus on the intrinsic sonic palette of electronic feedback), devised and directs Bath Spa's large-scale Behaviour ensemble, and was a former director of the Sonic Arts Network.

Ron Kuivila composes music and creates sound installations that revolve around the unusual home-made and home-modified electronic instruments he designs. He is an Adjunct Professor of Music at Wesleyan University. He was a fellow of the DAAD Artist in Berlin programme and an artist in residence at the Institute for Studies in the Arts at Arizona State University, California Institute of the Arts, the Banff Centre for the Arts, Tempo Reale and STEIM.

Alvin Lucier was born in 1931 in Nashua, New Hampshire. He studied at Yale and Brandeis and spent two years in Rome on a Fulbright Scholarship. Since 1970 he has taught at Wesleyan University where he is John Spencer Camp Professor of Music. Lucier has pioneered in many areas of music composition and performance, including the notation of performers' physical gestures, the use of brain waves in live performance, the generation of visual imagery by sound in vibrating media and the evocation of room acoustics for musical purposes.

Will Montgomery is RCUK research fellow in contemporary poetry and poetics at Royal Holloway, University of London. He is working on a book on the American poet Susan Howe and co-editing a collection of essays on Frank O'Hara. He makes electronic music and he has written as a journalist about experimental music for *Wire* magazine since the early 1990s.

Phill Niblock is an intermedia artist using music, film, photography, video and computers. Since 1985 he has been the director of the Experimental Intermedia Foundation in New York where he has been an artist/member since 1968. He is a retired professor at The College of Staten Island, the City University of New York.

Evan Parker is a saxophonist who has been part of many seminal free improvisation groups including Spontaneous Music Ensemble, Music Improvisation Company, his duo/trio with Paul Lytton/Barry Guy and the Evan Parker Electro-acoustic Ensemble, as well as working extensively as a soloist.

Tim Parkinson is an independent composer. He is also a pianist and performer, and has curated many concerts in the UK and abroad. He is a founding co-curator of the annual London-based concert series Music We'd Like to Hear. He studied at Oxford University, and then privately with Kevin Volans.

Michael Pisaro is a composer and guitarist, and founder and director of the Experimental Music Workshop. His music and several CDs have been published by Edition Wandelweiser (Germany). He is Co-Chair of Music Composition at the California Institute of the Arts near Los Angeles.

Edwin Prévost was co-founder in 1965 of seminal improvising ensemble AMM. He has also worked with numerous free-jazz and improvising musicians, as well as with musicians from other cultures. He has performed in the techno-ambient field and plays 'open-ended' compositions. During 1998 he made music for the Merce Cunningham Dance Company during their London season. He occasionally lectures on music, and as a writer has published the books *No Sound is Innocent* (1995), *Minute Particulars* (2004), and edited *Cornelius Cardew: A Reader* (2006). Since 1999 Prévost has convened a weekly improvisation workshop in London which has been attended by close to three hundred musicians.

David Ryan is an artist and writer based in London and Cambridge, who is also actively involved in contemporary music. He has been engaged with numerous exhibitions, concert organization, performance and audio-visual collaborations in the UK and abroad. Currently he is Reader in Fine Art at Anglia Ruskin University, Cambridge.

James Saunders is a composer, with an interest in modularity and series. He performs in the duo Parkinson Saunders, and with Apartment House. He is Head of the Centre for Musical Research at Bath Spa University, currently working on the composition and performance practice of text notation, and directs the ensemble Material.

Philip Thomas specializes in performing experimental notated and improvised music as a soloist and with leading experimental music group Apartment House. Recent solo projects have included surveys of the piano music of Christian Wolff, and concerts of music composed by improvising musicians. He is currently Senior Lecturer in Performance at the University of Huddersfield.

Jennifer Walshe was born in Dublin in 1974. She received a DM in Composition from Northwestern University in 2002. Her works have been performed by many ensembles and broadcast all over the world. She has been the recipient of many awards and fellowships. Walshe frequently performs as a vocalist, specializing in extended techniques.

Manfred Werder was born in 1965 and is a composer, pianist and performer, and curator. He lives in Zürich and is a member of Edition Wandelweiser. His work actualizes time and space by letting the world's natural abundance appear. His recent CD releases include *ein(e) ausführende(r) seiten 218–226* (EWR 0601) and *2006[1]* (skiti 01).

Christian Wolff, born 1934, in Nice, France, is a composer, teacher and sometime performer, and has lived in the USA since 1941. He studied piano with Grete Sultan. Since 1950 he has been associated with John Cage, also Morton Feldman, David Tudor, Earle Brown and Merce Cunningham, later with Cornelius Cardew and Frederic Rzewski. As an improviser he has worked with Christian Marclay, Takehisa Kosugi, Steve Lacy, Larry Polansky, Kui Dong and AMM. He taught classics at Harvard, and from 1971 to 1999, classics, comparative literature and music at Dartmouth College.

Foreword

A few years ago the French writer, critic and broadcaster Daniel Caux, who died in the summer of 2008, said that there had been three major new musical developments since the Second World War. By this he meant the appearance of radical changes of musical sensibility which had not been present earlier, nor which could be said to have evolved naturally from existing musical modes. He listed them as (i) the music of John Cage, (ii) American minimal music and (iii) English experimental music. The first two in his list are not surprising. Few would deny the overwhelming importance of the work of Cage – for me the major musical figure of the twentieth century – and there seems to be little obvious musical ancestry to his work. The appearance of 'minimal' music in the late 1960s was equally startling even if it is possible to locate its roots in the work and teaching of Cage, especially through the attendance of La Monte Young at Cage's classes at the New School for Social Research in 1958. (En passant it is worth, perhaps, noting that composer James Tenney felt that La Monte Young was the only 'minimal' composer – the others producing what he termed 'pulse-pattern music').

With English experimental music, however, the family tree is less clear, though it too can be shown to come indirectly from Cage. One source is clearly Cornelius Cardew, and the seeds of a new and peculiarly English music may be traced to his encounter with Cage and David Tudor in Germany in 1958, at the time that he was working as assistant to Karlheinz Stockhausen. Another source is the pianist John Tilbury who had studied in Warsaw. Both were aware of the music of the European avant-garde but were also alert to the lesser-known new music emerging in New York (Cage, Feldman, Wolff and La Monte Young).

When the two of them worked together in the mid-1960s they were proselytizing a range of new musics that covered more than Europe. Cornelius would talk about La Monte Young, for example, and write articles in the *Musical Times*, while John Tilbury was performing Cornelius, Cage, Feldman and Christian Wolff – later Terry Riley and other things of that kind. People like myself, Christopher Hobbs and John White appeared a little later and, while we looked up to Cornelius and John, they were like colleagues, not gurus. But Cardew did have a kind of magnetism – people were drawn to him and a lot of collective music-making happened through him – and it is a sign of his powerful influence that many who emerged to compose in the late 1960s disappeared when Cornelius abandoned his experimental position a few years later.

A very important element is the relationship with the visual arts and the role of the art schools of the period. Many experimental musicians found a supportive environment in art schools at a time when university music departments, conservatoires and music colleges – much more conservative then – were not really interested in employing this kind of musician. And at the same time there was a conceptual alertness in the world of fine art that was singularly absent in contemporary music, as well as an openness to the question of what might actually count as 'music'. After writing the first two paragraphs of *The Great Learning*, for example, Cornelius realized that what he needed for a work of this kind (and indeed for most graphically notated scores and text compositions) was a mixture of trained and untrained performers who were open to reading notational systems that were not conventional. The ideal performer was someone who retained a high degree of musical innocence yet at the same time was capable of being stimulated by visual and textual notations. And it was clear that such people were more likely to be located in the art school.

People there, staff and students, were game to try out some kind of performance – the whole area of performance within the fine arts, with Fluxus and so on, was already there. Some had rudimentary musical skills but all, of course, could read English and also interpret graphics in an imaginative way. One of the chief protagonists of Fluxus, George Brecht, lived in London at that time and collaborated on many performances. His *Water Yam* was one of the key works of the period. At Portsmouth, for example, I would work with students on *Water Yam* and works like Ichiyanagi's *Distance*, on prose pieces by Christian Wolff and La Monte Young. This kind of repertoire informed performances of Cardew's Fluxus-related *Schooltime Compositions*, for me one of his finest and most understated works in a line that goes from the completely graphic *Treatise* (which never fazed those close to fine art), through *The Tiger's Mind* and *Octet '61*. These artist-musicians were essentially the kind of people that Cardew needed for *The Great Learning* and the Scratch Orchestra probably really came about for that reason. It was formalized in June 1969 but once these people were together many other things were possible.

The relationship with art colleges was also important for the way in which then current fine art practice was able to inform musical composition and vice versa. For example, at Portsmouth there was a strong presence of what was called the Systems Group – painters such as Jeffrey Steele and Dave Saunders. Many within this group were sympathetic to experimental music practice and could see parallels with what they were doing in terms of producing art works from number systems, grids, matrices and even random material. To some extent this was not unlike the link between so-called minimal artists in America like Donald Judd and Sol LeWitt and a composer such as Steve Reich. The difference, however, was that in England this was not just some form of aesthetic kinship, but rather of people actually working together.

A further aspect of collective activity arose with the Experimental Music Catalogue, a publishing venture that was started in 1969 by Christopher Hobbs and is a good example of the kind of idealism and selflessness that characterizes so much of English experimental music – its innocence and lack of interest in commercial enterprise. It came about because there had been a lot of pieces written for John Tilbury, and John had acquired a substantial collection of manuscripts that he felt should be made more widely available. A catalogue was made of these and was advertised in the *Musical Times*. After a couple of years this had attracted many composers and the EMC became too big for Hobbs to handle alone so I ran it from 1972 until its closure in 1981, with editorial help from him and Michael Nyman. Pieces were put into anthologies rather than sold separately, and a number of pieces of more elegantly printed music were added – John Gosling's edition of George Brecht's *Water Yam*, Christian Wolff's *Prose Collection* and Tom Phillips's graphic scores (these two beautifully printed by the artist Ian Tyson). The EMC handled sales and printing but this wasn't publishing in the full sense in that there was no collection of royalties, no promotion; composers retained all rights and the purchase cost of the music was more or less the cost of printing. But the work was being disseminated and people outside the UK got to know the work. For example, there was a lengthy correspondence with John Adams, who was just starting to teach at the San Francisco Conservatory of Music in 1973, which resulted in the performances of many works in America the following year.

A measure of the increasing international awareness of this music came when, in 1973, there was a week of English experimental music at the Palais des Beaux Arts in Brussels as part of the month-long 'Europalia' which celebrated Britain's entry into the European Union. Then from 1975 Brian Eno's Obscure label issued several works by composers such as myself, Christopher Hobbs, John White, Michael Nyman, Tom Phillips, followed by a younger generation comprising David Toop, Max Eastley, Jan Steele, Eno himself, as well as the Americans John Adams (his first released recording) and Harold Budd.

Throughout its peak period, roughly from 1968 to the mid-1970s, English experimental music was noticeably without any official support (the Belgian performances were due to the enterprise of the Belgian organizer Hervé Thys, who researched music other than the mainstream repertoire provided by the BBC Symphony orchestra and others). There were no commissions from performing organizations (the Cheltenham Festival's commission of Paragraph 1 of Cardew's *The Great Learning* predates this period and, in any case, was not a comfortable one). There was little interest from broadcasters (apart from a recording of one piece for the BBC by John Tilbury in 1969, along with a piece by John White and one by Howard Skempton, which was edited to half its length; I had nothing on Radio 3 – then the Third Programme – until 1987).

But being outside was in no way a disadvantage, on the contrary it was almost relished and the apparent isolation had many positive consequences. The music was able to develop without composers seeking an external approval and there was no real interest in self-publicity. Composers accepted whatever resources were available – writing for fellow composers as performers could throw up unwieldy instrumental combinations – and did the best work possible within those constraints.

In the end there emerged music that was idiosyncratic yet conceptually clear; that was fiercely independent yet benign and welcoming; that was aesthetically challenging yet often deceptively attractive; and which, in spite of its acknowledged historical importance, is still little known.

But of course this is not ultimately something that would cause distress to any of these composers...

Gavin Bryars
Billesdon
January 2009

Acknowledgements

There are many people whom I would like to thank for their support in the production of this book. It goes without saying that it would not have been possible to realize this project without the considerable effort of the chapter authors and interviewees, through both the time and knowledge invested in their contributions here and the previous work that made the study possible in the first place. I am extremely grateful for everything you have brought to this volume. Thank you also to Heidi May at Ashgate for your continued patience when responding to my queries, with both the minutiae of manuscript preparation and more general questions of style, structure and content. The whole project would also have been impossible without the support of colleagues and students in the music departments of Bath Spa University and the University of Huddersfield. Much of the work on the interviews in particular was completed whilst on leave in the 2005–2006 academic year, supported by the University of Huddersfield and the Arts and Humanities Research Council through their Research Leave scheme. This time gave me the much-needed space in which to progress the text towards publishable copy. Finally, none of this would have been possible without the leave granted by my family to spend hours in front of a computer: Becky, Florence and William, thank you for giving me the time to complete this, and for your own experimental music.

Permission to reprint the examples have been kindly granted by the composers and their publishers as follows:

John Cage –	*Concert for Piano and Orchestra* (EP 6256); *Child of Tree* (EP 6705); *Music of Changes* (EP 6685). © Copyright by Henmar Press, Inc., New York. Reproduced by permission of Peters Edition Limited, London.
John Cage –	'Rolywholyover: A Circus', 12 September–28 November 1993. © Museum of Contemporary Art, Los Angeles. Photo Credit: Paula Goodman. Reproduced by permission.
Michael Finnissy –	*Folklore.* © Oxford University Press 1996. Reproduced by permission.
Jürg Frey –	*Lovaty.* © Copyright 1996 by Jürg Frey and Edition Wandelweiser GmbH. Reproduced by permission. All rights reserved.
Bryn Harrison –	*être-temps.* © Copyright 2002 by Bryn Harrison. Reproduced by permission. All rights reserved.
Joseph Kudirka –	*Beauty and Industry* © Copyright 2007 by Joseph Kudirka. Reproduced by permission. All rights reserved.
John Lely –	*All About the Piano.* © Copyright 2006 by John Lely. Reproduced by permission. All rights reserved.
Pauline Oliveros –	*Circle Sound Meditation.* © Copyright 1978 by Pauline Oliveros. Reproduced by permission. All rights reserved
Yoko Ono –	*Box Piece* and *Map Piece*, Yoko Ono, *Grapefruit.* © Copyright 1964. Used by permission. All rights reserved.
Tim Parkinson –	*piano piece 2006* © Copyright 2006 by Tim Parkinson. Reproduced by permission. All rights reserved.
Michael Parsons –	*Fourths and Fifths.* © Copyright 1982 by Michael Parsons. Reproduced by permission. All rights reserved
Michael Pisaro –	*ricefall; so little to do [harmony series 6].* © Copyright 2004, 2005 by Michael Pisaro and Edition Wandelweiser GmbH. Reproduced by permission. All rights reserved.
Karlheinz Stockhausen –	*Klavierstück Nr 1.* Klavierstücke 1–4	für Klavier	Nr. 2/UE 12251. Reproduced by permission. All rights reserved.
James Tenney –	(night) *For Percussion Perhaps, Or...* [from *Postal Pieces*]. © Copyright 1971 by Sonic Art Editions. Used by permission of Smith Publications, 2617 Gwynndale Ave., Baltimore, Maryland 21207 USA.
Manfred Werder –	*2005¹; 2006¹; 2006²; 2008³.* © Copyright 2005, 2006 and 2008 by Manfred Werder and Edition Wandelweiser GmbH. Reproduced by permission. All rights reserved.
Christian Wolff –	*Duo for Pianists.* © Copyright by C F Peters Corporation/ Henmar Press, Inc., New York. Reproduced by permission of Peters Edition Limited, London.
Christian Wolff –	*Fits and Starts.* © Copyright 1971 by Christian Wolff and Frog Peak Music. Reproduced by permission. All rights reserved.

Introduction

In the preface to the second edition of Michael Nyman's *Experimental Music: Cage and Beyond*, the possibility of a sequel is mooted.[1] This is not that book. It is not a history of experimental music, it does not present an exhaustive overview of current practice, and there is no attempt to categorically define experimental music. As the title suggests, *The Ashgate Research Companion to Experimental Music* is a sourcebook and commentary on selected work by experimental musicians. It is in two parts: nine authored chapters exploring aspects of experimental music, and fourteen interviews with experimental musicians, which contextualize and exemplify each other respectively. Whilst focusing on notated music, the texts encompass related aspects of performance, improvisation and sonic art, with many of the interviewees being referenced in the opening chapters as might be expected. Through both these approaches the book considers a range of issues pertinent to recent and historical developments in experimental music, including definitions of experimentalism and its relationship with a broader avant-garde; experimentalism and cultural change; notation and its effect on composition; realizing open scores; issues of notation and interpretation in live electronic music; the performance practice of experimental music; improvisation and technology; improvisation and social meaning; instrumentalizing objects; visual artists' relationship to experimental music; working across interdisciplinary boundaries; listening and the soundscape; and working methods, techniques and aesthetics of recent experimental music.

Although the book does not aim to define experimental music explicitly, this is an emergent feature of much of the writing, particularly with regard to its location in relation to other contemporary arts practices. As Christopher Fox points out in Chapter 1, 'Why Experimental?, Why Me?', the distinctions made by Nyman between experimental and avant-garde music seem less clear with time. The continuum of possible innovation fans out as we look back to work that now seems less diametrically opposed than might have been the case 35 years ago. Fox's chapter takes this as its starting point, before exploring the relationship of his own work, and that of Kagel and Volans, to the experimental tradition.

---

1   Michael Nyman, *Experimental Music: Cage and Beyond* (Cambridge, 1999), pp. xv–xviii.

Given this situation, it becomes meaningless to define experimentalism in a closed way: rather a series of indicators might suggest where much of this work is located. Such referents include not trying to build on the past, but starting from scratch; seeking to discover or test something as a prerequisite; not working with traditional formats (sounds, instruments, forms, media, institutions, people); challenging our assumptions about music, art and life, and the apparent boundaries between them; questioning the relationship between composer, performer and audience; having a nebulous relationship between score (where present) and sound, and between the end result and its constituent parts; accepting circumstantial outcomes as readily as planned outcomes; music in which the idea or concept is as interesting (if not more so) than the sound; existing only in the moment; and taking an idea or parameter and following it to an extreme degree. Other musics clearly present some of these features in isolation, but it is only through their intersection that the nature of experimental work begins to emerge.

The following three chapters address the relationship between composition, notation and performance. An examination of the role of notation as the mediator between idea and realization is one of the principal emphases of experimental music practice, and an understanding of the strategies its practitioners take to this information exchange is central to its study. Chapter 2, Michael Pisaro's 'Writing, Music', deals with the essentiality of inscription in its widest sense in the compositional process, exploring the ways in which the act of writing directly affects the resultant music. Pisaro suggests that written music must confront ideas about writing, and that this in turn leads to a consideration of the role and nature of the score. His chapter presents a framework for notational practice, exemplified by a catalogue of notational types, examining the way in which this variety leads and is required by the work.

As a result of this multiplicity of notational approaches taken by composers, the problem of developing a methodology for realizing scores is more pronounced than with music for which a clearer and more unified performance practice exists. The indeterminacy of much experimental music in particular allows for the presentation of multiple readings of the same text, all of which might retain a validity with regards to their authenticity despite radical differences. Whilst this could imply the need for consolidation, imposing narrow restrictions on realization strategies would render this work moribund. Instead, as Philip Thomas notes in Chapter 3, 'A Prescription for Action', it is vital that performers look within the work to find its implied (and often unique) performance practice, substituting investigation for a more generalized interpretation. In his chapter, Thomas explores David Tudor's idea of work-as-interpretation, discussing this within the context of classic and more recent examples of experimental music, as well as more prescriptive complexly notated work.

This situation is compounded by the development of live electronic music in the 1960s, where the growing use of networked systems and home-made instruments further destabilized the relationship between score (where present) and sounding result. In pieces such as Cage's *Variations* series (1958–67), the creation of a meta-composition requires much of the performer when preparing a realization: whilst the derived notation might be specific, the performed actions can result in a wider and often relatively uncontrollable variance. Ronald Kuivila examines this situation and the role of the score in live electronic music in Chapter 4, 'Open Sources: Words, Circuits and the Notation/Realization Relation in Live Electronic Music'. He comments on the way that these pieces were tied into the performance practices of individuals and the equipment they developed: the music was locked into their experience and circuitry as opposed to their more conventional location, the score. These relationships define the way this music evolved.

This movement towards utilizing more unpredictable devices whose potential for sound-making had not been fully explored formed part of a wider reconsideration of instrumentation, which encompassed extended techniques, invention, preparations and modifications, and treating 'the instrument as total configuration'.[2] Whilst electronics provided one approach to circumventing the learned assumptions of existing performance and composition practices, the appropriation of objects, of any sound producing means, provided a parallel way forward. Specific pieces of equipment found their way into many notated compositions, such as Kagel's *Acustica* (1968–70), for which newly constructed repertoires of performative actions were developed in order to actuate them. Such instrumentalizing has found its natural place in improvised music, however, where live investigation of the sounding potential of objects is arguably the purest form of experimentation. The extent to which the object, as opposed to its tradition (where one exists), leads this investigation is discussed in Andy Keep's 'Instrumentalizing: Approaches to Improvising with Sounding Objects in Experimental Music' (Chapter 5). Keep presents approaches to assessing an object's sonic properties, framed by discussions of creative abuse, notions of performer skill and the use of referents in experimental improvisation.

These investigations into the sonic potential of objects are the concern of both notated and improvised music, but it is the degree to which the former's appropriation of the latter's practical research occurs that can be seen as problematic in some contexts. The subject is touched on later in the book through the interviews with Rhodri Davies and Evan Parker, but it is a central tenet of Chapter 6, Eddie Prévost's 'Free Improvisation in Music and Capitalism: Resisting Authority and the Cults of Scientism and Celebrity'. Prévost argues that the collaborative nature of musical exploration is not fully acknowledged through the process of writing scores, of fixing sounds and their innovative techniques of production. The result of this appropriation of sound by composers is an embedded capitalism within music: it is perhaps a notion which defines a more chronological avant-garde, where as Philip Corner suggests 'You already see where the great tradition of Western culture is supposed to go; who's the genius who will get there first?'[3] Instead, the act of improvisation is an immediate moment of discovery, one in which all possibilities reside.

Appropriation of sound to a different end is considered in both the next chapters. Will Montgomery and John Levack Drever explore the way in which a broad

---

2   Ibid., p. 20.

3   Geoff Smith and Nicola Walker Smith, *American Originals* (London, 1994), p. 88.

spectrum of artists has approached environmental sound as material. In Chapter 7, Montgomery's 'Beyond the Soundscape: Art and Nature in Contemporary Phonography', the aural environment and its framing as art is discussed, considering the potential distinctions made between nominally discrete areas of activity such as phonography, sound art and music. The medial position much of this recorded work occupies is balanced, often precariously, by our understanding of its artifice and presentation as an acoustic reality, manipulating our experience of the world and commenting upon it. The practice of soundwalking on the other hand explores the soundscape without the mediation of recording. Here the framing of the everyday is immersive: as participants and listeners, the experience confronts us through layered modes of listening,[4] asking us to negotiate our interpretation of environmental sound without the distancing found in the presentation of a recorded soundscape. The varied practices and purposes of this activity are explored by John Levack Drever in Chapter 8, 'Soundwalking: Aural Excursions into the Everyday'.

This enmeshing of disparate activities has been a central theme of experimental music, in part due to many of its principal exponents having arrived from separate disciplines, artistic or otherwise. The forum such work has provided encourages the recontextualizing of concepts, the testing of ideas and the acceptance of failure: it is born of an intermedia investigation. A consideration of the role of visual artists in experimental music, both as creators and as participants, and the corresponding engagement with the institutions of visual art by composers, is the subject of David Ryan's '"We have Eyes as well as Ears…" Experimental Music and the Visual Arts' (Chapter 9). Ryan focuses on the relationship between experimental composers and the visual art world, considering both interdisciplinary practice and the impact of art schools as environments for experimentation

Ultimately this book is about work: it examines creative methodologies and considers how a particular group of musicians think and act. Taking the etymology of 'experimental', it is also a book about experience: the experience of making music, of Jasper Johns's desire to 'paint it and then see it',[5] or Alison Knowles's attitude of 'being on your toes at all times, of being aware of the moment in order to find things in it'.[6] It is also a reflective consideration of this experience, an evaluation of the things found in those moments, or as Ken Friedman puts it, 'Experimentalism doesn't merely mean trying new things. It means trying new things and assessing the results.'[7]

---

4   See Pierre Schaeffer, *Traité des Objets Musicaux* (Paris, 1977), or summarized in Dennis Smalley, 'The Listening Imagination: Listening in the Electroacoustic Era', *Contemporary Music Review*, 13/2 (Amsterdam, 1996): 77–107.

5   Jasper Johns, 'Untitled Statement', in Kristine Styles and Peter Selz (eds), *Theories and Documents of Contemporary Art: A Sourcebook of Artists' Writings* (Berkeley, 1996), p. 323.

6   Smith and Smith, *American Originals*, p. 151.

7   Ken Friedman, 'Fluxus and Company', *The Fluxus Reader* (Chichester, 1998), p. 248.

PART I

Why Experimental? Why me?

Christopher Fox

In 1990 I was asked to contribute an article to a forthcoming issue of *Contemporary Music Review* about English experimental music. They wanted something written from the perspective of a composer who was too young to have been in the Scratch Orchestra but for whom the work of composers like Cornelius Cardew, Gavin Bryars and Howard Skempton was an important influence. I wrote a few thousand words under the provisional title, 'Here Comes Everybody: beyond Cage and beyond', but then the issue was shelved and I gave up midway through the article, at the point where I was about to start discussing aspects of my own music. At the start of 2000 I was asked for something similar and wrote more of what appears here, only for that project also to founder. Returning to these words for a third time I have made minor revisions to what I already had and brought matters more or less up to date, but I have resisted the temptation to disguise the long evolution of my ideas. Indeed, as I will suggest later, the shifts in emphasis between the three generations of this text tell their own story.

In 1974 Michael Nyman published his book *Experimental Music: Cage and Beyond*. At the time I was an undergraduate in the music department at Liverpool University and as soon as I got hold of the book I became fascinated by its construction of an alternative to the established new music canon within which I was trying to locate my own compositional activities. Nyman described music which, unlike that of Birtwistle or Stockhausen, was not on the library shelves, not in the record shops, not on Radio 3; exactly the sort of music, in other words, to appeal to a 19 year old keen to get ahead of the game. The book also confirmed my suspicions that there might be ways of writing music that could be based on processes without being serialist, that could involve repetition without being rock, that could embrace tonal materials without being backward.

Over the following months and years there were memorable opportunities to add an acquaintance with the music itself to that first encounter with it through Nyman's prose. The boxed set of *Drumming*, *Six Pianos* and *Music for Mallet Instruments, Voices and Organ* came out in 1974; in 1975 the Philip Glass Ensemble came to Liverpool and made my ears ring with some of *Music in Twelve Parts*; somewhat later I was one of the minority to be delighted rather than dismayed by a concert that Gavin Bryars, Dave Smith and John White gave at the 1979 Composers' Weekend organized by the Society for the Promotion of New Music at York University. Later still I began to add words of my own to the growing critical literature around this music, with articles on Morton Feldman, Erhard Grosskopf, Christian Wolff and Walter Zimmermann for *Contact*, on John Cage, Steve Reich and Zimmermann for *Tempo*, and a portmanteau survey ('Après *Einstein*: la succession minimaliste') for *Contrechamps*.

At first I devoted a great deal of energy to trying to establish the defining features of 'experimental' music. In 'Walter Zimmermann's Local Experiments', for example, I suggested that a 'characteristically experimental' compositional approach was the 'distancing of creative will from created sound' and the rejection of the 'possibility of music as a direct and immediate outpouring of the creative will'.[1] This was both an echo of Gavin Bryars's definition of his aesthetic position as:

> stand[ing] apart from one's own creation. Distancing yourself from what you are doing … I'm more interested in conception than reality.[2]

and an attempt to maintain Nyman's distinction between experimental music and other 'avant-garde' composers.

As I suggested earlier, one of the most appealing features of *Experimental Music* was that Nyman argued that it was possible to 'isolate' the music under discussion in his book: in the introductory paragraph he claims that he will

> attempt to … identify what experimental music is … what distinguishes it from the music of such avant-garde composers as Boulez, Kagel, Xenakis, Birtwistle, Berio, Stockhausen, Bussotti, which is conceived and executed along the well-trodden but sanctified path of the post-Renaissance tradition.[3]

What followed was a panoramic study, ranging from experimental forebears (Ives, Russolo), through the 'permission giving'[4] work of Cage and, subsequently, Brown, Feldman and Wolff, to the various dissolutions of musical convention in the 1960s and the new focus on minimalism and tonal materials that succeeded them. As Keith Potter said at the time, 'At each stage Nyman picks out the essential points, asks and answers a lot of the right questions and gives liberal examples of pieces.'[5] For me and many other young composers the book was akin to a generously illustrated holiday brochure, full of exotic possibilities, even if many of them seemed too remote to visit.

But, compelling as *Experimental Music* then appeared, the book's central thesis, that a music called 'experimental' existed in a directly oppositional relationship to another music called 'avant-garde', now seems simplistic. Clearly Stockhausen epitomized an approach to the work of composition radically different from that of, say, Cage or La Monte Young, a difference he made clear each time he appropriated

1   Christopher Fox, 'Walter Zimmermann's Local Experiments', *Contact*, 27 (1983): 4–9.
2   Derek Bailey, *Improvisation* (Ashbourne, 1980), p. 136.
3   Michael Nyman, *Experimental Music: Cage and Beyond* (London, 1974), p. 2.
4   Morton Feldman, *Essays*, ed. Walter Zimmermann (Cologne, 1985), p. 37.
5   Keith Potter, 'Experimental Music: Cage and Beyond', *Contact*, 10 (1975): 39.

elements of their work in his own music. But Nyman's categorization of Kagel as avant-garde rather than experimental is hard to sustain, for example, if one considers the works that Kagel was creating at the end of the 1960s. Were Kagel's *Staatstheater* (1967–70) and *Ludwig van* (1970) so distinct from Cardew's *The Great Learning* (1966–71) or a 'Popular Classic' as defined in the Scratch Orchestra's Draft Constitution (1969)? Indeed was not the large-scale organization of continuity in *The Great Learning* actually less 'experimental' than that in *Staatstheater*?

Gradually my struggle to establish a theoretically satisfactory line with which to divide the avant-garde from the experimental led me to the conclusion that things were rather more complicated than Nyman had suggested, a conclusion that I realized I had acknowledged in the music I was writing some time before I finally abandoned my attempts to maintain the division in words. Unlike Nyman in 1974, I also had the great advantage of knowing that the experimental rigour of Reich's *Pendulum Music* (1968), with its indeterminate process and its minimalist concentration on a single sound-generating phenomenon, would eventually lead to *The Desert Music* (1982–84), music closer to Copland than Cage. I should add in Nyman's defence that he had already hinted at such complications, quoting Feldman's judgement on Boulez and Cage – 'what is interesting is their similarity' – and pointing out that the then freshly politicized Cardew saw both camps as sharing 'overriding similarities' rooted in the 'elitist, individualistic culture which has spawned both'.[6]

But if Nyman's attempt to establish experimental music as aesthetically discrete was flawed, his tracing of a musical history other than that of modernist orthodoxy was nonetheless an important early manifestation of the post-modernization of new music. Although *Experimental Music* was itself a typically modernist project in its insistence on a dialectical opposition between the experimental and the avant-garde, it nonetheless challenged a central tenet of modernism, that the remorseless progress of history could lead to only one future and that that future was made concrete in the work of the avant-garde. What Nyman made clear was that a work like *The Great Learning* had its own history, different from but no less valid than that of Stockhausen's *Momente* (1961–72), for example. What has become clear in the years since 1974 is that there is not just one true history, that of the post-1945 modernist avant-garde with, possibly, and in contra-distinction, a shadowy alternative history, that of experimental music: instead there is an abundance of histories. Furthermore these histories are themselves contingent on the perspectives adopted by the writers who fashion them and on the contexts in which the histories are recounted.

One of the most startling examples of this was Cardew's revision of the history of his own work in his book *Stockhausen Serves Imperialism* (1974), where what had once been claimed as musically progressive was instead attacked as socially regressive. Similarly the classic account of 1950s Darmstädter Ferienkurse as a crucible in which the associative impurities of music were burnt off to produce a new, pure, international soundworld could be retold by Hans Werner Henze as

---

6   Nyman, *Experimental Music*, p. 2.

'the ruling class's attempt to make music non-communicative … a thing apart from life … without any social dimension … to prevent people from seeing music as simple, concrete and comprehensible communication between human beings'.[7] Less radically, the period since the publication of *Experimental Music* has seen a broadening of the history of modernism itself to allow the re-adoption of figures such as Scelsi and Nancarrow, whose music had been marginalized by the avant-garde in the 1950s and 1960s.

The development of this plurality of musical histories has not been entirely straightforward. An attitude at the heart of modernism, that at each point along the vector of history one particular set of compositional approaches will be more important than any other, was still much in evidence in the 1980s and is retained by some commentators to this day. Richard Toop, for example, justified an article on four representatives of the so-called 'New Complexity' with the assertion that 'alongside Birtwistle and Ferneyhough they represent the few possible sources of light within a scene otherwise dominated by (to coin another catch-phrase) "The New Capitulationism"'.[8] Elsewhere, historical precedent was invoked as a means of excluding from discussion those musics which were not congruent with the modernist tradition. Thus Harry Halbreich remodelled the early 1980s in the mould of the 1920s, casting Brian Ferneyhough as 'unser Schoenberg' and Horatiu Radulescu as 'der Varèse unserer Zeit'.[9] Having assigned these roles, both central to the ancestry of the post-1945 avant-garde, Halbreich could safely dismiss as unimportant any other composer whose work was not related directly to Ferneyhough's post-serial 'complexity' or Radulescu's 'spectral' music.

Nevertheless there has been no shortage of composers prepared to embrace the creative possibilities implicit in the dissolution of the monolithic modernism of the post-1945 era. At various points in the last 30 years, composers as different as Clarence Barlow, Kevin Volans and Michael Finnissy could all be said to have been writing music which is essentially inclusive rather than exclusive, evolving musical languages for each new work that drew on a wide range of sources and doing so in such a way that the identity of both the composers' intentions and their various sources can co-exist. Volans's *White Man Sleeps* is a case in point, taking elements of the indigenous musics of southern Africa and articulating them through instrumental ensembles intimately associated with West European art music. In the first version (1982) of *White Man Sleeps* for two harpsichords, viola da gamba and percussion, the pitched instruments are retuned to an African tuning in which there are roughly seven equal steps to the octave. In the second version (1986) for string quartet, equal temperament, the conventional Western tuning of the last 400 years, is used.

In the 1982 piece our attention is caught by the strangeness of the music: instruments at the margins of mainstream concert music playing in an unfamiliar

---

7   Hans Werne Henze, *Music and Politics* (London, 1982), pp. 49–50.

8   Richard Toop, 'Four Facets of "The New Complexity"', *Contact*, 32 (1988): 4–50, at 4.

9 |Harry Halbreich, 'Müde Helden, neue Hoffnung', *Algorithmus, Klang, Natur: Abkehr von Materialdenken? Darmstädter Beiträge zur neue Musik*, 19 (1984): 56–9, at 59.

intonation; in the 1986 piece timbral variety, within classical music's most homogenous grouping, becomes a focus. In each case Volans's music tells us something about the distinctiveness of indigenous southern African music, but in so doing also emphasizes the great differences, social, political and economic, between the cultures in which that music is made and the culture within which European art music has evolved. Above all Volans would seem to have been acknowledging that composing today is an essentially conditional activity: *White Man Sleeps* may be based on an extant music but that music cannot be simply recreated through composition.

In making and remaking *White Man Sleeps* Volans demonstrated not only that composition has limitations but also, as Linda Hutcheon has said of postmodern parody in general, that it is both 'deconstructively critical and constructively creative'.[10] The same might be said of a work cited by Nyman as representative of experimental music in England, Gavin Bryars's *Jesus' Blood Never Failed Me Yet* (1971), in which an instrumental harmony slowly accumulates around a tape loop of a tramp singing the Victorian hymn of the title. Over time the listener is able to hear the formal qualities of the material – the idiosyncrasies of the tape performance and the complications this creates for the live musicians – and to reflect on the multiple ironies of the religious certainties of the sung text, the alienation of the singer within a society which is still at least nominally established on those same certainties, and the metaphorical re-assimilation into (musical) society that the harmonization of his voice implies.

Crucially, in neither *White Man Sleeps* nor *Jesus' Blood* is there the distinction between 'found' material and the composer's own 'voice' that one finds in modernist collages such as Stockhausen's *Telemusik* (1966) and *Hymnen* (1966–67) or the quotation-rich pieces of B.A. Zimmermann. Whereas in those works a hierarchy of meanings is set up in which the quoted and/or transformed fragments have a specific representational function, there is no similar distinction in Bryars's or Volans's works. The presentation of particular materials may be an act of deconstruction but at the same time these materials are all that the (newly created) music is. To quote Linda Hutcheon again, in this deconstructively creative music, 'complicity always attends its critique'.[11]

Since the work of both Bryars and Volans has qualities that, according to Hutcheon, can be generally ascribed to work within the category 'postmodern' and yet Bryars has also been located within the experimental camp, it might seem that these categories are mutually inclusive. However, as I argued earlier, satisfactory definitions of what constitutes experimental music are perhaps less easily achieved than is suggested by Michael Nyman's book. Furthermore, while some of the music that Nyman mentions would seem to satisfy postmodern criteria, other composers' work is more readily heard as modernist. Cornelius Cardew's music before 1974, for example, is quintessentially modern in its tendency towards self-referential closure. Scores like *The Tiger's Mind* (1967) or *Treatise* (1963–67) may offer new

---

10   Linda Hutcheon, *The Politics of Postmodernism* (London, 1989), p. 98.
11   Ibid., p. 99.

openings for the engagement of their performers but the music experienced by the listener is as wantonly obscure as anything from the so-called avant-garde.

Distinctions also exist between postmodernism's inclination towards eclectic inclusiveness and the tendency of (so-called) experimental composers (and Nyman as their advocate) to dismiss those musical possibilities that were particularly associated with (so-called) avant-garde music. This was an understandable consequence of an attempt to define by exclusion a musical territory whose borders were, as I have argued, less definite than Nyman had suggested. It was also a mirror image of the avant-garde's attitude to experimental music: if the avant-garde condemned experimental music for the banality of its metric regularity or the irresponsibility of its indeterminacy, then experimental musicians rejected the formal control of the avant-garde as totalitarian and its complexities as elitist. While Nyman's construction of the history of experimental music demonstrated the existence of another musical history, it was only within postmodernism that the heterogenous co-existence of different histories achieved theoretical justification. As someone who had become depressed at the mutual intolerance expressed by minimalists, neo-romantics, complexitists and spectralists I found the plurality of postmodernism a welcome development, especially since the music I was writing embraced aspects of all these supposedly antagonistic tendencies.

What the postmodern and the experimental do share is an awareness that there is a 'distance' between the music made and the maker(s) of that music, the distance that I had claimed as 'characteristically experimental' in my 1983 article on Walter Zimmermann. Whereas I had then implied that this distance could be imposed or removed more or less ad libitum, I now recognize that it exists as an inevitable product of the interlocking structures of language and meaning within which all our activities take place. Whether composers choose to acknowledge this distance, to be complicitous with it, is a matter of individual choice; it cannot, however, be wished away by some Nietzschean effort of the creative will. In my own music, perhaps needless to say, I choose to be aware that 'my' ideas arise from a particular set of circumstances and that concepts such as 'self', 'expression' and 'individuality' are fraught with complications. In recent works, for example, I have specifically…

And at that point my early 1990s thoughts stopped. When I returned to the article in 2000 I thought of submitting my younger self to the sort of corrective self-criticism to which Cardew subjects himself in *Stockhausen Serves Imperialism*, where even the endnotes enter the struggle, offering a strictly Maoist critique of the rather looser ideology of the main text. Unlike Cardew, however, I had not undergone a series of major ideological realignments since I began the article, although by 2000 I already found my earlier preoccupation with postmodernism rather doctrinaire, not to say smug. In the intervening years I had become increasingly impatient with the popular misconception of the term 'postmodernism' as a synonym for polystylism, multiculturalism and ahistoricism, used as a definition which can endorse all sorts of reactionary nonsense.

More seriously, I had come to realize that post-modernity *chèz* Baudrillard, where every utterance is a simulacrum of something already in the world, ran counter to the belief that through the deployment of experimental stratagems it was possible to create genuinely new work. While it may be interesting to reflect, after the compositional moment has passed, on the playful combination of signifiers that has been created, in the moment of musical genesis it is important to concentrate exclusively on the materials being used. This is the case in each of the works I want to discuss now, the audio collage *MERZsonata* (1993, revised 1998) and the ensemble works *Themes and Variations* (1992–96), *Strangers in our midst* (1999–2001) and *Everything You Need To Know* (2000–2001); each was created in the years after the first interruption of this chapter and each addresses aspects of the aesthetic issues which the original article had been exploring.

MERZsonata was made in the Radiophonic Workshops of the BBC in the summer of 1993 as part of a Radio 3 commission called *Three Constructions after Kurt Schwitters*. Schwitters was an artist whose work I admire enormously and whose career, with its mixture of domestic compromise, aesthetic adventuring and political exile, is a paradigm of one sort of artistic life in the twentieth century. In its broadcast form, the *Three Constructions* consisted of a short spoken introduction, explaining who Schwitters was and illustrated with brief archive sound-clips, followed by three longer sections, the 'Constructions', each of which was prefaced by a spoken title. In 1998 I revised the first of these longer sections for CD release, where it became the *MERZsonata*. It is, as the radio version said, 'A Biography in Sonata-Rondo Form', biographical because each sound in the piece has a significance in the story of Schwitters's life and a sonata-rondo because the structure of the piece is based on the final movement of Schwitters's sound-text masterpiece, the *Ursonate* (1922–32), which Schwitters himself described as being in sonata-rondo form.

Indeed there is a sense in which the *MERZsonata* is no more than a transcription of the Schwitters since it takes over his rondo-like arrangement of materials into a series of recurring modules (even preserving his exposition repeat) and matches each of his vocal sounds with an audio sample. For example, Schwitters's first subject is:

> *Grimm glimm gnimm bimbimm*
> *Grimm glimm gnimm bimbimm*
> *Grimm glimm gnimm bimbimm*
> *Grimm glimm gnimm bimbimm*
> *Grimm glimm gnimm bimbimm*
> *Grimm glimm gnimm bimbimm*
> *Grimm glimm gnimm bimbimm*
> *Grimm glimm gnimm bimbimm*

In *MERZsonata* this becomes a four beat figure: (1) 'oh' (Schwitters's voice); (2) 'hello' (Schwitters's voice); (3) dog bark; (4) 'Anna' (Schwitters's voice); as in the Schwitters this is repeated eight times. The first Schwitters sample comes from an archive recording of the *Ursonate*, possibly by Schwitters himself, possibly by his son Ernst, which was released on a Wergo CD in 1993. The other Schwitters samples come from his recording of his most famous poem, 'an Anna Blume', while the dog bark is a reference to Schwitters's fondness for barking like a dog before going to bed, noted by Dr Klaus Hinrichsen who was interned with Schwitters during the early months of the Second World War in the Hutchinson Square detention camp for enemy aliens on the Isle of Man. Elsewhere in the piece there is a baby's sneeze (because Schwitters used to perform a sneezing sound-poem, 'The Fury of Sneezing'), moments from the other three movements of the *Ursonate* (Schwitters himself in an extract from the first movement and Dr Hinrichsen in an extract from the third movement which became a shared greeting amongst Schwitters's fellow internees in Hutchinson Square) and many, many more biographically significant audio fragments.

The process of making *MERZsonata* – Schwitters memorabilia held within Schwitters's form – has both postmodern and experimental characteristics. It painstakingly parodies the form of the *Ursonate* finale, but whereas the relationship between the structure of the piece and the material which articulates that structure is organic in the original – to hear or perform the *Ursonate* is to have an intimate sense of Schwitters's own vocal physiognomy – it becomes conceptual in *MERZsonata*. This duality has perhaps contributed to the unusual reception *MERZsonata* has enjoyed. It has been used within BBC Radio as part of a training programme demonstrating the possibilities of sound editing. Translating the work back into the dimension of visual signs, the graphic designer Kelvin Smith has made a transcription using an often arcane system of audio-visual equivalences: the dog bark, for example, became an exclamation mark because in printing trade slang this symbol is know as a 'dog's cock'. Particularly gratifying has been the confusion over the work's authorship: on a number of occasions listeners have imagined they were listening to a sound-collage by Schwitters himself, high praise indeed.

The *MERZsonata* draws together sounds of very different provenance, preserving much of the original grain of the sounds, including the texture of their recording: scratchy voices lifted from old LPs sit next to clean digital samples. Within the *Three Constructions after Kurt Schwitters* the same sorts of juxtaposition also occur at the macro-structural level. The second 'Construction' was a studio recording of the piano piece 'Worthless Leather', a song without words which is also the central movement of my Schwitters song-cycle, *Louisiana*, and the third 'Construction' was announced in the radio version as 'Fragments from a Documentary Reconstruction', the thing reconstructed being the acoustic landscape of the interior of Cylinders Barn (between Elterwater and Chapel Stile in the English Lake District) where Schwitters made his last sculptural installation. (This installation, known as the Merzbarn, is now in the Hatton Gallery at the University of Newcastle upon Tyne.) This third construction was also revised for CD release in 1998 when it became *Cylinders Barn 1947*. It consists of location recordings made in my mother's garden shed, a space similar to that of Cylinders Barn, mixed together with the voices of Schwitters's Lake District acquaintances.

Thus the *Three Constructions* consist of a constructivist sound-collage, followed by a piece of domestic piano music, followed by *musique concrète* in which, as the art historian Wendy Frith once observed, 'you can actually hear the concrete being mixed'. In other words, they are unified by their relationship to Schwitters rather than by any consistency of material or compositional method from movement to movement. For some listeners these inequalities of tone and style might be disconcerting, but in a radio programme this sort of discontinuous form is not so remarkable: we are used to sound quality changes from studio to phone-line, or to differences in the way in which information is presented, from edited report to live interview to scripted link. Tested against the criteria for experimentalism which I proposed earlier, the *Constructions* also demonstrate the necessary distance between creative will and musical result, allowing the identities of composer and source material to co-exist.

I worked on the *Three Constructions after Kurt Schwitters* during the summer of 1993. By then I was already planning a substantial work for a group from the Netherlands, the Ives Ensemble, and I wanted this work to explore the same sort of discontinuities as the *Constructions* but within the context of the concert hall. *Themes and Variations* is a cycle of six separate works – *memento, à bout de souffle, tangled, intersections, triasse* and *string quartet* – each with a different combination of three, four or five instruments drawn from a pool of ten players. Each work within the cycle has a radically different soundworld. *memento* (violin, viola, cello, piano) begins with a mid-nineteenth-century piano quartet texture (although the tempo marking, 'andante risoluto' is a tribute to Charles Ives) which is progressively refined and filtered to extinction. *à bout de souffle* (bass flute, bassoon, drums) is spectral at first, gawkily exhibitionist by the finish. *tangled* (clarinet, trumpet, crotales, piano, violin) is intensely loud, bright and monolithic, appropriately likened by one critic to some sort of East Asian court music. *intersections* (alto flute, bassoon, trumpet, double bass) is musically repetitive but continually broken by pauses; *triasse* (clarinet, slit drums, piano) is dark and brooding, and *string quartet* (violin, viola, cello, double bass) is an ethereal composition in string harmonics, 'like a senile music box' wrote another critic.

Although each of these six works can be performed independently, they are intended to be heard together as half of a conventional concert programme. In a complete performance of the cycle the end of *memento* overlaps with the beginning of *à bout de souffle*, and a couple of false starts for *triasse* interrupt the latter stages of *intersections*. A complete *Themes and Variations* also involves an informal theatre of performance. The cycle begins with just the piano quartet on stage and other instrumentalists enter as they are required, breaching normal concert practice by walking in while their colleagues are playing. Once they are in the space of the music they stay there, moving from centre-stage into a surrounding square of chairs to form a collegial audience, becoming listener-performers. Their periods of relative inactivity are also a very obvious reminder of the cycle's rather inefficient use of personnel, a visible critique of the work's construction.

Why 'Themes and Variations'? At its most obvious the title pays tribute to John Cage, whose 1982 book has the same title. Less straightforwardly, each part of the cycle can also be regarded as both a 'theme' – that is, something self-sufficient – and a 'variation' – something which refers to, and in some way varies, another part of the cycle. Some examples: *memento* sets off from a C minor chord (see Example 1.1); *string quartet* refers to this when all the strings retune to notes from the C minor triad (see Example 1.2). *à bout de souffle* is in three sections, the first of which shares the same tempo and metric divisions as the last 95 measures of *memento*; each of the following sections of *à bout de souffle* compresses the dimensions of this first section while nevertheless attempting to fill the contracting space with the same amount of material. 'Variations' are most apparent where they involve some of the same instrumental personnel, as in *memento* and *string quartet*. In the same way, *triasse* (see Example 1.3) is obviously some sort of negative inversion of *tangled* (see Example 1.4), or perhaps an archeological assemblage based on long-buried fragments of *tangled*. Only once does an instrument appear in successive movements – the trumpet in *tangled* and *intersections* – significantly doing so at the cycle's mid-point, the point of its maximum discontinuity.

Each work within *Themes and Variations* is intrinsically coherent, but played continuously, with the audience being very clearly invited to hear them as a sequence, the discontinuity of the cycle is very apparent. The intention is that the work as a whole can only begin to make sense when the music stops, although there is a pause for possible early reflection when, after *triasse*, the strings retune in preparation for *string quartet*. As is the case in other cyclical works within the experimental tradition, such as Cage's *Sixteen Dances* (1950–51) or Walter Zimmermann's *Lokale Musik* (1977–81), which explore similar ideas of discontinuity, *Themes and Variations* is a work which is only completed some time after the music has finished, when listeners begin to play with their memories of what they have heard.

Themes and Variations, like the work of most composers, starts from the a priori assumption that it will be heard within the current conventions of musical presentation and even works like *MERZsonata* or *Cylinders Barn* are usually heard in the concert hall, or on a 'classical music' radio station, or on CD. The concert format has much to recommend it: not only does it imply quite specific expectations about listeners' attentiveness and a familiar temporal organization for their listening, but it is also an attractive way of spending time socially, a chance to eat and drink and talk and promenade, to be gregarious, to be private, to listen to music. It is, nonetheless, a format that can now often feel quite threadbare – far too few musicians think about ways of rejuvenating the way they present music to rows of people in a concert hall – and the experimental tradition, perhaps particularly in the work of Cage and Cardew, has repeatedly produced music which by its very nature demands different modes of presentation.

Two works written at the beginning of the current century stem directly from this interest, *Strangers in Our Midst* and *Everything You Need To Know*. *Strangers* consists of 45 minutes of music for five players: a cellist and four other musicians who play instruments suitable for performance in the street – euphonium, accordion, banjo and tenor saxophone. Over the course of a day, but individually and separately, the street musicians play their music within different urban locations. Their performances are fragmented, inconsequential, hesitant, unprojected – the antithesis of successful street music. But their performances are also personal: the score asks each musician to play a 'folk-tune', which is described as being 'a partially remembered performance of the melody from a piece of music which has particular significance for the performer', and to make a statement, 'a spoken

THEMES & VARIATIONS (ONE)

Example 1.1   Christopher Fox, *Themes and Variations: memento*,
bars 1–7

Example 1.2   Christopher Fox, *Themes and Variations: string quartet*,
             bars 1–5

THEMES & VARIATIONS (FIVE)

Example 1.3   Christopher Fox, *Themes and Variations: triasse,*
bons 1–5

Example 1.4   Christopher Fox, *Themes and Variations: tangled,*
first page

account by the performer, explaining something of their family origins and their relationship to their instrument'.

As they play, their performance and the reactions of passers-by is recorded on video, as if caught by surveillance cameras. At the end of the day all four outdoor players collect in an indoor location where they replay their music together with the cellist's music – a continuous piece, *inner*, which can also be performed on its own – and accompanied by silent video playback of their street performances. In this new, ensemble context family resemblances between all the music become audible and the fragmentary street music is now linked by cello music whose continuity is intended specifically to invoke the gradual and discursive evolution of story-telling. In its culmination as 'chamber' music the story of *Strangers* will always have the same trajectory but the incidents of that story will also always be different, coloured by the personalities of the musicians involved and their experiences that day.

The stimulus for *Strangers* came from two related late twentieth-century phenomena: the increase in social deprivation which has filled city streets and transport systems with people desperate for money, urging us to help them by playing to us or simply holding out a hand; and end-of-century retrospection. The twentieth century was above all the century of population dislocation, of homelands lost behind changing frontiers, whether economic, political or linguistic, and many of the desperate people on the streets of Western European cities are from these exiled communities. They are like us in their humanity but they are strangers too, alienated by culture and experience. It was appropriate that the work's premiere in Vienna in 2001 should be given by musicians from Bratislava, transposed over the border from Slovakia to Austria.

Strangers in Our Midst is an attempt to reflect and record these phenomena. Street musicians usually try to entertain but the street music of these *Strangers* is instead perplexingly unattractive and foreign and only at the end of the day does it come together; we have to follow the musicians 'home' to understand them. The video playback helps us to measure the distance between the individual as a figure isolated on the street and as a member of a coherent social and musical grouping. Just as *Three Constructions after Kurt Schwitters* mixed the conventions of radio programme-making with those of sound art, so *Strangers* mixes modes of musical performance and the technology of surveillance.

If *Strangers in Our Midst* was an exploration of the differences between the music of the street and the music of the concert hall, *Everything You Need To Know* was an attempt to transpose some of the conventions of installation art into the musical domain. When the Ives Ensemble commissioned *Everything* their only stipulation was that it should be a single 'production' but not a 'concert'; for want of a better description the resulting work is now categorized as an 'ensemble installation'. At its premiere in May 2001 it consisted of a set of twelve solo vocal pieces entitled *Catalogue irraisoné*, seven *Generic Compositions* for solo instrumentalists (since then I have added two further *Generic Compositions*) and five sections of ensemble music, each of which offers a different type of activity (processional, dance, mourning, interlocking pulses, slowly changing harmonies). Ten instrumentalists moved around in the performance area, left it and returned, performed individually, coalesced in various groupings, while a solo soprano acted as a guide to these various activities. The ensemble pieces constitute the spaces in which individual solo works, the *Generic Compositions*, are placed, all of it 'explained' by the singer as catalogue. But just as a scholarly catalogue or the annotations beside visual artworks can become a narrative in its own right (gallery visitors often spending longer reading notes than looking at the paintings to which they refer) so *Catalogue irraisoné* is a flight of vocal fancy, exploring different types of utterance such as the baby-talk of 'Babel' (see Example 1.5) rather than providing any sort of useful commentary.

Like an installation, the component parts of *Everything You Need To Know* are designed so that they may be reconfigured to fit any space, time and personnel

Example 1.5 Christopher Fox, *Catalogue irraisoné*, 'Babel', first three lines

available and since the premiere in 2001 there have been many performances of the material of *Everything*. Some have consisted of no more than a single *Generic Composition* or an individual movement from *Catalogue irraisoné*; others have been a heterophonic combination of solo and ensemble pieces. They have been given in spaces as different as the nineteenth-century gymnasium of a Belgian school, a former synagogue in the Netherlands and the National Portrait Gallery in London and have ranged in duration from 5 to 85 minutes. Most of the separate components of *Everything* are also flexible in their instrumental requirements, particularly the *Generic Compositions* which, as their title implies, generally focus on ways of playing (blowing, plucking, bowing and so on) rather than on specific pitches or timbres. *Generic Composition #1* 'for percussionist' can be played on any seven objects, #5 'for a sliding instrument' can be played either by a string instrument or by trombone (see Example 1.6) and *#8* 'for a sustaining string instrument' can be played on a cello with a Bachbogen, or on an electric guitar using feedback, or on a piano with e-bows.

Installations by artists such as Beuys, Kounellis or Boltanski have an extraordinary physical presence yet one knows that, were the same elements to be brought together in another space, their meaning would be altered. The collection of scores which constitute *Everything You Need To Know* are an attempt to create a compendium of materials which will similarly yield different meanings: is this a new version of the same work or a new work with the same title? The obvious precursors of this type of musical work as compendium are Kagel's *Staatstheater* and *Acustica* (1970), Cardew's *Schooltime Compositions* (1968) and Wolff's *Burdocks* (1970–71) and, pre-eminently, Cage's *Concert* for piano and orchestra (1957–58) and *Song Books* (1970), all of which can be said to experiment with the nature of the work identity. If *Everything You Need To Know* can be said to go 'beyond Cage' it is in the sense that each of its component parts offers order, albeit temporarily, rather than anarchy.

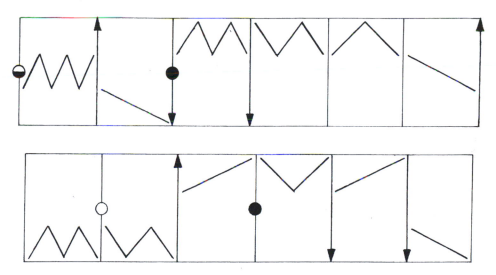

Example 1.6   Christopher Fox, *Generic Composition #5*, first two systems

A recurrent question for all experimental works which adopt this compendium model centres on the extent to which the work can be said to have been experienced when only some of its constituent elements have been heard. In Gavin Bryars's *The Sinking of the Titanic*, for example, the composer has always sanctioned performances which present only part of the available material (which has in any case progressively grown since the work was first performed in 1972), since any performance will always relate to the fundamental conceptual premise of the work, the disappearance of an ocean liner beneath the Atlantic. With *Everything You Need To Know* it has been suggested, most persuasively by the members of the Ives Ensembles whose two productions of the work have been the most comprehensive, that only performances which include all the different types of material within the work – ensemble pieces, instrumental solos and vocal solos – can really be said to represent the work's identity.

More recently this question has informed my composition of a set of seven pieces, *hearing not thinking* (2007–2008). The pieces are to be performed simultaneously and fall into two groups: three with the subtitle 'the erosion of memory', for trombone, woodwind instrument and accordion; four with the subtitle 'at the edge of time', for guitar, bowed string instrument, prepared piano and bass drum. Each individual piece explores the idea of music as a phenomenon which occupies and marks time and space and each may be played as a solo or in combinations of up to four pieces. This restriction means that in one sense the whole work can never be heard, but at the same time the effect of the music is always the same. Nevertheless the division of the pieces into two subsets is an acknowledgement that the ways in which these pieces occupy and mark time is subtly different. The 'erosion of memory' pieces string together sequences of changing sounds, whereas the 'edge of time' pieces are concerned with the reiteration of similar sounds. When performed individually the pieces retain the title of their subset, in combinations where one subset predominates the performance takes that title, and only when an equal number of pieces from each subset is played is the overall title *hearing not thinking* used.

That the same set of materials might have different identities and therefore different names suggests a multivalence which the aural transparency of each piece encourages: the music moves slowly and is often interrupted by silence. In addition, in ensemble versions of the work the instrumentalists are spread as far apart as possible within the performance space, a diffusion that is intended to allow each instrument to be heard both individually and through all the other instrumental layers; it means too that the experience of the music will be different in different parts of the space. Notation also affects the perception of the music: each piece occupies a single A3 sheet so that there is no distracting page-turning and no visual clue as to the passage of time. This, combined with the relative lack of differentiation in each instrumental part, is designed to thwart listeners' attempts to navigate their way from a beginning to an ending. As its main title implies, this is music which favours the sensual pleasure of hearing rather than the intellectual pleasure of analytical listening.

In 1990 I began this article by remembering the impact that Michael Nyman's *Experimental Music* had had on me as a student in the 1970s. Completing it now I am trying to remember the me who wrote those first few thousand words. In 1990 I think I felt, as I had done for the previous 15 years, that my compositional affiliations placed me at the margins of contemporary musical life. For English ears my work was too continental, while in the free-wheeling, improvisatory Berlin in which I lived in 1987 it was too composerly; for my complex colleagues at the Darmstädter

24

Ferienkurse where I was a member of the composition staff from 1984 to 1994 it was too minimal, while for my minimalist colleagues elsewhere it was too complex. I was sure of what I was doing, but less sure that I could easily find a context for it.

Since then a lot has changed. Most importantly, new generations of musicians have come along with fresh enthusiasm for musical adventure – in my career these are represented by the members of the instrumental groups, the Ives Ensemble and Apartment House, with whom I began to work in the 1990s and subsequently by the singers of EXAUDI. These groups have established considerable reputations for the quality of their performances of music from the experimental tradition – Cage, Feldman, Wolff, Cardew – but have also promoted the music of younger composers and have taken many of my works into their repertoires. While it would be an exaggeration to say that this music was completely neglected before the Ives Ensemble and Apartment House came along, these groups have revitalized its performance. In large part this is a result of the commitment with which the ensembles' directors, respectively the pianist John Snijders and the cellist Anton Lukoszevieze, approach experimental music. Unlike so many musicians in other ensembles, the people who play with Snijders and Lukoszevieze understand that indeterminate notations are to be taken just as seriously as any other set of music symbols rather than being tickets to a holiday from the usual disciplines of performance. More recently I have discovered the same degree of understanding in the work of the vocal ensemble directed by James Weeks, EXAUDI, who in 2005 began to record and perform my music. Their work on *American Choruses* (1979–81) was perhaps the most striking of all since the singers were more or less the same age as the piece itself.

Working with these ensembles has made me aware of the compromises I made in my attempts to convince earlier generations of professional musicians of my competence as a composer. In retrospect it is easy to see that as I made my way from the sheltered world of student music-making into the more hostile, time-constrained environment of professional work, I altered the ways in which I presented my ideas, more or less abandoning the graphic innovations of piece like *American Choruses* for more conventional notations. I wanted to write music which might be heard and for which I might be paid, and the musicians with whom this was possible simply did not have the time or, in most cases, the inclination to work on music which looked unconventional. With special musicians, like the clarinettist Roger Heaton or the recorder player Peter Hannan, there could be exceptions but in general I sacrificed notational ambiguity for efficient rehearsal. Within the history of my own music represented by this hop-skip-and-a-jump of a chapter it is also clear now that for early 1990s me notational indeterminacy was a less important aspect of experimentalism than the way in which compositional processes could mediate the relationship between creative intention and musical material. Latterly the experience of working with the musicians of the Ives Ensemble, Apartment House and EXAUDI has renewed my sense of indeterminacy as being the fundamental principle of all aspects of experimental music, informing every stage of music-making, from the choice of materials (instruments, time and space), to compositional processes, to the ways in which performers will be involved in the music's realization.

If I now feel much more optimistic that the sorts of music I want to create will find willing and gifted advocates I am conscious that the world in which that music is heard has also changed. Technical developments in music technology and communications have transformed the ways in which music can be produced and disseminated, while political developments in both local and global economies have shaken even the most established of cultural institutions. Over the same period many critics have begun to argue that notated concert music as a whole has become a cultural oddity within the global music market. In such circumstances the oppositional role to which Nyman's book consigned 'experimental music' is no longer available: how can some music be an 'alternative' to other 'mainstream' music when everything written by composers is now marginal?

Nyman subtitled his book 'Cage and Beyond' and it is to the aesthetic challenge of John Cage's music and ideas that my own work has perhaps been most consistently addressed. In the opening paragraphs of the essay 'Experimental Music' published in *Silence*, Cage says that 'times have changed; music has changed; and I no longer object to the word "experimental"'. He distinguishes between the composer as someone who 'knows his work as a woodman knows a path he has traced and retraced' and the listener who comes to the work 'as one [confronted] in the woods by a plant he has never seen before' and goes on to say that he has now 'become a listener and the music has become something to hear'.[12] This is usually interpreted as a description of Cage's adoption of chance operations in the making of compositional decisions within his music; Cage became a 'listener' because the chance operations produced events within the music that he had not expected. For me, however, it also describes an approach to composing in which the composer attempts to create music to which s/he has an unprecedented relationship, each new work an attempt not just at rearranging previously tested music formulae but at making something different. Not all composers need (or need be expected) to do this, but today, just as when Cage wrote his essay, this approach is still quite properly described as 'experimental', and it is what I do.

---

12   John Cage, *Silence: Lectures and Writings* (Middletown, Conn., 1961), p. 7.

Writing, Music
Michael Pisaro

Encountering Cage

My first contact with experimental music began, as it does for many, with the music of John Cage. Seeing his published scores for the first time, I encountered the work of a hand, and only later, because of the curiosity this created, that of a mind and ear. Looking at *Winter Music* (1957), the first score of his I saw – a page was printed on the back of George Flynn's magnificent 1974 recording of the piece[1] – I recognized an unfamiliar visual sensibility. It was simultaneously clean and clear, oddly formal and hard to decipher, as if it was inventing a new kind of formality based on a different kind of logic than what I had encountered. Everything, it seemed, was designed for the particular piece and was there to indicate a definite style of performance, but the beauty of the object was also striking, perhaps because it seemed like such an odd place to find beauty.

Later I learned that Cage had created the score by making points where there were imperfections on the paper he was using. These were turned into notes and the collections of points were aligned to staves and clefs to give the points relative pitch heights. The singular visual appearance grew out of direct contact with the page. The score was on paper, but it was also a reading of the paper. In a significant way, it *was* paper. It was the first music I had seen that had confronted the writing of a score as *material*, as a part of the composition itself. The score, while being instructions for making sound, was also an image, and, in the way one had to read it, a poem. Like a poem, it did not have to be read linearly (one could begin anywhere) and like a poem it seemed to demand multiple readings to be grasped.

Once you are attuned to this way of looking, and hearing, and thinking – where the writing of the score, the process of its creation and the object of the score, in all its materiality, are seen to play a decisive role in the music itself, you can find it everywhere in experimental music: in Morton Feldman's copying procedures, in Cornelius Cardew's *Treatise* and *The Great Learning*, in the curved eighths and the prose of Christian Wolff, in Lucier's *Queen of the South*, in *Water Yam* by George

---

1   John Cage, 'Winter Music', in *George Flynn, Wound/John Cage Winter Music*. Finnadar Records, QD 9006 (1974).

Brecht, even in Cage's 4'33". Through all this music it is clear that experimental music confronts ideas about writing.

Experimental music does not make a fetish of the score.[2] A score, no matter how beautiful, is still to be understood as a set of symbols whose goal is to be interpreted, in most cases, as sound (and silence). At the same time this music raises, again and again, fundamental questions about the conditions (that is, the mechanics, the system of reference, the function and the process) of writing: as an exploration of what the hand can do, as a way of giving performers directions, as a frame of reference for sounds, as a model for certain kinds of musical behaviour.

This practice has continued and has been amplified in much of the most challenging music being written today. Because experimental music is still a living practice and the full history of the practice has yet to be written, one can start anywhere. Because the network spans decades, with one composer picking up where another left off, and because the development of the ideas discussed here is not linear, but multi-dimensional, concept will be a better system of organization than chronology.

In a sense, within experimental music, the notion that the writing of the score is inseparable from the music is so pervasive, it may seem that there is nothing really important to say. There is some value to this idea: where this music really lives is in the doing of it, not the talking about it. Someone who has worked her way through the pieces, preparing performing versions of the scores, will know much more than if she has only read about what has been done. What might be most useful then, is to make a map with a legend, listing and briefly discussing some of the writing tools that continue to be used, without any attempt to be exhaustive in our explanations. We will follow some of the trajectories in this work to see where they have led and might be leading, with the hope that those who become interested will follow some of the many pathways down into this underground network.

The *Solo for Piano*

The *Solo for Piano* from the *Concert for Piano and Orchestra* from 1957–58 is a good place to start.[3] Its 63 pages contain a compendium of notational styles that, despite

---

2   It might be said that what is sometimes called 'graphic music' does make something of a fetish of the score – by giving priority to the visual image over the practical (or impractical) production of sound. However, no discussion of the writing of experimental music can avoid this lively discipline (and I will discuss a few examples of the music briefly in the 'Image' section of this chapter). The effect of the orientation towards the image in these works has also had a strong and continuing effect on the production of more traditional looking scores. Nevertheless my central focus will be on those ways of writing that stop somewhere short of the production of 'scores to be looked at' (though many of the scores discussed here are nice to look at) – and towards those ways of writing that are most oriented towards producing radical sounding results.

3   Here I will use the *Solo for Piano* as a starting point to discuss a great variety of notations, by Cage and others. An excellent and more extensive discussion of the *Solo*, however,

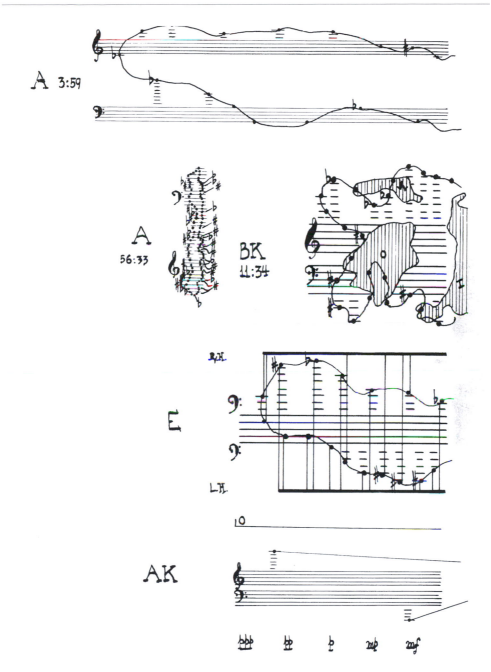

Example 2.1   Some of the notations found in John Cage's *Solo for Piano* from the *Concert for Piano and Orchestra* (1957–58), extract from p. 49

can be found in James Pritchett's *The Music of John Cage* (Cambridge, 1993).

some wonderful performances, seems far from being exhausted in implication and in practice, even 50 years after its creation. It begins as a collection of points. The point, as in *Winter Music*, *Atlas Eclipticalis* (1961) and *Music for Piano* (1952–56), will be the basic unit from which all of the other images spring. These points may occur by themselves, but more often are grouped to form simultaneities or attached in various ways to form lines (or melodies, explicit or implied, as in notation J). The points, along with lines, clefs, stems, dynamics and so on, form the basis of many other, more ambiguous kinds of objects. There are, for example, clusters of dots and lines that form complex patterns (notation AO), harmonic landscapes (A) and islands (T, p. 16), geographical [free hand] (BC, p. 47) or geometrical [ruled] outlines (such as G), overlapping geometries (AR, p. 31), collections of numbers (U, BI), exceptionally beautiful hybrids of numbers, shapes and musical notations (AY, BK), and drawings of the piano for locations (BT). The whole score is laid out with a sensibility for blank space, including three blank pages (15, 32, 61), that probably has Mallarmé's *Un coup de dés* as its inspiration. There are few rivals to this score in physical beauty (though there is obviously much more to the piece than this). One aspect of this beauty, and something we will return to a few times in this chapter, is the fact that this score is drawn entirely by hand. The character of Cage's handwriting communicates something important, if difficult to define about the character of the music itself. Cage's calligraphy is formal looking, clearly blocked and occasionally heavy though also capable of lightness. It is beautifully stylized – it is no accident that someone thought to create a John Cage font.[4] The writing encompasses a range of approaches: a ruler has often been used (for staff lines and other straight lines), a distinct and consistent style of lettering and quite a lot of 'freehand' lineation – which sometimes appears to me to be a performance unto itself, as if it were a question of simple transference to touch an instrument and make shapes with sound, in the manner of these drawings.

Much of what is notated cannot be simply and directly played. Work must be done to realize the notations, to turn them into sound. Cage, in his lengthy set of performance notes, provides many specifics about the realization. However, many details must be resolved or solutions to notations must be found by the performer. The gesture, harmony or shape of a notation can only be turned into sound by means of extensive interpretive work.

Something new and unexpected was happening in Cage's work at this time. He might well have made another decision: to work out, in detail, realizations of each of these ideas – for piano and/or other instruments. In fact this kind of work *was* being done at the time, by Stockhausen and Xenakis, among others. It is a matter of calculation and approximation, of assigning values in pitch space and in time to create the illusion of a line or a continuum, the outline or the volume of a shape. Works like *Gruppen* (1955–57) and *Metastasis* (1954) demonstrate that these kinds of points and shapes can become audible. Why then leave these notations in the form of unrealized images, what some might even call 'sketches', as suggestive

---

4   This was produced for the Museum of Contemporary Art in Los Angeles and the John Cage Trust by P22 type foundry (Buffalo, NY).

as they might be? Part of the reason might be Cage's oft-stated desire to remove his own desires from the composition of a piece, so that he could hear sounds as sounds, instead of as an expression of the composer.[5] What is clear, however, is that any sounding version of the piece will pass through the thought and practice of another musician (unless the performer happens to be Cage). In Cage's work, the music enters a totally new stage of its existence when the musician takes signs created by the composer, signs that are mute about some important aspect(s) of their sound, and transforms them into music. Making music is more than following instructions, and more than following someone's intention: it is the act of creating sound, of creating a space for sound that is alive to the moment. What is desired is a situation that is flexible enough to take on all of the minute inflections in sound appropriate to its time and place(ment). To give impetus to the becoming of sound – to take a role in making it, but also to observe it happen as the result of series of complex thoughts and actions – to be in a situation where one does not know when one is directing and when one is being directed – this is, in Cage's terminology, to be free in the creation of music and alive to what is created.

How did music get to this point? What had created the set of possibilities or the musical atmosphere in which Cage was able to operate? Starting perhaps with serial music, but then with Ives, Cowell and Varèse, it became more difficult to believe in the capacity of the notational conventions of Western music to deal with the conceptions of the composers. Already, with these three, it seemed cumbersome, even sometimes impossible to represent in a quickly comprehensible and elegant way the specific actions the musicians would perform and how these should sound.[6] The discrepancy in Cage's scores between how things look and how one thinks they will sound becomes so wide as to seem, at times, almost arbitrary (as anyone who has tried to follow the score of *Sonata and Interludes* for the first time knows). With the music of Cage around mid-century, this situation is brought to crisis, and seemingly all at once, the whole situation is transformed. Obviously there is much more to this tradition than alternate notation. It is an alternative way of thinking about music.

What we will do in the rest of this chapter is follow the emergence of this new thinking by looking at the way in which the scores are written – and then following the extension of these techniques to their implications for the performance and sound of music, occasionally touching on their implications for the potential of music to come.

Having explored in these first sections some of the broader issues associated with the changes in writing music, I would now like to provide an annotated glossary of some of the compositional practices and their use throughout in experimental music.

---

5   Whether such notations actually achieve this is another question. I believe the issue is much more complicated than that.

6   One thinks here of the lengths to which Ives went in his scores (and with the essays about the music) to convey something that seemed almost impossible to contain – in musical notation or for that matter, in language: as if all representation resources were going to be necessary.

A Catalogue of Experimental Music Writing

The point

Let us return to the *Solo for Piano*. As mentioned, is seems that the point (or dot) is the starting point for much, if not all of the notations created for this work. This of course must stem from the universal sign in Western music for a note. Cage's use of this dot or point, however, involves a degree of symbolic abstraction. With the *Music for Piano* series and later, in the aforementioned *Winter Music*, these dots, while still representing notes are determined in a way uncharacteristic of notes: as marks in the locations of imperfections in the paper. In *Winter Music* Cage introduces the further abstraction of allowing unplayable situations and by freeing up the relationship between note and clef. Later, in *Atlas Eclipticalis*, this dot, still often a note, is a transcription of the location of a star, and is meant to take its part amongst the constellations formed by the collections of instruments. With the *Solo for Piano* this point is treated in far more diverse and wide-ranging ways: in some cases it clearly indicates a tone, but in others it represents a limit mark or simply a generic sound.

As a shorthand for a musical event, this point, shorn of its typical accompaniments (such as lines and beams) can be useful. Works such as James Tenney's *Spectral Canon for Conlon Nancarrow* (1974) and his *Flocking* (1993), for two pianos tuned a quarter-tone apart, demonstrate the kinds of complex visual and aural patterns that can arise from this simplification.

Christian Wolff's use of the point, in pieces such as *For 1, 2 or 3 People* (1964), in *Burdocks* (1970–71) and other works, is more abstract still – without the staff it often looks like a point first and a notation second. Sometimes it *is* simply a note (perhaps with an indication of register), sometimes a version of it (an asterisk) is a noise. An 'x' (perhaps another version of this dot) is simply described as 'anything'.[7]

Perhaps the furthest point of abstraction occurs in many of the works in George Brecht's *Water Yam* collection. The status of the pieces in this collection *as pieces* for performance, might, in some cases be doubtful. One category of piece – such as *Time-Table Music* (1959), *Candle Piece for Radios* (1960) or *Motor Vehicle Sundown Event* (1960) – is very clearly meant for performance: each comes with fleshed-out instructions for specific actions. These scores occur alongside such pieces as *Flute Solo* (1962), with 'disassembling' and 'assembling' as its sole 'instructions'. In many of these pieces the instructions (if that is what they are) are preceded by a curious point, something like this: ●. As one keeps reading through the collection this dot or point becomes more and more odd seeming. It does not appear in every piece, but when it does occur it apparently has some role, it indicates something. The more abstract the piece is (that is, the less clearly it indicates performance), the stronger the function of this dot seems to be. Let's take a look at three works:

---

7   A rake being dragged across a church floor, perhaps, or a spoon in a jar of mustard.

SUITCASE

● from a suitcase

ORGAN PIECE

● organ

G. Brecht
1962

BACH

● Brazil

Example 2.2   Three notecard scores from George Brecht's
Water Yam

Perhaps it is just a bullet point, indicating the first item on a very short list. However, in my reading the dot is a point of demarcation. It functions as if to say (in the piece called *ORGAN PIECE*): 'something to do with an organ', or 'an action involving an organ', or perhaps most of all: 'the event called organ'. Point = Event. Many pieces by Brecht and the other Fluxus composers are, after all, called 'events'.

Flipping through the cards, we will at some point come upon Brecht's wonderful *SYMPHONY, 1962*, which consists of a very small, square card, in which, below the title and above the signature ('G. Brecht'), there is a single dot all by itself. Or rather, it is a hole, a perforation the size of the dot. One can look through the score and see the world. If you look through the hole, the score and the performance can be one and the same. (Needless to say this is not the only way of realizing such a score.) Another interpretation of this point/dot/hole is that it is open to an event of any kind whatsoever.[8]

In Antoine Beuger's *second music for marcia hafif* (1994) the point reappears as an indication for a simple event: a single short sound of some kind. The point is used for the entire 25-minute duration of the piece, inflected by differences in loudness and attack. Its role is to indicate a simple event that serves to mark off one point in time from another. Here the point approaches the meaning mathematicians assign to it: a location, pure and simple – it exists more as a break in continuity, or an infinitesimal stage of that continuity, than as a thing itself. This concept continues to operate in many works of Beuger from that time – though it is worth noting that as his music has developed, the duration of this gesture has expanded.

Finally, I will mention my own *a certain species of eternity* (1996). The score is a large collection of points and spaces aligned to a grid, laid out in columns and rows. Here the point is to be understood as 'one sound' (undefined) of some kind. Taking its cue from Spinoza's *Ethics*, the score concerns the sounding or not sounding of an event. The first page of the score presents a series of questions to the performer concerning the nature of the sound. These are not intended to address sonic requirements, but more the set of things to be considered in choosing the sound. Since the sound itself is open to determination by the performer[9] one question that gets raised here concerns the depth of the point. It is a given that a sound is already too present, that it takes up too much space and time to really represent a point. It must have some physical and temporal extension in order to exist in the sounding world. We learn, if we didn't know already, that words like 'one sound' or 'single sound event' or even 'one silence' are abstractions. *Actual*

---

8   It would be ungracious not to mention here the holes punched directly into the piano rolls by Conlon Nancarrow. The piano roll in Nancarrow's music must be considered another kind of writing. In Nancarrow's piano roll music, a hole is an action. I suspect that the similarities in appearance between Tenney's *Flocking* and some of the piano rolls of Nancarrow are not accidental!

9   Among others, there have been versions for wood blocks, sustained tones and even a proposed version in which the point would be represented by an entire movement of a Beethoven symphony – and lasting many days.

sounds are always multiple – there can be no end to the number of units, or the number of ways of breaking down a single sound. Simply put, there is no such thing as a single sound. But this does not mean we will not continue to refer to things as such and, more importantly, represent them that way in a score – one function of the score is indeed to consider its nature as an abstraction of an actual music situation.

Numbers

Another kind of symbol that is often present in the *Solo for Piano*, which of course has also had a very important role in the history of notated music, is number. Number in experimental music will be applied in a great variety of ways. In most cases, its use is not as fundamental to the ontological character of the music as the point. In other words, its use tends more towards the descriptive and less towards the nature of sound and event themselves. Numbers are ideally suited to the task of setting off or defining units of a multiplicity.

In *Solo for Piano* the abundance of numbers is immediately striking, as is the variety of uses towards which they are put. They are used to indicate proportions relating to subdivision of time or to the distribution of notes between the clefs, to indicate time in seconds (to a precision of two decimal places or in units of some kind), numbers of (indeterminate) events in a continuous situation (sections J and U), loudness (T), degrees of chromatic saturation (Y, AQ), generic numbers of tones, sounds or events (AY, BE, BP, BU), frequencies (BI) and harmonics to be depressed (BR), among still other more subtle uses. Stemming perhaps from Cage's use of the *I Ching* as a compositional tool, and his earlier use of numbers to generate proportional images, there was an increasing visibility of numbers on the score itself. The scale or range of numbers is also something one notices: the presence of a 64 number limit (that is, the number of 64 hexagram combinations) is often evident – and can imply a range of subtlety and exactitude to challenge any performer, as is clearly the case with the use of such numbers in a scale of dynamics.

Numbers can be used *abstractly*, as for instance, when they are used to indicate a quantity of indeterminate sounds in the graphic works of Morton Feldman. The score to *Ixion* (1962) consists primarily of a graph with numbers.

The other direction, towards the use of numbers to indicate *exactitude*, has been developed extensively by composers of microtonal music. This music has long called for inventive notations. While some of this development falls outside of what I would call experimental music, the recurrence, especially with just intonation, of experimental practices merits a few comments. In one direction, the music has worked as a refinement of the accidental. Along these lines, the systems of Ben Johnston and of Marc Sabat and Wolfgang von Schweinitz (called the Helmholtz-Ellis notation) are particularly interesting. The ratio numbers of just intonation are also fairly common and have played an important role in the music of James Tenney and others. When an even higher level of exactitude is required, composers have often prescribed specific frequencies or cents deviation from a particular pitch. The presence of a variety of these notations alongside indeterminate practices in the music of James Tenney and others demonstrates (along the lines of *Solo for Piano*) how indeterminacy and exactness in the writing of music can co-exist – how in this music, the one can be seen as the necessary complement of the other.[10] This is a theme that also surfaces often in discussions of the music of Alvin Lucier and in much recent experimental music where the apparent precision of number meets the 'fuzziness' (or indeterminacy) of language.

Irrational numbers might be said to have an infinite precision. My series *pi (1–2594)* (1998), attempts to approach this precision by setting the first 2,594 decimal places (after the initial number 3) of *pi*.[11] The score, after some initial explanation, consists entirely of these decimal place numbers, which indicate a number of repetitions of a single piano tone. A range of potential numerical patterns of *pi* becomes audible: in a way that at once suggests exactness (because the compositional system is rigidly constructed) and the indefinite (because the process of listening, by being located in time, tends to diffuse the precision of number by creating evasive, hard-to-remember contours).

Number can also be used as something equivalent to the point or dot – the main difference being that the number has the power of differentiation. In *Die meisten Sachen macht man selten (1)* (1994/7) for percussion, Jürg Frey asks the percussionist to find 100 instruments and/or objects that can be struck with a beater or with a hand. The score consists of a list of 200 of these numbers (including repetitions) that gives the order in which the instruments will be played. Small, barely perceptible patterns exist in the sequence of numbers, with some groups of them forming small motives that will be repeated a few times over the course of the piece. However, as the title indicates, the majority of the sounds occur only once or twice.

In Manfred Werder's series of pieces for from one to nine performers (*ein(e) ausführende(r)*, *2 ausführende* and so on (1999)), a number is always used to represent a *performer* who plays one sound (the dot, incidentally, is used here to represent silence).[12]

In each of the three pieces mentioned above, it is the power of number to distinguish amongst the multiple that generates the material of the score. One takes a number like 100 not because one has a specific group of 100 objects in mind, but because of the character of the number itself. In the Werder, it is the quantity of performers in the abstract that counts: these works will, over time, show the categorical difference between having, say, five or four performers in an ensemble.

10　Along these lines, I will also mention the series of pieces by Cage which feature incredibly exact durations, such as *31'57.9864" for a pianist* (1954). Here the proportional durations Cage had been using are precisely expressed throughout, and combined with indeterminate features.

11　The piece is meant to *suggest* this infinite refinement without of course actually achieving it (and it comes nowhere close to the current record (as of 2008) of 1,241,100,000,000 decimal places.

12　Werder, in his *stück 1998* uses pitch names as the equivalent of points. I will discuss both of these works later in this chapter.

Cage's series of number pieces, starting with *Two* for flute and piano (1987) takes the number of performers as the title of the piece. One can feel that, no matter what actually happens in the piece, as with Werder, the essential quality of a number piece is its twoness, or oneness, or threeness; its character as a group of seventy-four players or of seven. Cage and Werder are both edging towards the sense that first a number of people come together in order to make music, and only then can one decide what to play.[13]

This sense of a number of musicians of any kind taking precedence over instrumental requirements is taken still further by the series of number pieces by Antoine Beuger written from 2003 to 2005. These works require of the instrumentalist only the ability to sustain tones. Because the tones may be played in any octave, nearly every instrument can play any of the parts. In addition the music is designed so that, in its layout and in the way it instructs the musicians, it is truly a meditation on what it might mean to *be* two or twenty.[14] Starting always from the same principle, of a sustained tone with any tuning, Beuger arrives at strikingly different ways of conceiving of the group. One might call such an ensemble a society of a kind: a society that learns in the *peckinpah trios* how to get along or even to thrive as three, or as eighteen in the *badiou tunings for eighteen*. If there is a (very local) politics of such music, it is somewhere between communism – where each member of the group is counted only once – and anarchy, where, seemingly out of nothing, subgroups and even movements can be formed, only to disappear in the next section of the piece or with another number of players.

This example of one page from Beuger's *ockeghem octets* assigns the individual players (numbered) to one of two lines. All tones are sustained at a pitch anywhere between a half-step above and a half-step below the given pitch. The point of entry and the octave in which the tone is played are left unspecified. The result is an unusual but still faintly audible double canon. Each page assigns a different group of numbers to each part and, of course, changes the pitch context of the melody to be played.

This page from Beuger's *badiou tunings for eighteen* divides the group into subsets of three, six and nine. As with the *ockeghem octets* each page recasts the players assigned to the groupings. Each player selects *one* tone from the group they are given.

---

13   With Cage's number pieces the music can vary from piece to piece from contrasting parts – for contrasting instruments – to unassigned instruments with collections of tones or simply of sounds to play, creating a more conceptually homogeneous relation between the parts.

14   Another Beuger piece from this period is called, a bit more straightforwardly, *un lieu pour être deux* (2007).

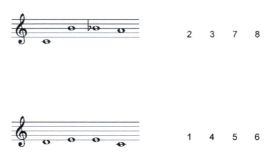

Example 2.3   One (unnumbered) page from Antoine Beuger's
            ockeghem octets (2004)

8   13   18

4   5   9   10   15   16

1   2   3   6   7   11   12   14   17

Example 2.4   One (unnumbered) page from Antoine Beuger's
              badiou tunings for eighteen (2005)

The grid

The layout of material in squares is well-known from the lattices created in serial music, spelling out the forms and transpositions of the row in two dimensions. Such lattices sometimes, however, in three or even four and five dimensions, are used in just intonation. Of course Cage often laid out his material on an eight-by-eight square to parallel the hexagrams of the *I Ching* (there are numerous grid-like notations in the *Solo for Piano*).

These tables of data in the form of graphs made their appearance in experimental music notation in some of the early works of Morton Feldman, notably the *Intersection* series for piano. The vertical dimension was used to distribute register and the horizontal for time – where, as in *Intersection 2* (1951), the pulse unit is simply one square on the graph. The visceral impact of a good performance of these pieces (by, for example, John Tilbury) is related to the directness of the score: one can in a very clear way *play* the surface features of pulse and density, without the unnecessary mediation of the staff and time signature.

The grid can also be understood as a way of organizing the space of musical performance (where the squares of the graph are understood as something like lines of longitude and latitude). In much of my recent work this grid has become a mapping of a sonic field – the creation of a landscape. Works like *ricefall* (2004), *A wave and waves* (2007) and *nachtstimmung* (2008) transpose this layout onto the performing space (see Example 2.5).

plastic 1	metal 2	rice 1	paper 2
metal 1	leaves 2	ceramic 2	wood 2
wood 1	stone 2	ceramic 1	paper 1
stone 1	leaves 1	plastic 2	rice 2

Example 2.5   The layout of performers with materials used as the basis for the rice landscape of *ricefall*

The layout of space and its representation in the score has also played a role in the music of Peter Ablinger – see for instance his *Weiss/Weisslich 5* (1992/94). In Ablinger's work this has also taken the form of seating chairs in a grid for listening, as with his *Listening Piece in Four Parts* (2001) (Example 2.6).

Example 2.6   Peter Ablinger – *Listening Piece in Four Parts*, 3. Los Angeles, Downtown. 4th Street/Merrick Street, Parking Lot (documentation)

The line

The line: as a stem, a beam, a staff line or a bar line, or, if curved, as a slur, is, along with the point, the basic graphic resource of Western music. The hand-drawn lines ntational elements or other images associated with drawing proper. Like a drawing its power is in suggestion rather than completion – composers draw, they don't paint. Sometimes it is what is left out that speaks.

In experimental music, within the relative freedom in which this drawing takes place, there is the understanding that a line might communicate more or be open to more than its typical function. A performer on an instrument, after all, also uses her *hands* (and sometimes her breath) to make music – another somewhat chaotic physical process. The music, however, is often content to suggest the possibility of a connection, to leave the relationship open, without being too specific about how exactly these lines are to be read.

There are times, however, when the relationship to real drawing can become explicit. In Cage's *Ryoanji* (1983–85), portions of rocks are traced onto the manuscript, making detailed lines with many small irregular features. Guidelines are given so that the performer can turn these into glissandi (that is, a continuous, microtonal tracing of the line created). The hand and eye can be a subtler indicator of minute variation than anything so far conjured up in microtonal accidentals. Here again the resulting sound would not have been imaginable without the intermediary of a method of writing.

The drawing of objects with sound is also the preoccupation of much of the recent work of Alvin Lucier. In *Still Lives* for piano and sine tones (1995) everyday objects are traced with sine tones, which because of their simplicity can easily suggest lines. A sine tone, as it moves in time, corresponding to the horizontal dimension, can easily be used to suggest straight (or unchanging), slanting (using glissandi) and even curved lines. This gives Lucier all the tools he needs to draw, using two or three voices (or lines), a hammock, a bread knife, a barbeque grill or a lampshade. The piano outlines the drawing of the shapes by playing tones that sound against the pure tones – usually at the unison, octave or another consonant interval. Since the pure tones are moving but the tones from the piano are stable in pitch, patterns of beating are created as the sounds approach or pull away – and these patterns, because they occur at various places in the room, due to the spatial nature of sound as waves, map or draw additional pictures in the space. What looks on paper to be two dimensional is four dimensional in the performance. As with most of Lucier's music, a simple, straightforward procedure creates very complex results. Other works in this vein trace the line of a mountain range (*Panorama* for trombone and piano (1993)), *Diamonds* for 1, 2 or 3 orchestras (1999) and the constellation *Cassiopeia*, for small orchestra (1998). In these last two the function of the sine tones is taken over by members of the orchestra.

In Craig Shepard's piece *Lines (1)* for performer (1999) the *process* of drawing a line on the page is made audible. By holding the paper in the air with one hand and drawing a straight line (with a pencil) with the other, the paper itself is turned into a kind of micro-resonator that lightly amplifies the movement of the pencil, turning the imperfections of the surface of the paper into a memorable source of sound.

It is worth remembering that the first version of Cage's *4'33"* (1952) marked off the duration of silence on the page with vertical lines – proportional to the required durations. I find the idea that a line can cut or divide a silence to be very rich. Where in any piece is that point that indicates the start? How is music really initiated? I have often had the experience, even with traditional music, that the music begins before the first sound, and especially, that it ends only after the silence following the last sound. There is something like a *passe-partout* in music as well as painting.[15]

---

15   The insightful discussion of the concept of the *passe-partout* by Jacques Derrida is (without knowing it) perhaps the deepest discussion of the implications of *4'33"* (see 'Passe-Partout' and 'Parergon', in *The Truth in Painting*, trans. G. Bennington and I.

The page

It is obvious that the paper on which a score is written or printed is an important part of its character, as Cage emphasized by tracing the imperfections of this paper, and transforming the resultant drawing into music. In the *Variations* series transparent pages are included. All of Cage's work, including his visual art, is highly sensitive to the unit of the page.

Morton Feldman was also highly conscious of how the music should fit on a page, even as he was writing his apparently (but deceptively) traditionally notated later scores. I cannot help but feel that behind this there is something that every composer understands: the superstition of the page (that is, the unwritten page, and the dream of what it might contain, the individual page understood as a unit of potential). *4'33"*, in its proportional version, approaches this notion: the performer is performing from a mostly blank or, in the case of page 3, an absolutely blank sheet.

A page is a unit of music. The pieces of George Brecht's *Water Yam* are inseparable from the appearance on a note-card size sheet. I don't think it was an accident that Earle Brown's *December, 1952*, and Christian Wolff's *Edges* (1968) appear on a single large page. It is important in all these cases to be able to see everything at once for the whole duration of the performance.

A page is usually also a part of the performance. In Beuger's *dialogues (silences)* (1993) and *things taking place* (1994), the beginning and ending times are marked on the pages, and thus the times (and) sounds of the page turns are part of the music. In my piece *leaves* (1994) the individual pages fall to the ground as they are finished being played. *braids* (1997), my piece for silent reader, consists, in its sounding material, of nothing but page turns.[16]

Image

Earle Brown's *December, 1952* was perhaps the first piece within experimental music to present an *image* or collection of images as a score. Without the performance instructions it might easily be taken for a drawing, perhaps because its visual orientation, as a series of lines and rectangles spread out on a single page, requires no explanation *as image*.[17] What is also clear, as soon as one attempts to play the piece, is that there will be no definitive or final interpretation. The ways of reading the score are so open, and there is so little that is fixed (such as instrumentation, duration, dynamics or pitch content), the score will, of necessity, be a jumping-off point for a great variety of realizations.

McLeod (Chicago, 1987), pp. 1–14 and 37–82).

16   The performer passes the time by reading a timed text of chance-determined lines from texts by Lao-Tzu, Baruch Spinoza and Allen Ginsberg.

17   Is this drawing perhaps indebted to the geometrical forms found in early twentieth-century abstract art?

To realize or make a version of a piece is not to compose one. David Tudor did sometimes write out versions of some of the pieces he played – for example the *Intersection* pieces by Feldman – as a discipline and as a way of making a reliable and accurate performance. But he seemed conscious of the fact that he was doing the work of interpretation, trying, as in all notated music, to represent as faithfully as possible whatever was indicated by the images and words of the score. Tudor's painstaking methods in preparing the indeterminate works of Cage, Wolff and Feldman from the 1950s, and his convincing performances of them are, as these composers have indicated, part of the reason why they kept writing this kind of music. Tudor made it clear that the realization of such music was just as challenging as learning the thousands of notes and rhythms required for the complex serial works emerging from Europe at the time. Unlike those works, however, the indeterminate pieces could be different in many or most of their sounding details with every performance. The performer could grow and change in his relationship to the image presented by the score. The discipline, with each performance, of returning to what was written or drawn, to decipher, with a slightly changed eye, the marks and spaces – and to re-imagine their sounding possibilities – is created by the necessity of interacting with someone else's vision. Imperceptibly, over the course of this extended process the performer might develop such a powerful vision of the work that it is no longer very clear whose music is being played.

John Cage's *Variations* series (1958–66) takes the use of the image even further, in having the performer *create* the image from the set of materials given – transparencies which are overlaid on a sheet of paper to create multi-layered score-images. The eloquence of means in *Variations III* (1963) is notable. A set of 42 circles, printed in black on a transparent sheet and cut out by the performer, is made to fall on a single sheet. The largest grouping of overlapping circles is determined, and then all of the other circles are cleared away. The result is so beautiful in its textural disposition of circles (it can look somewhat like a wall drawing by Sol LeWitt) that one struggles to find an interpretation worthy of the image. The actions one is to perform are not described, but a way of reading the circles, as a layering of interpenetrating variables, is. Cage leaves open the possibility that 'noticing' an environmental change could be understood as any number (including all) of the actions.

It makes a difference that these works are known to have been written by Cage. Although the context of the performance, and certainly the sounds, are not specified (just the opposite), the discipline Cage asks for, and the objectivity with which one needs to approach the task, virtually guarantee that, in a faithful performance, the juxtaposition of elements will not obey obvious stream-of-consciousness connections or a dramatic logic (both things that Cage abhorred). For me, one of beautiful paradoxes of Cage's work is that despite his stated goal of removing preferences (that is, his own likes and dislikes) from the process of writing music (in order to let 'sounds be themselves'), in a faithful performance, a Cagean character to the work ends up being reinstated.[18] There is no innocent

---

18   The *mechanics* of this are complex enough to be worthy of a separate essay, but I suspect

performance of a Cage score: the collective set of decisions that make up his music create a context in which other decisions may be made. Although much is open, there are limits to Cage's music – but these limits are interesting, and over time they become a part of the substance of a performance of his work. (This might be the most difficult thing to define about Cage's oeuvre: his sense of *taste*.) Nonetheless this score and the others in the *Variations* series probe a certain limit, one approaching a maximal distance between composer and the musical material. This topic is one that retains its liveliness in some of the graphic work by other composers that runs concurrently with that of Cage.

The inventions of Cornelius Cardew's *Treatise* (1963–67), as I mentioned at the beginning of this chapter, lie on the boundary of what I have chosen to consider here. As a work of score art it is probably unsurpassed – every page is filled with a free-wheeling (one is tempted to say 'psychedelic') invention. The impact of reading the work is unforgettable. For me it could only be compared to the impact of hearing, during one afternoon and evening, long ago, both books of J.S. Bach's *Well-Tempered Claiver*, all 48 Preludes and Fugues, in one sitting. Cardew's piece has something of the same over-the-top virtuosity. There have been many ideas about how to realize the piece and some excellent sounding versions. Nonetheless, probably the most important question here is whether in fact we are actually dealing with a score. Several years after completing the work, Cardew himself saw *Treatise* as providing nothing more than 'the visual aspect of a traditional score – an undefined, subjective stimulus for the interpreter'. Furthermore:

> *In performance, the score of Treatise is in fact an obstacle between musicians and the audience.*

> *Behind that obstacle the musicians improvise, but instead of improvising on the basis of objective reality and communicating something of this to the audience, they preoccupy themselves with a contradictory artifact: the score of Treatise.*

Summing up, Cardew says: 'Musical graphics are a substitute for composition.'[19]

Naturally, I am aware that this comes from a time (1974) in which Cardew, having recently converted to Communism, set out to provide a thorough-going criticism of the avant-garde in music, aiming directly at Cage and Stockhausen, but directing still more critical energy towards his own earlier work. Although there is something to what Cardew says here, he is probably being too harsh.

One could rather say that, in this case, *Treatise* functions as something like a screen or a filter through which a musical intention passes into performance. In the best performances it will have transformed in some subtle, but important way, the music that might otherwise have been created. Performers might improvise or

---

that many who have been deeply involved in the performance of Cage's work will agree with this assessment.

19   Cornelius Cardew, *Stockhausen Serves Imperialism* (London, 1974), p. 85.

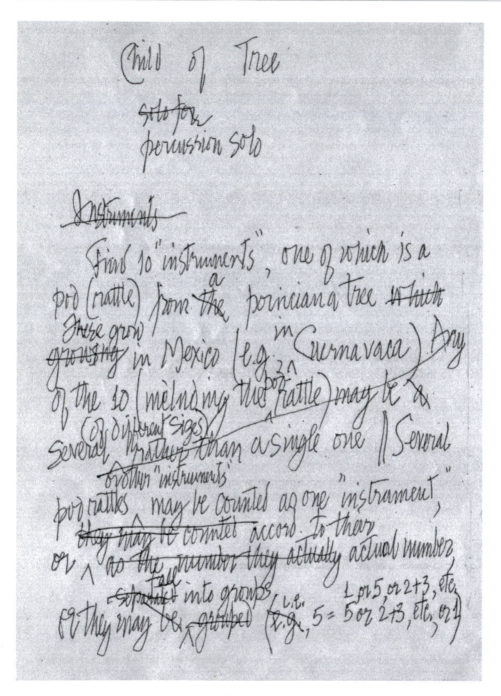

Example 2.7   A page of the sketch (in this stage, somewhere
                between a prose score and drawing) for John Cage's
                Child of Tree

compose realizations – having been inspired or challenged by the images Cardew created – *Treatise* acting here as a silent partner in the creation of one's own music. It is true that this process might look like a mystification of the work of making music. But something more directly musical can also happen, even if it is rare: a situation in which someone has been driven to make a more direct or less self-centred, less style-conscious music than they would have dared to make as an improviser or a composer. The images can, in such cases, release a desire in a performer they would not have known otherwise. This is, after all, comparable to the way in which any work of visual art can serve as a stimulus to any new musical work. But we are, as Cardew knew, now some distance from something that can easily be called a score.

Perhaps *Treatise*'s greatest impact has been to forever change the way certain musicians read music, and to define the something of a limit where the beauty of the image overwhelms the practical versions of it that can be made. This seems to be the case, at least for Cardew, who following *Treatise* produced *The Great Learning* (1968–71). It looks quite a bit more like a traditional (but experimental) score, but is also clearly indebted to the graphic sensibility Cardew had developed. *The Great Learning* remains one of the most inspiring scores of the period: it is so full of ideas, so eager to try things out, so optimistic about how humans can come together to make music and, finally, so accepting of the diversity of impulses that brings them together.

The period of experimentation with how a score could look, extending, in its first stage, from the early 1950s and continuing until the early 1970s, produced many beautiful documents. The pages assembled by John Cage and Alison Knowles for their book *Notations*[20] from a great variety of composers (not just limited to those associated with experimental music) could be the subject of an independent study. 'Graphic Notation' as this trend is sometimes called, has gone on to have a life of its own – and remains a constant challenge to the means of more traditional musical notation. The connection of this trend in notation to improvisation is deep and lasting, and, as composers such as Anthony Braxton and Wadada Leo Smith (among others) have shown, can lead to innovative music. New collections of the graphic impulses in notation have sprung up in recent years.[21]

Although my interest in this chapter is in those ways of writing music that have developed out of traditional musical notations, there is an indefinite border between these concerns and a broader set of questions, concerning the relationship between what we see and what we do, at the basis of much of the more consciously graphic work.

It is likely that this kind of thinking influenced works such as Christian Wolff's *Burdocks* (1971) – especially Section V, with its pinwheels or burdocks – and even some of the works of James Tenney, such as the layout of *Critical Band* (1988) – where the wedge created by the expansion of the harmony is visually represented in the score. A glance through many more recent scores – by Jürg Frey, Manfred Werder, Markus Trunk, Sam Mirelman, Michael Winter, Tashi Wada and many others, will

---

20   John Cage and Alison Knowles (eds), *Notations* (New York, 1969).

21   Just to mention two: T. Möller, K. Shim and G. Stäbler (eds), *SoundVisions* (Saarbrücken, 2005) and Theresa Sauer (ed.) *Notations 21* (New York, 2009).

demonstrate immediately that, even in scores whose primary function is to provide a set of instructions for making music, the visual image of the score is a crucial, if hard-to-define area of communication.

I want to close this section by briefly mentioning another kind of image – a kind of writing that takes place in (or on) the instrument itself. Alvin Lucier's *The Queen of the South* (1972) is a piece in which, building upon the discoveries of Ernst Chladni and Hans Jenny, vibration patterns are made visible on a surface by means of acoustical excitation. This score, like many written by Lucier, is a prose description – in this case making suggestions for how to get these patterns to appear, with lists of the various media and kinds of excitation that might work. It also includes some photographs of what the result might look like. As anyone who has worked on the piece knows, the production of the various patterns is dependent upon several hard-to-control variables: as with many of the effects produced in Lucier's music, the situation is fragile, inherently unstable. Much of the time one spends trying things out and failing. For one performance, composer Liam Mooney outfitted a vacuum cleaner with funnels and then placed them on the bottom side of some fairly large tom-toms with seeds placed on their heads. We waited for about five minutes while Liam attempted, by various means, to get the vibrations to produce recognizable patterns. When this did happen, the patterns appeared spontaneously out of the chaos of the bouncing seeds, remained visible for a while, and then disappeared just as suddenly, to be replaced by chaos again, or on rare occasions, a completely different pattern or image. One learns that the piece is really the whole process of making the images appear. But I had the sense that the score appeared before me – in way that truly connected the visual and the sonic – only in those moments when the patterns appeared.

Prose

Having reached one limit of this discussion, with the merging of image with sound, we will now look at one of the other great resources in the writing of experimental music: language itself. Many composers have written about music – some, including Cage, Feldman, Wolff and Tenney, in beautiful and enlightening ways. What I am interested in here, however, is the writing done in scores, as music. This seems to me, despite its frequent use in experimental music, to be an under-appreciated genre. It combines elements of technical writing, the instruction manual and various forms of literature – all geared towards getting a set of sonic results to happen. My conviction is that, far from just being a form of writing music that takes place outside of the symbolic territory of traditional Western music, this kind of writing also leads to new ways of making sound and opens up the ways we have of relating to music – and to people.

Let's begin with one of the classics of this form, Christian Wolff's score for *Fits and Starts* (Example 2.8).

One might actually begin anywhere in Wolff's *Prose Collection* to discuss the use of prose in music scores. Though unassuming in appearance and rhetoric the

Fits and Starts

Four or five of the following sequences represented to start with.

Any number of players; any one player playing one or more of the sequences; any number of players playing the same sequence.

Each player follows her own pulse, generally within the limits of one beat per 5/6 of a second to one beat per 1 1/3. Generally, though without straining to, avoid another's pulse.

The duration of a sound, unless some further articulation of it (which may include its stopping) is used to mark a rhythm, should not exceed about 2 1/2 seconds (and may be any shorter length).

1. 1 sound or articulation of a sound underway: every 21 beats, omitted every 6th time the 21st beat comes round.

2. 1 sound or articulation: at the 11th beat, then at the 12th, then 13th,, etc., always adding one.

3. 1 sound or articulation: at the 10th beat, the 29th, 60th, then 10th, 29th, 60th, etc., always repeating.

4. 1 sound or articulation: at the 120th beat; 2 sounds or articulations at the next 100th; 1 at next 90th; 2 at next 80th; 1 at next 70th; 2 at next 60th; 1 at next 50th; 1 at next 40th; 2 at next 30th; 1 at next 20th; 2 at next 10th; then 1 at next 20th; 2 at next 10th; then 1 at next 20th; 2 at next 30th; 1 at next 40th; 1 at next 50th; 2 at next 60th, etc., back to 1 at next 120th, then forward again, and back, etc.

5. 1 sound or articulation: 15 beats after 4 sounds or articulations heard; then 4 beats after 4 sounds or articulations heard; then 15 beats after 4 sounds, etc., heard, then 4 beats after 4, etc., always alternating; or (freely changing back and forth): 2 sounds or articulations: 21 beats, then 3 beats, then 50, then 21, 3, 50 always repeating, after 3 sounds or articulations.

6. 1 sound or articulation every 42 beats; or (alternating freely) 2 sounds or articulations every 29th or 58th beat.

Players may shift from one sequence to another at any point within a sequence.

When a player has a sense of the music of his rhythm(s) he may proceed simply on the basis of that sense, and hence to her own rhythms.

Example 2.8   Christian Wolff's score for *Fits and Starts,* from the *Prose Collection* (1968–71) collection represents an impressive array of writing strategies and of the kinds of music that can emerge from them. One of the characteristics of this music generally is that you do not really find out how the score functions until you try it out. The kind of reading one does for sense is obviously very different from the kind of reading one does when one has to act upon instructions.

For instance, with *Fits and Starts* when you get to the end of your first reading, you may have to reread in order to remember that you have to begin with only four or five of the six sequences. This implies coordination amongst the members of the ensemble in order to work out which sequences will be represented. If one has, say, three performers, the implication will be that at least one of the performers must switch from one sequence to another near the start of the piece; if one has 20 players, the group will have to decide which sequence (or two sequences) will *not* be available. In trying out the sequences themselves, it might become clear to a performer that they will need to write out the numbered pulse points in order to keep track of an involved counting procedure (such as that of #3).

One is sent back to the score again and again, in order to sift through all of the information necessary to stay within the boundaries of the piece. One will also have to read carefully to understand what has *not* been defined. For instance, what in this piece is a 'sound'? Nothing is said about this until the fourth sentence, and here it concerns only the parameter of duration. There are actually a few options in considering duration, the simplest being a sound lasting no more than 2.5 seconds, as a marker of the pulse. But the duration of the sound can also be (much) longer, which in this case becomes a carrier for the pulse, now understood as an 'articulation'.

Nothing at all is said about the instrument, pitch, colour or indeed the character of sound to be used. It might be almost anything, produced in just about any way, at any volume, at any pitch or without pitch altogether and so forth. In rehearsal one will probably make a whole chain of adjustments to the sound as one's sense of the realization develops. It is only after one has worked on the piece for a while that it becomes possible to understand what is meant by the last, most elusive sentence of Wolff's text – his permission to leave the instructions behind in order to proceed according to the music of one's own rhythms.

The result, when everything goes right, can be unlike anything one has heard before: a layering of individual pulses, making organically complex patterns that, in spite of their extreme polyrhythmic complexity, can sound quite natural, even gentle.

This somewhat lengthy summary of the procedure of working on the piece is an attempt to demonstrate just how close the reading of the score will be, and to give something of the flavour of the readings to which the piece has to submit. Working on this kind of music, I sometimes have the feeling that I am reading a legal document (the US Constitution?), and trying, as would a judge or legal scholar, to reach a settled interpretation of the score. Should one read for intent, attempting to glean 'spirit of the piece', or does one take the language more rigidly, doing only what is clearly stated? The method used might vary from piece to piece. In any event, with committed performers, there will always be different ways of reading the text and various ideas about what to do with it. This sets a singular chain of events in motion that will, eventually, become woven into the performance itself.

Each time I rehearse one of these pieces with a performing group, I am reminded of Wolff's skill in creating prose that stands up to repeated analytical and practical reading. This kind of writing clearly informs a lot of Wolff's other work as well – when prose is used in combination with Wolff's other notational practices.

Another feature of these prose pieces is that nearly anyone can do them. The entry level, in terms of the amount of previous musical training or technique one might need to perform it, is, compared to most classical music, quite low. It is usually possible to use sound sources that are available to just about anyone: the voice, everyday objects or some kind of simple instrument. The score also makes it possible, in most cases, to produce music right away.[22]

Pauline Oliveros, in her great, ongoing series of 'sonic meditations', uses the device of the text score to explore very sophisticated conceptions of music and sound. These pieces often begin by getting people to listen and to make sound with the minimal resources: their ears and mind, their voices and bodies.

In Example 2.9 the language used is simple and direct, with as little artifice as possible. The significance of this piece and so many like it by Oliveros, is in the doing of it. One might even wonder why such a score should be written at all – couldn't it just be given as a loose set of verbal instructions, which is, in fact, the way many of us encounter these pieces for the first time, in working with Pauline?

Circle Sound Meditation

Lie on your back with your head toward the center of the circle. After relaxing and easy breathing, listen then sound. Alternate between listening and sounding.

Example 2.9   *Circle Sound Meditation*, Pauline Oliveros, from the *Deep Listening Pieces* (1978)

---

22   One can also make the pieces very difficult, finding ways of doing them that would challenge even the most virtuosic musicians.

However, I think such scores demonstrate the power of language as a musical tool. Something apparently simple like this, which might appear to be something like an ear training exercise, is given an extra emphasis by being written out. Language has the ability to say: 'This *is* something.' In fact, the performance of such a piece is, in my experience, extremely complex. These apparently simple activities: lying, relaxing, breathing, listening and sounding, generate, in a decent size group, a host of layered, sometimes personally transforming moments of sonic awareness. Performing in this piece, and in others like it by Oliveros, I have occasionally thought about what the score would really look like, if one were to write out what everyone did in traditional notation. It could look very much like a complex contemporary score: a variety of extended vocal techniques and a multi-layered rhythmic structure, due to the fact that each person establishes their own network of rhythmic rates and durations based on their own breathing – a network which relates in some way to the others being performed – because one is, at the same time, influenced by the behaviour of the group. One sees the incredible efficiency of Oliveros's notation.

Such a score, to be sure, relies upon improvisation on the part of the performer. However, when one has done the piece a few times, one finds a certain consistency to it as well. The circle, the pattern of inward and outward direction, and the rhythm of the breath appear in every version. We find ourselves again in that grey area where so much music actually takes place: between the situation structured by the composer and the moment of performance.[23]

Prose also finds its way into the performance of pieces. John Cage's miraculous *Lecture on Nothing* (1950) combines text and performance in a way that can only be called compositional, using as it does proportional structure and duration, like other works of Cage from that time. This structure has a way of mediating the delivery of information – of allowing text to vacillate between sense and sound, or to become simultaneously sense *and* sound. The silences imbedded in the lecture reinforce the sonic situation of the environment in which they occur. This genre of the composed talk, sometimes mixed with Cage's poetic practice, resonates throughout his work from that point onwards.

It is a short step from Cage's initial work to the practice of many other composers who regularly write text to be performed. Robert Ashley has flooded his work with text. His *Private Parts (The Record)* (1977) is a spoken text, written by Ashley and accompanied by something like background music for tabla, synthesizer and piano. At first it might not seem to depart much from similar kinds of poetry and music combinations of the Beat era. But the genre of the text is ambiguous. It is not really a story or poem – it is more philosophical in orientation – perhaps it could be called a *meditation*. There is also something in the style of the text, the reading and the persistent music that makes it feel like it is always on the verge of song. It raises the question

---

23   This situation, and the inherent tightrope walk between what is asked for by the composer and the difficulty of reconciling this with the situation is the subject of Tom Johnson's brilliant and hilarious piece *Failing* (1975). The prose of the piece, as with many of Johnson's works, is planted into the performance of the piece itself.

whether, as in some sound poetry or even in some popular music (for example, some of the work of Bob Dylan), written text can in fact be a kind of music.[24]

Most of Ashley's work from this point on seems to grow directly from the writing, speaking and, eventually, the singing of prose, and can be understood as an extension of the resources of what was once called recitative. Many of the operas (in score form) have something comparable to the lineation of the *Lecture on Nothing*. They are written as text with numbered lines (where the line typically will have a fixed number of beats at a certain tempo), with a few sketched musical indications (a choice of rhythmic figures and melodies). The openness of the notation is conducive to a situation that prioritizes spoken or nearly spoken language, and a regular ensemble that knows the style. The rapidity and naturalness with which Ashley's troupe sing-speaks is beyond the resources of traditional musical notation.[25] And yet, the operas have the feeling and timing of highly structured works. This is in part due to their narrative structure – also quite radical.[26] But they have a strong musical identity as well, something that often lurks in the background of the music as a set of hinted at motives and harmonies.

One might almost call Ashley's use of language orchestral in its sense of the number of ways that American English can be spoken. There is something unmistakable in its combination of artistically rendered colloquial talking (and swearing[27]), its quasi-philosophical discussion (philosophy on drugs) and its self-referential narration (who am I now?). Perhaps here we ought to speak of a 'Third Practice', following about four centuries after the advent of the *seconda prattica* defined by Monteverdi.

With this heritage it becomes possible to work with ideas that might otherwise be considered too complex to follow in the context of music. Along these lines there has been some interesting work with actual philosophical texts, spoken or sung as a part of the music. Mike Richard's *Affects, Affections 1–4* (2002) takes the eponymous section from Gilles Deleuze's *Spinoza: Practical Philosophy* as the text for a kind of song cycle – the entire text here is spoken/sung with written-out instrumental accompaniment. The result stretches the time of reading considerably – it takes about 90 minutes to get through about three pages of text. One can read Deleuze's text along with the piece and develop a deeper relationship to it than one would be likely to have in a simple reading.[28] Richard has a created a system of

---

24   The answer to this question is, emphatically, YES. As with the history of the graphic score, the discussion of so-called sound poetry lies, for the most part, outside of this chapter, although it borders it at many points. An excellent discussion of the intersection between poetics and acoustics can be found in Adalaide Morris (ed.) *Sound States: Innovative Poetics and Acoustical Technologies* (Chapel Hill, 1997).

25   Much of what happens in this direction is also attributable to the use of the microphone in these pieces. The voices never have to strain to be understood.

26   Ashley's reworking of the opera seems to me to bear comparison to Jean-Luc Godard's work in film or the revolutionary re-evaluation of the novel carried out by writers such as Thomas Pynchon, David Markson and Joseph McElroy.

27   My favorite renderings of swearing occur in *Dust* (2000): 'fuuh' and 'shiih'. Their use, in the context of the scene in a hospital in which they occur, is heartbreaking.

28   A complete recording with the text can be found at this web address: http://www.archive.

harmonic and melodic motives that thread their way through the text – something he calls a 'secondary symbolic network'. The resultant opening of the text, in its poetic content and in the rhythm of its thought, is something like the discovery of an alternate kind of reading, one that takes time to meditate on each turn of the text and that appreciates (even in the English translation) its microstructure.[29] An era in which philosophical prose is used as the basis for extended experimental composition would appear to be just getting started.

The list

The compiling of chance events in the realization of a piece by Cage often involves the making of lists: of notes or sounds, of durations, of instruments and so on. The structure of a list is deceptively simple. It is an explicit device for creating similarity amongst various elements by appearing to give each one an equivalent amount of space.

Alvin Lucier's score for *Chambers* (1968) begins with lists of resonant environments and of ways of making them sound – followed by a few paragraphs that list some possible locations of performance, and ways of listening to and of recording the sounds made. Like many of Lucier's scores, the instructions appear rather unassuming – essentially a series of suggestions. However, each element on the list could take the better part of a day, or a week or a month to realize. Exploring the resonance of subway stations or of bays or bells could indeed be assignments for a lifetime. Or one could spend an entire cold winter exploring and recording the resonance possibilities inherent in freezing.[30] A body of art can be created from exploding as Cai Guo-Qiang has done, but how many, along the way, have explored the resonances that result? A list is a summary, but can also be an opening into a vast realm of experience and exploration, thus its appropriateness for experimental music.

Lists can also find their way into the actual performance material. The score to *calme étendue* (1996–97) by Antoine Beuger consists essentially of vast lists of notes, words or gestures that can be put into any duration between 45 minutes and 9 hours, with silences occurring between the sounding sections.

As one might learn from Whitman's *Leaves of Grass*, a list of words is nearly a poem. Because of the categorical way in which lists are often organized, it can be a very unusual one. We all know that the *ur*-list of a dictionary creates a multitude of unforeseeable juxtapositions. One of the oddest and most wonderful list pieces I know is Jürg Frey's *Lovaty* (1996). The work must be seen and heard to

---

org/details/mmm027 (accessed 9 September 2008).

29   This work, along with Antoine Beuger's *calme étendue*, was the inspiration for my own passage through Spinoza's *Ethics (Book 5)* called *Reading Spinoza*. In my piece, the entire Fifth Book of the *Ethics* is read, with a piano counterpart that is derived from the mathematical numbering system used by Spinoza to structure the book.

30   As any one who has experienced the sudden crack of ice on an apparently frozen lake would know, this could involve not only danger, but also a vivid experience of environmental sound.

be comprehended, but here perhaps a short description will give some indication of how the piece uses its materials. The score consists of two lengthy lists of names, coming to a total of about 2,200 words. The first list is of birds, which all come from a single source.[31] The second is of small locations – what in German are called *Flurnamen*, meaning features of a local landscape, such as sides of a mountain or a hill, parts of a valley, a pasture and so on, each of which has been given an individual name – all rendered in Swiss-German dialect.[32] Frey organizes the lists in a variety of ways. In general he works with the sounds of the words, in terms of their length and phonemic similarity/dissimilarity, and also with degrees of recognition. For instance, the first half of the list of bird names is such that a German-speaker wouldn't necessarily connect them with birds, although many of the names are quite suggestive. (There is one, for example, called 'Sprachmeister' or something like 'language-crafter'.) The second part of this list contains mostly names that clearly indicate birds – ending, for example, with '–vögel', '–gänse' or '–eulen'. There are also subsections that group together birds that have colours in their names or birds that have 'insults' as a part of their name – which might include words like 'complainer' or 'screamer' or 'thief' (in German).

With the place names, Frey for the most part ignores obvious geographical references – words like *Wald* or *See* or *Berg* (forest, lake, mountain). The order is in large part created by movement through adjacent areas of Switzerland – from the Lötschental, through the Alps and the Berner Oberland, on through the Seeland and the Jura, and ending near Basel. There is, within this large-scale organization, also an area where a series of one-syllable place names is used. These are incredible words: *Loo, Üech, Dy, Galm, Zälg* – one could easily quote the whole list.

The performance consists of a reading of the list by two performers. It is often a kind of solo reading. The role of the second speaker is to occasionally double the voice of the first. The only other variation that occurs in the reading of the list is the occasional and sudden but subtle acceleration of the regular tempo from 30 words per minute to 40 per minute.

The rate at which the words go by and the linguistic complexity of the names makes the work feel quite fast and dense at the beginning. The lists look rather simple, but (as with Lucier) they represent a significant amount of information, and one senses this. While listening one passes through times of concentration and fatigue, and there are passages that are inexplicably funny. The beginning of the second large section of the piece (about 35 minutes in) is the main event of the composition (Example 2.10).

The start of the section beginning with 'Siten' works as a kind of shock. One has not understood how acclimated one had become to the human language of birds (with all of its concomitant onomatopoeia and descriptions of appearance and character). In retrospect it is clear that the list was *speaking bird*, and then suddenly starts *speaking place*, a completely different language – one that is more direct and to

---

31   *Naturgeschichte der Deutschen Vögel einschlieslich sämtlicher Vogelarten Europas von C. G. Friedrich* (5th edn, 1905).

32   Place names were drawn from various maps of Switzerland at 1:25000 scale.

Rostdrosseln
Alpenamseln
Bleikehlchen
Falkensperlinge
Orpheussänger
Sperbergrasmücken
Fichtenammern
Karminhänflinge
Rosengimpel
Grosse Rohrsänger
Grosse Weidenblätter
Grosse Lerchen
Ungarische Sprosser
Schwedische Sprosser
Dänische Nachtigall
Diademwiesenschmätzer
Sandflughühner
Steppentauben
Gierfalke
Sternfalke
Blaufalke
Arabische Steppenhühner
Kaspische Reiher
Uralkäuze
Bleigraue Seeschwalben
Weissbindenkreuzschnäbel
Blassdrossel
Edelfasane
Ellernhühner
Schwarzbrüste
Tüpfelsumpfhühner
Bellhennen
Zwergbrachvögel
Kleinste Wasserhühnchen
Eulenköpfe
Rotbrüstige Säger
Lachseeschwalbe
Unsichere Teufelssturmvögel
Wanderne Albatros
Russsturmtaucher
Kleine Goldohren
Fluglose Alke
Harlekinsenten
Graue Strandläuferchen
Halsbandgiarole
Siten
Jäggu
Lejis
Hämu
Tönu
Nyffel
Birbe
Furli
Fälben
Fäili
Multen
Joneren

Example 2.10   An excerpt from *Lovaty* (1996), Jürg Frey. Italics
indicate the faster tempo

the point, but which also contains a greater variety of letter combinations. The piece in performance rarely has the effect of being 'just sound' – the meanings, which must in some deep way come from the things the names describe, communicate something beyond sound, even when one has no idea what the source word or words might be. In a list piece for solo speaker that followed this one, *Freichten* (1997), Frey felt capable of inventing his own words.

Poem

Cage's impact on modern poetics sometimes seems to be nearly as great as the impact he had on music.[33] In fact much of Cage's work seems to lie between poetry and music. Perhaps his best-known works in this direction are the many 'mesostics': a kind of poem in which a key (or repeated word or name) is embedded in a text, and which is then centred on the page, with the letters of the name capitalized. Sometimes Cage used this technique as a way of 'writing through' other works (that is, written by others), including four times through Joyce's *Finnegans Wake*. The second of these forms the basis of his seminal work *Roaratorio: An Irish Circus on Finnegans Wake* (1979).[34] The piece itself is remarkable, one of the richest and most beautiful sounding pieces that Cage produced. Also remarkable is his style of reading/singing – by itself a kind of theory of how a poem can become a song. There is also something undeniably poetic about the wording of certain scores, embedded, as it were, in the prose.[35] It is probably no accident that at the moment that Cage and others were exploring the tipping point between prose and poetry and their work, writers like Nathalie Sarraute, in a work like *Tropismes* (1957), and Samuel Beckett, in his short works from the 1960s onwards, were doing the same thing. Cage would have known about the prose-poems of Mallarmé and possibly also the work of Francis Ponge.

However, it was the members of the Fluxus group that took the concept of the prose/poem as music or action score and really developed it. Some scores by George Brecht or La Monte Young look as much like poems as anything else. Yoko Ono's collection *Grapefruit* (1964) has many such pieces. *EARTH PIECE* ('Listen to the sound of the earth turning') is identified as music because it involves listening – in this case an imaginary kind of listening. Others are absolutely poetic in sound and intent:

The very best are elegant, poetic and also quite practicable:

---

33 Cage is, for example, given a prominent position in Eliot Weinberger's excellent anthology of postwar American Experimental poetry: *American Poetry Since 1950: Innovators and Outsiders* (New York, 1993).

34 Mode Records 28/29 (1992).

35 Here, for example, is a sentence from *Variations III*: 'Some or all of one's obligation may be performed through ambient circumstances (environmental changes) by simply noticing or responding to them.'

BOX PIECE

Buy many dream boxes.
Ask your wife to select one.
Dream together.

1964 spring

Example 2.11   *Box Piece*, Yoko Ono (from *Grapefruit*)

MAP PIECE

Draw a map to get lost.

1964 spring

Example 2.12   *Map Piece*, Yoko Ono (from *Grapefruit*)

One spends a moment with such pieces, in part because the form allows one to write and to read so many of them. Occasionally one decides to do one – for a performance or another reason. This short form, which has been revived in recent years, is like a repertoire of poetic/musical notions that retain their potential, perhaps because potential is often the real subject of such scores.

James Tenney's *Postal Pieces* share some of the characteristics of this work, but some of the small differences are crucial. Some of the pieces, like *Having Never Written a Note for Percussion* (1971), make use of musical notation, however minimal. But this score is nearly a poem:

It is in part the lineation that creates the poetic effect. I am often reminded of a small section of Mallarmé's *Un coup de dés*:

> *blanchi*
>
> *étale*
>
> *furieux*
>
> (blanched, becalmed, furious)

Like a good poem, each word of the piece is necessary, but the words also refer to music: from the title (instrumentation) to the subtitle (performance indication) to the dedication (Budd is a composer and friend of Tenney's whose performance style must have influenced this piece). The list of instructions might very well be specific musical indications, including the word 'white' (for white noise). The whole, despite its poetic appearance, is a strong stimulus towards some kind of musical or performance action.

I have been involved in several performances of the piece and have experienced many wonderful renderings, without every hearing an unsuccessful one. These very few words seem to unleash a specific idea in the minds of the people who decide to perform the piece. It might be an orchestra of invented instruments playing soft white noises with tones peaking through; a large piece of Styrofoam being dragged across a cement floor for an hour; a white candle slowing burning in a small darkened room; a tube of toothpaste being slowly unravelled along a sidewalk – or, indeed, Harold Budd playing the piano softly and for a long time. Each of these seems to have captured the impetus of this set of instructions without agreeing in its essence. This demonstrates the power of poetic language to incite specified styles of reading or, in musical terms, of hearing.

These characteristics are also found in several works by Antoine Beuger. To choose one see Beuger's *ein ton. eher kurz. sehr leise.* (Example 2.14).[36]

---

36 Those interested in this aspect of Beuger's work might also wish to look at his *l'horizon unanime* for ensemble (1998), *évantail* for piano (1998), *tout à fait solitaire* (1998) for one performer and a series of pieces called *ins ungebundene* (1997–99). This translation of *ein ton. eher kurz. sehr leise.* (1998) is by the author of this chapter.

For Percussion Perhaps, Or . . . .

(night)

for Harold Budd

very soft

very long

nearly white

James Tenney
8/6/71

Example 2.13   *For Percussion Perhaps, Or...* one of the *Postal Pieces*
            by James Tenney

Here again we have a situation in which the verbal content of the score has been limited to only the words that are necessary. Beuger uses a kind of poetic licence in the elimination of what, in prose, would be necessary grammatical units.[37] The elegance of the description leaves open a multitude of ways of realizing the instructions – without clouding the set of clear actions indicated by the score with unnecessary considerations. The interactions between the two performers, arising from the separate decision-making process for each, and between them and their ever-present environment, suggest the complexity of a long-term relationship.

I will close this section on the poetic score with another recent piece by Manfred Werder.

---

37   'The materials consist of one tone, shared between the players, played softly and for a short time.' Here we would have seventeen words to Beuger's six.

one tone. rather short. very soft
for two performers

antoine beuger
1998

one tone.
rather short.
very soft.

once in the first half of each minute: one performer

once in the second half of each minute: the other performer

at some time one performer plays the tone no more and remains still until the
end of the piece.

at some time the other performer plays the tone no more and remains still
until the end of the piece.

duration of the piece: at least 30 minutes

Example 2.14   *ein ton. eher kurz. sehr leise.* (1998), Antoine Beuger
                (trans. Michael Pisaro)

eine anhöhe a hill

ein tal a valley

eine bergkette a mountain range

eine tiefebene a lowland

eine hochebene a plateau

ein flussdelta a river delta

ein fjord a fjord

manfred werder, *2008³*

Example 2.15   *2008³*, Manfred Werder

Title

Some of the pieces by George Brecht and by Yoko Ono consist, in large part, of their title. The reflexivity of Brecht's *TRUMPET* between title and action is enough to make one's head spin.

Let us consider the role of the title in some of the recent music of Manfred Werder. Example 2.16 shows, with somewhat condensed formatting, three of them.

Here we have a set of works that because of their apparent similarities call attention to the differences between them. Following the progress from one score to the next, one considers the difference between the indications 'time' and 'a time' or between 'place', 'a place' (with a description) and 'places'. The indication '(sounds)' is present in each. Like most of the work by Werder over the last 10 years, the title consists of a year it was written with the addition of a number next to it, to indicate the order of that piece within that year. The title, within the context of this very limited production, tells us something crucial: that in the year indicated, it was possible to add a piece to the chain of works stretching back to 1998. The titles emphasize the careful, deliberate process of thought, taking place over a relatively long period of time (given the brevity of the scores), which evaluates the necessity of adding to something that already exists. Werder's music mostly occurs as the slightest alteration in an environment: the presence of a performer (or performers) and the possibility (or the happening) of sound in time. Werder demonstrates that this infinitely rich set of circumstances – which is something like the infinite richness of reality, subtracted by the action of the music – can be approached again and again, each time from a slightly different angle, giving a slightly different colouring to an already present atmosphere.

Duration

One of the central developments in the music of John Cage was the treatment of duration itself as a musical material. His music up until 1952 understands this, but implements it mainly in the use of more typical rhythmic devices. As we have seen, the proportional system of micro- and macro-rhythms allowed for Cage to treat sound and silence equally. The next step along this path was the consideration of duration without the subdivision into rhythmic units.

The decisive transformation in this thinking becomes evident with the title of his *4'33"*. The title is, more or less, the work. It says that the material of the composition will be the time it takes. The piece demonstrates that the performance of the frame itself will be a sufficient requirement to create a musical situation. It reveals that the content of music is brought into being by duration, before any question of sound or silence occurs. Although one might not expect it, given the apparent simplicity of the instruction involved, the score itself seems to have presented challenges to Cage. It was as a carryover from his work with proportional durations in the works leading up to *4'33"* that he first notated these durations as proportions. It was only

ort
zeit

(klänge)

place
time

(sounds)

2005[1]
manfred werder

ein ort, natürliches licht, wo die oder der ausführende, die ausführenden sich gerne aufhalten

eine zeit

(klänge)

a place, natural light, where the performer, the performers like to be

a time

(sounds)

2006[1]
manfred werder

orte

eine zeit

(klänge)

places

a time

(sounds)

2006²
manfred werder

Example 2.16   Three pieces from 2005 and 2006 by Manfred Werder in its second version that Cage simply listed the durations of the three movements as time units.

Cage seems to have considered 4'33" his most important piece, and it is abundantly clear, in retrospect, that the compositional issues raised by the piece were truly significant. The realization of 4'33" seems to have opened the floodgates for Cage, in terms of the possibilities for *ways* of writing music. The following decade was a very productive time for him, including the series of pieces with exact durations as their titles and the *Music for Piano* series. There is also Cage's work with tape and electronic means in *Williams Mix* (1952), *Radio Music* (1956), *Fontana Mix* (1958) and *Cartridge Music* (1960). Finally the period includes the large-scale composition of the *Concert for Piano and Orchestra*, *Winter Music* and *Atlas Eclipticalis*.

However, viewed as a question of 'duration' itself, 4'33" was also something of a stopgap. It is only with 0'00" that Cage again picks up this particular thread, and with this work, it becomes clear, that the next step was indeed a very difficult one to make. That Cage was conscious of this connection is made clear by the score itself: 'This is 4'33" *(No. 2)* and also Pt. 3 of a work of which *Atlas Eclipticalis* is Pt. 1.'[38] As with 4'33" the title here says (almost) everything. This is a piece that posits a duration of 0'00" –that is, no experienced duration. Does the piece refer to the fact that a significant event can only be experienced as the trace of the event, and that its actual occurrence is somehow out of time or below a real-time duration? Is this what Cage really means when he says in the score that 'no attention [is] to be given the situation'? Is it in the nature of action to always somehow escape our attention? The work is a riddle and a limit – a demonstration that thinking about clock duration can be taken so far that it moves out of that realm altogether.[39]

The questions raised by these works have generated all kinds of creative responses. Cage himself returned in a relatively casual way to the question of duration with the number pieces, all of which use a time bracket notation[40] to open durational windows within the fixed total duration of the work.

The use of the clock or of the stopwatch has become commonplace in recent work. It allows one to simply say when an action or silence begins and when it ends or to give a duration, dispensing altogether with the bar as a unit of measure for longer durations. A silence of five minutes is a relatively straightforward thing and this notation corresponds to that fact. As one becomes accustomed to this way of notation one wonders why people hadn't thought of it before! It can also lead to musical ideas that might otherwise seem impossible. In Kunsu Shim's *expanding space in limited time* (1994) for solo violin, the use of clock timings allows Shim to

---

38   John Cage, *0'00"* (Peters Edition, New York, 1962).

39   I would also add, however, that the piece can and should be performed: it is more than a concept. Experience tells us that the problems raised by it generate fascinating, individual solutions, which would not have been imaginable without the score.

40   Here, in general, a starting time span (or single time) and an ending time span (or single time) are given. The player is generally free to place the sounds wherever she wishes within these brackets.

create durations of five minutes or more for single tones. This is combined in this work with an extremely tight control over how much of the bow will be used in that time (from a whole bow length to one-sixth of it). This sometimes produces a tone played so slowly that the sounding result is truly at the border of audibility, even when one is close to the instrument.

Much of Carlo Inderhees's music springs from the basic principles of human time-keeping. Many of Inderhees's pieces, including the two large cycles *für sich* (1997) and *STIMMEN* (2001–) last exactly one hour and derive their timings from proportional subdivisions of that hour.[41]

STIMMEN is a fascinating work. It exists mainly as a procedure for creating individual parts. Every part is designed to replicate the micro-rhythmic structure in the macro-rhythmic structure. The 60-minute duration is divided into 12 units of five minutes each. On the lowest rhythmic level, a 12-unit bar, with each unit corresponding to one second, is used as the rhythmic key for that part. The placement and duration of the unit within the bar will be repeated in each bar that follows, and will also map the span of the 60-minute duration used by that part. Thus, a part that has a one-unit duration beginning on unit one – with the following 11units having a rest – will map onto the large scale as the first five minutes of the 60 minutes – with the remaining 55 units being performed as a silence. A part having a four-beat duration occupying beats nine to twelve, will not start until minute 40, but will then continue until the end. These parts are conceived using a Fibonacci distribution of the total number of pitches needed over the nine central pitch places on the staff, without clef (this is determined by the performer). When a quartet is needed a set of four individual parts is assembled for the piece.[42]

The temporal requirements of Inderhees's joint project with artist Christoph Nicolaus (*garonne/für sich*) are even more extensive – involving the creation of a yearly calendar for the intermittent performances of the work.[43]

The question of long duration, as measured in something other than clock time, was a preoccupation of Morton Feldman's. The final works of Feldman treat duration as a question of scale. The magnificent *Nymphéas* (or *Water Lilies*) by Claude Monet housed in the Musée de l'Orangerie in Paris are so large in scale that one cannot see them all it at once – there are four murals in each of two oval-shaped rooms of the museum. One is constantly viewing *and* remembering, and the viewing experience includes also forgetting what one has seen, only to be reminded of it when one comes back around. This is an experience that will be familiar to aficionados of works such as the *String Quartet II* (1983) or *For Philip Guston* (1984). Having the

---

41 Other works by Inderhees are often, as in Cage, simply given a durational unit as a title: *SIEBENUNDVIERZIG MINUTEN* (47') for organ, *ZWANZIG MINUTEN* (20') for piano, *FÜNFUNDDREISSIG MINUTEN* (35') quartet and so on.

42 Inderhees sometimes decides to write a homophonic multi-voice piece, in which case all voices function rhythmically as one part, though with individual pitch assignments.

43 This project, as interesting as it is, is far too complex to describe here. Those interested can find more information on the Edition Wandelweiser website: http://www.wandelweiser. de/ (accessed 9 September 2008).

sense that one is adrift in time, on a scale that forgets the clock – that one will, sooner or later forget the beginning; that one will not be able to anticipate the end – that what has occurred early in the piece takes place not just within the scale of the piece, but in the scale of one's life[44] – all of this happens in another durational realm. It makes sense that Feldman arrived at these durations without apparent plan, as the result of adding to the music day after day until the piece was finished – the length of the piece corresponding approximately to the duration of the writing.

Beuger's *calme étendue* can last as long as *nine* hours for a single performance – a practice which grows out of his planning of *Ein Tag* [One day] events at the atelier of the visual artist Mauser in Cologne. For a performer or audience member who occupies the space for the full nine hours, this span begins to seem unbounded, as if it had never begun, as if one will keep doing it forever. The beginning and end of this duration seems relatively immaterial – the overriding perception is of being in *an infinite middle*.

Leaving things out

One characteristic of much of Feldman's music, late or otherwise, is the relative lack of dynamic indications. Early on Feldman got in the habit of simply writing, at the beginning of the piece, 'dynamics very low throughout' or 'dynamics are extremely low, and as equal as possible' or just 'extremely soft'. In a late work, typically, a single *ppp* at the beginning will apply to the entire piece. None of this of course means that every sound will have the same amplitude – far from it. The dynamic constraint applies mostly to the way in which the sound is played, but cannot really apply to volume as experienced. For what are very likely physiological reasons, there is simply much more perceived variation in volume at the low end of the scale than at the high end. Once one has been 'in' a late Feldman work for, say, 40 minutes, the scale of amplitude values can seem huge, approaching the infinite, like a vanishing point. The smallest changes become perceptible. The way to reach this complexity is not by indicating a dynamic for each sound, but to constrain them, to narrow the range of values. I think this functions like the way we perceive the sun at the horizon during sunrise or sunset. Because the horizon is there as a limit, many more changes become perceptible, in the size and shape of the sun, in its rate of movement, but especially in the character and colour of the light that one experiences.

Much of the experimental tradition concerns what can be left out of a score. A piece by Christian Wolff might say nothing about its total duration. Individual parts of his pieces might leave out clefs, or anything but the most general sense of rhythmic values. A score might say nothing specific about what kind of instrument can play it or about the alignment of parts. As soon as one begins to think along these lines there are many useful considerations concerning what might be left out

---

44 'It is now afternoon, but this morning, long ago, I have a vague memory of having heard that motive.'

of a score. Will it make the performance process more creative? Will a certain kind of openness with regard to instrumentation allow for a better performance because it will be available to any committed player, instead of just those who play that instrument? Will leaving out something specific, such as a complicated looking rhythm, actually increase the complexity of the result? Will the resultant clarity of a score create a sense of clarity in the performance? Are there things that will be played more subtly if the performer can concentrate solely on the sound instead of reconciling what is sounding with what is in the score? These kinds of questions are asked often in recent music – and represent an implicit theme of much of the music that I have been considering here.

In James Tenney's *Swell Piece for Alison Knowles* (1967) the only thing said to the ensemble about the pitches they should play is that they should be 'free and independent'. The score asks the performers to focus on the procedure of making a crescendo and decrescendo on a sustained tone (that is, any sustained tone). However, in performance after performance the resultant harmonies come together in a miraculous way – as if they had been composed to sound just the way they do – and by someone imaginative enough to break harmonic rules. When I first noticed this result I began to wonder why, over the centuries, so much time and energy had to be spent in creating logical and beautiful harmony, when it could be as easy as it appeared to be in this piece. In attempting to answer this question, I wrote a series of 34 pieces, titled, as a group, *harmony series* (2004–2006). Each of these works attempts to create conditions for a kind of functioning harmony without saying anything about the specific harmonies that should result. Example 2.17 shows one example.

Each piece in the series approaches the question from a slightly different angle: by varying the number of performers, the durational restrictions, the kinds of sustained sounds asked for or the patterns in which the sounds are deployed. But the basic question remains: How do we harmonize? In playing the pieces one develops a loose method for making decisions, even if one doesn't have a conscious sense of what the others will play. This is a very odd experience: an attempt at musical divination in which, it seems, an answer will always be found. This is not to say that every decision is equally acceptable or beautiful. It is almost as if each situation presents a specific organism, one that has a complex set of behaviours – that one learns more through immersion than analysis. It is, at first, a situation in which composition and improvisation seem to be indistinguishable. But as one keeps working, a version begins to develop, something that the collective decision-making of the group has begun to shape, and which appears to grow almost on its own.

Transcription

A significant part of the recent work of Peter Ablinger has revolved around the process of transcription. In many pieces there is a specific intent: to represent raw or recorded sound on an instrument or through language. This process can be fairly

So little to do [harmony series no. 6]
        for six or more performers playing sustained tones

Letter To La Monte Young

There is so little to do, and so much time to do it in.

—George Brecht

The duration (of each section) is 10 minutes.
A performance consists of at least one section, but the section may be repeated any number of times (with each new section beginning immediately after the previous has ended).

Each performer plays one tone (any tuning).
With each new section the tone may be retuned slightly, i.e., altered no more than 20 cents from the previous tone.

Tones are very pure, very soft, very clear.

At some time before the 9th minute the performers begin playing their respective pitches simultaneously and hold them until the end of the 10 minutes is reached. The entry point(s) for the group should be determined beforehand using a chance procedure.

Winds and perhaps bowed strings should alternate sound and silence (entering and leaving as imperceptibly as possible) for the duration of the playing time, in order to avoid fatigue.

Michael Pisaro
January/February, 2005

Example 2.17   The score for *So little to do [harmony series 6]* (2005), Michael Pisaro

simple, as in the pieces from the *Weiss/weisslich 11b* (1994–) series ('sitting and writing'), verbal transcriptions of the sequence of sounds in a specific environment over a specific length of time.

The *Voices and Piano* (1998–) is a more complex work. It is a projected series of around eighty pieces for compact disc and piano. The voices all come from found recordings of well-known figures from art, politics, entertainment and so on.[45] A recording of the voice is played and then accompanied by a live pianist. Ablinger describes the piano part as a 'temporal and spectral scan of the voice, like a coarse-grid [digital] photograph'. The writing here is actually the transcription of acoustical information, a process made possible by the ease with which a computer can manipulate sound data. The score often looks surprisingly like a kind of avant-garde piano music one might have seen in the Darmstadt years.[46]

Transcription has also been carried over by Ablinger into the purely mechanical realm, with a recently developed player piano that Nancarrow would have envied. This instrument can, with the aid of a computer, skip the score stage and go directly to spectral transcription.[47] These works are part of a large series that Ablinger calls *Quadraturen* (1995–). Here the basic principle involves squaring, or creating a frequency and temporal grid of a sonic 'photo', identifying a median sound for each quadrant and then making a transcription of that. These squares are then re-assembled into a grainy reflection of the sonic image – a process Ablinger calls 'phonorealism'.

Another principle of transcription reverses the procedure, moving from simpler graphic images towards sound.

Alvin Lucier's *Letters* (1992) transcribes capital letters onto the score according to a clear and simple set of rules. The space traced is within an octave from middle c to c^1. An octave cluster in the piano is a vertical line. Straight horizontal lines are represented by sustained tones. Curved lines are traced with glissandi. Using this simple vocabulary Lucier could spell anything in English! With a little practice listening, one can hear the letters as they go by. This procedure can be carried out using large proportions: each large C of the piece *Charles Curtis* (2002) takes six minutes to draw.[48]

The recent music of Chiyoko Szlavnics involves transcribing drawings made by the composer. As described by Szlavnics, the drawing process itself is done in stages, sometimes with several versions of a drawing being made, until a form of

---

45 Some examples: Guillaume Apollinaire, Jorge Luis Borges, Angela Davis, Morton Feldman, Martin Heidegger, Billie Holiday, Mao Tse-tung, Pier Paolo Pasolini.

46 Much of this and other works by Ablinger can be seen and heard on his website: http://ablinger.mur.at (accessed 9 September 2008).

47 There is a set of works by Ablinger that use this method, including a truly incredible piece that allows the piano alone to create the sound of Schoenberg's English speaking voice, German accent and all: http://ablinger.mur.at/txt_qu3schoenberg.html (accessed 9 September 2008).

48 Here, as with *Still Lives*, sweeping sine tones do the drawing and the violoncello part is created from patterns designed to play with the beating that may occur with unisons, octaves and occasional other intervals.

it emerges that is 'strong and convincing'. Next a complex series of calculations is used to align the linear structure of the drawing to the instrumental and the tuning situation.[49] In Szlavnics's work the many slanting lines are connected, by way of instrumental glissandi or sine tones, to a series of goals coordinated in to a harmonic scheme in just intonation. The sounding result in a work such as *Reservoir* (2006) for chamber ensemble and sine tones conveys a plasticity of time and space that can feel as if a new world has been created – as though we were finally getting to *hear* some of the outlandish conceptions of worlds to be found in the far reaches of mathematics.

Writing as process

The text score for Cage's *0'00"* is the written record of its first performance: the amplified writing of the score itself fulfilled the obligation of the instructions. In other words, the making of the score was the performance of the score. How does the writing of experimental music harmonize with the life of the people writing it? It is, of course, work – and, as I have tried to indicate, this is only a part of the work of the composer, especially if one is committed to all of the conditions of making music. The question of how this kind of work related to life in society was one of the great themes of Cage's writing.[50]

The ongoing work of many of the composers discussed here is (or was) a way of life. For some composers this is made explicit in the working process itself – where an individual project takes on a life of its own that runs parallel to the life of the composer.

One such ongoing project by Antoine Beuger is called *auch da*. Over a period of a few months, starting in August 2007, Beuger composed ten melodies of four phrases each every day, using a kind of notational shorthand. This quickly became a very large repertoire that Beuger has continued to add to, somewhat less regularly. The progress can be observed by the composer's musical friends by checking a website he created for this purpose. Having no particular instrumentation, each melody can be seen as a potential for a piece and this is in fact what Beuger is doing, by using this material as the basis for completed works. A series of these pieces, called *aus den liedern* assigns poetic texts by a mysterious process to some of the individual melodies from *auch da*. The effect of this (nearly) chance coming together of text and tune is surprising: it is as if the melody were lying in wait for the text, which, at the same time, is given new meaning by the contours of the tune. Consider for a moment the piece shown in Example 2.18, based on a text by Rajzel Zychlinski.

---

49 The procedure is described in detail in Szlavnics's article 'Opening Ears – the Intimacy of the Detail of Sound' (*Filigrane*, #4, 'New Sensibilities', 2006). Much of Szlavnics's work can be seen and heard at www.plainsound.org (accessed 9 September 2008).

50 It is something that pops up now and again in his *Diary: How to Improve the World (You Will Only Make Matters Worse)*.

aus den liedern (düsseldorf 2008)

Antoine Beuger, 2007/08
(Texte: Rajzel Zychlinski)

1 Der Wind, er wird dir   ver-trau-en, wie ein   klei-nes Schaf wird er   die Au-gen schlie-ßen.

2 Die Bäu-me rau-schen, der   Wind ist kühl und   bringt uns bald   die Nacht.

3 Ein Blick weckt   ei - ne Welt   mit-ten im   hel-len Tag.

4 ...heb   ich   den Stein   von der Er-de auf und es fällt auf mich ein Re-gen ü-ber herbst-li-chen We-gen.

Example 2.18   A page from *aus den liedern* (2008), Antoine Beuger

The meeting of text and music here breaks the sentence in unexpected places, by virtue of the structure of the melody and the irregular pattern of the text. But the halting rhythm thus created brings something new to the poem – the sense that this is thought rather than description.[51]

James Saunders's series #[unassigned] (2000–) is also an ongoing, modular work. Each piece in the series is composed for a specific occasion, and has a title designed to reflect the date of its one (and only) performance. The titles are created using a #ddmmyy pattern: thus the piece #200203 was performed (by the London Sinfonietta) on the 20 February 2003.[52] The series acknowledges the continuity of a composer's work by understanding all the variations that occur within the series as one piece; a piece that is the result of the intersection between the continuum of the composer's thought and work, and the necessities of producing a piece for a specific set of performers for a single date. (The poet Oswald Egger would call this 'discrete continuity.') Material from one piece might be used in another or might reappear transformed. A set of concepts governs what constitutes a unit, but these are shaped and developed over time, influenced by the things that have already occurred. The piece grows organically without any conception of a whole or an end. The individual units are not only site-specific, they are date and situation specific. There is something about the project that suggests a kind of organic Markov chain: it creates an (im)personal history that runs parallel to the working conditions and the life situation of the composer and of the (experimental) music world.

Perhaps the most ambitious of the long-term, situational and compositional projects are those designed by Manfred Werder. With both his *stück 1998* and the series of pieces for from one to nine performers (_ *ausführende*), Werder has created works of a length that easily transcend the limit for a single performance. *stück 1998* consists of a total of 120,000 actions, each having a duration of six seconds, followed by six seconds of silence, for a total performance time of 400 hours. The _ *ausführende* series consists of nine pieces, each of which has 160,000 actions, having the same 12 second duration, for a total time of 533 hours. The production of the pages, when they are required, is real work – a chart must be consulted and each event must be entered onto the score.

Each piece, however, is conceived to be part of a single, intermittent performance. In order to play one of the works, one has to be in contact with the composer, so that he can provide the next set of pages – enough, at eight minutes per page, for whatever the duration of the performance will be. Each page follows the same rules as all of the previous pages, but even so, in most cases, one will generally not, at least at first, have any idea of how the previous set of pages was performed (that is, for which performers, using which sounds, for how long, in what performance location

---

51   This is a piece for voice and chamber orchestra: each of the instruments chooses one (or two or none) of the pitches from the phrase and plays it softly and for a long time over the duration of the song.

52   An updated list of versions with the titles and performances (and more information on the series) is given on James Saunders's website: http://www.james-saunders.com (accessed 9 September 2008).

and so on). The composer himself only provides oversight of the distribution of the pages, not the actual form of the realization. Given that in most cases only a few to several of the pages will be performed each year, each piece is likely to be a lifetime commitment for the composer.

However, from another standpoint they are works that seem to have their own life, one only loosely guided but not guaranteed or even necessarily experienced by the composer. The trajectory and development of the piece will be largely independent of him, even when he himself is, from time to time, one of the performers. A community of performers who have taken part starts to form – people who have, in some way, contributed to the same ongoing thread. In this sense the time between the performances is also worthy of thought: these are silences, of a kind – times when the work goes underground but does not disappear. For a small portion of our lives we are conscious of being in this silent community.

Conclusions

Experimental music opens the entire process of creation to question and to investigation. We do not forget that writing is but one part of music-making – even if, within this tradition, it can be an important part of it.

By taking the whole process by which the music is conceived, written, performed and heard as an area for critical consideration, and then, for lovingly creative innovation, the music arrives again and again at unexpected ways of sounding and of being.

The novel visions that arise are ultimately collective: areas of innovation open to anyone who writes, plays and listens – and it is often the case that one composer will pick up in the neighbourhood where another left off, taking her idea further or putting it through another set of changes. What emerges is an ever-expanding network of possibility and of friends, a conspiracy against the way things are, a way of saying: there is also *this*.

A small manifesto

What writing music comes down to, in the end, is care. We create situations. We care about them and take care of them. And we care for the people involved.

A Prescription for Action

Philip Thomas

What distinguishes the interpretative approach of the experimental musician from that of other musicians? The pianist David Tudor, arguably the single most significant performer in the history of experimental music, described his emergent feelings in 1963 concerning performing experimental music:

> *When I play a piece that is notated, even though I may have a freedom of choice, for instance as in Stockhausen, I feel ... er ... it's a curious, er ... sensation that I'm trying to describe, but the whole thing is ... whatever you do, is like a stream of consciousness. And if I play something which is so notated I notice now, after having done it for several years, that it has the tendency to put me to sleep. It wants all the time to ... er ... recede into an area where my feelings are called upon more and more. And all the features which seemed to be so striking when the works were first composed now become much less striking. They don't seem so important and so the whole thing recedes into a stream which is mainly of feeling. Whereas if I play music which doesn't have any such requirement, where I'm called upon to make actions, especially if the actions are undetermined as to their content, or at least let's say undetermined as to what they're going to produce, then I feel like I'm alive in every part of my consciousness.*[1]

What Tudor seems be distinguishing between here is music which draws upon a consciously interpretative approach – one which involves what Tudor describes as 'feelings' – and music which requires one to do work – to 'make actions'. Perhaps these two types could be considered as music which is *projected* and music which is *investigative* (Tudor makes a point of linking the latter type with music the notation of which is indeterminate so that the resulting content is not predetermined). Tudor's use of the word 'actions' is revealing as it goes to the core of what it is to play an instrument. It is a word that is not generally encountered within literature relating to instrumental and performance practices, which are generally concerned with the development of 'technique' and 'interpretation'. There is a refreshing honesty

---

1   David Tudor and John Cage interviewed by Mogens Andersen in a broadcast of Danmarks Radio on 3 June 1963. Featured on the CD *David Tudor – Music for piano*, ed.RZ 1018-19 (2007).

about the term 'make actions' to describe what one does when playing music; it shrugs off centuries of tradition, schools of technique (here schools of pianism) and dismisses the mystique of 'interpretation'. Tudor's description seems to approach how a 'performing tradition' of experimental music might be expressed.

Literature (scholarly or otherwise) relating to experimental music on the whole focuses upon issues of compositional technique, notation and aesthetics. Through necessity, performance issues are discussed but these are generally restricted to descriptions of the performer's task (almost by default, the nature of much of the music requires analytical discussion to revolve around the implications and realization of the score). However, what the performer actually *does*, rather than what she is *required* to do, is a theme that needs investigating.

John Cage wrote 'Composing's one thing, performing's another, listening's a third. What can they have to do with one another?'[2] and Christian Wolff wrote 'Let playing be composition and composition playing.'[3] However, the experiences of both composer and performer[4] are very different, even if the composer is the performer. Performers act in response to that which a composer has created, generally (if there is a composer–performer relationship) in the form of musical notation and/ or other graphical elements, prose and/or written instructions. The relationship between both parties and the score is a defining distinguishing factor between composer and performer. Cornelius Cardew referred to the score's function as a vehicle for 'making people move'.[5] As with Tudor's remarks, the performer here is referred to as being *active*. The physicality of performance makes the performing experience wholly different to the composing experience. It is likely, then, that a performer's response to and understanding of a piece of music is different to that of the composer. It is also true that the experience is different from that of the listener, though the visual alignment with the performer's actions in a live performance creates an association of physicality with the music.

The point I am wishing to make here is that general understanding of what experimental music *is* – what its defining features are, and what it is *not* – tends to be shaped by the approach taken by the composer. Discussion of the music is generally centred upon the stages leading towards the creation of the notation, as well as the notation itself, but not what is subsequently done as a result of that notation. Whilst understanding the conceptual and aesthetical issues pertinent to the music being performed will doubtless affect the interpretative approach taken, a performer's decisions – her *actions* – may conversely shape understanding of the music itself and the extent to which it may be considered experimental.

---

2   John Cage, *Silence* (5th edn, London, 1999), p. 15.

3   Christian Wolff, *Cues: Writings and Conversations* (Cologne, 1998), p. 80.

4   For the purposes of this chapter, the term 'performer' is used solely in the context of the performer responding to some form of composed work, generally composed by someone other than themselves.

5   Cornelius Cardew, *Treatise Handbook* (London, 1971), reprinted in Edwin Prévost (ed.), *Cornelius Cardew: A Reader* (Matching Tye, Essex, 2006), p. 99.

This chapter examines what a performer does in response to a score (in the broadest sense of the term) of experimental music and attempts to understand whether or not that response – generally termed 'interpretation' – is significantly different to a score of music which might not be considered experimental. A variety of scores and notational types are examined and are used to move towards defining a common approach to the performance of experimental music. The examples used are mostly taken from the piano repertoire for the only (but significant) reason that it is my instrument and therefore if understanding of experimental music is to be furthered by performance practice it has to do so by performers writing about it – in this case, *me* drawing upon *my* experiences at the piano.

Choice and Intention

Discussion of experimental music, by both composers and commentators, is frequently littered with words and phrases such as 'getting rid of the glue', 'non-intention,' 'freeing sounds', 'investigation', 'allowing sounds to exist for themselves'. Paradoxically, literature relating to the performance practice of traditionally notated music is almost entirely concerned with issues of projecting unity, connectivity, intelligibility and so on. Indeed, performances are assessed and judged by such criteria. It could be argued that these factors are rendered insignificant to the performer of much score-based experimental music. Are events which simply occur one after another in time to be 'interpreted' or is it the performer's role to project them as clearly and with as much focus as possible but not to 'meddle' with them?

Naturally, as soon as performers move in response to a score they are engaged in an act of interpretation. Any performance, no matter how transparent or void of 'ego', betrays the performer's presence – her touch, her sense of time and tone, her allegiances (to instrumental and/or compositional 'schools') and so forth. In a similar manner, John Cage's music *sounds* like John Cage's music in that it betrays and is the result of the character and aesthetic sensibilities of the composer, no matter that the detail is composed using chance methods and/or is the result of a realization of indeterminate notation.[6]

Interpretation must be defined by the way in which a performer responds to a score. This includes the idiosyncracies of the performer's technique – if technique can be separated from what might be termed 'manner', the accumulation of years of training (most usually for players of notated music from within the classical music mould of practical exams, competitions, universities and the Academy) – but perhaps more significantly includes the way in which the performer understands and acts upon the score itself as the defining and sole context of the interpretation. I

---

6   I would argue that this is true of even the most open of the scores, such as *Variations I* (1958) and *II* (1962), as long as the performer follows the parameters of the score's instructions.

would argue that within experimental music, the score should not only be sufficient for all that the performer needs but should rule out external imposing factors such as matters of style and authenticity. If experimental music is concerned with investigation and creating a context within which sound is free to 'be', then the performance of such music must be free of interpretative impositions and instead be devoted to the actions required by the score.

The reality is not as dogmatic as has been suggested above. However, as a statement of interpretative position, the notion that the score itself provides all that is necessary for the music to be realized is a worthy goal and strikes to the heart of experimental music-making, wherein the interpretation and projection of ideas are made apparent in the abstract field of sound, without needing any further explanation, rationale or interpretation.

An example of such an approach is the *Duo for Pianists II* (1958) by Christian Wolff. The basic tenet of this score is that each pianist has blocks of material which are notated in coded form and require realization, either through notating a version or versions in advance or by creating a version in the performance moment. Example 3.1 shows one such block, requiring the pianist to play one of the two Ds notated in the first 1.5 seconds, followed by a quarter second of silence, a note drawn from collection 'a' in the next fifth of a second, followed by four seconds

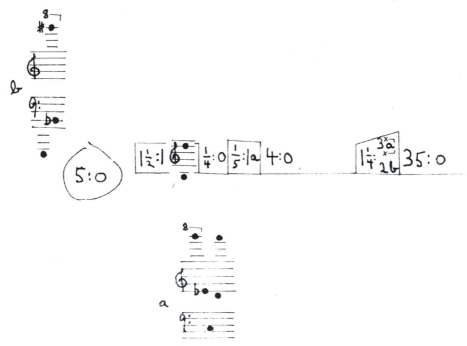

Example 3.1   Extract from Christian Wolff, *Duo for Pianists II* (1958) p. 2, 1st pianist

of silence, five notes drawn from the collections notated (three from collection 'a' in any octave other than that written and two from collection 'b') and ending with 35 seconds of silence. The order and point of entry of each event is determined entirely by what the pianist hears once she has completed any given block. The last sound (or length of silence) played by the second pianist once the first has completed a block determines which block to play next by means of a system of cues which precede each block (in Example 3.1 the cue is five seconds of silence). Despite the many ambiguities and problems the pianist must face when playing this work[7] it is an entirely self-contained score with absolutely no need to refer to external sources, performance practices or analysis to execute this work perfectly well. The role of the performer is to do what is required, to be focused upon the task at hand, which requires considerably more concentration in the performance moment than most works. John Tilbury, in an interview published in 1968, said 'Playing Christian Wolff's music is very complicated. You are so involved with actually making the sound that you have no chance of emotional indulgence; you have a job to do and it takes all your concentration to do it efficiently – i.e. musically. With this music you learn the prime qualities needed in performing: discipline, devotion, and disinterestedness.'[8] It is difficult to imagine a realization of any one of the blocks of material which would not sound right, the parameters are such that the freedom given, though considerable, will create a situation which is difficult to ruin. Likewise, if the performer is alert to the live situation, and the instructions of the score, a performance will always have a certain kind of continuity which is marked by both hesitancy and urgency, qualities which are the result of the performer responding to the score and not externally imposed.

However, few works manage to be so successful in negotiating their own performance practice solely within the confines of the score. The reality is that most demand some kind of interpretative approach worked out in partnership with the notational possibilities. The remainder of this chapter examines a variety of notational methods and examines the performer's role in defining the character of the music.

Complex Notation

The *Music of Changes* (1951) is arguably Cage's most dogmatic use of chance processes, in which almost every compositional decision and parameter is governed by chance. For the performer, however, the work is fixed and fully notated, albeit via a space-time form of notation which was not applied in order to create flexibility for the performer but rather to allow for nuances of timing which traditional metric

---

7   For further discussion of interpretative issues relating to this work, see Philip Thomas, 'Determining the Indeterminate', *Contemporary Music Review*, 26/2 (2007): 129–40.

8   'John Tilbury, 'The Contemporary Pianist (in conversation with Michael Parsons)', *The Musical Times*, 110/1512 (1969): 150–52, at 151.

schemes could not account for (reflecting explorations in tape music). Continuity and synchronicity are thus a product of chance (though, on the micro-level, some notes within a line may follow each other because they represent a stretched or compressed version of the original material). The pianist's job is to correctly realize the score, measuring lengths of and distances between events and relating these to the tempi provided (which may be constant or changing). This in itself demands considerable skill, away from the piano and with the aid of a calculator, as each inch is measured in relation to time (this involves some particularly complex calculations when the tempo is shifting from one to another). With neither metric scheme nor bar lines, each event is effectively a 'down-beat', none more or less significant than another (see Example 3.2). Interpretation of matters such as phrasing, shaping, continuity and prioritization are not of any concern to the pianist here. Instead she is to treat each event in isolation, regardless of what precedes or follows it, focusing upon the components which make the event what it is. David Tudor noted that one had to be 'ready for anything at each instant … I had to learn how to be able to cancel my consciousness of any previous moment, in order to be able to produce the next one.'[9]

Example 3.2   Line 5, p. 4 from John Cage, *Music of Changes I* (1951)

What interpretative decisions are there for the performer, then? First, the approach outlined thus far is clearly an interpretative approach – the choice *not* to manipulate continuity or prioritize one event over another is borne of an interpretative aesthetic which is associated with experimental (and in particular Cageian) ideology. Just as Cage's desire to remove his ego from his compositional endeavours in reality amplifies Cage's personality and aesthetic, so the interpretative approach advocated here (that of removing interpretative mannerisms to reveal the music as it is) also reveals the individuality of the performer (intellectually and technically). Second, events, noises, dynamics and articulations are 'interpreted' inasmuch as they will be filtered through the pianist's technical and intuitive response to such markings as well as her response to the acoustics of the concert

---

9   Victor Schonfeld and David Tudor, 'From Piano to Electronics', *Music and Musicians*, xx/12 (1971): 24–6, at 24.

hall and the qualities of the instrument. Third, obscurities in the notation itself require the pianist to make decisions, either intuitively or through reason. For example, if an event is likely to be obscured due to a particularly loud other event or events which surround it, the pianist must decide whether or not to balance the voicing so that it may be heard or to let it be obscured by the surrounding events, recognizing an emerging characteristic of Cage's work at around the time of composition which allowed for the unpredictable or the error to be accepted as a valid outcome. Likewise, when the notation produces a practical impossibility, the performer must make a choice; the choice could be determined using some chance method, or by means of assessing what is practically most viable, or by attempting the impossible in performance and accepting the outcome and so forth. Cage simply suggests in the preface to the score that 'the performer is to employ his own discretion'.[10]

The particular choices opted for by the performer may or may not have a perceptible impact upon the character of the music, but the point is that an interpretative approach needs to be adopted. There is nothing in the score to suggest that an interpretation which consciously seeks out shapes within the music, or applies phrasing (intuitive or otherwise), or tries to project one line over another, is *wrong*, but the performer who is aware of Cage's compositional aesthetic, or even of the performing tradition implied by David Tudor, would presumably seek to avoid such an approach. *Music of Changes* was the result of rigorous and laborious compositional endeavour on the part of Cage – once the initial compositional decisions were made (composition of material, arrangement of elements into workable grids, devising the method and so on) the realization of the composition required six coin tosses for every single decision (material selection, dynamics, attacks, durations, number of concurrent layers, tempi and so on). Performance of the work requires a comparable, selfless devotion to the realization of score to sound. The decision to avoid approximation and traditional interpretative impositions matches the intent of the composer. Though fixed in its notation, for the performer it is a thoroughly investigative, 'experimental' work.

Klavierstück I by Stockhausen, also written in 1951, is as complex as *Music of Changes* with respect to its notation of durations and dynamics. The subtleties of rhythm are equal to those of *Music of Changes*, though achieved by different means, and the nuances of attack due to the combination of note groupings and bar lines are as lively. It is, however, not as exploratory a work as that by Cage in terms of its use of the piano and exploration of resonance (that was to come in later *Klavierstücke*). It is useful to compare both works not only for their contemporaneousness but because they stem from a time when both composers were at the beginning of explorations into electronic music, Stockhausen with *Studie I* and *II* and Cage with *Williams Mix*. The rhythmic complexities of the two piano works are in large part the result of these new investigations and working methods. Through technology time was able to be measured to far greater exactitude than had previously been possible, and both composers responded to this new world in their instrumental

---

10   John Cage, *Music of Changes* (C.F. Peters, 1961).

music (Cage transferring the measurement of time in terms of fractions of inches of tape to a space-time notation in *Music of Changes*).

In the first four *Klavierstücke*, Stockhausen creates a nuanced liveliness in the durations through a development of traditional rhythmic notation, primarily through notating durational modulations over groups of notes. *Klavierstück I* features superimposed layers of durational modulations: Example 3.3 shows a bar of 2/4 which is subdivided into two units of two plus three quavers, at a modulated speed of five quavers in the space of four. The unit of two quavers is modulated further at a ratio of 7:8 demisemiquavers and the subsequent unit of three quavers moves at a rate of 11:12 demisemiquavers. As in *Music of Changes*, the pianist can calculate the relationships between events to a high degree of specificity (unlike Cage, Stockhausen does not notate actual tempi but states that the tempo should be as fast as possible. The pianist should presumably take the most difficult event, not necessarily the fastest, depending upon the way in which notes lie under the hand or leap across registers, as an indication of tempo). This is a useful exercise as it reveals the degree to which one group of notes is faster or slower than another which might not otherwise be obvious. In Example 3.3, if a standard quaver pulse were taken as being MM = 90, the first unit of the bar would move at MM = 98.4 and the second unit of the bar would move at MM = 103.1. Once such relationships have been established, each modulation acts as a catalyst to make the performer move, immediately shifting the pulse to a new gear. Though the rhythms are relatively simple *within* a particular group, the tempi shift so frequently that the performer is

Example 3.3   Bar 6 from Karlheinz Stockhausen, *Klavierstück I* (1951)

kept sufficiently alert. Stockhausen spoke of 'a new way of feeling time in music in which the infinitely subtle "irrational" shadings and impulses and fluctuations of a good performer often produce what one wants better than any centimetre guage',[11] reflecting again the ways in which composers often think of the function of notation in terms of movement.

---

11   Karl H. Wörner, *Stockhausen: Life and Work* (London, 1973), p. 32.

Rhythmically, then, *Klavierstück I* is as successful as *Music of Changes* and *Duo for Pianists* in requiring the performer to adopt an approach which focuses upon 'action' rather than 'interpretation'. The interpretation of other elements of the score is, however, more problematic. Texturally the music betrays the clear influence of Second Viennese School techniques, most notably a post-Webernian clarity, from which it and the subsequent three pieces fails to escape. The pitch material is serially organized, rather simply dividing the octave into two hexachord clusters and alternating between them. There is evident exploration of different types of grouping and degrees of activity (the work is generally accepted as being one of Stockhausen's first moves away from the extreme pointillism of preceding works). Groups of pitches seem to be registerally displaced according to notions of shape and continuity, even if the performer need not know how such features are ordained. All of which amounts to a considerable amount of external information which the pianist may draw upon to shape her interpretation as regards continuity, shape and phrasing. (When learning *Klavierstück III*, the pianist might like to draw upon a number of different analyses of the work to help shape their understanding of phrasing.[12]) Anecdotal evidence of Stockhausen's comments to performers encouraging an interpretative approach which relates to traditional notions of musical expression, and even to nineteenth-century composers such as Brahms,[13] suggests that for the performer of Stockhausen's music, an experimental, investigative performance approach is not going to be necessarily appropriate. It is difficult to adopt a 'tabula rasa' attitude to this music when the music of Stockhausen's European predecessors bears so heavy a weight upon the music.

If one were to disentangle the rhythmic techniques of *Klavierstück I* from its musical baggage, it would be true to acknowledge not only the radical and experimental aspects of its unprecedented notational complexity but also the functionality of the notation. It demonstrates well the capacity of broadly traditional notational parameters to stimulate the performer to move in new ways. Thirty years later, Morton Feldman used similar notations to imply a shift in the pulse in his late extended works, such as *Triadic Memories* (1981). As a general rule, Feldman restricts his use of modulations to one degree higher or lower than the number of beats in the bar (such as 4:3, 6:5, 7:8), suggesting that these are really just a way of nudging the tempo along or back a little. The bar line simply contains these modulatory shifts. In stating the case so simply and almost anonymously, with no other notational markings used, attention is focused more upon the material than upon other expressive factors. One can imagine the effect other methods, such as *accelerando* or *ritardando* or the use of other words, might have upon the performer. The performer responds to such notations almost physically, causing a perceptible shift in 'gear'.

---

12   Nicholas Cook, *A Guide to Musical Analysis* (Oxford, 1994); Paul Griffiths, *Modern Music and After* (Oxford, 1995); Jonathan Harvey, *The Music of Stockhausen* (London, 1975); Robin Maconie, *The Works of Karlheinz Stockhausen* (Oxford, 1976); Wörner, *Stockhausen*.

13   Private conversations with pianists Peter Hill and Philip Mead.

The relationship between action and perception in experimental music is often an interesting one. If, as Cardew stated, the function of notation is to make the performer move, then notation which is multi-layered and complex can create a situation in which the performer is reacting to a number of elements resulting in a sonic event which is the sum of but also other than the notation's appearance. Such notation, rather than binding the performer can act as a stimulus for the performer and push her beyond herself. Composers who work with complex notation in this way do so understanding that notation can never be a description of sound but instead a prescription for action. I would suggest that the intention is often to create a lively and unpredictable situation and is often as experimental in intent as many indeterminate scores, such as Wolff's *Duo for Pianists II*.

Bryn Harrison's *être temps* (2002) is a work which always provokes surprise whenever the score is shown to somebody who has just experienced a performance without having seen the score.[14] There is an apparent mismatch between the surface simplicity of the material and the detailed complexity of the notation. Page five of the score exemplifies this well (see Example 3.4): a single chord of three consecutive notes (F sharp, G, and G sharp) is repeated over and over, whilst the same chord is silently depressed two octaves lower, creating a cloud of resonance between each repetition. The chords are played with a variety of dynamics, from *ppp* to *ff*. The durations of each chord are all short, but vary between slightly less than a double-dotted semiquaver (bar 104) and a slightly extended hemidemisemiquaver (bars 92 and 101).

The temporal experience of the listener is radically different to that of the performer, who is counting intensely for the duration of the page, shifting tempi accordingly. Each chord is thus defined by a) its dynamic, b) its duration, c) its articulation, d) its rhythmic and metric context (how it relates to the bar-line and the beat), and e) its temporal context. Naturally, aspects of the pianist's technique, the instrument and the acoustic of the concert hall will also affect the sound to varying degrees. The result is a vivid sense of focus and energy accorded to each chord which it would be hard to imagine notated in any other way. The function of the notation is to make the performer move in such a way – a physical response to a complex and rigorous mental process – that the material is conditioned by, and can only exist in, the notation alone. And yet at the same time it acknowledges the notion that these physical and mental responses rely upon a deep-rooted understanding on the part of the performer of the implications of each notational detail, nurtured no doubt through years of training and experience within the arena of notated music.

One of the most valuable aspects of complex notation is that it has the potential to further the performer's sense of what is achievable, by taking the performer 'beyond herself', transcending technical, instrumental and experiential boundaries. One of the reasons John Cage was resistant to musical improvisation was that

---

14   For an extended discussion of this work from a variety of viewpoints, see Eric Clarke, Nicholas Cook, Bryn Harrison and Philip Thomas, 'Interpretation and Performance in Bryn Harrison's *être temps*', *Musicae Scienitae*, 9 (2005): 31–74.

Example 3.4   Page 5 from Bryn Harrison, *être temps* (2002)

it relied too extensively (consciously or subconsciously) upon the performer's previous experience, education/training and technique. This was true of his role as a composer and was borne out through his use of chance procedures in his compositions. Complex notation serves a similar purpose in keeping the performer alive to the moment and to new possibilities. Michael Finnissy, a composer who draws upon an experimental aesthetic a great deal whilst also acknowledging the performing traditions of a variety of other musical types, uses complex notation as one way of creating distance, or of guarding against an approach which relies upon expression as an imposed device. The briefest example, from the third section of the composer's *Folklore* (1993–94) will serve to illustrate this (see Example 3.5): the dynamic *ffff!* suggests as loud as possible and there are no articulation marks other than an accent on the first note of a phrase. All that the performer has to do is to match the pitches given to the notated rhythms.

The rhythmic complexities, combined with the extreme volume (and consequent physicality of playing as the pianist near-pulverizes the keys), the registeral leaps as well as the close intertwining of the hands due to the superimposition of a number of lines, result in a very particular kind of energy and focused intensity.

Example 3.5   Extract from Michael Finnissy, *Folklore III* (1993–94), lines 1–4, p. 48

I would argue that this would be impossible to notate in any other way and that any attempt to approximate or even improvise a comparable phrase would result in a loss of that energy. Interestingly, earlier works by Finnissy (such as *Jazz* (1976) and *English Country Tunes* (1977/82)) derive in part from his experiences as an improviser in classes at the London School of Contemporary Dance where he was accompanist. Yet the extreme complexity of the notation is an attempt both to reflect the complexity of those improvisations and also to bring a heightened sense of energy, physicality, intensity. The performer's attempts to just reach the right notes at the right time, whilst dealing with the textural and notational complexity, guards against complacency in performance and compels her to move beyond the normal technical and expressive requirements into unventured territory.

The difficulty in relating complex notations such as these to experimental music is that this type of notation is accompanied by extra 'baggage'. At the point at which one is dealing with bar-lines, note groupings, rhythmic relationships and so forth, inherent notions of gesture are brought into play. And these intimations of gesture are bound up with the canon of Western notated music, be it Mozart, Brahms or Webern. The most interesting composers are well aware of these associations and position their aesthetic clearly in relation to the Western musical tradition. This is true also of a number of composers who adopt a so-called 'action-notation' approach, such as Lachenmann, Spahlinger and others.[15] Though on the surface their music is well-suited to an essay such as this, and despite the notational and sonic innovations of their work, their music operates (in form, structure, continuity, gesture and so forth) within the sphere of Western (European) notated music. Performers responding to their often highly complex notational demands are doing so within that tradition. Harrison's *être temps* (and similarly the later works of Morton Feldman) manages to steer clear of these associations through the reductive properties of the material which forces the material to the foreground, instead of the mannerisms and interpretative prowess of the performer.

Indeterminate Music

Paradoxically, one of the most indeterminate scores (on the surface at least), John Cage's *Variations II* (1962), functions in much the same way as the complex scores discussed above. The 'score' consists of 11 transparent sheets, six with a single straight line on, and five with a single 'dot'. The performer is instructed to throw the sheets onto a surface and take the resulting configuration of lines and dots as the score. Measurements are then made by drawing perpendicular lines from the dots to the lines and assigning parameters to each line, such as time, frequency, amplitude, number of events. It can be played by any instrument or any number

---

15   For a fascinating discussion of the performer's role in interpreting these and other works, see Mieko Kanno, 'Prescriptive Notation: Limits and Challenges', *Contemporary Music Review*, 26/2 (2007): 231–54.

of instruments. Once realized, for the performer the work is as fixed as is *Music of Changes*, though of course further and radically different realizations may be made.

Clearly the performer has a major interpretative role to play here in that the selection of material and values from which measurements must be taken is left entirely open – literally any sound source would be valid. However, despite this considerable freedom, once each of the lines has been ascribed a value it is then down to the particular arrangement of lines and dots to determine how and when those values will be combined. There is no place for improvisation here and the work becomes as rigorous a process as *Music of Changes*. For the performer, whose choices of material type may or may not have been based upon (or limited by) their taste and/or experience, this is an exploration into some of the potential of their selected material and chosen sound source(s). The six values represented by the six lines mean that most if not all of the decisions concerning how to play are made and the performer must focus upon channelling these values into action.

A version I made in 2005[16] for solo piano combined seven different realizations using different kinds of source material which explored a range of plucked, muted, struck and normally played sounds as well as various percussive sounds around the frame of the piano using a variety of objects with which to strike. The final result (which I notated using units of a second as a structural grid) embraced periods of silence as well as sections of great complexity. Two of the most interesting products of the realization for me as a pianist were a) the combinations of struck and plucked harmonics, many of which took considerable time finding along the strings, and b) the sections which involved my playing normally struck keys, muted and plucked strings, and percussive noises on various areas of the piano's interior and exterior all within a short space of time. These involved considerable physical movement on my part (increasing my appreciation for Merce Cunningham's frequently impossible chance-derived movements) but more significantly advanced my understanding of timbral and pitch relationships across a variety of extended techniques at the piano.

Approaches to other indeterminate works by Cage are likely to be similar, with performers applying Cage's own compositional techniques to performance decisions to engage in a situation which is not reliant upon their judgement. It is not surprising that other composers may use indeterminate notation for other purposes, and are more inclined to allow improvisatory elements to play an important role in any performance. Indeterminate, or aleatoric, techniques are perhaps too often regarded as allowing for an 'anything goes' approach, partly the result of the blurring of the performer/composer divide whereby a number of significant performers and composers work within both composed and improvised genres. Engaging performers in an exploratory, investigative mode of music-making requires composers to be clear about the parameters of any indeterminate score, either through the use of verbal instructions or through the score itself. Without

---

16   Philip Thomas, *Comprovisation*, Bruce's Fingers, 66 (2007).

clear parameters in place performers are more inclined towards improvisation and less inclined towards experimentation.[17]

The comments by Tudor with which this chapter opened also seem to limit the possibilities for improvisation, though here Tudor is referring to 'interpretation' more generally. However, both words suggest more often than not a reliance upon experience: improvisation relies in large part upon the player's technique and stylistic affiliations, from which the player then hopefully moves to further both. Interpretation of notated scores also derives from these but performers are usually required to move between and adopt different stylistic codes dependent upon the repertoire being performed. My argument from the performer's perspective is that music which could be said to be 'experimental' requires a stylistically non-interventionist approach, whereby performers respond to the demands of the score, without reference to any external stylistic code, and focus upon the production of sound within the parameters of the score.

It is unsurprising, then, that composers who wish to avoid traditional notions of gesture, continuity and style choose instead to adopt some form of process as the formal basis of their work. This process may be one of rigorous chance procedures, as in Cage, or may rely upon the live performance situation, as in Wolff, or may be more transparent in its aural reality, such as Steve Reich or Alvin Lucier. The role of the performer in Lucier's music is to be both catalyst and medium for a particular sonic peculiarity. However, Lucier's music tends not to exploit the situation but rather to present it clearly and honestly with only the minimum of performer intervention.[18]

Piano Phase (1967) by Steve Reich would seem to be an exemplar for the kind of approach advocated here. The performers must simply do what is required – either keep the same 12-note pattern (in the first part of the work) at a constant tempo, or accelerate the 12-note pattern ever so slightly so that the two parts progressively interlock a semiquaver apart – and focus all energies upon doing this very task. The only interpretative licence is accorded the second pianist who may vary the number of repetitions, though this is within limited parameters and is generally the result of the time taken to do the work. If I have a criticism of this work it would be that its extremities can too easily shift the focus away from the material towards the

---

17 I am not suggesting that improvised music cannot be experimental. Indeed I would argue that the most investigative musicians working today are to be found within the arena of free improvisation. However, this chapter is dealing with music concerned with the negotiation of a score as the cue for musical investigation through performance. Composers who choose to work with notation (be it staff, graphic or text-based) must deal with it responsibly in full awareness of its potential and function.

18 The score to Lucier's *Vespers* (1968), for performers with echolocating devices, includes the instruction 'Decisions as to speed and direction of outgoing clicks must be made only on the usefulness in the process of echolocation. Any situations that arise from personal preferences based on ideas of texture, density, improvisation, or composition that do not directly serve to articulate the sound personality of the environment should be considered deviations from the task of echolocation' (in Alvin Lucier, *Reflections* (Cologne, 1995), pp. 312–14).

stamina and technique of the performers. Yet it is no more extreme than a number of works that are discussed, or could have been discussed, here, such as *Music of Changes*, Feldman's *Triadic Memories*, Walter Zimmerman's *Beginner's Mind* and so on. The difference is perhaps in the degree to which this is music which is projected through *attack* (rather than *locating* the sound) and which is centred upon the process and the combination of materials rather than the material itself.

In *Piano Phase* the performers 'speak' through their physical and mental virtuosity, a virtuosity which paradoxically requires them to present themselves as anonymous slaves to the process. I hope to have demonstrated above that performers of *Music of Changes*, *Variations II* or indeed most chance-ordained works by Cage reveal themselves through the focus on touch, technique and time required to allow the material to be revealed. Through their desire to be inquisitive about material – sound and silence – experimental performers willingly adopt a performance approach which is non-interventionist. With alert ears and responsive bodies, experimental performers attend themselves to the task at hand. All the performer can do in a work such as Michael Parsons' *Fourths and Fifths* (1982), consisting of a string of dyads, spanning intervals of either a fourth or a fifth and tracing a permutational line over the course of the piece (see Example 3.6), is to *play*, allowing as little to get in the way of the music as possible.

Example 3.6   Lines 1–4, p. 2 from Michael Parsons, *Fourths and Fifths* (1982)

What, then, of those indeterminate scores which are more ambiguous about the nature of the task? The first, and probably most famous, entirely graphic score was Earle Brown's *December 1952*. Like contemporaneous works by Brown, such as *Four Systems* (1954) and *Twenty-Five Pages* (1953), the score features only horizontal and (unlike the other works) vertical lines of different lengths and thicknesses, distributed within an empty canvas. The limitations of the vocabulary used (no curves, diagonals, connections and so forth) are such that performers will likely ascribe meaning to those features that *are* defining of the work. Like Harrison's *être temps*, the reduction of the material focuses the performer's attention towards the production of the material itself, making sounds that correspond to the various qualities of the lines. The austerity of the score suggests interpretations which avoid gesture but encourage imaginative and investigative approaches to sound.

Cornelius Cardew's *Treatise* (1963–66) is a less straightforward work, due to the greater complexity of the graphic material. There is not the space here to examine this work in any detail, but experience of performing this work with a variety of different musicians and in a number of different contexts has shown that this is a work which requires negotiation between players and that a wide variety of interpretative approaches can be adopted. One of the greatest dangers is that it simply becomes an excuse for improvisation and the score gets gradually left out of the equation. However, whether or not an approach is adopted which ascribes meanings to each and every symbol and is effectively (or actually) notated, or the score is used as a reference point within a more improvisatory approach, the purpose of the notation remains as a catalyst for action. The performer must respond to it in some way. That Cardew does not specify *how* the performer should respond does not lessen the function of the notation. Performers may respond to the graphics much as they might to an acoustical property of the performance space, a noise outside, or to the sounds from other players, or perhaps from a radio (which a number of musicians have used as representing the circles within the score). In this way the score of *Treatise* is as much a self-contained set of instructions as the *Duo for Pianists II* or *Piano Phase* – no other interpretative reference is necessary to perform it and in the absence of any performance instructions (the *Treatise Handbook* muddies the waters to such a degree that performers can only turn back to the score for guidance) the score becomes the sole point of reference.

Recent Responses

Notational types discussed thus far have touched on extreme complexity (though there are many *more* extreme examples that could have been used) and extreme indeterminacy, such as *Treatise* and *Variations II*. Interpretation has been shown to rely upon performers absolving themselves from traditional interpretative decisions concerning the production of sound, though frequently performers are called upon to make interpretative choices concerning the *realization* of scores. Performers concentrate upon the work necessary to the production of sound in response to the score alone.

Some of the examples discussed were composed over 50 years ago and as understanding of the aesthetic, technical and performance concerns of this music has increased so composers have responded to a kind of performance tradition which has emerged over the years. Essentially this is characterized by a focus upon material in the immediacy of the moment, a concern to involve oneself with the production of sound (whether this is the sound of a violin harmonic, a muted piano tone or electronic feedback), and an acceptance of the sonic result which may or may not have been intentional. The performer's physicality, intellect and character is wholly engaged with this act, and *not* with the projection of shapes, phrasing, line and so on. My experience is that this approach forces one to deal with the instrument itself in a far more technical and physical way than does much other music. One's attention is solely on the production of sound and the means of doing so and as a result one's understanding of the instrument is often considerably furthered.

Perhaps recognizing the ambiguities of many open scores and the consequent licence given to the performer, much of the most interesting music being composed today is organized in such a way as to provide clear and restrictive parameters within which the performer may move. The focus is upon what the performer *does* rather than how she interprets. Consequently (and ironically) a performing tradition is implied which follows the approaches described in this chapter. Three recent examples will serve to illustrate this approach:

Tim Parkinson *piano piece* 2006

The score is fully notated in terms of pitch, rhythm and tempi. Markings such as 'legato', tenuto marks, occasional dynamics and slurs feature in some of the sections. The music is notated using standard computer notation software but sections are delineated on the page through restarting a line at the beginning of each new section. There is a clarity about the music's presentation which is somewhat anonymous due to the software used and the framing of an uncluttered (though sufficiently detailed) notation upon the clean white paper. Pages 4–8 present the pianist with choices to make concerning the selection of material, in that the pianist must choose which of two blocks of material to play at a number of points. These last only a short number of bars and choosing one block over another does not significantly alter the character of the music as they are very closely related.

The title positions the work within a broadly abstract aesthetic and none of the performance indications allude to any external interpretative traditions. Instead all the indications tell the performer what or how to play. If the pianist attends to the written details and focuses upon the execution of these details as clearly as possible then the piece would seem to work. However, as discussed earlier, musical notation evokes responses associated with a variety of other musics. In order to avoid the kind of imposed expressive mannerisms that, for example, the first line of page 4 (see Example 3.7) might conjure up, the pianist would need to be aware of and familiar with a style of playing which derives explicitly from the experimental tradition as engendered by David Tudor, John Cage, Christian Wolff and others. Herein lies a problem, namely the tendency towards inertia that Tudor implied. As soon as performers position a work within a tradition and thus within a particular interpretative mode they are recalling a way of playing which has the potential to disengage them from the activity. Despite this, Parkinson's work challenges performers still to engage with the production of sound and the furthering of technique in response to the live performance moment. Trying for the kind of plainness of sound implied by the notation is not an easy task and the pianist must manage to balance the imperfections of the instrument, any irregularities in her technique (stronger/weaker fingers, difficult stretches and so on) and quirks of the performance moment in order to achieve a focused and unmodulated sound.

Example 3.7   Line 1, p. 4 from Tim Parkinson, *piano piece* (2006)

Joseph Kudirka *Beauty and Industry*

The clarity with which the instructions for this score are specified is characteristic of Kudirka's work in general (much of which, though not all, consists of text-based scores such as this). The performer's task is unambiguous though not without its freedoms: obviously choice of sound is free so long as its duration is characterized by the physical properties of the instrument/sound source or player; the performer can choose whether to slightly shift each new sound up or down in pitch, meaning that at one extreme a player might oscillate between two pitches for the duration of the piece or at the other extreme might progressively and consistently move down or up a microtonal scale; and performers can choose to make those choices in such a way as is determined by a structural plan or by listening to other musicians and responding accordingly in some way.

Like Wolff's *Duo for Pianists II*, it is hard to imagine a performance which, if the performers obey the instructions, could fail. Yet at the same time the work is clearly aligned to an experimental aesthetic which is post-Cageian, minimalist (reductionist?), non-teleological and articulates the material alone as subject. Despite there being no indication with respect to dynamics, an interpretation by any player which 'plays around' with these dynamics and attempts to impose some kind of shape would likely be inappropriate, drawing attention to the player rather than the material. The focus instead is on achieving consistency of sound whilst also balancing the minute changes required. Arguably, a performing tradition is assumed which aligns the performer's interpretative response to the composer's adopted aesthetic.

The score for this work reads as follows:

Beauty and Industry
for two or (many) more players

A performance of the piece is as many minutes long as there are players.

Each player should start playing at some time within the first minute and stop at some time within the last minute of the piece.

Each sound that a player makes should be conditioned by physical properties of the player/instrument; for instance, the entire length of a bow stroke, the amount of time it takes for a percussive object or plucked string to fully decay, the length of a wind player or singer's breath, etc. Given this constraint, each sound should be as long as possible. After each instance of playing, a player should rest for the length of their previous tone.

Each player's first tone is of their own choosing. After this, each subsequent tone should vary slightly in pitch (1/4 tone or less) from the last. Performers playing instruments of fixed pitch should play the same tone throughout the piece, unless playing a chordal instrument. If able to play chords, a player may (but need not) change one note from the chord in each period of playing.

Joseph Kudirka
2007

Example 3.8   Joseph Kudirka, *Beauty and Industry* (2007)

John Lely *All About The Piano* (2006)

Lely takes the risk here of leaving a number of aspects of the score open to the performer. The piano score consists of fragments (notes, chords, occasional decorative figures) spread across four pages fairly randomly (with differing spaces between them) from which the pianist may select as she sees fit, in any order, with any amount of repetition or omission (see Example 3.9). Concurrently, recording devices are set in motion to both record the piano part in real time and subsequently playback the recorded piano sounds. This can be done repeatedly so that subsequent recordings may also record other recordings as well as the continuing piano part. Gradually the pianist should play less and less whilst the recordings will likely become more dense. Very different performances and interpretations are possible, with the following variables being the most free: order of piano events, total duration, type of recording equipment (from lo-fi devices such as dictaphones to more recent technology such as Max/MSP), number of recording devices (or layers of recordings) being operated, routes through a space, use of alternative means for distributing sounds.

Despite these variables, the piano part will likely remain relatively consistent – the scope for interpretative innovation will more likely be explored through the recording processes. As the tape part(s) becomes more present the pianist enters into a dialogue with these other recorded sounds. At this point the degree to which the result is truly experimental or otherwise is negotiated by the pianist's response: if a sense of argument, of call and response, or playful interaction with the recorded parts is the aim (and such an approach is not forbidden by the score) then immediately the attention is turned from the material to the pianist's interaction with the material – the focus becomes the *interpretation* and not the material, and

Example 3.9   Page 1 from John Lely, *All About the Piano* (2006)

the openness to surprise and the unknown is superseded by cliché and missed opportunities (disappointment). If, however, an approach is taken which simply presents the piano material in conjunction with but not dependent upon the recorded material then the result is something else – connections are made that are not reliant upon the manipulations that the performer makes but derive from the simultaneity of the musics.

Concluding Remarks

It is perhaps perverse to end a discussion about experimental performance by examining what could effectively be called a 'performance practice' of experimental music. However, if it *is* a performance practice it is one with a difference: instead of being defined by a search for authenticity it is marked by inquisitiveness and investigation. The experimental performer engages with a task and pursues it with rigour and devotion, and is open to the multiplicity of options which have the potential to radically change each performance of the same piece. Rather than involve interpretative factors from outside of the parameters of the score and which are generally associated with the performance of *other* musics, the experimental performer remains open to and accepting of the sonic peculiarities engendered by the work.

Instead of regarding the kind of approaches discussed here as being non-interpretative, anonymous or even devoid of personality, the reality is that performers consciously partner with composers to join with them in an act of investigation and experimentation. The personality of the performer is revealed by their engagement with the work to be done. This is consistent with the fact that many such performers are also active as improvisers and/or composers. Any performing tradition that has emerged over the last 50 years of music has done so as a result of performers sharing the artistic concerns of experimental composers but also being desirous of a situation which provokes them to be curious. The scores which are most successful in achieving this are those which engage the performer in an act of work rather than interpretation, in order that intellect, ears and technique might be altered.

Open Sources: Words, Circuits, and the Notation/Realization Relation in Live Electronic Music

Ronald Kuivila

The term 'live electronic music' can be regarded as simply descriptive of any work that involves electronic means in performance. This would include myriad works ranging from the nightingale's song in Ottorino Respighi's *Pines of Rome* (1924) to the theremin in the Beach Boys' *Good Vibrations* (1966). However, it also has a far more specific connotation as an identifier of a collection of pieces and approaches to performance with electronics that evolved in the 1960s and 1970s and continues to this day in approaches such as circuit bending, electronic instrument building and some forms of laptop performance. These works favoured custom or homemade circuitry over commercially produced electronic equipment. The configurations of electronics used were more often treated as situations than as instruments. As David Behrman wrote for a 1971 recording of his piece *Runthrough* (1971):

> *Runthrough is made from cheap circuitry put together at home. Three or four people can use it to make improvised music. There is no score. The circuitry consists of sound generators and modulators, with dials and switches which can be worked by one or two people, and a photocell distribution circuit which two others can play with flashlights. The sound is best heard coming from four or eight large loudspeakers placed in a circle around players and listeners. No special skills or training are helpful in turning knobs or shining flashlights, so whatever music can emerge from the equipment is as available to non-musicians as to musicians. The generators and modulators provide a large reservoir of particular sound possibilities which can be gotten at by the players in the course of operating the various controls. Because there is neither a score nor directions, any sound which results from any combination of switch and light positioning remains part of the 'piece.' (Whatever you do with a surfboard in the surf remains a part of surfboarding).*[1]

---

1   Sleeve note by David Behrman from *Electronic Sound*, Mainstream, MS/5010 (1972).

This description, with its emphasis on a deskilled context open to all, underplays the importance of the sensibility shared by the composer/performers who first performed the piece. All were affiliated with and were influenced by the pioneering work of David Tudor and John Cage with live electronic systems; all provided music for the Merce Cunningham Dance Company at one time or another. It also attempts no description of the very specific musical properties of the electronics themselves that are constitutive of the 'sound world' that is the piece. Those properties were as often discovered as designed. The processes of experimentation and performance accumulate an oral and aural trace that defines the piece to the composer and performer alike. Because key attributes of the piece are physically rendered by the electronics, they can be left unnotated, unspecified and, in some cases, not fully understood.

In the particular case of *Runthrough*, an oscillator used to create the pulsing articulations characteristic of the piece had a varying amount of DC offset. The effect of this offset was to create a continuous transition from tremolo to articulation as the oscillator's level is increased. This property is not immediately obvious from the patch diagrams that describe the work. However, it was discovered when a digital realization of the work was prepared by Mark Trayle for a performance at California Institute of the Arts. The translation from one enabling technology to another exposed features that required additional specification. That digital simulation is in many ways a realm of pure notation is an issue to which we will return at the end of this chapter.

Cage/Tudor

The origins of the live electronic approach can be found in the slowly evolving relation between notation and realization at the heart of the indeterminate notations characteristic of the compositions John Cage wrote in the 1950s and 1960s. But these pieces are in many regards the polar opposite of live electronic works such as *Runthrough*. The notations of pieces such as *Fontana Mix* (1958) or the piano solo of *Concert for Piano and Orchestra* (1957–58) provide varying means for determining the sounding music but do not describe any specific, stable sound image. These pieces were explicitly *not* conceived as performable by performers of indeterminate background. Rather, John Cage repeatedly states that these pieces were composed for the very specific virtuosity of a very specific virtuoso, David Tudor. The origins of the live electronic approach can be traced to David Tudor's passage from virtuoso pianist to composer of electronic music.

The first work publicly presented as Tudor's or, more precisely, *not* presented as another composer's work, was *Bandoneon!* (1966), from the Nine Evenings of Theatre and Engineering. The programme notes for that piece state:

> *Bandoneon! is a combine incorporating programmed audio circuits, moving loudspeakers, TV images, and lighting instrumentally excited ... Bandoneon!*

uses no composing means, since when activated it composes itself out of its own composite instrumental nature.[2]

It is significant that Tudor describes this piece as a 'combine', Robert Rauschenberg's term for an artwork that is neither painting nor sculpture. As a combine, *Bandoneon!* is not quite a composition in the traditional sense, and Tudor does not claim the role of composer. The electronic components, designed by Lowell Cross, Robert Kieronski and Fred Waldhauer, create an electronic configuration that imposes a set of material constraints on a musical performance. Tudor acts as the interpreter and performer of a composition that 'composes itself' out of these constituent parts. Understanding this idea where collaborative enterprise obviates the need for composition requires a review of the interplay between fidelity and freedom that Tudor characterized as central to the evolution of indeterminacy and how, in his own music, these are fused in a new concept of instrumentality.

Notation/Realization

For Tudor, the most important aspect of the early period of chance composition was a change in musical perception triggered by his performances of Pierre Boulez's Second Piano Sonata (1948) and John Cage's *Music of Changes* (1951).

> *Both pieces were a radical departure, a different musical consciousness, though Cage's turned out to be more radical than Boulez's. The Boulez is where I learned I really had to change the way I thought about musical continuity, and that you don't necessarily go on in a linear progression. When I came to the Cage I had to work on the moment-to-moment differences. Music of Changes was a great discipline, because you can't do it unless you're ready for anything at each instant. You can't carry over any emotional impediments, though at the same time you have to be ready to accept them each instant, as they arise. Being an instrumentalist carries with it the job of making certain physical preparations for the next instant, so I had to learn to put myself in the right frame of mind. I had to learn how to be able to cancel my consciousness of any previous moment, in order to be able to produce the next one. What this did for me was to bring about freedom, the freedom to do anything, and that's how I learned to be free for a whole hour at a time.*[3]

A central characteristic of the *Music of Changes* is that chance specifies every detail. The performer has no choice but to follow the dictates of the chance process

---

2 Programme note for *Bandoneon!*, David Tudor Papers, Box 16, Folder 2, Getty Research Institute Archive.

3 Victor Schonfeld and David Tudor, 'From Piano to Electronics', *Music and Musicians*, xx/12 (August 1972): 24–6.

as accurately as possible. There is little room for the supplemental presence of interpretation. It seems completely appropriate that the first explorations of chance-determined music would be completely rigorous in their application of the chance mechanism and require perfect compliance with its results. How else to discover just what chance provides? The demand of fidelity to a score was also entirely congruent with Tudor's training as a classical pianist under the tutelage of Irma Wolpe.

Cage came to reject the attempt to fully specify all details of the sounding music he had made in the *Music of Changes*. He began to see the demands for purely precise execution it placed upon the performer as the creation of 'an object more inhuman than human'.[4] Correcting this naturally leads to the concept of indeterminacy: the creation of notations that circumscribe a field of musical possibility out of which an unrepeatable stream of unique sounds and actions can emerge. Superabundance became the creative discipline appropriate to the new understanding of composition. The paradoxical goal was to create a musical situation where both notation and imagination fail. Notation fails because the repetition inherent in any finite set of symbols suggests relations where there are none. Imagination fails because it is beyond the ability of any individual to comprehend or conceive limitless difference. The music can be 'heard' only when it sounds. In this way, the performer regains his/her own centre in relation to chance processes.

Beginning with *Winter Music* (1956–57) Cage adopted increasingly abstract notations where the performer more and more directly determines the specification and detail of the sounding music. In an interview with John Holzapfel, Cage indicates that Tudor's 'interest in puzzles invited the whole thing of indeterminacy. And so what you had to do was to make a situation that would interest *him*. That was the role he played.'[5] It might be more precise to say that Tudor was looking for the simplest – and, thereby, most open – formulation of the composer's idea. For example, he says about Stockhausen's early *Klavierstücke*:

> *All his works of those days were composed as theoretical forms, structures dealing with numbers, and whenever it came to making a score he had to translate his original material into musical form. Many's the time I would ask him why he didn't publish the original idea instead of the realization he had made from it, but he always refused.*[6]

The *Concert for Piano and Orchestra* represents a crucial point of closure in Cage's initial work in this direction. While the orchestral parts are notated relatively strictly and simply, the *Solo for Piano* is an encyclopedia of 84 different notations. Like most concerti, the *Concert* is a showpiece for a solo virtuoso. This appears to be in tension with a sensibility that shuns personality and ego, if not outright contradiction.

---

4   John Cage, 'Composition as Process: Indeterminacy', *Silence: Lectures and Writings* (London, 1968), pp. 35–40, at p. 36.

5   John Holzaepfel, *David Tudor and the Performance of American Experimental Music, 1950–1959* (CUNY Graduate Center, 1994), p. 59.

6   Schonfeld and Tudor, 'From Piano to Electronics', pp. 24–6.

In interviews, Cage often invoked Sylvano Bussoti's designation of David Tudor as a 'minotaur of the pianistical mythology'[7] quite literally, without the facetious undertone that was Bussotti's intent in his letter to Tudor. Coomaraswamy, whose thought Cage invoked repeatedly throughout his career, distinguishes between the types and archetypes in Platonic thought and in Indian thought as follows:

> But whereas Platonic types are types of being, external to the conditioned universe and thought of as absolutes reflected in phenomena, Indian types are those of sentient activity or functional utility conceivable only in a contingent world. Oriental types are not thought of as mechanically reflected in phenomena, but as representing to our mentality the operative principles by which we 'explain' phenomena.[8]

In this sense, Tudor can be imagined as an 'archetype' of music for Cage who literally embodies music. One can appreciate both the power and the restrictiveness of this understanding.

After completing the *Concert for Piano and Orchestra*, Cage began to explore even greater flexibility by remaking notations from the *Solo for Piano* as reconfigurable transparencies. James Pritchett refers to these transparencies as 'tools',[9] because they really function as decision-making devices that can be applied in new situations independent of the original piece. Tudor's approach to the realization of *Cartridge Music* (1960) and *Variations* (1958–1967) can be considered prototypes for the live electronic music he subsequently developed. Tudor discussed both of these pieces and his understanding of the composer/performer distinction during an interview with Teddy Hultberg in 1988.

> *TH: When we look at some of the scores of John Cage, were you not in a sense a co-composer when you realized them? How do you draw the line between interpreter and co-composer?*
>
> *DT: Oh, I think it's a great line. I crossed over it with great difficulty because I always wanted to be a faithful interpreter and my whole early training was for absolute realization of a score which is a very complicated proposition. For instance, nowadays, I feel that many people don't read John Cage's score in the sense that they don't realize why the instructions are difficult to understand. Now, when you look at a score that somebody presents to you and you see that you are following the instructions and the way they are laid down, you are the composers' helper. If you have to select a medium for yourself in which to realize those materials, then you have to think about how far you have to go in order to realize it. One example is John Cage's Cartridge Music. All the instructions were given. All you had to do was*

---

7   David Tudor Papers, Box 174, Folder 2, Getty Research Institute Archive.
8   Ananda Coomaraswamy, *The Transformation of Nature in Art* (New York, 1956), p. 17.
9   James Pritchett, *The Music of John Cage* (Cambridge, 1993), pp. 126–37.

to do what it said quote unquote and bring about a performance score for yourself. However, in doing that, there are a lot of small things which cause you to actually alter the readings you got from the score. For instance, for the determination of time, John Cage had employed a clock on transparent paper which goes around from one to sixty. Well, one thing which I discovered very early on was that when you are performing, there are lots of things you have to do besides looking at a stopwatch or thinking about the time. So after a while, you think, 'Oh, I was so late, what am I going to do? I'm supposed to hurry,' or, 'the time is so long, I have nothing to do, what shall I do?' So after looking back on it you decide, well, it's not important what minute it is, it's only important what second it is, so then you see that if you make your determination only reading the second hand and it does not say what minute it is, then all of a sudden you are giving yourself a freedom of interpretation which you didn't have before.

It was years later, because John and I performed this piece for many years, that I found out that he had done exactly the same thing in his own realization. And another thing which I had done was with reading a time bracket. If you take a time bracket, it says you start at :05 seconds and you stop at :35 seconds. It's also possible to read the bracket backwards. I mean, what difference does it make? And John was also doing that himself, but he had never told me. He had never told any of his performers that that was possible. But that's also given in the score material. If you look at it, precisely, you see that there are those possibilities.[10]

The change in the role of the time brackets from fixed grid to flexible collection of selectable constraints is a profound departure from Cage's initial insistence on specific time brackets – even for *4'33"* (1952). It is striking that *Four⁶* (1992), Cage's very last piece, is notated as a series of flexible time brackets.

Words

Throughout the later 1950s there had been a kind of dialectical collegiality between Stockhausen and Cage. In this period, Cage offered a course in experimental music at the New School for Social Research that, as Liz Kotz has pointed out, sought to introduce the innovations of Darmstadt to the American musical context. The student response to Cage's course went in quite a different direction. The pieces of this younger generation avoided the technical virtuosity and procedural complexity that seems so much a part of both Darmstadt and the New York School. Instead, they

---

10   Teddy Hultberg, '"I smile when the sound is singing through the space": An Iinterview with David Tudor by Teddy Hultberg in Düsseldorf May 17, 18 1988', available at http://www.emf.org/tudor/Articles/hultberg.html (accessed 30 April 2009).

began to work directly with naturally occurring chance processes and to compose brief, elliptical texts that might be conceived as scores, instructions or poems. The tactic was adopted by others not directly involved in the classes and, within a few short years, became an identifying characteristic of Fluxus performance.

George Brecht's initial response to the course was to compose pieces where the indeterminate structure of the piece arose directly from the action rather than being predetermined. His later event scores were 'private, like little enlightenments I wanted to communicate to my friend … Later on, rather to my surprise, I learned that … others had made public realizations of pieces I had always waited to notice occurring.'[11] Yoko Ono's word pieces[12] are quite similar to Brecht's but they involved a play between public and private spaces in which reading a text effectively performs it or individuals are asked to break a taboo in a context of mutual responsibility. In contrast, La Monte Young's text pieces were quite public in conception, with an occasional dose of intergenerational brattiness. For example, recalling Tudor's performance of 4'33", La Monte Young's *Piano Piece for David Tudor No. 2* (1960) asks Tudor to continue to open and shut the keyboard lid until he does so silently.

The first buddings of this work were received warmly by both Cage and Tudor. Tudor was directly involved with presenting the earliest of these pieces, performing works by George Brecht and La Monte Young in Cologne and participating in the loft concert series organized by Young and Yoko Ono in the winter and spring of 1961. In interviews around this time, Cage explicitly acknowledges Young as making work close in spirit but different in kind from his own. (George Maciunas, perhaps because of his hostility to Stockhausen, met with a much more reserved reception.)

This kind of work appears to have exerted some influence on both Cage and Tudor. In his analysis of Tudor's realization of Cage's *Variations II* (1961), James Pritchett details Tudor's approach, which was based on the specification of actions and tendencies (complex versus simple) rather than the specification of sounds.[13] In an interview, Tudor explicitly acknowledges that this realization was a departure:

> *DT: Now, John Cage had a series of Variations. In the First Variation, we both followed the score and made precise determinations. We commonly decided upon the time length and everything fell within that time length and the proportion that we had read. When it comes to Variations II, the material given by Cage began to be much freer and so many more determinations were necessary. One thing you had to determine was what instrument you had to use and in the case of Variations II, it didn't matter what instrument. That is, it didn't have to be one instrument, it could have been many instruments. This was a new piece and I wanted to make it a new experience so I wanted to experiment. I decided to do it for amplified piano. I had been assimilating*

11   George Brecht, 'The Origin of "Events"', in Julia Robinson and Alfred M. Fischer (eds), *George Brecht – Events – A Heterospective* (Köln: Walther König, 2006), p. 236.

12   See *Cut* and *Touch* in Yoko Ono, *Grapefruit* (New York, 2000) pp. 242 and 252.

13   James Pritchett, *David Tudor's realization of John Cage's Variations II*, available at http://www.rosewhitemusic.com/cage/texts/Var2.html (accessed 30 April 2009).

experience using electronic equipment. I looked at the score and thought, 'how can I realize these parameters using electronic equipment?'. Now involved in my decisions was the fact, that John Cage always makes his electronic notations according to numbers. For instance with the gain control, he looked at how many gradations there were on the dial. Well, gain controls can be made in different ways: you can turn the control almost all the way up and there is no change in gain or it can happen very immediately half-way through the control and there is no further effect. I had to find some relevant means of using this amplification as part of the instrument. It's not just amplifying the instrument, but the whole thing taken together is an instrument of its own.

So I began to look at the parameters and I made certain decisions as to what was important and that enabled me to make a score of my own. I looked at it and I said, 'well, this whole proposition is so fraught with chance-happenings, that I have to be able to have a score which itself incorporates all those possibilities, at the same time being faithful to the readings which I make from John Cage's material.' So I made a series of nomographs. They had every notation I had made but I could see every parameter at one glance. It was like a sign to me saying that you have to realize this within a certain time bracket.

Well, when you go that far, then in a sense you are co-composer. However, I still would be unable to call myself a co-composer. I call it my electronic version and I give my name as it's being my version.[14]

At roughly the same time as *Variations II*, Cage wrote *0'00"* (1962) which adopts the instruction format and bears a dedication to Toshi Ichiyanagi and Yoko Ono. In its call for a maximally amplified 'disciplined action. With any interruptions. Fulfilling in whole or part an obligation to others',[15] it can be seen as both emulating and critiquing the event scores of Fluxus. But it can also be seen as a theatrical generalization and simplification of Tudor's electronic realization of *Variations II*. If you are no longer forming and shaping a purely abstract music and instead accepting a physical process, why not make it one that does something useful? Whatever the case, by the time these two pieces are completed both time structure and the conception of sound as a vector of parameters have been set aside. These pieces also mark the beginning of a long hiatus where Cage is more involved in the organization of large-scale performances than creating works for David Tudor. In *For the Birds*, Cage remarks on the double absurdity of composing *Song Books* with Tudor in mind: Tudor was devoting his energies to electronic composition and, in any event, did not sing.

---

14   Hultberg, '"I smile when the sound is singing through the space"'.
15   John Cage, 'Solo for Voice 8', *Song Books Vol. 1* (New York, 1970), p. 31.

Circuits

Word pieces are highly fungible – they can appear on gallery walls, books or postcards. In the early 1960s, they provided a means of growing an international art movement with many disparate participants on a limited budget. Technology provided a similar means of organizing collaborations with more privileged and powerful participants. Beginning with Le Corbusier's Philips Pavilion in 1958, the association of artistic invention with technology became a basis for corporate, foundation and university support of artistic projects large and small. In the case of Le Corbusier, authorial identity was jealously guarded. So jealously guarded, that Iannis Xenakis had to threaten to resign in order to receive any public acknowledgement of his role in the design and conception of the Philips Pavilion. In the early 1960s, a more democratic and anarchic model of collaboration evolved out of Robert Rauschenberg's encounter with engineers from Bell Laboratories, Experiments in Art and Technology (EAT).

Cage had attempted to build a centre of new music research throughout the 1940s and his status as a 'musical inventor' was well established. So, it is not surprising that he engaged these emerging possibilities with his customary organizational energy. It is also easy to recognize that the combination of intellectual challenge and precise, meticulous preparation required for such technological collaborations to succeed would be appealing to David Tudor. Once engaged, Tudor would be drawn to interact with the possibilities of the technology as directly as possible.

For the Nine Evenings of Theatre and Engineering, Tudor was scheduled to provide his own concert as well as to assist with many others, ranging from Cage to Deborah Hay. The extent of the involvement of engineers from Bell Labs steadily increased, initially out of their own interest. As the project became more and more publicized, it became an important matter of public relations for the corporation that the events be a success. (EAT employed the same tactic, with catastrophic results, during the development of the Pepsi Pavilion for Expo '70.) Tudor's description of the overall project suggests that it was understood to be an inherently ephemeral exploration:

> It seems most of the ideas that emerged during Nine Evenings could be realized again and again, each time with current state of the art technology no matter how far different from the means originally used. Nine evenings bent the concepts of systems engineering, celebrating the arrival of technology rather than using it: no blame for either engineers or artists.[16]

However, the actual engineering concepts had a longer lasting impact on Tudor than this might suggest. Much of the technology developed for Nine Evenings was based on elements of the phone system familiar to the participating engineers. In particular, tones and narrow band filters were used to create multiple channels of control. Modulation techniques allowed one sound to control another. In this context, sound is no longer a dissociated, ephemeral experience but a means

---

16   David Tudor Papers, Box 16, Folder 2, Getty Research Institute Archive.

of command and control. The ideas underlying this 'instrumentalization' of sound could not hold appeal to Cage, a composer whose goal was a completely dissociated experience of sound that would make any and all sounds fascinating. However, for Tudor, this instrumentalized sound created the possibility of a new musical instrumentality. *Bandoneon!* was an initial exploration of this terrain where the sound of the bandoneon acted as a control source that would determine the details of a multimedia environment of lighting, video projection and sound. The goal was an environment so complex as to be 'unscannable' by the performer. The bandoneon extended by these sonically based systems of control became a *situation* in which the roles of notation and realization collapse together, making room for an entirely different kind of music-making and an entirely different kind of musician. This was the first of his own projects to be based, in John Fulleman's words, 'on his ability to assert just enough control over the equipment to get through a concert'.[17] In the six years following Nine Evenings, Tudor's involvement with electronics steadily grew and his distinctive approach evolved. Tudor's own description of that approach is as follows:

> I need to observe something in a way that I don't put any prejudice. I want to see what it tells me. My experience with Alvin [Lucier] is that he approaches things more like a romantic, so that he's an appreciator of these phenomena, and he appreciates their specific beauty. Then, when he goes to compose the work, he wants to display those characteristics, which seem beautiful to him. Whereas, in my case, I want to show it as something in nature. You know, I don't want to display it, I want it to display itself, you see.[18]

Given the distilled simplicity and acoustic specificity of Alvin Lucier's music and the technological complexity of Tudor's, the comparison Tudor offers is quite extraordinary. What does it mean to 'show something in nature' in the entirely constructed realm of live electronics? Possibly he is referring to his tendency to work 'against the grain' by directly engaging the physical principles of an electronic device rather than accepting the original intent of its design. Towards that end, Tudor tended to take any technological paradigm or device that interested him and attempt to invert its terms. *Rainforest* (1968–72), the first of his pieces for which he actually identified himself as a composer, typifies this. Loudspeakers are prized for their ability to produce all possible sounds, while the concept of *Rainforest* is that loudspeakers should have their own voice. Tudor's own description of the idea is as follows:

---

17   John Fulleman, Introduction to 'An Interview with David Tudor in Stockholm May 31 1984', *The David Tudor Pages*, http://www.emf.org/tudor/Articles/fullemann.html (accessed 30 April 2009).

18   Larry Austin, 'David Tudor and Larry Austin: A Conversation (April 3, 1989, Denton, Texas)', *The David Tudor Pages*, http://www.emf.org/tudor/Articles/austin.html (accessed 30 April 2009).

*it came about because of a sudden idea which occurred to me one day: that one
didn't have to think of the generation of electronic music from signal source
to the reproducing output, but one, instead, might just as well start from the
other end and go back and arrive at a signal source.*[19]

Rainforest is the best known of Tudor's pieces, in part because the concept is
readily understood. One selects an object and the object constrains and shapes all
subsequent sonic choices. As one prepares material for the piece, discoveries are
made; some sounds 'work' for many objects, others do not. To realize the piece,
you must collaborate with the object you chose. As a composition, all that must be
stipulated are the basic terms of that collaboration, the rest will unfold as 'nature'.
In its initial form, the objects were small and produced small sounds that required
amplification. In that form, the piece was similar to *Cartridge Music* (1960), but
with a level of indirection. Small sounds requiring amplification were activated
by other small sounds rather than by the performer's physical manipulation of
an object. As *Rainforest IV* (1972), the concept becomes the basis for a wonderfully
open introduction to Tudor's approach to electronic music. A presentation of
Rainforest IV, part concert, part science fair, part cocktail party does not exclude
and distil as Lucier's music does. Instead, adopting the model of 'fault tolerance
through redundancy', it trusts that the piece will emerge out of the tuned space of
objects and overlapping social activity. (Tudor does make one explicit exclusion:
no composed music should be used in *Rainforest IV*.)

As Tudor's work continued to develop, the defining concepts became lodged
more and more deeply 'inside electronics', becoming less and less accessible
to others. Tudor built some of his own devices and used many built by others.
Designers of those components, like composers of indeterminate notations, had no
clue as to how he used what they had made. Tudor acknowledges this:

*In my electronics, I work with an instrumental principle ... They become my
friends. They have personalities that only I see, because of my use of them. It's
an act of discovery. I try to find out what's there and not to make it do what
I want but to, you know, release what's there.*[20]

In later years, Tudor spoke wistfully about the passive and early transistor
electronic devices where he could treat outputs as inputs and inputs as outputs
and produce useful results. About commercial synthesizers, he commented, 'I
hated the way those machines were so predictable and it's very difficult to make
them sound, you know, different than they're supposed to ... So I put all my gain
stages into a single oscillator and the poor thing doesn't know what it's doing.'[21]
Clearly, tactics such as these are difficult to discuss outside of the specific context
of the devices themselves, so here are two simple examples. The 'stirrer' was a

---

19   Schonfeld and Tudor, 'From Piano to Electronics', pp. 24–6.
20   Austin, 'Interview'.
21   Fulleman, 'An Interview with David Tudor'.

specially designed potentiometer. These devices, the basis of volume knobs and tone controls, normally have three terminals and can be turned about 240 degrees. The stirrer had five terminals and could be turned all the way around repeatedly. One terminal attached to a wiper that moves closer and further away from the other four terminals. The device could be used to 'pan' a sound to four distinct outputs or, 'backwards', to select one of four inputs. All of the possibilities are identified in an article Lowell Cross wrote about the device in *Source* magazine.[22] Of course the inversion could be conceptual rather than literal. In *Dialects* (1984), for example, Tudor used a device intended to remove the pops created by surface noise on records instead to isolate those transients as a source of rhythmic articulation.

Conclusions

Tudor's own explanation for his departure from the piano is cast in somewhat critical terms:

> *One of the reasons I gave up the piano was because people from all over the world would send me scores knowing I was a pianist and they didn't interest me ... I wasn't interested in playing a game or dealing with a set of finite circumstances but rather in the fact that the world was completely open, and through a set of finite circumstances one could be led into something completely open. This was always uppermost in Cage's works, but a lot of the pieces I was getting seemed to be more attracted by the idea of structures rather than by the possibilities these open up.*

> *Christian Wolff never delineates a universe. He deals with possibilities which one could use if one wanted to. That's what is so beautiful about his pieces, because they don't express a composite view.*[23]

It is significant that Tudor singles out Wolff as well as Cage as an exception. At about the same time that Cage began to work with transparencies, Christian Wolff voiced some dissatisfaction with the fixed nature of the realizations Tudor was in the habit of preparing of indeterminate notations. Wolff developed an alternative approach, based on contingency, which attempted to make such preparations impossible. Simply put, Wolff developed notations that stipulate specific actions to be taken *based on the sounding music*. In *Duo for Pianists II* (1958), the choice of a loud or soft sound by one pianist directly determines the possible actions of the other pianist. In such situations, it becomes increasingly difficult, or even impossible, to preplan the performance. The introduction of this kind of 'real-time' decision-making was a fundamental expansion of the indeterminate mechanisms Cage

---

22   Lowell Cross, 'The Stirrer', *Source, music of the avant garde*, No. 4 (1968): 25–8.
23   Schonfeld and Tudor,'From Piano to Electronics', pp. 24–6.

and Tudor were evolving together. Certainly contingency is part of how Wolff composes without, in Tudor's words, expressing 'a composite view'.

The conception of live electronic music as a liminal situation caught between composition and performance characteristic of Tudor's work is a logical extension, perhaps even a logical conclusion, of his role as a performer of indeterminate scores. Electronic configurations, unlike transparencies, produce their own temporal behaviour. This creates a musical situation where advanced planning is only partially useful, perfect compliance is impossible, and the concepts of contingency and action are essential. In such situations, Tudor could act as a collaborator, diplomat and wayward influence on the actions and interactions arising from the confines of his electronic and electroacoustic systems.

Today, the tactics of live electronic music are part of a common lexicon found in contemporary electronic genres involving circuit bending, the kraakdoos, laptop computers and so forth. But there are immediately audible differences when these configurations are approached as extended instruments rather than embodied notations. In the former, the possibility of an unimpeded expression of will and associated images of power (the power of the performer over the sound and the audience) tend to emerge. In the latter, the configuration leads to a breakdown of continuity similar to that Tudor ascribed to the *Music of Changes* and the Second Piano Sonata. The problem of performance becomes the same: an ability to move forward through a complete and continual breakdown of continuity. In this context, Cage's approach to time structure as an empty vessel to be filled with sound that the performer can observe rather than 'feel' is a central point of reference. For example, when the Merce Cunningham Dance Company performs 'events', the musicians are free to perform any material they choose. After a performance that Tudor found unacceptable, he instructed the performers to determine time brackets using the *Cartridge Music* notations and use them in the next performance.

The development of digital systems capable of modelling live electronic configurations alters the nature of live electronics in fundamental ways. The programs that define a digital system are texts that are independent of their physical substrate. In that sense, they are *pure notation*. What was once wayward, unrepeatable and unreliable becomes immediately and readily replicable. For these reasons, Tudor was never attracted to digital computers but was delighted to devote attention to neural networks realized with analog circuits. In a conversation with the author describing a potential digital synthesizer, Serge Tcherepnin revealed a similar view commenting that, whatever the details of his design, it would never provide an ability to store settings. In the digital domain, the live electronic approach often adopts physical and social constraints to maintain an ever-changing relation to the material. For example, in Yasunao Tone's *Solo for Wounded CD* (1985) series, compact discs are physically mutilated and then played through an early compact disc player that skips, stutters and misreads, but does not mute. The performers of the Hub specify their pieces textually but each member produces their own realization on their own system. Michael Schumacher conceived of a virtual gallery of digitized soundworks with only one limitation, the buyer of the collection cannot control which piece plays when. All of these can be understood as attempts to maintain the wayward autonomy of live electronics in a world where bits are readily replicated.

Instrumentalizing: Approaches to Improvising with Sounding Objects in Experimental Music

Andy Keep

Within improvised experimental music the need to define a musical instrument can be superseded by acts of bespoke, and often temporary, uses of any sounding object. The performer's perspective of a musical instrument is also effectively changed from the traditional role of being a predetermined *thing* that realizes a musical language outside or indifferent to its self, to being an *act* that explores an object for its inherent sonic properties. This exploratory process seeks to create artistic statements that are responsive to the emerging sonic properties of an adopted or appropriated sounding object. The combination of artistic approach and performer activities that underpin this practice are considered here as the notion of *instrumentalizing*.

Instrumentalizing seeks to discover the performability, intrinsic sonic palette and possibilities for sonic manipulation of objects. It can be exercised on any object that has the potential to sound or manipulate sound in real time, and it need not be complex. Sticks, combs, tables, cases, shoes and vegetables are a few of the objects that have been successfully explored as sound-making devices for improvised performance. There are also many examples of the 're', or more accurately 'de', contextualizing and adaptation of a wide range of technologies. This includes those designed for music production to equipment that was intended for use in telecommunications, medicine, electrical engineering, entertainment and toys, road safety, surveillance, radio technology and domestic appliances.[1]

The process of instrumentalizing can provide the resulting artistic content of an improvisation, and may also become the performance strategy. There is a symbiotic

---

1   For current examples of artists exploring the artistic and performance possibilities of many of these technologies, see Nicholas Collins (ed.), 'My Favorite Things: The Joy of the Gizmo', *Leonardo Music Journal*, 17 (2007), in particular the collection of artists' statements on pp. 29–50; Brian Marley and Mark Wastell (eds), *Blocks of Consciousness and the Unbroken Continuum* (London, 2005), and David Toop's insightful observations in *Haunted Weather* (London, 2004).

relationship between the exploration and the emerging sonic material being discovered. Recordings of performances by artists that engage with this practice can exhibit many examples of the sonic potential in the objects they are instrumentalizing. However, there has been little discussion about *how* one approaches the activity of exploring a sounding object as a musical performance tool.

The aim of this chapter is to outline a practical method that can offer new performers and interested listeners an insight into this, all too often elusive, artistic practice. It is also an appreciation of how improvising and experimental performers can skilfully approach sounding objects as the core materials for performance. Of course, such a discussion will never be comprehensive. Every performer offers a personal aesthetic with a related personal practical approach in their exploration of sound-making objects and the subsequent rationale for organizing sound. For many the very idea of deconstructing an approach to performance may be an arbitrary exercise, and even counter to the musical aesthetic they are engaged in. This is especially the case if the very nature of the work is to question, confuse or even undermine its own rationale.

Historical Context: The Emancipation of *All Sounds*

The introduction of new sounding acoustic objects has been slowly augmenting Western music's palette of instruments over time. This has included developments in mechanical technologies which led to complex chromatic additions such as the piano and the saxophone. Through the twentieth century a combination of aesthetic, cultural and technological advances instigated the notion that *any* sound could contribute to the musical palette. Composers in the early part of the century, such as Varèse and Russolo, began to shift music-making away from the dominance of equal temperament and the organization of pitch towards 'the organization of sound'. Cage's (now canonic) 1937 lecture 'The Future of Music: Credo'[2] articulates the excitement of introducing the emerging experimental aesthetics being explored within other art forms into a musical arena. 'The sound of a truck at fifty miles an hour. Static between radio stations. Rain. We want to capture and control these sounds, to use them not as sound effects but as musical instruments.'[3] Two years later Cage composed *Imaginary Landscape No. 1* (1939), which Nyman cites as being the first composition to incorporate live electronics.

> It uses two microphones, one to amplify the two 'regular' percussion instruments (a large Chinese cymbal and a piano played in an unorthodox manner by sweeping the bass strings with a gong beater, or by muting the strings with the palm of the hand while playing the keyboard). The other

---

2   John Cage, 'The Future of Music: Credo', in *Silence: Lectures and Writings* (London, 1980), pp. 3–6.
3   Ibid., p. 3.

> *microphone picks up the sounds of the primitive electronic 'instruments' – recordings of constant frequencies which are test recordings used in acoustic research and radio stations. These are played on variable speed turntables.*[4]

As had been the case for 'exotic' sonorities during previous centuries, sounding objects that could not contribute pitched material were often presented or perceived as percussion during this early period. Again, Cage heralded the trend by suggesting that 'Percussion music is a contemporary transition from keyboard-influenced music to the all-sound music of the future. Any sound is acceptable to the composer of percussion music; he explores the academically forbidden "non-musical" field of sound insofar as is manually possible.'[5] However, listener interpretation could shift between the referential, the conceptual or a purely sonic experience, as many newly discovered or 'found' musical instruments had resonances with the *objet trouvé* of the visual arts. For example, Cage's *Water Music* (1952) incorporated the use of kitchen and domestic appliances, and Christian Wolff's instructional composition *Stones*, from his *Prose collection* (1968), was performed predominantly on stones.

In line with the pioneering developments occurring in studio composition, emerging audio technologies, such as the phonograph, magnetic tape, microphones and oscillators, were also being explored for their unfamiliar sounds and 'foreign' performance techniques. 'Composers of the musical avant-garde championed such instruments precisely because of their unique sonic characteristics and their explicit rejection of past musical technique.'[6] The use of new technologies in performance became accepted practice, and Chadabe comments that 'an electronic musical instrument can look like modules in a rack, or like a computer, or like a lot of grey boxes on a table, or like a violin, or for that matter, like virtually anything'.[7]

In contrast to the fixed nature of a studio composition, forever committed to tape, compositional strategies for experimental live performance could explore greater degrees of indeterminacy. Many composers began to offer less 'notation', instead exploring the use of graphic or text-based scoring systems for performers. This loosening of composer instruction came with an expectation on the performer to create, or improvise, much of the detail within a performance. The shift in the hierarchical grip of musical instruments became an important precursor to the development of 'free' improvisation. Bailey points out that free improvisation ultimately emerged as a cohesive movement in the early 1960s, as a result of the philosophy and extensions in indeterminate compositional approaches in European 'straight' music, combined with greater freedoms in jazz music.[8]

---

4   Michael Nyman, *Experimental Music: Cage and Beyond* (London, 1999), p. 45.

5   Cage, 'Future of Music', p. 5.

6   Paul Théberge, *Any Sound You Can Imagine: Making Music/Consuming Technology* (London, 1997), p. 44.

7   Joel Chadabe, *Electric Sound: The Past and Promise of Electronic Music* (Englewood Cliffs, NJ, 1997), p. 215.

8   Derek Bailey, *Improvisation: Its Nature and Practice in Music* (New York and London, 1992), p. 84.

In combination both of the above developments in experimental music liberated traditional notions of musical sounds and the musical instrument. They also created a performance practice outside of the composer-performer paradigm that has its primary focus on the exploration of new sonic territories. As *any* sound had come to meaningfully contribute to musical experience, then any sounding object could be considered a potential music-making instrument. Perhaps the need for a line between what is and what is not a musical instrument was firmly broken at the same time as the traditional polarities of noise and music became an artistic continuum. Théberge suggests that 'an instrument is never really completed at the stage of design and manufacture at all; it is only made "complete" through its use'.[9] In experimental improvisation this notion needs to be extended, accommodating temporary or fluid acts of instrumentalizing. The creation of a music-making tool need not have any intentional design process, or ever reach any sense of an instrument's 'completion'. How a performer approaches the practical techniques of 'playing' such a loose definition of a musical instrument is addressed in the following sections, beginning with the artistic notion of creative abuse.

Creative Abuse

Creative abuse is a fundamental element of instrumentalizing, as it offers an artistic approach that seeks to exploit a sounding object by any means necessary in order to access its potential sonic palette. Atkinson and Landy define it as an approach that explores 'instruments, objects and/or digital protocols for use in manners that differ greatly from those known generally'.[10] The term has come to be an umbrella term for varying degrees of remove from the intended function of any sounding object or technology, offering a performer access to new sounds and extended parameter manipulation in acoustic, electronic or digital domains.

For existing musical instruments creative abuse encompasses 'prepared' and 'extended' techniques.[11] Bailey points out that in free improvisation 'the unorthodox technique is commonplace'. 'An extension of technique might have certain musical implications which might in turn produce further technical implications, which might reveal further musical implication.'[12] As extended techniques become more exaggerated there is a point at which the original intention of the instrument design is forgotten, or is so fractured that it becomes a new sounding object in

---

9 Théberge, *Any Sound*, p. 50.

10 Simon Atkinson and Leigh Landy, *EARS: ElectroAcoustic Resources Site,* http://www.mti. dmu.ac.uk/EARS/ (accessed 11 July 2008).

11 For example, see Bertram Turetzky, *The Contemporary Contrabass: The New Instrumentation* (California, 1974) or Claus-Steffen Mahnkopf and Peter Veale, *The Techniques of Oboe Playing: A Compendium with Additional Remarks on the Whole Oboe Family* (Kassel, 1998) as clearly documented accounts of possible extensions and preparations.

12 Bailey, *Improvisation*, pp. 99–100.

its own right. This more open approach moves far beyond the possible stigma of classifying sonic explorations with the codified notion of extended technique.[13] It can even include the sonic possibilities of the instrument's case, any associated maintenance tools that may be at hand or anything that may be on the concert platform during performance.

Michael Nyman states that 'experimental music exploits a [musical] instrument not simply as a means of making sounds in the accepted fashion, but as a total configuration – the difference between "playing the piano" and the "piano as sound source"'.[14] Eddie Prévost encourages participants during his free improvisation workshops to discover 'the sounding properties of the objects you have', restating Nyman's notion that 'the musical instrument is just "material"', so 'no part of the instrument should be left unexplored'.[15] A clear example of this in context is performer Graham Halliwell's approach to 'the saxophone as a variable acoustic chamber with its own unique properties, enabling subtle changes in pitch, timbre, and harmonics'.[16]

Another form of creative abuse can be seen in John Richards's notion of 'bastardization', which describes a conceptual approach to the use of technology. He describes it as 'forcing a system into a state in which it was never intended, or appropriating something for a use other than what it was initially designed for. For example, in analogue terms, this may involve circuit bending or hacking a sound generating device, or forcing a circuit to oscillate through a feedback loop.'[17] Often, the use of extreme parameter combinations, and even manipulations of the expected supply voltages to battery-operated equipment, can push electronic or digital/virtual systems into the fruitful 'edge boundaries'[18] of unstable sonic activity. This is exemplified by David Tudor's recognition that

---

13 John Butcher's comments on the 'crude' terms used by journalists to describe his technical explorations: 'Much of that terminology is derogatory for sounds that 30 years ago people might have found unusual.' 'Slap-tongue automatically associates a sound with vaudeville and is dismissive of the fact that, the more you explore a technique, the more degrees of subtle differentiation you find inside it. My distrust of sounds labelled as "extended technique" comes from the world of composerdom, where there is a school of conventional instrument playing and other things added on top' (John Butcher, quoted in Philip Clark, 'Between Thought and Expression', *The Wire*, 289 (2008): 28–32, at 32.

14 Nyman, *Experimental Music*, p. 20.

15 Guidance and instruction given by Eddie Prévost at an improvisation workshop, held at the Cube Microplex Bristol 14 June 2008, attended by the author.

16 Graham Halliwell, 'What Are You Doing With Your Music?', in Marley and Wastell, *Blocks of Consciousness*, pp. 52–3.

17 John Richards, '32Kg: Performance Systems for a Post-digital Age', *NIME 2006 Proceedings* (Paris, 2006), pp. 283–7.

18 Ben Nevile, 'An interview with Kim Cascone', *Cycling '74*, http://www.cycling74.com/community/cascone.html (accessed 12 December 2007).

an electronic component can seem to have a personality ... If you really examine a device that you might buy, like a filter or a small mixer, and you actually try to experience its capabilities, you have to push it, to ask it to do something that it's incapable of doing. When you make those experiments you find out that unique things are happening.[19]

Marley and Wastell conclude that 'one of the characteristics of free improvisation is its hunger for new sounds, new ways of making sounds, and new ways to (dis)order them. Often these sounds are realized through the misapplication of a piece of music technology (such as Sachiko M's empty sampler) or the personalized modification of an existing instrument (such as Andrea Neumann's inside piano).'[20] Creative abuse is therefore at the core of instrumentalizing, providing the artistic licence to approach objects in whatever way is necessary to evoke sound.

Assessing an Object for Sound and Playability

Assessing the artistic and performative potential of a sounding object involves an exploration of its sonic capability combined with the physical possibilities to excite, influence and shape that sonic capability. Pressing cites auditory, tactile and visual as three key areas of performer feedback used when learning a musical instrument.[21] The same is true within instrumentalizing, as aural feedback focuses on emerging sounds, whilst tactile and visual feedback contribute towards an appreciation of the object's playability.

Consciously acquiring information aurally is often referred to as 'active listening'.[22] John Young suggests that for the composer aural analysis is 'a process of gaining understanding of the materials that will give rise to the musical "outcome", and for the musicologist, analysis dissects and contextualizes the final musical "fact"'.[23] During the process of instrumentalizing the performer needs a third type of aural analysis that is responsive to real-time activity. Experimental performer Xavier Charles considers this a 'virtuoso listening', where 'listening quickly doesn't

---

19 Teddy Hultberg, '"I smile when the sound is singing through the space": An Interview with David Tudor by Teddy Hultberg in Düsseldorf May 17, 18 1988, available at http://www.emf.org/tudor/Articles/hultberg.html (accessed 24 June 2008).

20 Marley and Wastell, *Blocks of Consciousness*, p. 4.

21 See Jeff Pressing, 'Improvisation: Methods and Models', in John Sloboda, (ed.), *Generative Processes in Music* (Oxford, 1987), pp. 129–78 and 'Cybernetic Issues in Interactive Performance Systems', *Computer Music Journal*, 14/1 (1990): 12–25.

22 See Barry Truax, *Acoustic Communication* (Stamford, Conn., 2001); Pauline Oliveros, *Deep Listening: A Composer's Sound Practice* (Lincoln, Nebr., 2005); Michel Chion, *Audio-Vision: Sound on Screen* (New York, 1994).

23 John Young, 'Sound Morphology and the Articulation of Structure in Electroacoustic Music', *Organized Sound*, 9/1 (2004): 7–14.

mean hurriedly, but rather being able to move to a listening of the elements at play in an improvised moment'.[24]

The language of experimental music is not restricted to, or reliant upon, the arrangement of pitch-based material, often not referring to it at all. Therefore virtuoso listening has a primary focus on what Rodolfo Caesar refers to as the 'interiority' of sounds, addressing the sonic qualities of mass, grain, spectral content and dynamic envelope.[25] This notion of interiority has its roots as a studio compositional tool, with the assumption that sonic material will be both fixed in nature and isolated from its original source, cause and context.[26] Within improvisation sounds are generally emergent or in constant flux, not affording the performer the luxury of contemplation or exact repetition during assessment. Attempts to define a fixed typological categorization of the nuances available from the unstable oscillations of a hacked electronic circuit, or the complex spectral resonances of a scraped cymbal, could prove futile. For this reason a more fluid 'topology' of available sonic behaviours offers a useful way to map an elusive sound palette during performance.

In the context of instrumentalizing, sonic activity cannot be detached from the simple cause-and-effect relationship the sound has with its physical object or technological source. As a performer demands more responsive interactions with the object's sonic behaviour it becomes necessary to track the relationship between excitation method or parameter adjustments and the resulting sound. Audible changes can be correlated to physical manipulations. Actions can be repeated to re-access fruitful results, though, as mentioned above, these are often likely to be reactivated sonic behaviours rather than exact events or gestures. This activity ultimately begins to create a map of the object's available sonic palette. Some of the parameter interactions will be generic, such as gain and equalization, whilst others will be specific to that object. Many technologies being explored will incorporate a high percentage of sonic colouration and behaviours that are artefacts of their own sound-making medium or processing routines. For example, a dictaphone will have an intrinsic colouration due to tape surface noise, tape speed and the sound quality of the in-built speaker.

Lee Patterson clearly describes his process of assessing the sonic potential of objects, linking sonic results with developing playing techniques.

---

24   Xavier Charles, 'What Are You Doing With Your Music?' in Marley and Wastell, *Blocks of Consciousness*, pp. 88–9, at 88.

25   Rodolfo Caesar, *The Composition of Electroacoustic Music*, PhD Thesis (University of East Anglia, 1992), p. 52.

26   Caesar's notion of interiority is an extension of the acousmatic composition tradition, and owes much to the lineage of Denis Smalley's 'Spectromophology' (1986, 1997) and Pierre Schaeffer's original 'Typo-morphology' (1998, originally 1967). Both are comprehensive tools for interpreting and categorizing sounds within *music concrète*, acousmatic and/ or tape-music composition. See Dennis Smalley, 'Spectro-morphology and Structuring Processes', in Simon Emmerson (ed.), *The Language of Electroacoustic Music* (London, 1986), pp. 61–93 and 'Spectromorphology: Explaining Sound Shapes', *Organized Sound*, 2/2 (1997): 107–26; Pierre Schaeffer, *Solfege' de l'objet sonore* (Paris, 1998).

> *Often, when a new kind of object is identified as a source of interesting sound,*
> *or as a potential instrument, then almost obsessive collecting of similar*
> *objects ensues. This is done in order to explore the range of sounds available*
> *from any particular type of object … Sound as a material property of objects*
> *is uncovered by detailed sonic investigations … As part of the same process,*
> *new playing methods are developed.*[27]

An object's playability is defined by its physical interface. The focus of instrumentalizing is on exploring or exposing the sonic properties of objects, rather than instrument design. This can create a challenge, as the performer is forced to work with interface controls that were only designed to access the object's original function. Assessment of these controls is based on both tactile and visual cues. However, when working with electronics, tactile feedback is rarely akin to a more haptic exchange, whereby the object gives a physical sensation that indicates a sonic change to the performer.[28] The fixed-scope dials and buttons inherent on a 'found' electronic instrument may not give any responsive mechanical behaviour. Their manipulation can result in the sound becoming saturated through gain or even degraded into complete collapse, but nothing in the feel of the controls would indicate this. The knowledge that a button is in or out, or a dial has reached the end of its scope, is only useful when considered in conjunction with aural and visual feedback.

Visual information proves valuable when learning a musical instrument where the physical interface is clearly mapped out, and its effects are 'literal', such as the frets on a guitar or a piano's keys.[29] With acoustic objects such as wine glasses or saucepans this visual reference becomes an important resource. Through experience it may also be possible to visually edit control parameters for instrumentalized electronics to revisit known areas of sonic activity. However, controls may be relative, multi-function and in the case of feedback oscillators they are even non-linear, and therefore not literal enough for visual appearance to be a reliable indicator.

It is possible to create a detailed sonic and playability mapping of an object with the use of these assessment methods. However, a performer can also consciously leave assessment findings fluid or unresolved, choosing to reinvestigate or rediscover fruitful interactions during subsequent performances. An outline of general practicalities for performer interactions is discussed below as sound-shaping.

---

27   Lee Patterson, 'What Are You Doing With Your Music?', in Marley and Wastell, *Blocks of Consciousness*, pp. 120–35, at pp. 127–8.

28   See Pressing, 'Improvisation' and 'Cybernetic Issues'; Brent Gillespie, 'Haptics', in Perry Cook (ed.), *Music Cognition and Computerized Sound: An Introduction to Psychoacoustics* (Cambridge, Mass., 1999), pp. 229–45.

29   Pressing, 'Cybernetic Issues', p. 15.

Sound-shaping

Sound-shaping techniques are the practical activity of instrumentalizing, and can be used during initial assessment and in subsequent performances with an object. It is here that the freedom afforded by creative abuse really comes into play, as a performer can explore and exploit *any* fruitful actions on the object or its available parameter controllers. Examples are presented across three levels of performer interaction: *facilitate*, *influence* and *impose*.

Wishart suggests that 'any sound has an *intrinsic* and an *imposed* morphology',[30] where an intrinsic sonic shape is predetermined by the object making sound, as opposed to external gestural shaping imposed by the performer. Young extends this notion for use in the analysis of electroacoustic music. He considers an inner morphology to be the 'inherent shape characteristics of naturally occurring sound objects', and an outer morphology to include 'the morphological artefacts of signal processing routines'.[31] Within live electronics Stan Templaars contributes a third tier to the inner and outer morphology notion, thus creating more of a continuum of possibility than an opposition. He distinguishes between '*internally generated* micro-modulation, which results from the properties of the instrument itself, and *externally generated* micro-modulation, which results from a performer's input'. Additionally one can make global-modulations that 'affect aspects of the entire sound, such as pitch and general loudness'.[32]

When combined, the notions of Wishart, Young and Templaars can accommodate internal sonic complexities, either inherently from the object or the result of performer control, and an outer sonic morphology, imposed by the performer. These resulting three tiers can be simplified into the interaction levels of *facilitate*, *influence* and *impose*. Facilitate and influence both explore intrinsic sonic potential, whilst sound-shaping techniques that occur outside of the intrinsic can impose external spectral or temporal characteristics. The practicalities of each are discussed below.

The first interaction level is that of facilitating an object's intrinsic sonic properties. Methods for facilitating are based upon the acts of configuration and excitation. Configuration is perhaps more of a concern when working with combinations of sounding electronics or objects mediated through microphones, amplification or sound processing. The order in which an audio signal passes through processors or self-oscillating audio equipment has a profound affect on the resulting sound. Configuration can be considered a form of instrument design, and ultimately a compositional decision. It also includes the loading of any predetermined source material onto the likes of turntables, dictaphones or samplers. Burns and Burtner note that in 'working with feedback, much of the composer's control over the musical result is invested in the original design of the recursive system'.[33]

---

30   Trevor Wishart, *On Sonic Art* (Amsterdam, 1996), p. 177.
31   Young, 'Sound Morphology', p. 7.
32   Quoted in Chadabe, *Electric Sound*, p. 242.
33   Christopher Burns and Matthew Burtner, 'Recursive Audio Systems: Acoustic Feedback in Composition', *Leonardo Music Journal*, 13 (2003), Leonardo Electronic Almanac,

To simply facilitate an object into sounding there has to be a neutral excitation. For example, acoustic objects can simply be struck, or dropped, and electrical or electronic objects can be 'turned on' to initiate what they do. A child's musical toy may be triggered to play its start-up melody, or a food blender's whir engaged by pressing the 'on' button. This facilitating level of interaction can be dictated by the simplicity of the object itself, but it could equally be artistic intent.

Influencing is the second level of interaction, which involves shaping the object's intrinsic sound through the use of available parameters or controls. The performer is consciously trying to influence the development of interior sonic attributes. A deeper level of excitation comes into play here, as it can also be a persuasive form of influencing. For instance, manipulating the regularity of the on/off switch, or bowing, scraping and rubbing as a way of both initiating and sustaining acoustic sonic activity.

With electronic equipment, manipulations that offer immediate change through switches and buttons are considered discrete, or continuous where controls such as dials and faders allow gradual change.[34] Choices made during configuration affect the availability of editable parameters, though these choices need not be restricted to a preparatory activity. Reconfiguring signal path routings to access new parameter editing potential can also be explored in real time. Hugh Davies describes any experimental electronics that have recursive feedback at their core as 'oscillators'.[35] The technology used is unlikely to have been originally conceived as an editable signal generator, but there may be many similarities to the sound design principles of synthesis. The sonic results of Tudor's pioneering output-to-input connections with off-the-shelf audio equipment, such as mixing desks and guitar effects pedals, offer examples of such oscillators. The sound of these bespoke oscillators can be influenced and shaped by using the objects' original editable parameters, but they are profoundly affected by the amount of system gain introduced by any internal volume or equalization.

The third interaction level explores Wishart's notion of an 'imposed' morphology, and occurs when the performer is sound-shaping 'outside' of the electronic system or object. This external activity can use spectral and temporal manipulation to change the sound's outer morphology, and includes volume shaping, filtering or equalization, and spatial processing such as reverb and delay. All offer extensive control on the final output signal. Imposed amplitude envelopes enable gestural shaping over a continuous resonance or oscillation. External filtering can help spectral placement when performing with multiple instruments, or create textural activity in static behaviours such as white noise or radio interference. One can also impose an outer morphology upon acoustic objects through the use of amplification

---

http://www.mitpressjournals.org/doi/pdfplus/10.1162/096112104322750827 (accessed 10 January 2004).

34   Pressing, 'Cybernetic Issues', p. 14.

35   Hugh Davies, 'Electronic Instruments, IV, 6, iii: Electronic Oscillators', in *Grove Music Online*, http://www.grovemusic.com/shared/views/article.html?section=music.08694.4.6 (accessed 28 June 2008).

and signal processing. For example, a volume pedal placed between the amplifier and a contact microphone that is attached to a resonating string can create a varying amplitude contour during the string's sustain.

Although discussed here in abstract, the levels of facilitate, influence and impose can be freely navigated in practice, and are often inseparably merged. Their use in no way indicates or prescribes any artistic, sonic or musical outcomes, but as a performer's experiential awareness of techniques within each level accumulates it is likely that a pool of skills will develop for use during future instrumentalizations. It is also important to note that the activities of the previous three sections are often completely intertwined. Object assessment is carried out from an artistic approach of creative abuse, using sound-shaping techniques.

Notions of Skill

The notion of performer skill within experimental music does not have the same aspirational allure that it does in most other forms of music-making. During instrumentalizing the acquisition and display of skill is guided by a combination of aesthetic and artistic choice, and the potential control intimacy afforded by the object being performed upon. Bailey offers insight into the perceptions of an improviser's skill.

> *Opinions about free music are plentiful and differ wildly. They range from the view that free playing is the simplest thing in the world requiring no explanation, to the view that it is most complicated beyond discussion. There are those for whom it is an activity requiring no instrumental skill, no musical ability and no musical knowledge or experience of any kind, and others who believe it can only be reached by employing a highly sophisticated, personal technique of virtuosic dimensions.*[36]

Bailey also adds the pithy comment that 'virtuosity doesn't have to be empty',[37] for it can be wrongly interpreted as an indicator of more traditional performance values. Many performers consciously challenge audience expectations of skill by placing a primary focus on seemingly simple tasks or procedures that facilitate sounds to be 'free' of performer intention, or invite degrees of indeterminacy. Within composition Cage made a call to 'free sound from all psychic intentionality. Sound is sound and man is man. Let sound be itself, rather than a vehicle of human theory and feeling.'[38] In the following interview extract with Hultberg, Tudor describes Cage's principle from his own performance context.

---

36   Bailey, *Improvisation*, p. 85.
37   Ibid., p. 100.
38   Wim Mertens, *American Minimal Music*, trans. J. Hautekiet (London, 1983), p. 106.

TH: Like Cage, you have said that you are interested in leaving sound to itself, that sounds should be themselves, that sounds have to be free. Do you still hold that view?

DT: Yes, I certainly do.

TH: Why do you want to free sounds?

DT: (laughter) It might be presumptuous of me to think that I could free them. The thing is I want them to be free. As we were talking before, when the sound appears to be live in the space, then it's free, it seems to flow by itself and not to be caused by some specific intention, especially of an intellectual nature. If you put yourself in a situation of unpredictability and then find that it's completely possible to accept it, then you become an observer. Then you see that the sound can be free. I know it's hard to be clear about that, because a sound is something that you receive, but when you put sounds together, they are in a context and if that is burdened by an intention to conquer or an intention to impress, then ... well, if I find myself in that situation, I'm rather unhappy. I smile when the sound is singing through the space.[39]

Navigation through the previously discussed interaction levels of facilitate, influence and impose can be viewed from Evan Parker's notion of instability-to-control during performance.[40] If desired, one can acquire a balance of general skills such as manual dexterity and response speed, although performers are not judged by their ability to control an object. However, there are times when artistic intention may require greater levels of skill. There are two more specific skill areas important to instrumentalizing, each representing experiential knowledge acquired through practice. The first is a performer's ability in the actual process of instrumentalizing; the second is a performer's skill on a particular instrumentalized object.

A skilful ability to assess any object's potential through a wide range of excitation and sound-shaping techniques enables confident explorations of new objects within a live performance situation. This includes having an eye for a fruitful object to perform on in the first place. In fact for many, being guided by the spontaneous discoveries of sonic properties in the object becomes the primary content of a performance. Prévost describes this exploratory approach in his own work as *heuristic*, stating that 'the intention is making music, and listening to it, as if for the first time', by 'transcend[ing] all previous experience of music production and music consumption.'[41] He also expands this into a wider improvisation principle by saying that heurism 'is the practice of problem solving during performance.'[42]

---

39   Hultberg, '"I smile when the sound is singing through the space"'.
40   Evan Parker, in conversation with the author May 2007, during a collaborative Sonic Arts Network/PRSF commission with Bath Spa University's Behaviour ensemble.
41   Edwin Prévost, *No Sound is Innocent* (Matching Tye, Essex, 1995), p. 3.
42   Edwin Prévost, *Minute Particulars* (Matching Tye, Essex, 2004), p. 53.

Although Tudor is cited as an example of 'setting sounds free' the breadth of his work also offers an example of this exploratory, or heuristic, technique. He stated that 'I put myself into the most difficult and complex situation and try to get out of it.'[43] Gray suggests that 'Tudor's goal was always to control the situation. [But] if ever he fully achieved this goal, he would change the parameters of the whole setup to force himself once again into a new level of complexity. In many ways he enjoyed the hunt as much as the end result.'[44] Repeatedly placing himself in unfamiliar and unstable territory gave Tudor a high level of exploratory skill in performance. Adams recalls that 'his ability to control multiple stages of amplification without the system "taking off" was simply virtuosic'.[45]

The level of exploration, or heurism, can be increased still further when high degrees of inherent object indeterminacy are combined with live circuitry construction or configuration. Pentos Fray Bentos's 'unstruments' are 'a form of real-time "sonic Lego". The starting point is a "feedback element" – which could be a simple oscillator or something more complex – to which electronic components are spontaneously added.'[46] Similarly, John Bowers's 'ad hoc instruments' are constructed during the course of performance through responsive interaction.[47] Much skill is needed in the exploration process for such precarious situations to be successful.

Having a detailed and informed knowledge of a particular object being performed upon forms the second skill area important to instrumentalizing. A type of control intimacy of the object is acquired, mapped through familiarity gained in assessment and/or accumulative improvisations. This in turn can lead to practised operational skills, more decisive excitation and more subtle sound-shaping of timbral nuances. Prévost suggests that the relationship a performer may have with a particular object is akin to traditional instrumental ability, establishing the development of 'neural pathways in the body (in golfing parlance "muscle memory"). In effect the musician is physically reshaping the body to enable particular actions.'[48]

The distinction between the specific and the more general instrumentalizing skills can at times be unclear. This is in part due to the fact that performers may gravitate towards particular known objects they perform on, slowly evolving the internal details, configurations and combinations, but also introducing new objects and sound-shaping methods. Many performers have a pool of instrumentalized objects on which they have developed an informed knowledge, making it possible for them to engage with differing performance situations. It is also not uncommon

---

43   Hultberg, '"I smile when the sound is singing through the space"'.

44   D'Arcy Philip Gray, 'David Tudor in the Late 1980's: Understanding a Secret Voice', *Leonardo Music Journal*, 14 (2004): 41–7.

45   John D.S. Adams and D'Arcy Philip Gray (eds), *The David Tudor Pages*, http://www.emf. org/tudor (accessed 23 April 2005).

46   Pentos Fray Bentos, 'Feedback at the Limits of Precise Control', *Resonance Magazine*, 9/2 (2002): 30–32.

47   See John Bowers and Nicolas Villar, 'Creating Ad Hoc Instruments with Pin&Play&Perform', *NIME 2006 Proceedings* (Paris, 2006), pp. 234–9.

48   Prévost, *Minute Particulars*, pp. 54–5.

for performers to be associated with their prowess or skill on a particular object or specific type of technology. Again, using the instabilities of electronic feedback as an example, Aufermann recognizes that 'after some time a player will develop some intuitive understanding of the instrument and will be able to predict roughly how and when the sound will change'.[49]

Another key criteria when considering the acquisition of performer skill on a particular object is the object's ability for diversity. Is it a one-hit-wonder, perfect for 'that' moment, or does it contain enough nuance and complexity to enable differing performances in a variety of musical situations?[50] A successful rating within Sergi Jordà's musical instrument diversity mapping is dependent upon the activity needed to play being neither too simple nor too complicated, and having a potential for progression towards virtuosity with a learning curve that is rewarding to the performer. Jordà makes the important point that a successful instrument 'will allow its performers to play music and not only to *play with music*.'[51]

Jordà's diversity levels of 'macro, mid, and micro' reflect possibilities of expressivity and 'the freedom the instrument can offer the performer'.[52] Macro-diversity (*MacD*) 'determines the flexibility of an instrument to be played in different contexts, music styles, and varied roles'. Mid-diversity (*MidD*) 'indicates how different two performances on the same instrument can be'. Micro-diversity (*MicD*) also has an affect on 'how two performances of the same piece can differ', but here it is more related to expressivity. 'Differences and nuances from one performance to another, from one performer to another.' '*MicD* is indeed essential for turning a musician into a potential virtuoso.'[53]

Instrumentalized objects generally have a low *MacD* due to a limited control interface and an 'abstract' sonic palette. However, many allow high *MidD* potential, with a large amount of variation possible from performance to performance on some objects. They can also score well in the area of *MicD*. With enough practice and acquired knowledge high degrees of sonic nuances and individual performer approaches can be achieved. As can be seen from the descriptions of Tudor's performances with feedback electronics, a certain level of randomness or instability in the instrument can actually help the 'development of a finely tuned skill and expressive control'.[54]

The following comment by Bailey encapsulates the elusory nature of skill within an experimental performance.

---

49   Knut Aufermann, 'Feedback and Music: You Provide the Noise, the Order Comes By Itself', *Kybernetes: The International Journal of Systems and Cybernetics*, 34 3/4 (2005): 490–96.

50   For an interesting discussion on the artistic merits of sounding objects that have a very limited playability, see Bowers and Archer's paper on 'infra-instruments': John Bowers and Phil Archer, 'Not Hyper, Not Meta, Not Cyber But Infra-instruments', *NIME 2005 Proceedings* (Vancouver, 2005), pp. 5–10.

51   Sergi Jordà, 'Digital Instruments and Players: Part 1 – Diversity, Freedom and Control', *NIME 2004 Proceedings* (Hamamatsu, 2004), pp. 59–63.

52   Ibid., p. 59.

53   Ibid., pp. 59–60.

54   Ibid., p. 61.

Although some improvisers employ a high level of technical skill in their playing, to speak of 'mastering' the instrument in improvisation is misleading. The instrument is not just a tool but an ally. It is not only a means to an end, it is a source of material, and technique for the improviser is often an exploitation of the natural resources of the instrument.[55]

Referents for Performance

The activity of object assessment and explorations into sound-shaping techniques can lead to instrumentalizing skill through the development of a detailed knowledge base in an object's performance potential. This knowledge base can subsequently develop a web of possible referents for use in performance. Pressing suggests that 'to achieve maximal fluency and coherence, improvisers, when they are not performing free improvisation, use a *referent*, a set of cognitive, perceptual, or emotional structures (constraints) that guide and aid in the production of musical materials'.[56] As an example Pressing cites the chord chart, or cyclical harmonic sequence, used by jazz musicians as an implicit structure to maintain cohesion between ensemble members. Referent material in experimental improvisation can guide a performer in a range of areas, from the subtle attraction towards a previously discovered fruitful sonic area, to arranging coincidences of ensemble events on pre-arranged cues.

It may take a number of improvisations to develop an informed relationship with a sounding object. Some of these can be in more private sessions, away from the pressures of live performance. Roger Dean and Hazel Smith add a valuable perspective on improvisational performance approaches by suggesting delineation between 'pure improvisation' and the preparatory process of 'applied improvisation'. Pure improvisation consists of completely unprogrammed events unfolding in front of an audience. In contrast, applied improvisation does not normally occur in public, and it is a step towards producing a work that will eventually be played to audiences. It is not looking for the 'right' solution, and has a readiness to accept any possible outcomes.[57]

Applied improvisation is also referred to as 'lab' or 'process' improvisation, and for many it allows a great sense of exploratory freedom, unhindered by durational constraints and audience gaze. The activity is often used as a preparation for performance, and a space to bench-test newly found objects to instrumentalize. When working with electrical or electronic objects it often leads to the consolidation

---

55 Bailey, *Improvisation*, p. 99.
56 Jeff Pressing, 'Psychological Constraints on Improvisational Expertise and Communication', in Bruno Nettl and Melinda Russell (eds), *In the Course of Performance: Studies in the World of Musical Improvisation* (Chicago, 1998), pp. 47–67.
57 Hazel Smith and Roger Dean, *Improvisation, Hypermedia and the Arts since 1945* (Amsterdam, 1997), p. 27.

of a particular combination or configuration of equipment. During this process possible referents readily arrive that can be used in subsequent live performances.

Referent strategies may simply involve setting a 'territory' for improvisation, such as:

- Sonic – a descriptive sonic landscape, dynamic, or contour
- Aesthetic – such as the indication to work very quietly, or with much ambient space
- Technological – working with previously discovered practical tasks on an object
- Organizational – time structures or arrangement ideas, with or without an expectation for a particular sonic content.

One particular referent strategy that can be readily perceived by the listener is the use of 'looped' sound material. Originally this was explored through lock-grooves on vinyl and 1/4" tape loops. The advent of electronic looping and delay units such as the Digitech PDS-800 EchoPlus Delay in the early 1980s made the process more immediate. They enabled fragments of improvisation to be captured and used as a texture-bed under further explorations. All three of these technologies are still very much in use today, alongside the software emulations and more sophisticated digital buffering systems. Software capture and looping may profess to be the most malleable, but perhaps the most ubiquitous looping tool, seen in the technical set-up of countless improvisers, is the Boss RC-20 Loop Station foot-pedal.[58]

The combination of a unique instrumentalized object(s) and the repeated use of a successful style of subtle referents across a number of performances can also aid the creative identity of a performer. Improvisations can occupy a particular referent territory for a number of performances, or use a similar approach strategy to different objects, on a continuous thread of exploration through a phase of a performer's work. An awareness of referents proves a very useful tool when seeking to understand the rationale or underlying thread behind a concert, as it is not uncommon to see familiar 'routines' performed by certain improvisers.

Artists can also work with referents that could almost be defined as compositional strategies, focusing a performance with the aid of a mental map of key activities or sonic events to present. This is perhaps a direct lineage to earlier experimental composer-performers who created bespoke compositional strategies to frame procedures with electronic instruments, such as Gordon Mumma, Alvin Lucier and Nicolas Collins. Mumma recognizes the implications of bespoke instrument design as a form of creating or 'coding' a compositional strategy for performance, and considers himself a 'designer-composer-performer'.[59]

---

58   See http://www.bosscorp.co.jp/products/en/RC-20/ (accessed 24 June 2008) for manufacturer details.

59   Barry Schrader, *Introduction to Electro-acoustic Music* (Englewood Cliffs, NJ, 1982), p. 205.

Summary

Instrumentalizing has been presented here as an exploratory performance approach that encompasses a number of key notions and activities central to improvised experimental music. The inclusion of *any* sound into the musical palette by the pioneers of experimental music through the early twentieth century, and the notion of creative abuse, which exploits objects for uses far beyond their intended function, form the artistic context to instrumentalizing. Practical activity often begins with an assessment of the music-making potential in an object, both its sonic capabilities and its physical playability. This is intertwined with a range of sound-shaping techniques that seek to manipulate available parameters of the sound's interior qualities. These are executed through degrees of extended techniques and general creative abuse, and occur across the performer interaction levels of facilitate, influence and impose.

Objects may require a learning curve to develop knowledge about the physical interface, the available sonic palette and the relationship between parameter adjustments and the resulting sound. As a consequence of prolonged engagement with a sounding object, awareness of effective performer activities is acquired. Whether gained during preparatory explorations or in live performance, this knowledge base can lead to the development of performer skill. However, perceived skill is not always an indicator of a performer's improvisatory ability or artistic integrity, as emerging sounds may be intended to be free of performer intention. Experiential knowledge can also lead to the discovery of a web of possible referents that a performer may choose to draw upon to focus improvisations. These referents can also move seamlessly into loose compositional strategies, ranging from a very open single word description or instruction, to more elaborate sonic or orchestration design.

As stated in the introduction, this model of instrumentalizing does not profess to be a comprehensive explanation of approaches used in improvised experimental music. Ultimately, a performer's activity is driven by artistic intent, and in fulfilling that artistic intent the techniques discussed here may be adopted wholeheartedly or in part, where elements of a certain activity may simply be referred to momentarily. However, with an openness to all sound as a musical material and the practice of creative abuse, the combination of a focused object assessment, tiered sound-shaping techniques and the use of loose referents become powerful tools for discovery and performance activity. They can also aid in developing clear artistic themes during phases of an improviser's work. For many performers the role of a musical instrument has changed its perspective from being something that can realize a musical language outside or indifferent to its self, to being an object that can create a music responsive to its inherent sonic properties. Any fixed definition of a musical instrument may be too concrete for sounding objects that remain in the fluid domain of instrumentalizing.

Free Improvisation in Music and Capitalism: Resisting Authority and the Cults of Scientism and Celebrity

Edwin Prévost

There is a strong argument for not aligning the two topics contained in the title of this chapter. Music is one thing and capitalism is another. Except, of course, they intercept. A discussion about capitalism is inevitably political. It is a critique of how human society works. All of us, in some way, are involved with the cash nexus. Free improvisation in music is also a site for human activity in which there is also the potential for exchange.

Listening to music is mediated mostly through the market place. The listener has in some way to purchase the opportunity to hear the music through attending concerts or purchasing recordings.[1] The major exceptions to this appear to be religious music and what is left of unmodified folk musics, although listeners to these musics have to pay with something other than money. The motivation for making and listening to music need have nothing to do with whether it is a commodity or not. However, it is extremely difficult to escape the cash nexus. In a capitalist society everything, even our leisure,[2] is measured by the dominant social and economic criterion – the monetary equivalent.

In most cases we purchase musical instruments (or the materials and tools if we make them ourselves). We are likely to purchase tuition. Even if we organize a free concert then it is likely that the space for the performance will have to be rented or

---

1   Downloading from the internet for free might seem to counter this suggestion. However, there is a difference between something which is freely available and something which can be freely obtained. Downloading for free makes the recipient feel as if they have got something for nothing (that is something that they might otherwise have to pay for). In a capitalist ideology it is this characteristic (that is 'theft') that makes it feel that something of worth has been obtained without payment.

2   It could be argued that the concept of leisure is predicated upon its opposite: waged labour.

some arrangement made so that the owner of the premises can make some return on the transaction (for example by selling beer and food to listening customers). Of course, the capitalist system is the normal socioeconomic environment. Most people will see nothing unusual or wrong with the idea of music being made to be purchased, and whether the music is successful in the market place often becomes the measure of its value. In other words many consumers believe that if music is worth paying money for then it must be good. Conversely, if the music is given away freely then it must, by definition, be worthless.[3] This is ideology at work.

It is within the conditions outlined above that a music like free improvisation has to contend. And its practitioners are not immune from the basic requirements of existence (within capitalism) which enable them to continue living. Certain material conditions have to be met before any music can be made. Given that the social and economic background is so uncongenial for musics that fall into the broad category of free improvisation or experimentalism, it is somewhat surprising that this music exists at all. In some sense, however, we could posit that it exists precisely because of the socioeconomic strictures of a capitalist culture. That is, it is a form of music which (I suggest) counters the ethos which characterizes capitalism; with its emphasis upon market relations, and all the social forms and attendant attitudes, that follow in its wake. In this respect free improvisation follows an artistic and a cultural trajectory that is familiar to the history of jazz.[4] Wherein, despite the close kinship that early jazz had with vaudeville and its continuing links to show business, there have existed radical pockets of resistance to mainstream white-dominated US culture and an assertion of an alternative set of cultural values and mores. Very little of this cultural self-assertion was consciously anti-capitalist. It was mostly the intuitive response of a community under pressure from some of capitalism's uglier henchmen – its racists.[5] Jazz became a secular part of the cultural self-definition for a beleaguered community in which some white dissidents also felt at home.

There are examples of musics being part of a counteraction to the strictures of capitalism but it would be an exaggeration to claim, for example, that jazz was intrinsically political and therefore anti-capitalist or anti-anything in particular. Some jazz musicians were more overtly political than others, such as Max Roach. In a similar way I think that we can claim that free improvisation in music is an alternative cultural form.

However, perhaps this mirrors the growing disaffection of some people in the so-called advanced industrial capitalist societies in Europe (the white populations in

---

3   Here I am suggesting that a dialogical process is as much an exchange – a reciprocal act of giving and receiving – as is the more usual notion of money exchanging hands for goods and services.

4   Free-jazz began the task of apparently deskilling (or reskilling?) jazz from the technocratic leanings of be-bop (which became more and more formalized and subsequently used in formal music training). It also put intuition back on the creative agenda and reasserted collectivism.

5   Black resistance to racism has rarely let itself turn into a counter-example of the affliction it was defying, although some black communities have rightly been wary of white liberal affiliations.

particular), in which there are very few models of positive cultural responses (other than those contained in religion and other superstitious systems) and no adequate models of resistance to the prevailing individualistic culture. However, although many free improvising musicians may be apolitical, there is something in the manner of their working, and their general relations within the form, that suggests an alternative to the kind of context that capitalism thrives upon – namely market relations.

At this point we need to outline what is it in free improvised music that distinguishes it from other ways of making music. Hopefully, this will enable us to categorize its structural moments that make it, both potentially and inherently, a vehicle for cultural renewal. In *No Sound is Innocent*[6] I began to flesh out the twin-analytical propositions of heurism and dialogue which seem to me to be at the heart of collective improvisation. In brief I suggested:

a) that in a so-called normal piece of formal music, for example a Beethoven string quartet or even a pop song, most of the technical problems of preparing for a performance are solved and refined before the intended presentation.

b) that the relationships between the musicians are mediated through the manuscript which normally represents the score.[7]

The contrast of these analytical propositions with those of improvisation are:

a) that improvising musicians are searching for sounds and their context within the moments of performance.

b) that the relations between musicians are directly dialogical: their music is not mediated through any external mechanism such as a score.

What we are talking about here is the process of discovery in music-making. In relation to the AMM improvising experience Cornelius Cardew wrote:

> We are searching for sounds and for the responses that attach to them, rather than thinking them up, preparing them and producing them. The search is conducted in the medium of sound and the musician himself is at the heart of the experiment.[8]

It is this activity which leads to what I have referred to as self-invention. This is how and where enquiring musicians find and develop a unique voice to represent their individuality and their general aspirations. Together with this is the implicit

---

6   Edwin Prévost, *No Sound is Innocent* (Matching Tye, Essex, 1995), pp. 171–2.

7   A score being (among other things) a document in which ownership of the music can be enshrined and legally protected. Subsequently it becomes the means by which value can be extracted from musical performances by way of royalties.

8   Cornelius Cardew, 'Towards an Ethic of Improvisation', in *Treatise Handbook* (London, 1971), reprinted in Edwin Prévost (ed.), *Cornelius Cardew (1936–1981): A Reader* (Matching Tye, Essex, 2006), pp. 125–34, at p. 127.

collectivism of the activity – the dialogical: '*we* are searching for sounds' (emphasis mine). It is people working closely with others in a mutual process of making music: a creative and a continual social-invention.

Of course, it is unlikely (although not impossible) that anyone decides to listen, or play, freely improvised music on the basis of some already formed political judgement of the value of the music in question. And, it has been a continuing regret that many people that I know, who consider themselves to be politically intelligent, still cannot identify with the radicalism that clearly resides within the process of free improvisation. For many left-wing radicals this kind of music remains incomprehensible – mostly, it would seem, because free improvisers create a music without conventional tonality and familiar rhythms and have a conscious disregard for any populist (market?) appeal. Whilst, for many listeners, some ersatz folk-cum-rock music (or even world music[9]) – as long as it has an appropriately radical lyric or some historical political allusion – seems to fit the bill, and it continues to work for them even though they are quite aware of the compromises that most popular musics have to make with capitalism in order to continue to exist. It does not seem to occur to many left-wing ideologues that changes in social relations will have to be reflected in all manner of human activities – including (?) music. Meanwhile, many practitioners of musics which owe their genesis to free improvisation are now finding that certain facets of this creative approach are amenable to exploitation within a burgeoning sector of the leisure market called 'art'. All this should be very discouraging for those who think that freely improvised music can in some way be a vehicle, or a model, for the kind of society – other than a rampant free-for-all capitalism – in which they would prefer to live.

However, before we turn away disillusioned, let us examine what is happening in this, albeit minor, capitalist appropriation of free improvisation. For years I have thought that some of the exceptionally discordant sounds and general dislocation of expectation would have resisted marketing. I am familiar with responses to experimental and the freely improvised musics where listeners do not comprehend these things as music at all! Whereas for myself and numerous others it is this otherness in the sonic world that we find attractive. But what seems to have happened is that in certain contexts, and for a section of the audience, discord and dislocation have become tolerable (or tolerated?) experiences. Maybe this was what Cardew was referring to when he observed (during the 1960s and 1970s) the bejewelled bourgeois clientele at, for example, the Venice Bienalle or those who attended Merce Cunningham Dance Company performances.[10] They listened

---

9   World music is the development of a new genre in which folk forms are combined with mostly Western forms of pop music. Although jazz and even Western classically orientated music have also embraced this fusion.

10   During the 1970s the Cunningham Dance Company had begun to become fashionable especially in France. Occasionally Cardew had been employed as one of the accompanying musicians.

attentively and politely applauded the music of John Cage *et al*.: 'The bourgeoisie have learnt to take their medicine.'[11]

What does the avant-garde have to do to shock now? Well, nothing: as Chris Cutler suggests with convincing illumination, 'the avant garde is dead'.[12] Many audiences have learned to applaud politely at almost any occasion – just as long as they have been persuaded (sometimes through media hype) that their acquiescence serves some fashionable cause, and there is always the after-concert drink and dinner in prospect! I have always supposed that the avant-garde was where new cultural horizons could be explored. That the avant-garde was the site for an implicit rejection of the status quo. Such activity consists of alienation strategies: atonality, chance procedures, using new technologies to make sounds, making new sounds with old instruments. These actions are intended to disturb the perceptive, cultural and sometimes the social equilibrium. However, many of these procedures are reactive. The intention is to negate what is already perceived as a negative situation. There is, as I hope to show, another role for some of these apparently disruptive procedures.

During the early 1970s some hair-shirted Maoists of my acquaintance (some of whom had been avant-gardists) were not alone in perceiving the antics of much of the avant-garde as the tiresome excesses of bourgeois individualism. But by confusing positive and creative features of individuality with individualism they threw the baby out with the bath water. In their desperate (and forlorn) haste to usher in the era of the dictatorship of the prolelariat they sought to denigrate and rob others of a conduit for dialogue and creative understanding. For them, from thence on, only the party leadership could decide on what cultural manifestations mattered. We need not shed too many tears here; for their fundamentalist confidence in Mao was soon to be shattered, although not before much damage was done to creative initiatives, cultural relations and even friendships. The idea of the avant-garde is, of course, dead the moment it becomes classified and, given that so much of what is now accepted as art has become so relativized ('everything can become art' or 'all sound is music'), then it follows that it matters little – except as a leisurely diversion – if we pay any attention to what goes on in the name of art. The Maoists of my acquaintance found it easy to convince themselves that modern art was merely a bourgeois indulgence, because (presumably) that is what they had been indulging themselves with whilst they were avant-gardists. However, there has always been another strand in creative life that was attached to cultivating and enhancing a sense of personal and social being. For example, the avant-garde in black jazz of the 1960s in the USA was self-consciously social. It often prided itself on its technical excellence and its community spirit. The idea of 'anything goes' in a casual pose of 'it is art if I say it is art' attitude would not do. A sense of black pride went with a determination to be as good, and preferably better, than any representative

---

11   In a remembered conversation that John Tilbury had with Cardew.
12   Chris Cutler, 'Thoughts on Music and the Avant Garde', in Chris Culter, Hanns-Werner Heister, Wolfgang Martin Stroh and Peter Wicke (eds), *Musik-Avantgarde. Zur Dialketik von Vorhut und Nachhut* (Oldenburg, 2006), pp. 52–73.

of the oppressing culture. It must be said that jazz no longer maintains such a social and political (or even artistic) profile in the black community of present-day USA. However, I suggest that similar motivations can continue to exist within the practice of free improvisation.

By the 1950s – and as the world emerged from the privations of the Second World War and moved into the ideological climate of the Cold War – a sense of a new world was offered to Western culture by the experiments of the New York school of composers that we associate with John Cage, and the ruminations of the total-serialists of Darmstadt. These activities were concurrent with the emerging musical initiatives – largely inspired by jazz – which led to the development of a new musical aesthetic which we can now broadly refer to as free improvisation. They all, in some way, impacted upon each other. Although free improvisation drew very little following and support (official or otherwise) in comparison to that which Darmstadt or Cage and company acquired. However, free improvisation was contentious enough for Cage, Boulez, Stockhausen and many of the major new music protagonists to comment upon.[13] There were also some significant overlaps: for example the composer and young associate of John Cage, Christian Wolff, improvised with AMM in the late 1960s; Boulez and Berio wrote articles discussing free improvisation; Anthony Braxton admired Karlheinz Stockhausen. One might even say that Boulez and Stockhausen actually flirted or dabbled with improvisation, but the procedures they adopted and the results have little in common with the general aspirations and artistic objectives that continue to sustain an 'improvisational' musical life as we know now. However, although Cage and the Darmstadt school were thought of in some ways as competitive, they had, in my view, significant things in common that separated them fundamentally from their free improvising counterparts.

The quasi-mathematical calculations required in John Cage's *Variations I* (1958), in which transparent overlays are used to create random relationships between dots and lines from which sounds/music are constructed, mirrors (perhaps in a comical way) a much more rigorous attitude instructive of total serialism. Cage, however, was famously against improvisation. This chimes with his general philosophy about the use of chance within his compositions which puts great emphasis upon letting sounds be themselves: somehow allowing sounds to have a life outside of, or beyond, human intention. His inspiration for these methods of creating objective or neutral sounds, and configurations of sounds, was the I Ching (or Book of Changes), the first book of the Confucian classics. Perhaps a more famous user of the I Ching in Western culture is the analytical psychologist C.G. Jung. The I Ching's attraction for Jung seems to me to be precisely opposite to the claims that John Cage made for its procedures. Jung was impressed by how the ritualistic and random falling of the yarrow stalks (or the three coins in the short

---

13   Pierre Boulez, 'Constructing an Improvisation', *Orientations*, ed. Jean-Jacques Nattiez, trans. Martin Cooper, (London, 1986), pp. 155–73. Luciano Berio, *Two Interviews with Rossana Dalmonte and Bálint András Varga*, trans. and ed. David Osmond-Smith (New York, 1985).

form of the divinatory method) allowed questioners to get into their unconscious. Cage was only interested in getting beyond consciousness. Jung, I am sure, would have questioned the possibility of escaping the persona and would have claimed that using the yarrow stalks actually brought the individual closer to the totality of their being by integrating, or tapping into, their unconscious motivations and insights. However, and interestingly, both Cage and Jung were enthralled by the I Ching because the manipulations proceeded mechanically and 'left no room for interference by the will'.[14]

Cage may well have been looking for a system of randomization. In which case, given the perceived modernity of the project, why did he choose a method that had so many historical, exotically foreign cultural and mystical overtones? There are important issues here. For example, is it possible to arrive at a state of complete psychological neutrality, and is such a state desirable? Cornelius Cardew, who had initially been Cage's great advocate in Europe, subsequently noted, for example, that when John Cage and David Tudor themselves performed *Variations I* that:

> *Their performances were full of crashes, bangs, radio music and speech etc. No opportunity for including emotive material was lost. And musically they were right. Without the emotive sounds the long silences that are a feature of the piece in its latter stages would have been deprived of their drama and the piece disintegrated into the driest dust.*[15]

At best John Cage, with his silent piece, 4'33", and chance methods of construction, posed a series of challenging questions about the nature of music. He gave us all a fresh insight into the possible meaning and beauty of sounds that were previously considered to be outside of the territory of music. He encouraged a certain kind of freedom of thought. However, as David Tudor remarked in an interview, 'I had to learn how to cancel my consciousness of any previous moment in order to produce the next one, bringing about the freedom to do anything.'[16] This is a comment from John Cage's right-hand man, so to speak. It is clear from many accounts (including my own) of preparing for Cage pieces using the prescribed chance mechanisms that any so-called 'freedom' is totally dislocated from any human objective – except the (perverse?) satisfaction of carrying out an irrelevant instruction. Perhaps Tudor, in the above quotation, was explaining some of his own strategies for trying to escape 'the anticipated' in performance. But there is something (self-)deceiving in the idea of trying: 'to cancel [one's] consciousness of any previous moment'. This practice is nigh impossible as well as being perhaps of no particular consequence.

Cage's music had assumed the soubriquet of the 'experimental'. This was in contrast to the term 'avant-garde' which those who gathered at Darmstadt

---

14   C.G. Jung, *Memories, Dreams, Reflections*, ed. Aniela Jaffe (London, 1963), p. 342.

15   Cornelius Cardew, 'John Cage: Ghost or Monster', in *Stockhausen Serves Imperialism* (London, 1974), reprinted in Prévost, *Cornelius Cardew*, pp. 156–61, at p. 158.

16   Victor Schonfeld and David Tudor, 'From Piano to Electronics', *Music and Musicians*, 20 (1972): 24–6.

(during the immediate post-Second World War period) assumed. The Darmstadt enterprise seems to have had much more intellectual intensity. There was a serious sense of rigour applied to the new music arising from a development in serialism following on from Schoenberg and Webern. Pierre Boulez, together with Karlheinz Stockhausen, was considered a prominent figure in this total serialist movement. Boulez seems to have been searching for and developing what he called an 'active analytical method' which for him was indispensable:

> it must begin with the most minute and exact observation possible of the musical facts confronting us; it is then a question of finding a plan, a law of internal organization which takes account of these facts with the maximum coherence; finally comes the interpretation of the compositional laws deduced from this special application.[17]

There is none of the playful and often poetic mischief one can detect in John Cage's music. Nor is there any apparent freedom for the musician. And although performing in this arena of music is totally outside of my own experience, John Tilbury, in one of his more robust descriptions of the demands that total serialist music made upon musicians, described it as being 'a very complicated way of laying the dinner table, except that there was never a meal at the end of it'.[18] This highly technocratic formula for making music clearly places the musicians in a subordinate and functionary role as far as the creative outcome of the music is concerned.

The heyday of serialism and indeterminacy may be considered by many to have passed, and that newer musics have moved away from any affiliation or attachment to either school. Certainly the subsequent formulations appear to be more eclectic and disparate: Minimalism, New Complexity and the various micro-tonal forms have vied with numerous other postmodern expressions, and even some forms of free improvisation can be said to have engaged with Cagean aesthetics and embraced micro-tonality. However, we live in a time that is more at ease with the apolitical and ahistorical discourse. The capitalists have been gloating that the ideological battle has been won, although there is currently some back-tracking going on about the notion of the end of history. Music seems to be lingering in a twilight world in which it exists for its own (and the market's?) sake. Yet I would contend that positions proposed by the serialists and the indeterminists (who emerged in a time where polemics were an anticipated part of any cultural proposal) regarding the relations of musicians to sound, musicians to fellow musicians and musicians to the wider cultural landscape remain essentially intact and in position. I would argue therefore that a review of what was proposed and subsequently developed from serialism and indeterminacy is still worth pursuing for it will shed light on the lingering tendencies which persist in their wake. What was on offer appeared to

---

17   Pierre Boulez, *Boulez on Music Today*, trans. Susan Bradshaw and Richard Rodney Bennett (London, 1971), p. 18.
18   In conversation with the author.

be the (alleged) objectivity of total serialism and the neutrality of random products of indeterminism. On the one hand there was the unalterable order of the tone row (and its extension into other parameters of music). This was perceived as a metaphor for some kind of scientific democracy (for a new world order?). On the other hand we were offered the (alleged) anonymity of sounds selected by chance procedures as a metaphor for some kind of liberal freedom. Cage's obsession with removing the will from the music-making equation, by virtue of mechanisms for random choices for sound selection, and the strict mathematical discipline of total serialism led to very similar ends. The interpreting musician could make very little difference to the artistic outcome. Cornelius Cardew, who had been an assistant to Karlheinz Stockhausen in the early 1960s, had become increasingly uneasy with the rigidities of the new music. Cage and company initially seemed to offer something of a liberating respite. However, through the deception of randomization, the real message behind the new procedures of making music was not freedom but its opposite: authority. Cardew's initial response to this – as seen in his own indeterminate works (arising out of, but going beyond, these influences) – was to begin to display 'people processes'.[19] This culminated in Cardew ceasing to compose for a while and becoming a member of the improvising ensemble AMM, where it was no longer enough simply to make sounds. The sounds had to be understood, nurtured, enjoyed and even personalized – and placed within a human (that is, a socialized) context.

Modernism in general has been equated with a new form of scientific culture. Stockhausen recounts the move (traceable to Varèse) of music towards scientific enquiry and more specifically towards collaborations with companies at the forefront of new technologies, such as Bell Telephone Laboratories.[20] Boulez took this a step further with the founding of a research institute in Paris (IRCAM) in which composers joined with engineers and scientists for what was described as 'a disciplined joint programme for the advancement of musical and acoustical science'.[21]

Meanwhile, John Cage and associates offered a scenario in which anything and everything could be music.[22] Between them (and much of that which has since followed) they offer us anaemic musics squeezed dry of the life-giving blood cells of meaningful participation. And so often, what replaces the possibility of social involvement is the projection of celebrity. For, whoever makes the most outrageous claims for their music, and appeals to the exclusive market in 'high' modern art (mostly through publicity mechanisms that favour notoriety and scandal), becomes the most celebrated. Not, of course, that the less intellectually revered musics

---

19   Michael Nyman, *Experimental Music: Cage and Beyond,* 2nd edn (London, 1999), p. 6.
20   Robin Maconie (ed.), Stockhausen on Music: Lectures & Interviews (London, 2000).
21   Ibid., p. 176.
22   Here I am referring to many of the extreme performance pieces, such as La Monte Young's *Piano Piece for David Tudor #1* (in which the performers are instructed to feed the piano hay) which works the first time around (to surprise or disorientate an audience?) but, in my opinion, barely deserves to be repeated except as a bit of harmless fun.

were ever immune to such self-regarding and inflated views. Jelly Roll Morton had apparently claimed that he was the inventor of jazz, whilst more recently others have had artistic originality thrust upon them like some kind of virgin birth: Ornette Coleman has been acclaimed as the creator of free jazz and Derek Bailey as the inventor of free improvisation. All of which is palpable nonsense (and has nothing much to do with the musicians concerned) but it makes good media copy and propagates the myth of celebrity.

Many of the musics referred to above are marginal and completely outside of the experience of the majority of the population. Yet they are the sites of cultural debate and in some cases the recipients of huge state funding. For where capitalism has not found the arts to be a source of both financial profit and doctrinal comfort, it is quite prepared to influence the use of public resources for ideological purposes.[23] Certainly Stockhausen serves capitalist culture – even if we cannot go so far as to follow Cardew's provocative assertion that Stockhausen serves imperialism.[24] Why else would Stockhausen have been lauded so much? Perhaps it would be more accurate to say that capitalism serves Stockhausen, but this still begs the question. Why the cult of genius and celebrity when he was but one of many making innovatory moves in music?

The scientism[25] perhaps reached a new level with Stockhausen's *Helicopter String Quartet* (1992/3).[26] For the first performance in Amsterdam, the four musicians of the Arditti String Quartet were positioned individually in helicopters that flew around in the air space near to the venue. Their playing parts were radioed down to the concert hall, where the composer sat at a mixing desk controlling the sounds (moderating the mixture of sounds from musicians and helicopters) that were eventually heard by the audience. I leave it to the reader to ponder upon the potential cultural value of such a piece. However, from a practical (and financial?) point of view I wonder why there is any need for helicopters and string quartets if the sounds that these elements produce are going to be controlled and electronically modified. On the other hand it was a huge publicity coup.

There has to be a reason why examples such as the above (and perhaps not so extreme) are not just tolerated but encouraged, all at great financial cost and with no observable benefits for the advancement of mankind except as some kind of great pantomime – and perhaps something akin to firework displays on

---

23 In Britain currently we see the diverting of 'the people's money' for the benefit and leisure of the rich through the use of Lottery Funding to the arts. The system is different in structure in the USA. Large private endowments (often representing hundreds of thousands of dollars per recipient) are available to musicians many of whom would be regarded as avant-gardists and be considered outside of the mainstream of arts, such as Anthony Braxton, Steve Lacy, George Lewis and John Zorn, to name but a few.

24 Cornelius Cardew, *Stockhausen Serves Imperialism* (London, 1974), reprinted in Prévost, *Cornelius Cardew*, pp. 149–227.

25 I use the term 'scientism' to describe an area of discourse which uses the language and nuances (and to some extent the authority) of science without necessarily being scientific.

26 A 20-minute piece that was part of Stockhausen's opera cycle *Mittwoch aus Licht*.

New Year's Eve. These works are propagated (and given exposure) as the better and more representative examples of positive modernism or as worthwhile experiments.[27] The truth is that some of Stockhausen's works owe their genesis to other works by other composers (and is it not always thus?). *Mikrophonie I* (1964) for tam-tam and six players surely owes a debt to La Monte Young.[28] Reading Stockhausen talking about the development of this 'composition' it becomes very clear that his own explorations with the tam-tam proved to be difficult to notate or even to repeat with any hope of accuracy.[29] The question one has to ask is, why not let the musicians themselves make theses sonic enquiries? Why does Stockhausen (via his supporters) maintain the idea that unpredictable sounds emerging this way (that is, via the performers) constitute his 'composition'? As a long-standing tam-tam player myself, I know and rejoice in the uncertainties of the instrument.[30] I am always amazed that different people using the same kind of instrument seem to manage to produce such a diversity of sounds. All this, to me, seems to be a signifier and a celebration of humanity and not at all scientific, even though a playful sense of enquiry is at the heart of the exercise. The interface between materials and the person has a special individual imprint. Such a free and spontaneous approach (which is the general modus vivendi of an improviser) is an unmediated and an unfettered response to the world. It is not (thankfully) subject to some scientific calculation. It is not repeatable, and there is no good reason why it should be repeated, except to capture and exclusively enslave the sounds – and maybe exploit them financially.

So, why is this notion of the composer/controller-genius maintained? Much better, to my mind, for musicians to be directly involved in discovering sounds for themselves rather than being directed to try this or that procedure. There are other works of Stockhausen that are perhaps collaborations for which compositional contributions have never adequately been acknowledged,[31] whilst his Intuitive Music mystical formulations hijack a whole range of practices, sentiments and aspirations that were commonplace (if valuable) to schools of improvising musicians elsewhere in Europe and North America prior to the time of his own outpourings. At best, Stockhausen was participating in a worldwide enquiry, yet so much of this material is perpetrated as the work of a single genius. Capitalism cannot, of course, allow any credibility to the potent mix of self-assertion and collectivity that free improvisation thrives upon and consequently encourages. Where would it all lead?

---

27 Many of the participants of this movement initially felt that they were working together on a common humanist programme. But as Hans Werner Henze reflected: 'Slowly but surely we became, or were made into, competitors in the same market.' Hans Werner Henze, *Music and Politics: Collected Writings 1953–81* (Ithaca, NY, 1982).

28 La Monte Young, *Studies in The Bowed Disc* (1963).

29 Maconie, *Stockhausen on Music*, pp. 76–87.

30 My 2006 solo CD featured a tam-tam. Edwin Prévost, *Entelchy*, Matchless Recordings, MRCD67 (2006).

31 See Cardew's account of his work for/with Stockhausen on *Carré* in Cornelius Cardew, 'Report on Stockhausen's "Carré"', *The Musical Times*, 102/1424 (October 1961): 619–22. Reprinted in Prévost, *Cornelius Cardew*, pp. 23–37.

Of course the current myth of celebrity has to some extent superseded the somewhat over-inflated myth of genius itself. This is because most celebrities cannot, by any stretch of imagination, be afforded the soubriquet of genius. And most do not want it. Celebrity is now held to be far more important than any recognition of work done.[32] Given the currency of ambiguity and ambivalence in so many features of US culture and society, particularly since the 1960s and 1970s, one wonders at the precise significance of Andy Warhol's memorable (if alleged) response when asked about what had been his greatest achievement: 'keeping a straight face'. Music is promiscuous. I have already sounded a number of warning notes about how easy it is for a cultural objective to be undermined or subverted. A musician may be working towards the production of a collaborative piece of work only to find that the collaborators are using the material for their own (and other) ends. Even reviewers, consciously or otherwise, often represent things according to the prevailing capitalist ideology. I recall the release of AMM's first album.[33] There was nothing to suggest, in the music or the accompanying sleeve notes, that the music or the ensemble was anything but a collective. There were two prominent reviews: one called AMM 'The Cornelius Cardew Ensemble' (*Musical Times*) and the other referred to AMM as 'The Cornelius Cardew Quintet' (*Jazz Journal*). Apart from nicely revealing the specific cultural baggage of the journals in question, they raised the spectre of capitalism's anti-communitarian programme. Cultural perception as a maker of historical fact!

My general critique has often been portrayed as anti-technological. This is because most of the negative examples I have noted – for what I see as abuses occurring in music (such as the oppressive use of electronically induced volume and the indiscriminate, often careless and uninspired usurpation of material by means of sampling) – happen to occur through the medium of electronic machines and computers. I have been cast in a Luddite mould. But, as I think is clear from a more careful reading of my earlier texts, it is not the machines I blame but some of the machine-minders.[34] We do well to remember Marcuse's caution about man's subjection to his production apparatus.[35] Science and technology – even in music – have been viewed as progressive features in our culture. Little or no account is taken of the ideological dynamic in human activity which can attach itself to the machine and to science or scientism. Robin Maconie, in his 'Afterword', writes that 'Technology can create images which are themselves exciting, and it can also

---

32   Arguably capitalism's effect on jazz was to develop the careers of but a few tenor saxophonists. Each label had one or two stars. Yet when I first went to the USA in the late 1960s it seemed as though there were brilliant saxophonists around every corner. The market apparently could not tolerate the existence of more than a few stars.

33   AMM, *AMMMUSIC*, Elektra EUK 256 (1966). Later re-released as AMM, *AMMMUSIC*, ReR AMMCD (1989).

34   Edwin Prévost, *Minute Particulars* (Matching Tye, Essex, 2004).

35   Herbert Marcuse, *One-Dimensional Man* (London, 1991).

suggest new ways of generating images which, because they are self-sufficient and unanswerable to traditional ideas of taste, lead to exciting and revealing results.'[36]

If Maconie's words reflect the general ideology of his subject and his followers (as it seems reasonable to suppose) then we have to ask whose (and which) definition of 'exciting' is being applied here? There is something very deterministic going on which ironically has much in common with Cage's own liberal anarchistic brand of excitement. Whether through the 'self-sufficient' and (worryingly) 'unanswerable' use of technology or through the use of chance methods to find and fix futures, the audience and the rest of the world are held hostage. 'The genius of capitalism is not simply that it gives consumers what they want, but that it makes them want what it has to give.'[37]

Much the same can be said of what passes as art music from Cage to Boulez and beyond. If we – as musicians and listeners – have any choice when confronting the morality of capitalism, then it must be to do rather than to be done to. We must decide who we are rather than be given an identity. In our freely improvised music there is the opportunity to apply a continual stream of examination. We search for sounds. We look for the meanings that become attached to sounds. And we have to decide – on the basis of observable responses – on the musical, cultural and social values that reside in whatever configurations emerge. The search is surely for self-invention and social-invention. This is an opportunity to make our world. If we do not act to make our world then somebody else will invent a world for us.

---

36   Maconie, *Stockhausen on Music*, pp. 176–7.
37   Timothy Garton-Ash, 'Global capitalism now has no serious rivals. But it could destroy itself', *The Guardian*, 22.02.2007.

Beyond the Soundscape: Art and Nature in Contemporary Phonography

Will Montgomery

The 'blurring of the edges between music and environmental sounds is the most striking feature of twentieth century music', observes R Murray Schafer in a 1973 pamphlet.[1] This chapter, which will explore some of the contemporary ramifications of this remark, is occasioned by the proliferation of field recording activity in recent years – field recording is now commonly encountered both as a distinct artistic practice and as a component of experimental music and sound art.[2] I will consider the aesthetic status of field recording itself and the extent to which recordings of environmental sound show signs of the structuring or artefactual characteristics of an artwork, whether musical or not. My concern is not the tendency of contemporary music, under the distinct pressures exerted by Russolo, Schaefer, Cage or Schafer himself, to incorporate non-musical sound into its own processes. Rather I will focus on phonography itself, discussing works that are certainly artworks and that share much ground with some forms of experimental music.

This chapter will address the aural manifestations of a very old problem: the distinction between the world and its artistic representation. Schafer writes of the need to turn from the Romantic-expressivist paradigm that continues to guide the mainstream of Western art music, towards a view that treats 'the world as a

---

1   R. Murray Schafer, 'The Music of the Environment', in Christoph Cox and Daniel Warner (eds), *Audio Culture: Readings in Modern Music* (London, 2004), pp. 29–39, at p. 34. In a later version of this statement Schafer is more cautious, substituting 'may eventually prove to be' for 'is'. See his *The Soundscape: Our Sonic Environment and the Tuning of the World* [first published as *The Tuning of the World*] (Rochester, 1994 [1977]), p. 111.

2   I will generally use the term 'phonography' to distinguish the work I discuss. In this I am following Douglas Kahn's description of an activity that 'replicates the entire world of sound, including those sounds arising from other art forms and other media'. See 'Audio Art in the Deaf Century', in Dan Lander and Micah Lexier (eds), *Sound by Artists* (Toronto, 1990), pp. 301–24, at p. 324.

macrocosmic musical composition'.[3] The founder of acoustic ecology and the inventor of the term 'soundscape' had an explicit hierarchy of sound in mind, counterposing the 'hi-fi' of the pre-industrial rural soundscape to the 'lo-fi' of the city street corner, where signal (good) and noise (bad) are indistinguishable.[4] Citing Goethe on feeling 'the presence of the Almighty' as the poet presses his ear to the grass to hear the 'humming of the little world among the stalks', Schafer asserts that human hearing was infinitely more sophisticated in the pre-industrial past: '[f]rom the nearest details to the most distant horizon, the ears operated with seismographic delicacy. When men lived mostly in isolation or in small communities, sounds were uncrowded, surrounded by pools of stillness, and the shepherd, the woodsman and the farmer knew how to read them as changes of the environment.'[5]

While all of the artists I will be discussing have been influenced by soundscape theory, all take issue to at least some extent with Schafer's position on natural sound. I will suggest that the most adventurous contemporary phonography never seeks to present a quasi-photographic recovery of numinous natural sound in a fallen world.[6] On the contrary, such work often involves or implies a far more complicated treatment of the relationship between art and the natural world.

The complexity of this relationship can be felt in the difficulties many have in demarcating different forms of phonographic, artistic and musical activity. In a brief contribution to the recent book *Autumn Leaves*, Tobias Fischer discusses the German Gruenrekorder label, noting the imprint's parallel series of field recordings and audio art.[7] He suggests that the label has done much to bring down barriers between areas of activity that had hitherto remained distinct. In support of his argument, he cites the musician Jason Kahn's remark: 'More and more I wonder about what the point of organizing sound into music is. Just walking down the street sounds so great. Everywhere you go, it's already there.'[8] It is hard to ignore the Cagean fingerprint here (as in so many contemporary discussions of sound, art and music): 'Walking down the street is now equivalent to reading *Finnegans Wake*',[9] he asserted in a 1967 radio dialogue with Morton Feldman. Such rejections

---

3   Shafer, *Soundscape*, p. 5.
4   Schafer's definition of the term 'soundscape' covers both the 'sonic environment' and 'abstract constructions' such as soundscape compositions. See Schafer, *Soundscape*, pp. 274–5.
5   Ibid., p. 44.
6   On the relatively slow development, compared to art photography, of an 'artistic practice of phonography', see Kahn, 'Audio Art in the Deaf Century', pp. 301–3.
7   Gruenrekorder is one of a number of independent labels releasing field recordings in contexts that suggest an overlap with artistic or musical practices. Others include and/OAR (US), Winds Measure (US), Room::40 (Australia) and Sirr (Portugal).
8   Tobias Fischer, 'Gradual Changes: The Gruenrekorder Label', in Angus Carlyle (ed.), *Autumn Leaves: Sound and the Environment in Artistic Practice* (Paris, 2007), pp. 115–16, at p. 116.
9   John Cage and Morton Feldman, *Radio Happenings I–V*, trans. Gisela Gronemeyer (Köln: MusikTexte, 1993), p. 137. Available in streaming form at www.radiom.org, Part 2, at 9'50" (accessed 16 June 2008).

of the lines drawn between artwork and natural world are commonplace and contemporary phonography has flourished between the two. It is far from unusual now for musicians to work as sound artists, for phonographers to perform their work live and for sound artists to release CD versions of installations on labels normally associated with musical genres. Issues of definition are hotly disputed on mailing lists such as soundasart, with many accepting a version of Schafer's 'blurring of edges' as one of the givens of the contemporary aural arts.[10]

Writing against the grain of this consensual hybridity, Andy Hamilton, in the course of his recent book *Aesthetics & Music*, seeks to distinguish music from sound art and natural sound. Yet, while Hamilton argues strongly for a universal definition of music, he concedes that music is 'on a continuum with non-musical sounds arts, differing from them in the preponderance of tonal material'.[11] Hamilton's concept of a continuum is accepted by this chapter – I make no attempt to erect an impermeable barrier between phonography, sound art and music but I do believe that each term describes a distinct conceptual area.

In his recent book on sound art, Alan Licht discusses the relationship between the Land Art/Earthworks movement of the late 1960s and early 1970s and early sound art, noting the sound component in Earthworks-influenced pieces by Bill Fontana, Walter Marchetti and Bruce Nauman. He particularly stresses the influence on this work of Robert Smithson's Non-site series, in which arrangements of sand, earth and rocks were installed in galleries.[12] Sound art, he argues, derives from a general turn in the 1960s away from the hypostasized artwork of Greenbergian modernism and towards an art that recognized the spectator's experience of the artwork in specific contexts. This controversy was also felt in debates on the role of experience and context in minimalist art in the 1960s, to which I will return towards the end of this chapter. In my view, these discussions about the relationship between world and artwork are developed in striking ways in the acoustic field by the phonographers whose works I discuss.

The thought of the German philosopher Gernot Böhme, which is informed by ecological concerns, is helpful in thinking these issues through with regard to the soundscape. His notion of the 'atmosphere' develops out of a phenomenological description of bodily awareness. 'Atmosphere is a kind of tuning, *Stimmung*, that colours perception', writes Heinz Paetzhold of Böhme's work.[13] 'It exists in space,

---

10   I use the terms 'phonography', 'sound art' and 'music' in the awareness that each is contested. See sound artist Jez Riley French's blog, www.jezrileyfrench-inplace. blogspot.com (accessed 7 July 2008), for interviews with several artists working at the interface of these areas of activity.

11   Andy Hamilton, *Aesthetics and Music* (London, 2007), p. 46. Hamilton's definition of 'tonal' is broad and is not restricted to music that uses a discernible key: '"Tone" … is a relational concept which refers not just to the nature of component sounds but also to how they are structured through rhythm, melody and harmony' (p. 49).

12   See Alan Licht, *Sound Art: Beyond Music, Between Categories* (New York, 2007), pp. 78–85.

13   Heinz Paetzhold, 'Adorno's Notion of Natural Beauty: A Reconsideration', in Tom Huhn and Lambert Zuidervaart (eds), *The Semblance of Subjectivity: Essays in Adorno's Aesthetic Theory* (Cambridge, Mass., 1997), pp. 213–35, at p. 224. Böhme's ideas in

althought its parameters cannot be defined.' Böhme himself, in an article written for *Soundscape: the Journal of Acoustic Ecology*, writes of atmospheres as the meeting point between perceiver and world:

> *Atmospheres stand between subjects and objects: one can describe them as object-like emotions, which are randomly cast into a space. But one must at the same time describe them as subjective, insofar as they are nothing without a discerning Subject. But their great value lies exactly in this in-betweeness.*
>
> *[...]*
>
> *Today we can say that music occurs when the subject of an acoustic event is the acoustic atmosphere as such, that is, when listening as such, not listening to something is the issue. This requires further elaboration. But one can say off the top that music in this case need not be something made by humans.*[14]

Such a notion of 'atmosphere', neither subjective nor objective, pervades much of the work I discuss. Böhme's description of 'listening as such' usefully leads us to a conception of musicality in the natural world that does not impute a quasi-divine aesthetic order to that world. In what follows I will discuss work by six phonographers – Chris Watson, Peter Cusack, Kiyoshi Mizutani, Toshiya Tsunoda, Jacob Kirkegaard and Stephen Vitiello – who use field recordings in ways that transcend the straightforwardly mimetic and which reach a musical or aesthetic form of expression.[15] Several of the phonographers discussed have a background in experimental music.[16] However, each produces work that no longer seeks to push at the boundaries of music. Instead they all show a commitment to the musical qualities of environmental sound if these are understood to include the perception of minimal structure, quasi-tonal or quasi-rhythmic qualities, or textural affinities with the broad sound palette of twentieth-century and contemporary experimental music.

Böhme neatly observes that 'what from the perspective of music was an expansion of musical materials, was, seen from [the] perspective [of acoustic ecology], a discovery of the musicality of the world itself'.[17] The relationship

---

relation to sound are discussed in David Toop, *Haunted Weather: Music Silence and Memory* (London, 2004), pp. 62–3.

14   Gernot Böhme "Acoustic Atmospheres: A Contribution to the Study of Ecological Aesthetics", trans. from the German by Norbert Ruebsaat, *Soundscape* 1/1 (Spring 2000): 14–18, at 15, 17.

15   I have limited this chapter to works released on CD. This necessarily excludes the site-specificity that some would argue is integral to sound art but has the significant benefit of allowing others relatively easy access to the material under discussion.

16   Watson, Cusack, Mizutani and Vitiello. Many of those involved in acoustic ecology either came to field recording through contemporary music or remain active in composition: David Dunn, Douglas Quin, Hildegard Westerkamp, Annea Lockwood and Bernie Krause are cases in point. See Toop, *Haunted Weather*, p. 50.

17   Böhme, 'Acoustic Atmospheres', p. 16.

between 'musicality' and sound, from the viewpoint of the figures I discuss, has an almost circular quality. The 'music' such work acknowledges and references is itself put under pressure to the point of collapse by the post-Cagean imperative to come to an accommodation with non-musical sound.

The notion of representation implicit in the work I discuss appears to be in agreement with Brandon LaBelle's suggestion that the presentation of the aural experience of place in recordings always at the same time involves an acute sense of displacement, a 'backside to soundscape compositions' emphasis on immersion and origin'.[18] Place is never represented in this work without an awareness that listening to one place in another place is intrinsically unsettling, even as it draws the auditor into a powerful identification with the phonographer's original listening experience. This 'sense of displacement' colours the passage from place to sound recording to finished artwork, replacing the holistic, healing ambitions of some soundscape composition with a commitment to a more self-reflexive, formally self-conscious mode of activity.

*

The first phonographer I want to discuss is Chris Watson. The three 18-minute tracks on his *Weather Report*[19] display an interest in narrative structure. There is in this work a clear desire to intervene in the representation of the natural environment and to make explicit the editorial activity of the sound recordist. 'Ol-Olool-O' compresses recordings made over 14 hours of one day into a single piece. 'The Lapaich' edits together recordings made between September and December in a valley in the Scottish Highlands. 'Vatnajökull' is, from one perspective, an even greater feat of compression: 'the 10,000 year climatic journey of ice formed deep within this Icelandic glacier and its lingering flow into the Norwegian Sea'.[20]

Watson has worked often in film, television and radio and his experience in organizing acoustic events into persuasive narratives is evident on each of these recordings. Such editing is not new in the field of soundscape composition. Hildegaard Westerkamp's *Transformations*[21] would be a classic example – Westerkamp's voice playfully intrudes at one point on 'Kits Beach Soundwalk', for example, to describe the eq-ing she is using in the studio; she also filters the traffic noises in 'A Walk Through the City' in order to extract pitched sounds that are combined into chords. However, Watson's recordings on *Weather Report* are at a distinct remove from Westerkamp's desire to move from 'noise to silence, from the external to the internal, from acoustic onslaught to acoustic subtlety, from worldly to sacred experiences' or indeed the lost Eden recovered of Schafer's 'macrocosmic musical composition'.[22] Watson's is a desacralized soundscape, attuned to its

---

18   Brandon LaBelle. *Background Noise: Perspectives on Sound Art* (London, 2006), p. 211.
19   Chris Watson, *Weather Report*, Touch, TO:47 (2003).
20   Sleeve note to *Weather Report*.
21   Hildegaard Westerkamp, *Transformations*, empreintes DIGITALes, IMED 9631 (1996).
22   Westerkamp, cited in LaBelle, *Background Noise*, p. 210.

subtle textures but shorn of the larger aspiration of the reconciliation of human and natural worlds through a regenerative act of listening. Instead Watson seems entirely comfortable with his work's relationship to forms of quite jarring electronic music or electroacoustic composition.[23]

'Vatnajökull' is the most extreme of the album's tracks and also, in its structuring of sonic events, the most reminiscent of a musical piece. The beginning of the track features deep thuds and groans of ice, and the sound of water splashing. The swooping tones of the wind gradually insinuate themselves into the mix. After several minutes, a crash (a huge block of ice falling into water?) ushers in another set of pitched tones that sound like wind instruments. At such carefully timed moments of drama, the quasi-musical qualities of the piece, if these are understood to include a purposeful structuring of acoustic material, are powerfully in evidence. A change of direction occurs when the sharp cries of gulls and other birds are set against the near-white-noise effects of the wind. The piece moves to its end with the anxious clacking of pistol shrimps' claws, closing a condensed creation narrative that began with the juddering pangs of the ice floes and ends with the melt-waters meeting the ocean.[24]

It is significant that detailed information on the sources of particular sounds is withheld from the listener. The acoustic qualities of such sounds are clearly prized above their status as the record of a particular natural phenomenon or a particular species in a particular habitat. If the conventionally mimetic field recording aspires to present a realistic 'slice' of the natural world, Watson's *Weather Report* emphasizes instead the artificiality of its own construction. Watson is not concerned on *Weather Report* with whatever integral harmonies the soundscape might harbour or with the possibility of mimetic reproduction. These soundscape compositions gesture towards 'imaginary landscapes' but at the same time they return to the component sounds' status as sounds in themselves. They can be heard both for their indexical function (pointing towards a vague idea in the listener's head of what such an Icelandic landscape might be like) and for their abstract function, as sounds whose complexity and ordering invoke a quasi-musical conception of composition. Böhme's term 'atmosphere' is again helpful in describing the aesthetic space between subjective and objective that Watson synthesizes in the edit.[25] The delicacy and subtlety of Watson's work leads the listener into an encounter with 'acoustic atmosphere as such', with a narrative organization of naturally occurring environmental sound that achieves its effects through the telescoping of larger time frames.

---

23 Watson releases his work on the Touch label, which is associated with experimental electronic music.

24 The shrimp passage was discussed at a sound recording workshop given by Watson at London's Museum of Garden History in November 2007. Watson, who had made similar recordings in many locations, remarked that he believed this sound, normally inaccessible to humans, was the most common sound on earth.

25 See Toop, *Haunted Weather*, pp. 51–5 for lengthy citations from emails in which Watson describes the centrality of sound in creating 'atmosphere'.

Peter Cusack's *Baikal Ice* (Spring 2003)[26] is, like Watson's 'Vatnajökull', a recording organized around the gradual liquefaction of ice. The recordings were made on and around the world's oldest and deepest lake, in Siberia, during the spring thaw. They contain none of the dramatic editing of Watson's *Weather Report* album. Instead, the listener is offered a series of untreated recordings, most very short.[27] Local dogs bark, a girl sings, the Trans-Siberian railway roars and the phonographer prises himself out of his sleeping bag in the morning. What makes the album remarkable, though, are the underwater recordings of the ice breaking up, made using home-made hydrophones.[28] These move between gentle watery sounds, the tinkling of icicles hitting one another and the crunching and scraping of the break-up of the ice. The listener is constantly made aware of the change of state from solid to liquid, happening across a vast expanse of lake.

The ice recordings exemplify the convergence between contemporary nature recording and the forced opening of Western art music to the sounds of the world. It is hard to hear the intense tinkling effects without recalling Xenakis's groundbreaking *Concret PH* (1958), which used a recording of crackling embers as its source material. As is well known, the piece was performed at the Philips Pavilion through 40 speakers alongside Edgar Varèse's *Poem Eléctronique* (1958) at the Brussels World Fair in 1958.[29] *Concret PH* was constructed out of countless miniature events produced by slicing the embers recording into very small segments, piecing them together into sound textures and then layering combinations of these. As Agostino di Scipio remarks, the extreme brevity of the individual fragments produces an indeterminacy of pitch: 'frequency and its perceptual attribute, pitch, are hardly controllable here, as it is impossible for human ears to integrate differences of pitch and amplitude in such brief moments.'[30] Di Scipio goes on to claim that 'each fleeting creak of sound in *Concret PH* is a point of catastrophe and discontinuity; it represents a tiny explosion which transforms a bit of matter into energy'.[31]

While it is unlikely that the Xenakis piece even crossed Cusack's mind as he assembled his field recordings, he is sure to be familiar with such landmarks of experimental music. Cusack has been active for many years as an improvising

---

26   Peter Cusack, *Baikal Ice (Spring 2003)*, ReR Megacorp, ReRPC2 (2004).
27   My guess is that nothing more than subtle equalization has been applied to the recordings.
28   Cusack explained this in a posting on the Yahoo! Phonography listserve, 8 December 2007.
29   The pavilion was effectively designed by Xenakis, though le Corbusier, his architectural mentor, initially claimed responsibility. See Nouritza Matossian, *Xenakis* (London, 1985), pp. 116–21. This and other multimedia work by Xenakis is discussed as a precursor of sound art installations by LaBelle, *Background Noise*, pp. 183–93. *Concret PH* is referred to in Hildegard Westerkamp's narration for 'Kit's Beach Soundwalk'.
30   Agostino Di Scipio, 'Compositional Models in Xenakis's Electroacoustic Music', *Perspectives of New Music*, 36/2 (Summer 1998): 201–43, at 204, available at http://www.jstor.org/stable/833529 (accessed 1 July 2008). Di Scipio's article includes sonographic analysis of sound events in *Concret PH*.
31   Ibid, p. 213.

musician, specializing in guitar, bouzouki and baglama (a Turkish instrument), and was a founder member in the 1970s of the London Musicians Collective. His sense of 'musicality' is correspondingly broad. In the accompanying note to a CD entitled *Noises Off: Sound Beyond Music* that he curated for *Leonardo Music Journal*, Cusack writes: 'although many of the pieces have starting points and connections "beyond music", the end results show a high degree of musicality. Perhaps that is just the bias of my curatorial choice, but maybe there is an inherent tendency in all of us to search for the aesthetic in our everyday hearing.'[32] Cusack neither speculates on an objectively present musical ordering in natural sound nor claims music for the domain of human activity. The musical is simply available in the experience of the environment, its 'atmosphere'.

Like Xenakis's *Concret PH*, Cusack's underwater ice recordings portray a process of energy conversion, as solid ice warms and breaks up into icicles and then water. The tinkling of the countless icicles resembles the thicker textures of Xenakis's layered embers and the sound of the water itself is sometimes close to the undifferentiated rush of white or pink noise. At the fringes of this recording of a natural process, I would argue, is a tendency to perceive natural sound not as natural sound but as an outgrowth of the explorations of those at the frontiers of musical experimentation in the twentieth century. Although Cusack's work engages closely with acoustic ecology it does not contain the atavistic yearnings for an unsullied natural state discernible in some of the positions adopted by Schafer and Westerkamp. On the contrary, Cusack's ability to discern a musicality in environmental sound makes him representative of a cultural moment in which the very concept of musicality is under immense pressure. The 'in-betweeness' that Böhme remarks upon in the concept of the 'atmosphere' is again apposite: neither 'music', nor 'sound art' is sufficient to pin down the operations of this phonographic activity.

The 'musicality' of *Baikal Ice* is dependent on perceptual events that operate according to no discernible pattern. The coherence lies in para-rhythms and the relatively unified sound field involved – the ice recordings, although dense with detail, use a quite narrow 'palette' of sounds. Sound travels more quickly through water than through air, and underwater recordings such as those of Cusack (and parts of Watson's *Weather Report*) consequently often have a disorienting spatial quality. There is no pretence at mimetic aural representation at such moments – these are conditions that could not be experienced by the human ear.

On one hand, then, the slow melting heard in *Baikal Ice* and 'Vatnajökull' cannot be heard without an awareness of the effects of global warming. Yet, on the other hand, Cusack and Watson do not set out with the explicit aim of documenting a vanishing soundscape. What they capture and present through hydrophones is a quite artificial version of wilderness available only through the tools of the very same advanced technological modernity that has provoked ecological crisis.[33]

---

32 *Leonardo Music Journal*, 16 (2006): 69–70, at 70.
33 See Toop, *Haunted Weather*, p. 50, for discussion of the esoteric 'ghost zones' – geological events, insect activity, plant-sourced sound – that are explored by contemporary phonographers. Toop remarks on the similarity of many of these environmental sounds

The listener is presented in these recordings with a sonic environment that is aesthetically conceived and presented in terms that depend on human agency.

*

Releases by Japanese phonographer Kiyoshi Mizutani such as *Scenery of The Border: Environment and Folklore of the Tanzawa Mountains*[34] work both with and against the conventions of field recording. The title, indeed, plays with the way ethnographic recordings are typically presented. Mizutani has a background in Japanese noise music.[35] Solo recordings such as *Transcend Sideways* and *Waterscape*,[36] display an interest in feedback and, in the case of the latter, in the noise-generating capacities of everyday objects such as a child's swing or a damp cloth. His more recent field recordings often focus on the interpenetration of human activity and the natural. On several such Mizutani pieces wind rumble, microphone handling noise and passing aircraft – levels of impurity that would be unacceptable to more conventional recordists – are discernible. In interview Mizutani has remarked on the challenge nature presents to the 'musical':

> *I am made to think by the sound of nature 'what is the music'. The sound of nature contains a lot of musical messages. It is a signal and information from the nature. It is a musical element included in the nature.*[37]

In Mizutani's view, musical 'messages' or 'elements' are not the same as music per se, with his recordings inhabiting the state of 'inbetweenness' that is brought into play by the most challenging field recording. On his *Bird Songs* CD,[38] he revitalizes the archetypal nature recording, the capture of birdsong (itself a conspicuously acculturated emblem of human aesthetic endeavour). Mizutani's version of this form of recording is to combine 'nature' with extraneous material: scraping a wire fence, the squeaking of polystyrene or feedback. All of these interventions represent the kind of degenerate man-made 'noise' that might for an acoustic ecologist be set against the purity and complexity of the natural 'signal', the beauty of birdsong. Like other of the phonographers discussed in this chapter, then, Mizutani is questioning an essentially Romantic vision of nature that, mediated by contemporary ecological imperatives, counterposes a dream of innocence and a fallen mankind.

---

to electronic sound.

34   Kyoshi Mizutani, *Scenery of the Border: Environment and Folklore of the Tanzawa Mountains*, And/OAR, and22 (2006).

35   He was a member, with Masami Akita, of Merzbow, the most influential group of the genre. Merzbow has functioned as a pseudonym for Akita since Mizutani left the group in the late 1980s.

36   Kyoshi Mizutani, *Transcend Sideways*, Artware Production, Artware 19 (1997) and Kyoshi Mizutani, *Waterscape*, e(r)ostate, ErosCD 001 (1997).

37   http://jezrileyfrench-inplace.blogspot.com/ (accessed 7 July 2008).

38   Kyoshi Mizutani, *Bird Songs*, Ground Fault, GF010 (2000).

On many of the tracks on the *Scenery of the Border* double CD Mizutani stresses the human presence in the landscape. Sometimes this is manifest in recordings of Buddhist or Shinto ceremonies, and sometimes in the recordings made near a power plant or an electricity substation – natural sounds are presented against a background of persistent electronic hum. Elsewhere nature or animals – birds, the wind, a river – are presented in isolation. The second of the two CDs is, unusually, an 'enhanced' CD, containing photos and a high-resolution map of the Tanzawa area. Mizutani puts considerable effort into the documentation of a specific place across different media. He remarks:

> *The recorded sounds can be divided into categories such as natural occurrences, animals, man-made structures and folk traditions. The combination of elements found in a particular location determines the character of its atmosphere. To make this CD, I put the different combinations together in a manner of a sonic photo book. Rather than looking for a meaning in individual sounds, I suggest listening with the feeling of gazing at various landscapes, one after another. In any case, the cognitive consistency one maintains when listening to contemporary music is not a requirement here.*[39]

Writing with classic soundscaper's attention to overall picture rather than particular detail, Mizutani suggests that a form of listening that is analogous to the gaze is more helpful to the listener than the kind of focused attention that would be directed at music. He wants to stress the relationship between environmental sound and musical sound at the same time as cancelling any attempt to assimilate the two to one another. He suggests a distinction between the 'cognitive consistency' of musical listening, in which an implied coherence is projected by the listener on to the acoustic experience, and the less interpretative gesture of the contemplative gaze. Mizutani, then, juxtaposes distinct but related soundscapes with the aim of constructing a slowly evolving, impressionistic rendering of the atmosphere of a particular place.

Mizutani's note also stresses the historical significance of the Tanzawa mountain region, a relatively isolated border area that has, over the centuries, been the site of many conflicts.[40] The implication, in the strong version of this idea of acoustic representation, is that features of this troubled history are somehow encrypted in the aural environment. A weaker version of this idea would cause the listener to project an awareness of that history into the listening experience, imbibing a richer awareness of 'place' than would be possible with the sounds alone. In either case, the sounds serve as the platform for a larger investigation into the cultural resonances of a specific place. Mizutani's audio recordings on this release, therefore, engage both the visual and the conceptual spheres, setting in motion complicated interactions between listening and looking, place and displacement, natural and man-made, signal and noise. His interest in the historical dimensions

---

39 http://www.and-oar.org/pop_and_22.html (accessed 25 June 2008).
40 Ibid.

of place suggests that sonic atmospheres can help communicate the shifting drama of mutual interference between man and environment.

*

Another Japanese phonographer, Toshiya Tsunoda, demonstrates a more radical and interventionist attitude towards natural sound in his explorations of place. Tsunoda, a founding member of the WrK artists' collective, often works with very sensitive contact microphones or miniature conventional microphones, attaching them to objects in order to probe those objects' acoustic qualities. On many of his recordings he has explored interior spaces by placing microphones inside bottles or funnels or between sheets of metal – the recordings thus produced are therefore a specialized kind of non-electronic acoustic 'processing' of sound and vibrations that find their way to the microphones from outside the enclosing medium. On other recordings he has attached contact microphones to interior or exterior walls, windows and air ducts, seeking out the vibrational qualities of built space. More than Watson and Cusack, then, he directs the ear towards what is not available to ordinary experience, offering what Brandon LaBelle reads as 'an altered understanding' of the spaces we inhabit.[41] Tsunoda's work, in this view, reveals a network of linked acoustic systems that encode forms of human activity.

Often his recordings are presented in ways that juxtapose natural sound with the sound of human activity, feedback or oscillators. The album *Pieces of Air*,[42] as well as exploring the acoustic properties of pipes and bottles, features relatively conventional recordings of crickets chirping and a windy day by the beach. Yet in these cases wind, crickets and water can all be understood as approximations to electronic sound. Two tracks incorporate low-frequency sine tones. The album *O Respirar Da Paisagem*[43] contains a recording of cicadas combined with a creaking window, which sounds like a minimal electroacoustic composition.[44] Another sound source is presented in two forms, via the medium of 'air' (that is, with conventional microphone) and that of something 'solid' (with contact microphone). Even more challenging to the listener is Tsunoda's *Low Frequency Observed at Maguchi Bay*.[45] This album combines a set of four contact miked field recordings with filtered versions that remove all material above 20hz, more or less the threshold of human hearing. The filtered recordings – half of the album – are, therefore, literally unlistenable. In the domestic set-up I have, both loudspeakers and headphones register the sounds only as ultra-low throbs and buzzes indicating distress to the hardware. While Maguchi Bay may be an attractive spot, *Low Frequency*'s filtered recordings

---

41   LaBelle, *Background Noise*, p. 239.

42   Toshiya Tsunoda, *Pieces of Air*, Lucky Kitchen, LK016 (2001).

43   Toshiya Tsunoda, *O Respirar Da Paisagem*, Sirr, sirr012 (2003).

44   Schafer, *Soundscape*, p. 39, compares the cicada's sound-producing mechanism to 'a tin lid when pressed in by the finger', the kind of metallic surface that fascinates Tsunoda.

45   Toshiya Tsunoda, *Low Frequency Observed at Maguchi Bay*, Hibari, Hibari 11 (2007).

translate the natural setting into another format altogether, dominated by the distant vibrations of otherwise imperceptible human activity. Everyday human acoustic perception is thus relativized and, strikingly in this instance, shown to occlude man-made sounds.

Many recordists use high-pass filters to remove the low-frequency sounds that our ears habitually edit out for us (these can sound intrusive when listened to through loudspeakers at above ambient levels). Tsunoda reverses this principle, leaving the listener with the acoustic vibration at the border of hearing and feeling. For him, this is a means of arriving at a faithful but non-mimetic representation of place:

> *Vibration is sustained like the sound of the heartbeat of the space. This is the inherent phenomenon of the space. The vibration is proof of the place's identity/existence. Therefore, as for physical vibrations, all of the incidents/ occurrences are reflected in the space ... When one considers the time and space of the vibration phenomenon, there appears to be a big gap in our consciousness regarding common/ordinary spaces. Through observation, our attention gravitates towards the relationship between the actual world and our perception of it. We thus encounter the intrinsic nature of the place. What's interesting to me is that by recording an actual phenomenon, you can extract the intrinsic quality of an actual existing space.*[46]

Despite the apparent abstraction of his work, Tsunoda shares with Mizutani, Watson and Cusack a desire to communicate the aural features of 'actual existing space'. In his case, however, the truth of that representation lies not in what is manifest but in what is hidden. There is a 'gap' between our after-the-fact reorganizations of perception and the 'actual world'. Tsunoda invites us to engage in an expanded form of listening, even if this involves using microphones as an aural prosthesis to uncover hidden layers of sonic information. Again, his renderings of acoustic environments are thoroughly imbued with the imperatives of aesthetic investigation. As with the work of Jacob Kirkegaard and Steven Vitiello, which I will now discuss, concealment and the active intervention of the recordist are integral to an aestheticized form of research practice.

*

One of the more extreme sound artists currently working with field recordings is Jacob Kirkegaard, from Denmark. I will comment briefly on two recent releases on the Touch label, each of which is built around a relatively simple concept. The recordings in each case have a textural complexity that has much in common with the further fringes of musical experimentation. With *Eldfjall*,[47] Kirkegaard, like

---

46   Toshiya Tsunoda, 'Toshiya Tsunoda', in *Extract: Portraits of Soundartists* (Vienna, 2007), p. 86.
47   Jacob Kirkegaard, *Eldfjall*, Touch, T33.20 (2005).

Chris Watson, uses recordings gathered in Iceland. Rather than glaciers, though, he recorded near the geysers of Krisuvik, Geysir and Myvatn. On these recordings, Kierkegaard, like Tsunoda, is interested in vibration. He inserts accelerometers (very sensitive contact microphones) into the earth and these pick up volcanic activity ('eldfjall' means 'fire mountain' or 'volcano'). Unlike Watson's often rather dramatic narratives on *Weather Report*, Kirkegaard's tracks each present a relatively unchanging quasi-musical idea. In this, they recall the animus against harmony, melody and musical development in much electronic music of the 1990s and 2000s (itself often a revisiting of ideas in the work of La Monte Young, Tony Conrad, Eliane Radigue and others in the 1960s and 1970s). Each piece has a claustrophobic and tightly focused quality, as if it were putting a particular acoustic phenomenon under the microscope. Sudden opening and closing fades accentuate the jagged, bruitiste aspects of the work. It is regrettable, perhaps, that Kirkegaard chooses as his track titles such words as Al-Lat, Aramaiti and Izanami – the names of earth goddesses from different points around the world, thus adding a spurious mythic patina to work that counts a demythologizing impulse towards the environment among its strongest features.

As with Tsunoda, the process of revealing sonic substrata to our experience is constitutive of the artistic event. Kirkegaard in interview demarcates his work from that of scientists in ways that are revealing: 'I am not sure whether scientists think too much about hidden layers, secret messages, whisperings or songs emitted from souls from other frequencies, when they explore the VLF vibrations through their receivers. Maybe they do. In any case there exists a motivation for me there, in the dreams of other spaces, missing links or black holes, as there always are more sides to a fact.'[48] Kirkegaard here presents himself as a kind of technological shaman, alert to messages that cannot be deciphered through the procedures of scientific investigation. The pieces on *Eldfjall* develop from an aesthetic of hiddenness, with the artist offering a speculative decoding of a world thickly populated with occult meanings.

Kirkegaard's album *4 Rooms*[49] is specifically concerned with the cultural significance of the acoustics of buildings. In these recordings, Kirkegaard revisits and inverts Alvin Lucier's renowned *I am Sitting in a Room* (1969).[50] Kirkegaard alters Lucier's process by recording not voice but silence. The pathos of this act of subtraction is the more marked because he uses abandoned public spaces in Chernobyl: a church, a swimming pool, a gymnasium, an auditorium. The resulting

---

48   Kirkegaard interviewed by Diane Ludin in January 2005 for the New York-based internet art portal The Thing. The interview is archived at www.touchmusic.org.uk/archives/reviews_jacobkirkegaard/ (accessed 16 June 2008).

49   Jacob Kirkegaard, *4 Rooms*, Touch, Tone 26 (2006).

50   Lucier recorded himself reading a short text. He then played back the recording in the same room, using a second tape machine to record the original recording. He then played back and recorded the second recording, repeating the process until nothing was left of his voice, which had been transformed into a complex, multi-layered drone exhibiting the resonant frequencies of the room itself.

recordings are ambiguously pitched drones, rich in overtones. The conceptual dimension of the work is obvious, with the drones serving as the ghostly remainder of the population that left the area after the nuclear reactor disaster of 1986. Sound is conjured from absence in a gesture of collective channelling.[51]

Kirkegaard's work combines an austere ear with a curious desire for re-enchantment: ghostly voices and earth goddesses. He makes available to the listener sounds that would otherwise be unimaginable and which sit comfortably alongside avant-garde musical experiments. On these releases, environmental sound is transformed by the use of unusual recording techniques. The work emerges through the creative use of technology by the recordist, who assumes a more composerly role than in the work of some of the phonographers discussed above. If there is a flaw to this suggestive, acoustically rich work, it lies in the suspicion that sound's materiality is used to cloak a fascination with spirit.

*

The last example of field recording use that I want to discuss is a reflection on place, environment and art. American sound artist Stephen Vitiello's *Listening to Donald Judd*[52] uses recordings made during a residency at the Chinati Foundation, Donald Judd's museum in Marfa, Texas.[53] Unlike all of the artists discussed hitherto, Vitiello has processed almost all the recordings he made, using time-stretching and other techniques. These original recordings, a liner note explains, were made in and around the Judd buildings and installations. Microphones were attached to Judd's 'specific objects', placed on the floor of the studios housing them, and positioned in the surrounding countryside. Recordings were made from a glider, in fields of grasshoppers and in a street. Marfa is, Vitiello notes, 'a very quiet town'. Among the few recognizable unprocessed sounds is that of the train that passes through the town daily. These recordings span a number of linked contexts: artwork, exhibition space, natural environment, urban environment. As with Kirkegaard's Chernobyl recordings, Mizutani's Tanzawa release and Tsunoda's *Maguchi Bay* album, there is

---

51 Cf. Peter Cusack's Chernobyl recordings. On Gruenrekorder's *Autumn Leaves* online compilation (2007) are two tracks, 'Chernobyl Dawn' and 'Chernobyl Frogs'. Cusack writes: 'Since the nuclear catastrophe of April 26 1986, and in complete contrast to human life, nature at Chernobyl is thriving. The evacuation of people has created an undisturbed haven and wildlife has taken full advantage. Animals and birds absent for many decades – wolves, moose, black storks – have moved back and the Chernobyl exclusion zone is now one of Europe's prime wildlife sites. Radiation seems to have had a negligible effect.' Text available at http://www.gruenrekorder.de/?page_id=181 (accessed 1 July 2008).

52 Stephen Vitiello *Listening to Donald Judd*, Sub Rosa, SR245 (2007).

53 Vitiello's career as a sound artist took off following a six-month residency at the World Trade Center in 1999 when, among other things, he attached contact microphones to the building's windows. This work has, needless to say, gained enormously in retrospective significance. An excerpt can be heard at www.ubuweb.com/sound/vitiello.html (accessed 2 July 2008).

an assumption that a particular place has a specific acoustic signature. Although many of the sounds have been processed beyond recognition, scattered and reassembled as data through digital reconfiguring, Vitiello's contention is that he is still, in a sense – more than ever before, perhaps – 'listening to Donald Judd'.

One of the conceptual fields engaged by this CD's treatment of environmental sound is the controversy that surrounded minimalist art. In the words of one of the foremost opponents of this new 'literalist' art, Michael Fried, minimalism depended on a quality of 'theatricality' that stressed the context and the particular experience of the viewer at the expense of the properly autonomous artwork. For Fried, 'Literalist sensibility is theatrical because, to begin with, it is concerned with the actual circumstances in which the beholder encounters literalist work. [Robert] Morris makes this explicit. Whereas in previous art "what is to be had from the work is located strictly within [it]", the experience of literalist art is of an object *in a situation* – one that, virtually by definition, *includes the beholder.*'[54]

Fried contrasts the modernist painting or sculpture, which transcends its own objecthood and exists in a condition of presentness or grace, to the three-dimensional objects of minimalism. These are greatly limited as artworks, he argues, by their emphasis on duration, context and the spectator. Judd, on the other hand, spurns Fried's transcendent 'presentness', insisting on the actual encounter with the specific artwork. David Batchelor's commentary on Fried's rejection of Robert Morris's ideas – 'what for Fried is the negation of art, is for Morris, the condition of its continuation and renewal' – is equally applicable to the ideas of Judd.[55] When Judd began buying land and buildings in and around Marfa it was with the intention of establishing a suitable architectural environment to house his work. Vitiello is clearly sympathetic to this emphasis on context. By capturing the acoustic experience of Marfa, Vitiello offers us a single sensory aspect of Judd's artworks and their surroundings, tipping the balance away from artwork and towards context. By processing and recombining much of the audio he resituates Judd's work, translating both art and context into another realm altogether. Both are simultaneously invoked and estranged through presentation in the medium of sound.

By multiplying the contexts of the works' reception in this way, Vitiello directs our attention to the very fact of context. While Guy Marc Hinant's claim in his liner note that Judd's 'specific objects have been absorbing the landscape' seems overstated, *Listening to Donald Judd* depends absolutely on the interdependence of artwork and environment. The drone-like qualities of parts of the work are analogous to the emphasis on simplicity and duration in some minimal art. Yet Vitiello's sonic compositions, with all their roughness and variability of texture, achieve something rather different from the austerity and formal purity that is typically attributed to minimalism.[56] Going further than Judd, he opens the gallery

---

54 Michael Fried, 'Art and Objecthood', in *Art and Objecthood* (Chicago, 1998), p. 153. Fried cites Morris's 1966 essay 'Notes on Sculpture'.

55 David Batchelor, *Minimalism* (London, 2001), p. 67.

56 See Robert Morris on minimalism's conflicting impulses towards the material and

door on to the surrounding countryside. Judd's attention to obtrusively man-made objects is displaced by the natural sound that leaks in. Here Schafer's conception of signal and noise is reversed, with natural noise productively contaminating the purity of the artwork.

*

In all of the work discussed above, there is a wariness of any attempt to obscure the inherent mediatedness of recordings of the natural world. Nature is certainly not made available in a state of prelapsarian grace. Human intervention in the landscape and conspicuous artifice in the recording or editing of these sounds qualifies the idea of the natural. In this form of phonography, natural beauty and artistic practice are mutually dependent and no absolute antithesis between the sound of music and the sound of the world is implied. Such recordings of nature are, on the one hand, always understood to be profoundly cultural and, on the other, close to the musical or aesthetic organization of sound.

My discussions of an 'in-betweenness' that characterizes these developments and critiques of the soundscape can usefully be compared to Robert Smithson's radicalization of the idea of the 'picturesque' presented in the eighteenth-century writings of Uvedale Price and William Gilpin and, in the following century, realized in the parks of Frederick Law Olmsted:

> The contradictions of the 'picturesque' depart from a static, formalistic view of nature. The picturesque, far from being an inner movement of the mind, is based on real land; it precedes the mind in its material external existence. We cannot take a one-sided view of the landscape within this dialectic. A park can no longer be seen as a 'thing in itself', but rather as a process of ongoing relationships existing in a physical region – the park becomes a 'thing for us'. As a result we are not hurled into the spiritualism of Thoreauvian transcendentalism, or its present-day offspring of 'modernist formalism', rooted in Kant, Hegel and Fichte. Price, Gilpin and Olmsted are forerunners of a dialectical materialism applied to the physical landscape. Dialectics of this type are a way of seeing things in a manifold of relations, not as isolated objects. Nature for the dialectician is indifferent to any formal ideal.[57]

Leaving aside the awkwardness of the application of 'dialectical materialism', Smithson's notion of ceaseless interchange between an obdurately material

---

the transcendent: 'Minimal art was the attempt to recuperate transcendent Puritan values by reencoding them via an iconoclasm of austere formal spatial purity. At the same time its ambition was to transpose and redeem utilitarian industrial processes and gestalt forms into an aesthetic space of the phenomenological.' See 'Size Matters', *Critical Inquiry* 26 (2000): 474–87, at 480.

57   Robert Smithson, 'Frederick Law Olmsted and the Dialectical Landscape', in *Robert Smithson: Collected Writings*, ed. Jack Flam (Berkeley, 1996), pp. 157–71, at pp. 159–60.

landscape and the aestheticizing human hand is a fertile concept. This 'manifold of relations' points us to the kind of dynamic interaction between artist and environment that the phonographers discussed in this chapter achieve. There is in this work, which I find more rewarding than most music released in the same period (that is, since the turn of the century), a radical openness to the aesthetic potential of acoustic atmospheres. The peculiar status of sound in our experience of the world is recognized and manipulated in ways that extend and enrich that experience. The lived experience of 'atmosphere' is re-presented in the highly artificial situation in which we listen to these recordings, mediated by loudspeakers or headphones. The use by phonographers of hydrophones and contact microphones opens up still further dimensions of sound. In these ways, we are both drawn into and distanced from acoustic environments that we might never encounter or that would be impossible to encounter without the aid of specialized technological equipment.

Pure artifice on the one hand, and the natural 'in itself', on the other, are rejected by Smithson in favour of the interaction between the two. The natural is denatured to varying degrees in the phonography discussed in this chapter, while never yet quite relinquishing a residual objectivity. That limit state of otherness is what continues to challenge our notions of aesthetic ordering and what persists in frustrating our attempts to draw it once and for all into the realm of culture. The ungainsayable beauty of such sound exists as a kind of shadow to the beauty we discern in music, a bulwark against aspirations of fully achieved subjective expression. The specificity of both subject and aesthetic object is preserved in this work. Between these poles complex perceptual atmospheres take shape. Advanced phonography of the kind discussed in this chapter makes compelling claims on our attention because of its peculiar ability to offer us not the world but the relationship between the world and its representation.

161

Soundwalking: Aural Excursions into the Everyday

John Levack Drever

> *When you take your ears for a soundwalk, you are both audience and performer in a concert of sound that occurs continually around you. By walking you are able to enter into a conversation with the landscape.*[1]

Soundwalking – a persistent yet markedly peripheral activity of experimental music and sound art – in its most fundamental form, in the words of soundwalker/composer/acoustic ecologist Hildegard Westerkamp, is 'any excursion whose main purpose is listening to the environment. It is exposing our ears to every sound around us no matter where we are.'[2]

The concatenation of locomotion with a state of readiness for attentive unprejudiced listening that protracts beyond the walls of the consecrated sites of dedicated otic practices (that is, concert hall, church, lecture theatre) form the commonality that is soundwalking. Within this definition, however, motivation, methodology and manifestation radically vary. It can be a linear, dare I say, composed affair, scored for ensemble or solo (collective or hermetic). Conversely, eschewing such predetermined prescriptions it can take the form of an extemporized performance, contingent on the vicissitudes of the environment in correspondence with the whims of the composer as sherpa (remembering Heraclitus' philosophy of perpetual flux: 'You cannot step twice into the same river; for fresh waters are ever flowing in upon you').[3]

A more and more prevalent method is reliant on headphone mediation, where audience/participant is ordained as pathfinder within an open structure with location-specific psychogeographically devised sonic material being released on cue aided by GPS technology, such as Teri Reub's *Trace* (1999). And soundwalking has even assumed the form of a book, as with Janet Cardiff's *The Walk Book* (2005). In

---

1   R. Murray. Schafer (ed.), *The Vancouver Soundscape* (Vancouver, 1978), p. 71.
2   Hildegard Westerkamp, 'Soundwalking', *Sound Heritage*, III/4 (1974). Reprinted and updated in Angus Carlyle (ed.), *Autumn Leaves: Sound and the Environment in Artistic Practice* (Paris, 2007), pp. 49–54.
3   Bertrand Russell, *History of Western Philosophy* (London, 1991), p. 63.

fact soundwalking is something that composers have habitually done *ad infinitum*, and as such it straddles that grey area between fieldwork and arts practice.

Whatever the level of composerly determination and technological mediatization (which at the least may ask for a good pair of walking shoes), the hierarchical roles of composer, performer and audience are often indivisible, or at any rate authorship is almost always problematized.

As we shall go into, soundwalking asks questions of our engagement with the outside world with a bias towards aural sensibilities. On one level it demands the reverence of concert hall listening, yet we find ourselves physically placed and passing through the everyday: a state that naturally prompts everyday behaviour, which is at odds with the contingencies of concert hall listening. Thus discernment between signal or noise, foreground and background, aesthetics and function (that is, what does the composer intend us to listen to and how should we be listening to it?) becomes a matter of shifting attitudes and sensitivities.

This chapter provides a historical perspective and theoretical context on the trajectory from peripatetic composer to soundwalking as a mode of participatory experimental music in its own right. Moreover, as walking is the means and the physical action of soundwalking, the chapter also expounds on artistic forays in the 1960s into pedestrian behaviour, a trope that crosses over with the experimental music culture of the day, and helped give soundwalking credence.

The Everyday

The salient concern in soundwalking is everyday life. Bringing into play the everyday suggests a shared tacit knowledge, whilst validating individuals' behaviour, perception and interpretation. It accesses notions of reality that are mundane and whose processes are transparent, whilst unwittingly engendering the particular, and due to its very everydayness, habituation renders them invisible, silent and unspoken. Henri Lefebvre, who has championed the study of the everyday, attempted to define the field as '"what is left over" after all distinct, superior, specialized, structured activities have been singled out by analysis'.[4]

As we cross the threshold of the auditorium, we adopt the (albeit) vestiges of ritualistic practices of classical musical performance governed by highly conventionalized sonic and social relationships and behaviours. To borrow the adjectives designated by Lefebvre, a concert hall performance can be considered a 'distinct', 'specialized' and 'structured activity', supported by the institutions of knowledge: musicology, performance practice, journalism and so forth. It has to be

---

4   Henri Lefebvre, *Critique of Everyday Life: Volume 1*, trans. John Moore (London, 1991), p. 97.

said that concert listening is coated by the everyday[5] and spills in to the everyday,[6] but the actual contractual *focus* of the concert hall bifurcates from its realm.

Despite the occasional occurrence of symbolic representation of *extra-musical* sound (for example Janequin, Vivaldi, Mozart, Mahler, Russolo, Respighi, Varèse, Messiaen and so on), Western music culture has spent five centuries increasingly retreating from the sounds of everyday life – enclosed 'behind padded walls' of the concert hall, where 'concentrated listening becomes possible'.[7] It remains anathema for street sounds to spill into the auditorium[8] or the recording studio for that matter, cocooned in its acoustically *neutral* bubble. Such a system is predicated on a notional unbroken circuit from composer to score to performer to listener.

Taking the everyday as its context, soundwalking mingles in the everyday but is not of the everyday. Akin to other modes of cultural performance, such as the classical music concert, it is a kind of limbo activity, where the goals and stresses of everyday life are temporarily lifted, and the sensation of partaking in a performance event is invoked, but distinctively in soundwalking the relationship between participant and everyday life is conspicuously porous. In the jargon of Victor Turner,[9] it is a kind of liminoid activity, 'the quasi-liminal character of cultural performances',[10] that 'originates outside the boundaries of the economic, political, and structural process, and its manifestations often challenge the wider social structure by offering social critique on, or even suggestions for, a revolutionary re-ordering of the official social order'.[11]

Thus one of the underpinning goals of soundwalking is about circumnavigating habituation, in a process of de-sensitization and consequently re-sensitization, in order to catch a glimpse (*un coup d'oreille*) of the 'invisible, silent and unspoken' of the everyday.

---

5   'To music is to take part, in any capacity, in a musical performance, whether by performing, by listening, by rehearsing or practicing, by providing material for performance (what is called composing), or by dancing.' Christopher Small, *Musicking: The Meanings of Performing and Listening* (Middletown, Conn., 1998), p. 9. Small even includes the cleaners and the ticket sales in this definition.

6   See Tia DeNora, *Music in Everyday Life* (Cambridge, 2000).

7   R. Murray Schafer, *The Soundscape: Our Sonic Environment and the Tuning of the World* (Rochester, 1994), p. 103.

8   Bridging the noise gap between the political turmoil of the Paris streets and the relative quite of the theatre, in Antonin Artaud's *mise-en-scene* direction for Roger Vitrac's *Coup de Trafalgar* (finally performed in 1934) he proposed that: 'From the very beginning of the Act, a background noise will be established in order to make one feel the constant presence of life outside.' (Antonin Artaud, 'Deux projets de mise en scene' (1931), *Oeuvres Completes*, vol. 2, p. 147, quoted in Denis Hollier, 'The Death of Paper, Part Two: Artaud's Sound System', *October*, 80 (Spring 1997): 27–37, at 35.

9   Victor Turner, 'Liminal to Liminoid, in Play, Flow and Ritual', in Edward Norbeck (ed.), *The Anthropological Study of Human Play* (Houston, 1974), pp. 53–92.

10 Mathieu Deflem, 'Ritual, Anti-Structure, and Religion: A Discussion of Victor Turner's Processual Symbolic Analysis', *Journal for the Scientific Study of Religion* 30/1 (1991): 1–24, at 14.

11 Ibid., p. 15.

In situ

The everyday in turn invokes notions of corporeal emplacement and the concomitant geographical concept of *in situ*: as the surrounding *texture* in which an object is embedded informs its narrative. In the case of soundwalking, the audience's own physicality and actual embodiment in the *here and now* within the environment is put into the equation in a way that concert listening customarily denies – although this is a sliding scale, as in some walks the audience is brought into an awareness of dislocation (for example Janet Cardiff, Christina Kubisch, Duncan Speakman); a feeling of being cut off from one's immediate/contiguous environment. The audience and the sounds they encounter whilst in transit inhabit the site (albeit fleetingly); they are *in situ*. The dynamic temporal and spatial relationship engenders a dialogue between listener, sound and location (that is, *locus sonus*), and narrative unfolds.

The *aural texture* of the soundwalk is formed first of background noise from which a signal surfaces amongst other competing signals. For Michel Serres background noise is 'that incessant hubbub, our signals, our messages, our speech and our words are but a fleeting high surf, over its perpetual swell'.[12] This is not simply a superfluous backdrop, however: in the study of the everyday even background noise can be the very stuff of research and its influence should not be overlooked. Referring to it as 'our perennial sustenance',[13] Serres reminds us that 'We are in the noises of the world, we cannot close our door to their reception, and we evolve, rolling in this incalculable swell.'[14]

The second order of *aural texture* is informed by the overall sensorium[15] via the exteroceptive senses (that is, audition, gustatory, haptic, olfactory, optic, vestibular) of an individual member of the audience. Sense data garnered from the outside world (although privation of a particular sense most commonly achieved by blindfold can be a deliberate compositional strategy, for example Ben Patterson's *Tour* (1963), which will be discussed later) forms a composite of affects and triggers a matrix of signification. Thus the audience's multi-modal integration through the literacy of the signs of any given environment that they have exposure to will inevitably colour the experience. Moreover the relative sensitivity to what is present, on a phenomenological level will also help shape the individual aesthetic experience and reading of that experience.

Due to the ostensible simplicity and universality of soundwalking (most of us can simultaneously walk and listen) and its link to everyday life, such practice can summon the utmost interdisciplinary study, be that experimental music,

---

12   Michel Serres, *Genesis*, trans. Geneviève James and James Nielson (Ann Arbor, 1995), p. 6.
13   Ibid., p. 7.
14   Michel Serres, *The Parasite*, trans. Laurence R. Schehr (Minneapolis, 2007), p. 126.
15   'The sensorium is dynamic, relational and political (not the private world psychologists posit), and our senses extend as far as our culture's technologies of sensing (corporeal and extracorporeal) permit them.' David Howes (ed.), *The Empire of the Senses: The Sensual Cultural Reader* (Oxford, 2005).

architecture, acoustics, cultural geography, sociology, natural history, choreography, meteorology, urban design and so on. Perhaps because of these multiple identities it finds itself at the periphery of more established cultural forms.

Composer as Aural *Flâneur*

Walter Benjamin, in his vast network of fragmentary observations and quotes vis-à-vis nineteenth-century Paris that goes to make the seminal cultural history that is *The Arcades Project* (started in 1927 and abandoned in 1940), citing his old teacher Georg Simmel, distinguishes big cities, 'by a marked preponderance of the activity of the eye over the activity of the ear'.[16] Simmel's conjecture for this 'uneasiness' was due to the long time that people had to spend in the presence of each other in public transport. This ocular predisposition is evident throughout *The Arcades Project*, where for the *flâneur*, the urban stroller, 'who goes botanizing on the asphalt',[17] the Paris arcades were akin to a 'diorama'. Benjamin finds one exception, posited by Pierre Larousse from his *Grand Dictionnaire Universel* (Paris, 1872), a kind of the aural *flâneur*:[18] 'A noise, insignificant to every other ear, will strike that of the musician and give him a cue for a harmonic combination.'[19] The muse for this model was Beethoven, who, mythology retells 'was seen walking each and every day ... around the ramparts of the city of Vienna ... who, in the midst of his wanderings, would work out his magnificent symphonies in his head before putting them down on paper'.[20]

It was not only in the landscape of the metropolis; the figure of Beethoven traversing the countryside has been a popular theme for artists since the first half of the nineteenth century. However, this is distinct from Benjamin's archetypal *flâneur*,[21] Baudelaire, exemplified in his most famous/infamous collection of poems, *Les Fleurs du Mal* (first published in 1857). With its themes of sex and death, garnered form the urban spectacle, Benjamin considered Baudelaire's attitude analogous to that of an explorer in the *wilderness*:[22] 'There is an effort to master new experience

---

16   Walter Benjamin, *Charles Baudelaire* (New York and London, 1997), p. 38.

17   Ibid., p. 36.

18   'It was Adorno ['Radio Physiognomik' (1939)] who pointed to the station-switching behavior of the radio listener as a kind of aural *flânerie*.' Susan Buck-Morss, 'The Flaneur, the Sandwichman and the Whore: The Politics of Loitering', in the *New German Critique*, Second Special Issue on Walter Benjamin, No. 39 (Autumn, 1986): 99–140, at p. 105.

19   Walter Benjamin, *The Arcades Project*, trans. Howard Eiland and Kevin McLaughlin, prepared on the basis of the German volume ed. Roy Tiedemann (Cambridge, Mass. and London, 2002), p. 453 [M20a,1].

20   Pierre Larousse quoted in Benjamin, *The Arcades Project*, pp. 453–4 [M20a,1].

21   This is in contrast to a slightly earlier generation of *flâneurs* (circa 1840), whom, Benjamin recounts, took 'turtles for a walk in the arcades' (Benjamin, *Baudelaire*, p. 54), the turtle setting the pace.

22   Patrick Süskind's protagonist Jean-Baptiste Grenouille in *Perfume: The Story of a*

of the city within the framework of the old traditional experience of nature. Hence the schemata of the virgin forest and the sea.'[23]

In recurring depictions of Beethoven, however, the representation of his deportment betrays his attitude, one of self-containment and preoccupation: 'he saw nothing; his mind was elsewhere'.[24] This environmentally detached behaviour is concordant with the prevailing bourgeois culture, in an era when walking was elevated from peasant predicament (that is, in order to get from A to B such as the itinerant *jongleur* and troubadour of the Middle Ages) to cultural pastime and an aid to philosophical musings, warranted in part by John Thelwall's tome *The Peripatetic* (1793). Echoing Rousseau, Thelwall relates thinking with walking: 'In one respect, at least, I may boast of a resemblance to the simplicity of the ancient sages. I pursue my mediations on foot.'[25]

Romantic Ecologists

The 'ancient sages' in this regard are Aristotle and his school, the Peripatetics, who were said to have conducted their lectures on foot, pacing up and down the colonnade: an account without solid foundations, yet from the eighteenth century, a revered practice[26] that pervaded nineteenth- and twentieth-century thought. It feeds into the cult of the pastoral idyll and the metaphysical figure of the lone artist tackling vast landscapes that propel the individual into the sublime; this is the era of the romantic ecologists Wordsworth and Coleridge. Although contexts and agendas differ, in Rebecca Solnit's history of walking practices *Wanderlust* (2002), she articulates what walking has to offer the artist:

Murderer (1985) provides us with a refreshing yet sinister shift in the bias of the senses, this time an olfactory *flâneur*: 'He would often just stand there, leaning against a wall or crouching in a dark corner, his eyes closed, his mouth half-open and nostrils flaring wide, quiet as a feeding pike in a great, dark, slowly moving current. And when at last a puff of air would toss a delicate thread of scent his way, he would lunge at it and not let go. Then he would smell at just this one odour, holding it tight, pulling it into himself and preserving it for all time.' Patrick Süskind, *Perfume: The Story of a Murderer* (London, 1987), p. 35. His highly acute sense of smell would lead him through the streets of eighteenth-century Paris, and whilst the *flâneur* is detective-like, Grenouille is driven to homicide in his desire to *grasp* smell: 'No matter what trail the *flâneur* may follow, every one of them will lead him to a crime.' Walter Benjamin, *Baudelaire*, p. 41.

23   Charles Meryon and Pierre Alexis Ponson du Terrail, quoted in Benjamin, *The Arcades Project*, p. 447 [M20a,1].
24   Pierre Larousse, quoted in Benjamin, *The Arcades Project*, p. 454 [M20a,1].
25   John Thelwall, quoted in Rebecca Solnit, *Wanderlust: A History of Walking* (New York, 2002), p. 14.
26   Ibid.

Walking, ideally, is a state in which the mind, the body, and the world are aligned, as though they were three characters finally in conversation together, three notes suddenly making a chord. Walking allows us to be in our bodies and in the world without being made busy by them. It leaves us free to think without being wholly lost in our thoughts.[27]

In that regard Mahler comes to mind. For Mahler, taking long hikes in the Tyrol was a congenial even obligatory compositional process, although this activity was curtailed in later life by heart disease (c.1908). In a letter to Bruno Walter he laments his wanderings:

For years I have grown used to taking strenuous exercise, to walking in forests and over mountains and boldly wrestling my ideas from nature ... I have never been able to work only at my desk – I need outside exercise for my inner exercises ... the desired effect of forgetting my body.[28]

His neurosis however led his mind back to his body with continual monitoring of his pulse. He was even known to have carried a pedometer[29] to restrain his pace.

Of course singing (mental or actual), or humming and whistling often accompanies walking, albeit unwittingly. Percy Grainger's *Walking Tune* for wind 5-some (*Room-Music Tit-bits No. 3*, 1904) is one such example, the quasi-Celtic tune coming to the 18-year-old Grainger whilst he was on a three-day trek in Western Argyllshire (Scotland) in the summer of 1900. Charles Amirkhanian based his homage to Grainger on *Walking Tune*. Amirkhanian's *Walking Tune (A Room-Music for Percy Grainger)* (1986–87) blends synclavier sounds, Grainger pastiche and field recordings, including the sound of tramping and a swarm of humming birds, plus ambient recordings from Australia.[30]

For Beethoven, Mahler or Grainger, or to that mind Elgar – a keen cyclist, whose music often calls for 72 beats a minute, the average rate of a heart beat[31] – these perambulations take the role of catalyst for fantasy. The resulting exhilaration can provide tempi, and untethered from everyday concerns, help promote a creative frame of mind. The sounds they encounter *in situ* can act as a prompt, but the semblance to the *real world* in such work tends to be symbolic in intent and delivery. Peppered throughout the poetry and prose of the Lake District poets we often find allusion to sounds of the *wilderness*. Attributing a 'voice to nature',[32] Coleridge

---

27 Ibid., p. 5.
28 Mahler quoted in Edward Seckerson, *Mahler* (London, 1984), p. 119.
29 Ibid.
30 A similar eclectic yet considered mix of field recordings and synclavier are brought together in his homage to Samuel Beckett, *Pas de voix* (1988), including recordings made in the lobby and environs of Beckett's apartment in Paris.
31 Jerrold Northrop Moore, *Spirit of England: Edward Elgar in his World* (London, 1984), p. 105.
32 Jonathan Rée, *I See A Voice: A Philosophical History* (London, 1999), p. 56.

writes of the 'the brook's chatter' and 'the breeze, murmuring indivisibly'.[33] But these notions have less to do with the sounds themselves and the context that gave rise to them, and more to do with romantic ideology. This is analogous to, say Mahler's mimicking of bird song in *Der Trunkene im Frühling* (The Drunken Men in Spring), from the fifth song from *Das Lied von der Erde* (1907–1909), which functions as a harbinger of spring. And in the fifth movement of *Symphony No. 3 in D minor* (1893–96) where we hear a children's choir imitate the bells, the movement had the working title of 'What the Morning Bells Tell Me' (and later, replaced by 'What the Angels Tell Me'). This double-edged relationship with the sound world that the composer extrapolated from is demonstrated in Ken Russell's psychodramatic film *Mahler* (1974): on composing the Fourth Symphony, Mahler complains to Alma about the noises (for example sparse sound of cows mooing and a distant church bell) (1899–1900) penetrating his composing hut at the utmost picturesque location of Maiernigg on Wörthersee.[34]

Satie

In October 1898, Erik Satie relocated to Arcuil, 10 km from Paris, where he stayed till his death (1925). From here he would set off on a daily walk to Paris (sporting, one can only assume, one of his seven identical grey velvet suits until he changed his guise for the final time in 1906). This was no hike, rather a peripatetic stroll, with generous hiatus for refreshment and composition en route; it was reputed that Satie notated 'ideas at night on foot which he would then work on in cafés during daytime'.[35] In a conversation on Satie with John Cage (another walking composer and champion of Satie, whom we will return to), Roger Shattuck and Alan Gillmor, Shattuck suggested that:

> the source of Satie's sense of musical beat – the possibility of variation within repetition, the effect of boredom on the organism – may be this endless walking back and forth across the same landscape day after day, and finally taking it all in, which is basically what Thoreau did: the total observation of a very limited and narrow environment.[36]

Robert Orledge, stimulated by this notion, goes further to suggest that, 'the absence of expressiveness and sentimentality surely reflects the drab and often

---

33   Coleridge, 'Lines written in the Album at Elbingerode' (1799), quoted in Rée, *I See A Voice*, pp. 56–7.
34   Russell takes a liberal approach to chronology, as Mahler met Alma Schindler in 1901.
35   Robert Orledge, *Satie the Composer* (Cambridge, 1990), p. 20.
36   John Cage (with Roger Shattuck and Alan Gillmor), 'Erik Satie: A Conversation', *Contact*, 25 (Autumn 1982): 21–6, at 25.

dangerous areas through which he walked',[37] suggesting that the 76 beats per minute pulse of *Parade* (1917) echoes Satie's walking speed. It is plausible that this may be a two-way process, as the gait and actual walking speed of the composer at work is adjusted in correspondence with the allure and tempo of the music that is being unfolded and reworked as a mental walk through.

Satie's *Vexations* (c.1893) – a short ostensibly simple homophonic work scored for piano, yet containing beguiling harmony, to be repeated 840 times with the tempo marking of *Trés lent*[38] – is a pre-Arcuil work, yet it demonstrates his predisposition to repetition and simplicity over long durations (that is, scale[39]). The effect of *Vexations* on the listener is similar to going on a long walk through homogenous topography. The scenery remains pretty much the same, but the light changes with the passing of the day through which we encounter intermittent showers (Satie was known for walking in all weathers). When John Cage mounted a performance (reputedly the first) in 1963 in New York with a relay team featuring luminaries from the New York scene, the total duration was 18 hours and 40 minutes. Cage noted an ambient quality of the work that acknowledges the here and now, enabling us (and with Robert Rauschenberg's canvases in mind) 'to see such things as dust or shadows. Whereas, if we had the shadows carefully painted, as in Rembrandt, any other shadow entering the situation would be a disturbance and would not be noticeable, or if noticeable, a disturbance.'[40]

Moreover, as with the long trek simile, as one would expect, during a performance of *Vexations* concentration drifts, fatigue and hunger take precedence, long forgotten memories are recalled, and like the ailing Mahler you are brought to mind of your own physicality through discomfort. If you are in a group this shared discomfort can lead to a welcome solidarity. Cage and the other performers and members of the audience of the 1963 performance were struck at how they were transformed by the performance, during and even more profoundly, by the morning after:

> What happened was that we were very tired, naturally, after that length of time and I drove back to Stony Point … – and I slept I think for, not 18 hours and 40 minutes, but I slept for, say 10 hours and 15 minutes. I slept an unusually long period of time, and when I woke up, I felt different than I had ever felt before. And furthermore, the environment that I looked out upon looked unfamiliar even though I had been living there. In other words, I had changed and the world had changed.[41]

---

37   Orledge, *Satie the Composer*, p. 18.

38   For a fuller description, see Gavin Bryars, 'Vexations and its Performers', *Contact*, 25 (Autumn 1983): 12–20.

39   'Up to one hour you think about form, but after an hour and a half it's scale. Form is easy – just the division of things into parts. But scale is another matter. You have to have control of the piece – it requires a heightened kind of concentration. Before, my pieces were like objects; now, they're like evolving things.' Feldman quoted in *Universal Edition Composer Brochure: Morton Feldman* (Wien, 1998), p. 3.

40   Cage, Gillmor and Shattuck, 'A Conversation', p. 22.

41   Ibid., p. 24.

Well into his Arcuil lifestyle, Satie even attempted to foster dispassionate meandering and chatting in the presence of a performance of his music. He tried out his *Musique d'ameublement* (1920), a forerunner of ambient music, during the intervals of a performance of music by Les Six, with the performers spread throughout the auditorium to provide a surround sound effect. Ironically, the result was that the audience stopped talking and headed back to their seats. Satie cried out at his audience to: 'Go on talking! Walk about! Don't listen!' Of course all his peroration achieved, even despite a note in the programme to 'pay no attention',[42] was in fact to draw more focus to the music, rather than less.

Thoreau

Like Satie, Henry David Thoreau (1817–62) – another marginal figure whose oeuvre was frequently referenced by Cage – took to daily saunters.[43] During two years and two months he lived hermit-like in Walden Pond in Concord, Massachusetts, on land owned by Emerson, daily traversing the territory. He wrote up this experience and musings back in 'civilized life'[44] resulting in *Walden* (first published 1854). But unlike Ken Russell's portrayal of Mahler, Thoreau indicates that during his sojourn he did not assume an antagonistic relationship with the environment, quite the contrary:

> *My vicinity affords many good walks; and though for so many years I have walked almost everyday and sometimes for several days together, I have not yet exhausted them. An absolutely new prospect is a great happiness, and I can still get this any afternoon. Two or three hours walking will carry me to as strange a country as I ever expect to see ... There is in fact a sort of harmony discoverable between the capabilities of the landscape, and the threescore years and ten of human life. It will never become quite familiar to you.*[45]

Thoreau composed and recomposed his walks within a defined territory, proclaiming that combinatory variation could not be exhausted within the span of a lifetime.[46] This approach corresponds with one of Jean-François Augoyard's characterizations of walking practices (expounded in *Step by Step: Everyday Walks in*

---

42   Darius Milhaud, quoted in Robert Orledge, *Satie Remembered* (London, 1995), p. 154.

43   Thoreau's preferred term (Henry David Thoreau, *Walking* (1861), in Jeffrey Kastner and Brian Wallis (eds), *Land and Environmental Art* (London, 1998), p. 235.)

44   Henry David Thoreau, *Walden* (Oxford, 1924), p. 1.

45   Thoreau, *Walking* (1862), available at http://thoreau.eserver.org/walking2.html (accessed 28 August 2008).

46   'The length of his walk uniformly made the length of his writing. If shut up in the house, he did not write at all.' Ralph Waldo Emerson, *Thoreau*, in Joel Myerson (ed.), *Emerson and Thoreau* (Cambridge, 1992), p. 422.

a French Urban Housing Project, first published in 1979) as analogous to the rhetorical figure[47] of the *metabole*: 'A bound spatial set is walked at one's pleasure, according to combinations whose variety seems endless … Metabole is always carried out in one's walks with a poetic, ironic, or playful tone. The space walked is always valued for itself.'[48]

Notwithstanding this creative cartographic spatial practice, Cage was impressed with this attitude of perpetually renewed interest within a limited territory and topography,[49] yet resulting in fresh perception and affect, noting that 'Many people taking such a walk would have their heads so full of other ideas that it would be a long time before they were capable of hearing or seeing. Most people are blinded by themselves.'[50]

It is worthy of note that in antipathy to Cage's professed stance, Thoreau aligned himself with the romantic ecology canon,[51] bound up in a heroic quest – seduced by

47   Augoyard's concept of relating walking to rhetorical figures was picked up by Michel de Certaeau in *The Practice of Everyday Life* (first published in 1980). On surveying Manhattan from the 110th floor of the World Trade Center, de Certeau is ordained with the 'voluptuous pleasure in "seeing it all"': 'It allows one to read it, to be a solar Eye, looking down like a god. The exaltation of a scopic and gnostic drive' (Michel de Certeau, *The Practice of Everyday Life* (Berkeley, 1988), p. 92). On his return to ground level to continue his analysis of the spatial practice, in order to get beyond 'graphic representations alone', de Certeau, displaying his semiotic proclivities, comparing 'pedestrian processes to linguistic formations' (ibid., p. 103):

    The act of walking is to the urban system what the speech act is to language or to the statement uttered … it is a process of *appropriation* of the topographical system on the part of the pedestrian (just as the speaker appropriates and takes on the language); it is a spatial-acting out of the place (just as the speech act is an acoustic acting-out of language); and it implies *relations* among differentiated positions, that is, among pragmatic 'contracts' in the form of movements (just as verbal enunciation is an 'allocution,' 'posits another opposite' the speaker puts contracts between interlocutors into action). (ibid., pp. 97–8)

    Despite employing the metaphor of *rhetorics* and the tantalizing wide ambit in *The Practice of Everyday Life*, disappointingly de Certeau defers to a more literary *scoping* of the city.

48   Jean Francois Augoyard, *Step by Step: Everyday Walks in a French Urban Housing Project* (Minneapolis, 2007), p. 52.

49   Cage finds a similar manner of recomposition in his perception of the canvases of Rauschenberg that Thoreau found in Walden Pond: 'Over and over again I've found it impossible to memorize Rauschenberg's paintings. I keep asking, "Have you changed it?" and then noticing while I'm looking it changes.' John Cage, *Silence: Lectures & Writings* (London, 1978), p. 102.

50   Interviews with Lisa Low (1985), quoted in Richard Kostelanetz, *Conversing with Cage* (London, 1989), p. 45.

51   'Most of the experiences he describes in Walden are defined by literary and philosophical allusion in a sort of freefloating Platonic realm of traditional ideas' (Louise Westling, 'Thoreau's Ambivalence Toward Mother Nature' (1992), in Laurence Coupe (ed.), *The Green Studies Reader: From Romanticism to Ecocriticism* (London, 2000), p. 265).

overloaded hyperbole:[52] 'for every walk is a sort of crusade'[53] – for transcendental spiritual reality accessed through the perception of the wildness of nature:

> *all good things are wild and free. There is something in a strain of music, whether produced by an instrument or by a human voice – take the sound of a bugle in a summer night, for instance – which by its wildness ... reminds me of the cries emitted by wild beasts in their native forests.*[54]

Hence, Thoreau's avowal: by adopting a greater sympathetic 'free' and 'wild' disposition and lifestyle in alignment with the *natural world*, we can begin to approach those 'good things'.

Walking *Zazen*

Cage was renowned for his eclectic transcultural accrual and concatenation of ideas developed throughout a lifetime, providing a coherent patchwork of compositional procedures. But it has been noted that where he was open to verbalized ideas, he was less interested in related 'bodily practices'.[55] For example, despite profuse recourse to the writings of the Japanese Zen master Dr D.T. Suzuki, to such an extent that his name became synonymous with Zen, Cage did not practice *zazen* per se. Consequently, it would be more precise to say that Cage's attitude was tangential to Zen, as Suzuki clarifies:

> *Personal experience is strongly set against authority and objective revelation, and as the most practical method of attaining spiritual enlightenment the followers of Zen propose the practice of Dhyana, known as zazen [that is, to sit in mediation].*[56]

In Zen mediation, walking *zazen* is customarily used as physical respite between sittings, nevertheless the practitioner attempts to maintain the same quality of focus whilst walking very slowly, step by step around the room in a group. The Vietnamese Zen Buddhist monk Thich Nhat Hanh has led a number of silent Peace Walks in Los Angeles (2005 and 2007) with groups of about 3,000, practising what he calls mindfulness (a popular metaphor for Zen). This is a sharp contrast to the customary barrage of noise that normally accompanies public protests. Beyond the

---

52 'The writing of one's steps produces at the same time a reading that magnifies the site' (Augoyard, *Step by Step*, p. 57).
53 Thoreau, *Walking*.
54 Thoreau, *Writing the Wilderness* (1862), quoted in Coupe, *Green Studies Reader*, p. 24.
55 Douglas Kahn, 'John Cage: Silence and Silencing', *The Musical Quarterly*, 81/4 (Winter, 1997): 556–98, at 566.
56 Daisetz Teitaro Suzuki, *An Introduction to Zen Buddhism* (London, 1991), p. 34.

spiritual goal – 'when we practice walking meditation beautifully, we massage the Earth with our feet and plant seeds of joy and happiness with each step'[57] – the spectacle of thousands of people walking slowly and 'mindfully' in silence is a powerful political act. Regardless of its outward manifestation such practice is at heart centripetal.

Walking *zazen* has found its way into experimental music via a Deep Listening exercise[58] harnessed by electronic music pioneer Pauline Oliveros. Oliveros's instructions are similar to the Zen practice, however, as the title, *Extreme Slow Walk*, suggests, it has a kind of Bhutto-like task-based orientation, where the brief focuses the practitioner on one's bodily awareness aided by the challenge: 'you can always go slower'.[59] Whilst walking *zazen* does not encourage inference of external stimulus, which can cause a distraction from the exercise in hand (that is, mindfulness), one practitioner has recounted how the experience of the *Extreme Slow Walk* led him to a greater aural awareness of the prevailing landscape:

> *the creaking wood floor beneath my feet, the shuffle of socks against the lacquer, and the swish of jean fabric against itself … All of these auditory elements combined to play as a sort of soundtrack to the act of walking, which was transformed into an art.*[60]

Cage the Forager

Cage was known for rambling in the countryside during his free time. In August 1954 Cage moved from the relative privacy of downtown New York into a communal living farmhouse for artists, in rural Stony Point, New York State, up the Hudson River, set up by friends from Black Mountain College, 'living in the attic with a wasps' nest for company'.[61] Ironically, despite eschewing the buzz of New York, Cage did not take to the crowed living space. Long walks in the neighbouring woods offered him the mental space he strived for. It was here that his knowledge of mushrooms became encyclopaedic, an interest that had gown out of sheer necessity for nutrition in 1934 during the Great Depression.[62] After his time at Stony Point, walking continued to be a means of hedonic foraging for mushrooms, something that he made time for in his itinerant lifestyle around the

---

57 Thich Nhat Hanh, flyer for a Peace Walk, 2007, http://www.zcla.org/, (accessed 2008).
58 'These exercises are intended to calm the mind and bring awareness to the body and its energy circulation, and to promote the appropriate attitude for extending receptivity to the entire space/time continuum of sound' (Pauline Oliveros, *Deep Listening: A Composer's Sound Practice* (Lincoln, Nebr., 2005), p. 1).
59 Ibid., p. 20.
60 Andrew Taber, quoted in Oliveros, *Deep Listening*, p. 60.
61 David Revill, *The Roaring Silence: John Cage: A Life* (London, 1992), p. 180.
62 Ibid., p. 43.

globe, which was aside to his artistic practice and thought:[63] 'I was involved with chance operations in music, and thought it would just be a very good thing if I get involved in something where I couldn't take chances.'[64]

By the time Cage arrived at Stony Point he had already instigated a paradigm shift in the prevailing music culture – that has certainly helped engender soundwalking as a valid offshoot of experimental music – exemplified in the *untitled event* in Black Mountain College and his 'silent work' 4'33", both presented in the summer of 1952.

untitled event

Although accounts differ concerning the duration and even the date of the *untitled event*, which used the unconventional venue of the dining hall at Black Mountain, we do have a vague sense of the scenario, thanks to William Fetterman's collation of first-hand accounts:[65] simultaneous and staggered performances which individually did not intentionally support any other element. The elements included Cage, M.C. Richards and Charles Olson reciting text up ladders, David Tudor playing Cage's *Water Music* (1952), Robert Rauschenberg playing Edith Piaf records, Rauschenberg and Franz Kline paintings suspended around the room, Merce Cunningham (who was chased by a dog at one point) and other dancers moving around the audience, projection of films and slides, and so on.[66] Cage provided time brackets so performers had a sense of when to start and stop performing, and there was a plan charting out where performers were to be positioned. So duration and approximate location was a given, but it seems that everyone had freedom as to what to present. The audience was seated in a configuration of four triangles forming a square, with space for performers to move between the triangles, and space in the middle suggesting a theatre in the round. The perimeter of the dining room was the spatial frame for the performance.[67]

Of relevance to soundwalking in *untitled event*, the customary focal point of a concert experience is exploded. There is no dedicated front or back orientation for the audience: foreground or background. And it called for a juxtaposition and superimposition of many different media and genre. As a result performance spills into the everyday, as it is unclear what is inside or outside of the performance, the perimeter of the room defining the limits of the performance space. And akin to the everyday soundscape, phenomena collide, coalesce and bifurcate in a haphazard manner regardless of intention.

---

63 Although he did say that 'mushrooms allowed me to understand Suzuki' (John Cage, *For the Birds* (London, 1995), p. 188).
64 Yale School of Architecture (1965), quoted in Kostelanetz, *Conversing with Cage*, p. 15.
65 William Fetterman, *John Cage's Theatre Pieces: Notations and Performances* (Amsterdam, 1996).
66 For a collation of accounts of *untitled event*, see ibid., ch. 5, pp. 97–104.
67 Ibid.

This event helped spur Cage's interest in theatrical works, including the humorous *Music Walk* (1958) and *Water Walk* (1959). Although walking was a minor feature of *Water Walk*, it was manifest as an integral element in *Music Walk*. In a version done with Jill Johnston in New York in 1962 (*Music Walk with Dancer*), among other elements, Philip Corner, interviewed in 1989, still had a clear impression of the quality of movement:

> *There was a lot of movement. I remember this being very lively. David Tudor and John Cage had to get up and go to other places to do things, and turn on things and do other things, so there was that whole theatrical aspect, the conjunctions in space. The movement from one point to another was very much a fast movement. Efficient. No hesitancy. It wasn't a slow drag by any means, but I wouldn't say it was hectic – it seemed like it was totally under control. They gave themselves enough time to get wherever they were going.*[68]

And in the *Musicircus* (the first version done in 1967) events – 'a multi-media event of simultaneous and independent performances, often presented in non-traditional performance spaces, with a large number of participants, and lasting for several hours'[69] – it is the audience who are required to manoeuvre, and through their multiple locomotion and trajectories the work is given form.[70]

As well as the many different circumstances and combinations of *Musicircus* that have been performed even after Cage's death, the method of the mobile audience has led to open air works such as *Fifty-Eight* (1992) for Landhaushof (mansion courthouse) in Graz, where 58 musicians are placed in the 58 arches of the courtyard, generating a 58-point source polyphony. A work with a similar homogenous, albeit more continuous texture is James Tenney's *in a large open Space* (1994) for variable orchestra (12 or more players), where he invites the audience to physically move through the harmonic series (based on a double bass F) spread throughout the site and maintained by the performers who are assigned a harmonic, for an indefinite duration: an otherwise static sonic field is made fluid through movement. Unlike the more hectic *Music Walk*, in the *Musicircus* approach the audience tends to move slowly, with generous lingering.

---

68   Philip Corner, quoted in Fetterman, *John Cage's Theatre Pieces*, p. 58. For a collation of accounts of different performances and versions of *Music Walk*, see ibid., ch. 3, pp. 47–59.

69   Ibid., p. 125.

70   Umberto Eco had already noted this trend from a European perspective in 1962. 'Contemporary poetics proposes a whole gamut of forms – ranging from structures that move to the structures within which we move – that call for changing perspectives and multiple interpretations.' Umberto Eco, *The Open Work*, trans. Anna Cancogni (London, 1989), p. 24.

4'33"

This problematizing of intention and focus of the concert hall performance is taken to polar extremes in *4'33"*.[71] David Tudor, who gave the first performance of *4'33"* in Woodstock, New York in 1952, recounted that 'There was a tin roof and it rained during the second movement – not during the first or third.'[72] Although the rain was not notated, what is groundbreaking here is that the sporadic sound of the rain did not contaminate the work; rather it was as valid an element as any other sonorous occurrence within the time brackets of the three movements: 'Those [sounds] that are not notated appear in the written music as silences, opening the doors of the music to the sounds that happen to be in the environment.'[73]

In his collection of short anecdotes and aphorisms to be retold as an accompaniment to Merce Cunningham's dance *How to Pass, Kick, Fall and Run* (1965), Cage retells the story of a piano performance by Christian Wolff which includes chunks of silence in the score. The performance took place whilst the windows happened to be open, consequently the sounds of 'traffic, boat horns' spilled in the room, masking much of the piano. On being encouraged to perform the work again with the window closed this time, Wolff remarked that 'he'd be glad to, but that it wasn't really necessary, since the sounds of the environment were in no sense an interruption of the music'.[74]

With a nod to his chess teacher and first generation Dadaist Marcel Duchamp, whose notion of the *readymade*, for example *Fountain* (that is, a urinal) (1917), proposes that 'the artist cannot make, but can only take what is already there',[75] in *4'33"* Cage extends the aural frame from stage onto the extant soundscape: Nyman calls this an act of 'decentralization'.[76]

Cage had witnessed Rauschenberg's white and black canvases of 1951–52, which were ostensibly blank (in fact consisting of a layer of domestic paint), encouraging the viewer to acknowledge the dust settling on the canvas, and the glare of the gallery lighting as a here-and-now functioning of the artwork. With a similar nerve, Cage uses the concert hall context to *facilitate* a time-based listening frame out of a mute musical act (that is, *musicing*), allowing all that is listenable, audible and musical: 'I have felt and hoped to have led other people to feel that sounds of their environment constitute a music, which is more interesting than the music which they would hear if they went into a concert hall.'[77]

---

71 Much has been written on the genesis of *4'33"* founded on Cage's self-proclaimed account. For a debunking of some of the myth, see Kahn, 'John Cage', p. 566, and Dickinson's interview of Tudor in 1987 (Peter Dickinson (ed.), *Cage Talk: Dialogues with and about John Cage* (New York, 2006)).

72 Tudor, quoted in Dickinson, *Cage Talk*, p. 88.

73 Cage, *Silence: Lectures & Writings*, pp. 7–8.

74 John Cage, *A Year from Monday: Lectures & Writings* (London, 1968), p. 133.

75 Douglas Crimp, *On the Museum's Ruins* (Cambridge, Mass., 1993), p. 71.

76 Nyman, *Experimental Music*, p. 25.

77 Cage, quoted in Kostelanetz, *Conversing with Cage*, p. 65.

The phenomenologist Don Ihde, reflecting on the habitual filtering of audible information, bifurcates incoming sound as either *fringe* or *focal* phenomena; the reading of which is continually shifting due to cultural convention and contingencies of the site:

> *I go to the auditorium, and, without apparent effort, I hear the speaker while I barely notice the scuffling of feet, the coughing, the scraping noises. My tape recorder, not having the same intentionality as I, records all these auditory stimuli without distinction, and so when I return to it to hear the speech re-presented I find I cannot even hear the words due to the presence of what for me had been fringe phenomena.*[78]

Cage's 4'33" upsets the status quo of the concert hall, bringing *fringe* phenomena into the foreground, becoming *focal*. Moreover the listener is embodied in the space. Cage, however, did not limit performances of it to the concert hall. In collaboration with Nam June Paik, Cage took this work onto the streets of Manhattan. On making a film version of 4'33", they randomly selected locations to record the ambiences of Manhattan using a map and the I Ching: 'to simply hear what was there to hear'.[79] Cage also performed the work on piano in Harvard Square, Boston, in 1973.

Although much of Cage's work is positioned in the classical music context of the concert hall, James Pritchett notes that it is ultimately not a question of letting the sounds of the world in, rather, 'he opens it to let the world invite us out'.[80]

> *the music I prefer, even to my own or anybody else's, is what we are hearing if we are just quiet. And now we come back to my silent piece. I really prefer that to anything else, but I don't think of it as 'my piece'.*[81]

Thus for Cage, 4'33" is not context specific, and it does not require the ritualistic paraphernalia of *musicing* paraphernalia of concert performance: shifting it from compartmentalized composition in a concert hall into a listening attitude emplaced in the everyday. It is apposite to compare this approach to Westerkamp's definition of soundwalking. Both maintain an attention to listening to the environment whatever the context, however underpinning Cage's stance is the oft-quoted mantra: 'New music: new listening. Not an attempt to understand something that is being said, for if something were being said, the sounds would be given the shape of words. Just attention to the activity of sounds.'[82]

In his critique and demystification of the genesis of 4'33", Douglas Kahn articulates the limitation of this attitude: '[Cage] did not incorporate the social, or

---

78   Don Ihde, *Listening and Voice: A Phenomenology of Sound* (Athens, OH, 1976), p. 74.

79   John Cage, from CD Booklet for *Roaratorio*, Wergo WER 6303-2 (1994), p. 14.

80   James Pritchett,, *"Something like a hidden glimmering": John Cage and Recorded Sound*, www.rosewhitemusic.com/cage/texts/glimmering.pdf (accessed 28 August 2008).

81   Cage, quoted in Kahn, 'John Cage', p. 561.

82   Cage, Silence: Lectures & Writings, p. 10.

the ecological for that matter, into the immediate materiality of sounds, but only simulated their compass and complexity through undifferentiated totalization.'[83]

It is in the artists working in the aftermath of 4'33",[84] in particular the Neo-Dadaist and Fluxus artists, that we find an acknowledgement and for some an embracement of the social and/or ecological, resulting in a plethora of walking-based activities.

Fluxus Walks

Paradoxically it was Cage's own students in his Experimental Music Composition class at the New School for Social Research in Manhattan (where he taught from 1956 to 1960) who resolutely reintegrated the social, although refracted through Cagean precepts of chance and indeterminacy. The class included George Brecht, Al Hansen, Dick Higgins, Allan Kaprow and Jackson MacLow, a veritable role call of the first generation American Fluxus movement.

Brecht, like the rest of this group, was not content with framing his work within the rubric of music, rather he adopted the notion of 'an expanded universe of events'[85] where 'each event comprises all occurrences within its duration',[86] yet within an event, 'sound is deemed incidental'.[87] He adopted the notational device of the 'event score': pithy, haiku-like performance instructions printed on cards, a technique that became a pervasive device for Fluxus art.

For example, in *Water Yam* (a collection of event scores on cards that he worked on between 1959 and 1963), on a card titled *Air Conditioning* the instructions are 'move through the place'. There is a parsimony in the delivery of the instruction, and a simplicity in carrying it out, albeit open to interpretation and influence by contingencies of the site, resulting in an ephemeral act that anyone can perform, demonstrating an everyday orientation: suggesting there is no boundary between art and life.[88]

---

83   Kahn, p. 589
84   'Every young artist tried to define himself/herself as going past Cage but this was very difficult because the Cagean revolution was very thorough' (James Tenney, quoted in Douglas Kahn, *Noise, Water, Meat: A History of Sound in the Arts* (Cambridge, Mass., 1999) p. 225.
85   Ina Blom, 'Boredom and Oblivion', in Ken Friedman (ed.), *The Fluxus Reader* (New York, 1998), p. 68.
86   Liz Kotz, 'Post-Cagean Aesthetics and the "Event" Score', *October*, 95 (Winter 2001): 55–89, at 75.
87   Anna Dezeuze, 'Brecht for Beginners', *Papers of Surrealism*, Issue 4 (Winter 2005), available at www.surrealismcentre.ac.uk/papersofsurrealism/journal4/acrobat%20files/dezeuzepdf.pdf (accessed 2008): 2.
88   Friedman, *Fluxus Reader*, p. 247. Brecht's attitude to music is laid bare with a jibe at Cage in his *Virtuoso Listener*, with the instructions 'can hear music at any time' (Jill Johnston, 'George Brecht, the Philosopher of Fluxus', *The Johnston Letter*, 2/7 (2007), http://www.danceinsider.com/jill_johnston/j041907.html (accessed 2007)).

Intentionally performing everyday life is bound to create some curious kind of awareness. Life's subject matter is almost too familiar to grasp, and life's formats (if they can be called that) are not familiar enough.[89]

There are many text scores that ask for some kind of ambulatory activity, most famously La Monte Young's *Composition 1960 No. 10*, a performance score consisting of the instruction, 'draw a straight line and follow it', Takehisa Kosugi's *Theatre Music* (date unknown) with the instruction, 'keep walking intently' and Dick Higgins' *Gángsáng: For Ben Patterson* (1963):

One foot forward. Transfer weight to this foot.
Bring other foot forward. Transfer weight to this foot.
Repeat as often as desired.
Stockholm, February 27, 1963[90]

Clearly these works are open to interpretation, which could quite easily take on a metaphorical reading. Characteristically, Yoko Ono's *Walk Piece* (1964) takes on a wholly conceptual/poetic mode:

Stir inside of your brains with a penis until things are mixed well. Take a walk.[91]

Other Fluxus works that are walking based include Alison Knowles – *Shuffle* (1961), Ben Vautier – *Run* (1963), Milan Knizak – *Walking Event* (1965), Bengt af Klintberg – *Forest Event Number 6* (1966), Wolf Vostell – *Circle II* (1966).[92]

In *Tour* (New York, 1963), by double bass player Ben Patterson (despite being an American he emerged out of the Cologne Fluxus scene working with George Maciunas), interpersonal relationships and one's extra-visual spatial awareness of the everyday are explored. Participants are blindfolded and led through an environment by a guide. The guide chooses the route, leading the participant for over 45 minutes.[93] Patterson has continued his interest in site, in *The Liverpool Song-Lines* (2002): shifting the concept of the Australian Aborigine song-line to Liverpool, he provides an aural map, guiding the listener though the city using the names of public houses and places of worship as signposts.

---

89   Allan Kaprow, *Essays on the Blurring of Art and Life* (Berkeley, 2003), p. 187.
90   Geoffrey Hendricks, *Critical Mass: Happenings, Fluxus, Performance, Intermedia, and Rutgers University, 1958–1972* (Piscatawy, NJ, 2003), p. 11.
91   Edward Strickland, *Minimalism: Origins* (Indiana University Press, 2000) p. 141.
92   The text-based score of these and other performance scores can be found at Fluxus Performance Workbook (Ken Friedman, Owen Smith and Lauren Sawchyn, *Fluxus Performance Workbook*, supplement to *Performance Research*, 7/3, 'On Fluxus' (2002), available at http://www.thing.net/~grist/ld/fluxus.htm (accessed 2008).
93   Achille Bonito Oliva (ed.), *Ubi fluxus ibi motus 1990–1962* (Milan, 1990), p. 241.

Judson Dance Theater

Concurrently with the flourishing of Fluxus and in the light of minimal sculpture by such artists as Carl Andre, Dan Flavin and Donald Judd, the dance world was rebelling against the erstwhile obligatory dance training and deference to the balletic canon, with a refocusing towards the abstraction of pedestrian movement. This was most pronounced in the work of Yvonne Rainer and Steve Paxton of the Judson Dance Theater, based in Judson Memorial Church, New York, which was directed by Merce Cunningham colleague and Cage student Robert Dunn.

For example, in striving to eradicate dance's predilection for phrasing, development and climax, variation, character, performance, the virtuosic feet and the fully extended body,[94] in *Trio A* from *the Mind is a Muscle* (1966), Rainer substitutes these aspects for a minimal aesthetic founded on 'found' movement, task like activity, singular action, engendering a neutral state of performance.[95] 'Emptied of all ambiguity, of any traditional dramatic content or climax, Rainer's work leaves movement itself, as it were, walking on its own feet.'[96] In fact, a faithful presentation of *Trio A* demands a new kind of virtuosic, yet pedestrian, discipline.

Bruce Nauman's Studio Walks

Bruce Nauman's starting point for his studio films was the context of the artist's studio and reflection on the kind of mundane activity that goes on there. He found that he paced around a lot (in a peripatetic manner) while he worked, and that developed into an interest 'in the sound of pacing and just the activity of pacing'.[97] He consequently started to film himself pacing around his studio and with the advice of Meredith Monk (another Judson Dance Theater associate), validated by knowledge of Cage and Merce Cunningham's[98] outlook and harking back to Eadweard Muybridge's staggered motion picture capture from the late nineteenth century (whose studies, as well as equestrian subjects included the human figure in

---

94 Yvonne Rainer, 'A Quasi Survey of Some "Minimalist" Tendencies in the Quantitatively Minimal Dance Activity Midst the Plethora, or an Analysis of Trio A', in Mike Huxley and Noel Witts (eds), *The Twentieth-Century Performance Reader* (London, 2002), pp. 327–34, at pp. 328–9.

95 Ibid., p. 329.

96 Suzi Gabilk, 'Minimalism', in Nikos Stangos (ed.), *Concepts of Modern Art* (London, 1991), pp. 244–55, at p. 253.

97 Janet Kraynak (ed.), *Please Pay Attention?: Bruce Nauman's Words: Writings and Interviews* (Cambridge, Mass., 2002), p. 166.

98 Cunningham had already worked with non-dancers in 1952 at Brandeis University. The students were asked to do 'simple gestures they did ordinarily … these were accepted as movement in daily life, why not on stage?' (from *Merce Cunningham's Changes: Notes on Choreography* (New York, 1968), quoted in Coosje van Bruggen, *Bruce Nauman* (New York, 1988), p. 230.

motion), he elaborated the process via a range of strategies. The result was a series of dance/movement exercise-based films, enacted by himself, with the camera in a fixed position taken in one unedited take. These included *Playing a Note on the Violin while I Walk around the Studio* (1968), *Dance Exercise on the Perimeter of a Square* (1968),[99] *Slow Angle Walk* (aka *Beckett Walk*) (1968) and the silent film *Walking in an Exaggerated Manner around the Perimeter of a Square* (1968).

In *Slow Angle Walk* (aka *Beckett Walk*) (1968) we literally get documentation of a soundwalk, an 'apparently real-time record of human activity'.[100] We hear amplified footsteps, which act as percussive punctuation of the step, as Nauman abstracts an awkward clownish gait of 'stiffened legs without bending a knee or stopping',[101] the movement, an amalgamation and variation on the protagonists' gaits from Beckett's *Molly* and *Watt*.[102] Even when Nauman stumbles out of shot the resonant footsteps continue.[103] The step sound is varied by a 'scraping sound caused when he makes the turn from one end of the studio to go back to the other'.[104] The duration (60 minutes) is defined by the amount of time it takes for Nauman to complete all the possible variations of the rules that he set in the task. Again, after Satie and Thoreau we have 'the possibility of variation within repetition and the effect of boredom,'[105] and another example of Augoyard's *metabole* in action.

Scratch Orchestra and Walking

In England between 1969 and 1972 we find a thriving of experimental activities that interfaced with the everyday, spearheaded by the collective Scratch Orchestra of Cornelius Cardew (who had performed *Music Walk* with Cage and Tudor in 1958). The group was influenced by the New York School and Fluxus events going on in America and continental Europe, and stimulated by George Brecht's move to England in 1968. Michael Parsons writes that their 'more collective approach to performance reflected its loose and informal sociability, which was based on mutual respect and tolerance rather than on adherence to any preconceived structure or set of rules'.[106]

---

99   Where his movements are kept in time by a metronome.
100 Ibid., p. 116.
101 Bruce Nauman, *Image/Text 1966–1996* (Wolfsburg, 1997), p. 69.
102 Steven Connor, 'Shifting Ground', http://www.bbk.ac.uk/english/skc/beckettnauman/ (accessed 2008). This is the English version of an essay published in German as 'Auf schwankendem Boden', in the catalogue of the exhibition *Samuel Beckett, Bruce Nauman* (Vienna, 2000), pp. 80–87.
103 Similarly, in *Playing a Note on the Violin while I Walk around the Studio*, where Nauman played, 'two notes [on a violin, an instrument that he was not adept at playing] very close together so that you could hear the beats in the harmonics' (van Bruggen, *Bruce Nauman*, p. 230), when he walks out of shot the double stopping continues.
104 Ibid., p. 115.
105 Shattuck, quoted in Cage, Gillmor and Shattuck, 'A Conversation', p. 25.
106 Michael Parsons, 'The Scratch Orchestra and Visual Arts', *Leonardo Music Journal*, 11

Shunning the concert hall, their chosen performance platform included shopping centres, the underground and isolated coastal areas.[107] Among their vast collection of graphic notions and event scores in *Scratch Music*[108] are a number of walking pieces, including *Parsons' Walk* (1969), for any number of people walking in a large public space. In keeping with the Scratch Orchestra's proclivities, the work was performed in Euston Station, London. Parson recounts:

> *this involved walkers individually criss-crossing the space at different randomly determined speeds, waiting for different lengths of time at chosen points and then setting off in another direction. At Euston this naturally intersected with the activities of bona fide travelers as they hurried or waited for their trains.*[109]

In contrast to Rainer's minimalist aesthetic and Nauman's endurance and discipline, the Scratch Orchestra made different versions of *Walk* inviting participants to select from a repertoire of walks, including walking backwards and imitating the iconic John Cleese silly walk (of *Monty Python's Flying Circus*, first aired in 1970).

This English eccentricity also surfaces in the *Sounds Heard* projects (1976–77), by experimental composer and instrument builder Hugh Davies, who encourages creative listening in different environmental contexts. *At Home* (1978) calls for a home-made sheepdog on wheels which is taken on a walk.[110] Nevertheless the eloquence of this Scratch Music text score, speaks for itself.

> *Walk music.*
> *Movement music.*
> *Stop – watch – listen.*
> *Continue.*[111]

(2001): 5–11, at 7.

107 Ibid.

108 Cornelius Cardew (ed.), *Scratch Music* (London, 1972).

109 Parsons, 'Scratch Orchestra', p. 8. We find a contemporary take on the blurring between participants and the general public in the Noise Memory Gesture project. From March to May 2007 a number of flashmob silences instigated by Ross Brown were convened around London. Participants were invited to attend a given space at a given time to memorialize something. The exact nature of that something was not clear: The idea was that the stories were to be found within the prevailing soundscape.

110 Hugh Davies, *Sounds Heard* (Chelmsford, 2002), p. 48.

111 Cardew, *Scratch Music*.

Field Trips and Lecture Demonstrations: Beyond 4'33"

Returning to listening and walking, in 1966 Cage associates and regular performers of his music Philip Corner and Max Neuhaus separately developed aural excursions through the everyday as a logical next step to or perhaps, as in the words of Corner, 'the ultimate consequence'[112] of 4'33" *et al.*.

Corner

In the summer of 1966, Philip Corner, Fluxus artist, resident composer and musician to the Judson Dance Theatre (1962–64) and co-founder of the Tone Roads Ensemble (1963–70) – which was an 'important force behind the Charles Ives renaissance, and also gave influential performances of works by Cage, Feldman, Ruggles and others'[113] at the New School for Social Research – started to take people on walks 'around the block' in New York (documented in his note book/stream of consciousness style publication, *I Can Walk Through the World as Music (first walk)*, 1980). His instructions were again simple: 'Just listen to sounds as given as if at a concert (with that attention)'.[114]

In a frenzied mind map, Corner puts Cage's maxim to task, scribbling 'what kind of "just listening?"' and in reference to his own practice: 'Why didn't Cage (John) go this far?'[115] He poetically sets the scene:

> *That morning I decided no museums no other art, but belief in This reality*
> *To act it and spend a day within That other place where everything from This*
> *one Time To pure meaning. Oh! – it became three weeks long of it.*[116]

For Corner, attentive listening to the everyday has continued to be a central activity, and fed into subsequent projects. For example, in 1995 he led a 'listening walk' at a fabric factory, Lanificio Bonotto in Italy, an event, which he recorded, where 'the regular workers were the conductors of that music made by the machines … each part of the mill with its own sound; all in rhythmic counterpoint.'[117] On the CD release of the recording he identifies the work as 'pieces of (acoustic) reality and ideality'.[118]

---

112 Philip Corner, *I Can Walk Through the World as Music (first walk)* (New York, 1980), p. 7.
113 Larry Polansky, 'Philip Corner', Grove Music Online, http://www.oxfordmusiconline. com/public/ (accessed 2008).
114 Corner, *I can Walk*, p. 7.
115 Ibid.
116 Ibid.
117 Philip Corner, http://www.mimaroglumusicsales.com/artists/philip+corner.html (accessed 28 August 2008).
118 Philip Corner, *Pieces of (Acoustic) Reality and Ideality*, Alga Marghen, C 2NMN.013 (1997).

LISTEN: A Demonstration in Situ

Also in New York in 1966, the percussionist Max Neuhaus began to organize listening excursions in New York. Neuhaus had made his name interpreting works of avant-garde composers such as Stockhausen and Cage, and his distinctive harnessing of acoustic feedback in performance. Through his role as performer he had witnessed the opening up of everyday sounds into the concert hall:

> I saw these activities as a way of giving aesthetic credence to these sounds – something I was all for. I began to question the effectiveness of the method, though. Most members of the audience seemed more impressed with the scandal of 'ordinary' sounds placed in a 'sacred' place than with the sounds themselves, and few were able to carry the experience over to a new perspective on the sounds of their daily lives.[119]

In a sense the notoriety of 4'33" within the context of the classical music canon had hijacked its simple message and, unlike the rain, had contaminated the work. His answer was, instead of bringing sounds in, to take people out.[120] In this regard, in 1966 Neuhaus organized an event for a small group of invited friends. At the initial rendezvous, with a rubber stamp he branded the hand of each member of the group with the imperative 'LISTEN', and led them down West 14th Street in Manhattan towards his studio in lower East Side, where he concluded with a performance of some percussion works. These were the first tentative steps towards a series of extra-concert hall excursions which he explored for the next ten years, where listeners went on 'Field Trips Thru Sound Environments'. In future excursions-cum-'lecture demonstrations' he excluded his own musical interventions, content with the sound environment as found to do the talking/sounding. Starting from the mundane, locations became more elaborate, including trips to industrial locations normally inaccessible, such as the Consolidated Edison Power Station, Hudson Tubes (subway) and the New Jersey Power and Light Power Plant. Rather than the concert performance and composition status that 4'33" maintains, it is interesting to note the deference of the 'field-trip' mode of presentation billed as 'Lecture Demonstrations' – Neuhaus regarding the rubberstamp as 'the lecture and the walk the demonstration'.[121]

Bearing the mark of 'LISTEN' bore multiple functionality for the audience: as mnemonic (in case one forgot to listen), as score and as concrete poem: 'The simple clear meaning of the word, to pay attention aurally, and its clean visual shape – LISTEN – when capitalized.'[122] Its simplicity, in tandem with the quality of

---

119 Max Neuhaus, 'Walks', *Max Neuhaus*, http://www.max-neuhaus.info/soundworks/vectors/walks/ (accessed 2008).

120 Max Neuhaus, *Max Neuhaus: Inscription, Sound Works Volume 1* (Ostfildern, 1994), p. 130.

121 Neuhaus , 'Walks'.

122 Ibid.

the environments that were traversed, also provoked one to reflect on what it is to listen, and hence helped foster a refocusing of 'people's aural perspective'[123] – the hitherto untapped aspiration of *4'33"*.

As a follow-up, Neuhaus created a series of LISTEN branded works including postcards and posters: most famously superimposed on Brooklyn Bridge – South Street (1976). This was not the first time that 'LISTEN' had function as a score. In 1960, Dennis Johnson reduced non-intentional music as a Fluxus event score with the single word 'LISTEN'. He proclaimed to La Monte Young that with this one word he had produced a work that 'was entirely indeterminate and left the composer out of it'.[124]

Cage's Demonstration of the Sounds of the Environment

Not to be left out, responding to an invitation to do a guest lecture, in the Fall of 1971, Cage adopted a similar lecture/demonstration approach to Neuhaus and Corner, that he titled *Demonstration of the Sounds of the Environment* (which was also considered a *Musicircus* as the audience members were the performers, structuring the work though their own movement and perception, albeit following each other in a single file for 90 minutes through the campus). In an interview with Joan Retallack, Cage responded to the notion of soundwalking:

> *I think that was done at Oh, I haven't done it as a composition, so to speak, but I've done it. At the University of Wisconsin, I think Milwaukee rather than in Madison, I gave what was called a 'demonstration of sounds' in which we set out from the hall where we had met to make a chance-determined [using the I Ching] walk though the campus. And we were to walk silently, so that we would hear the sounds of the environment. Then came back to the hall and talked briefly about what we'd heard. I gave sort of a lecture.*[125]

It is worth noting that the group numbered approximately 300,[126] so like Thich Nhat Hanh's *Peace Walks*, it would have been an impressive sight.

---

123 Ibid.
124 La Monte Young, 'Lecture 1960', *Tulane Drama Review*, 10/2, (1965): 76–7, quoted in Branden W. Joseph, *Beyond the Dream Syndicate: Tony Conrad and the Arts After Cage* (Cambridge, Mass., 2008), p. 102.
125 Joan Retallack (ed.), *Musicage: Cage Muses on Words, Art, Music* (Hanover, NH, 1996), p. 186.
126 Revill, *Roaring Silence*, p. 166.

Acoustic Ecology

Vancouver in the late 1960s/early 1970s saw soundwalking decisively put on the map with the critical mass of the World Soundscape Project (WSP) team directed by R. Murray Schafer, based at Simon Fraser University. This group developed methods to analyse, communicate and educate people about the soundscape, inaugurating the interdiscipline of acoustic ecology. Central to the WSP endeavour is the concept of *soundscape*, articulated by WSP member and composer Barry Truax as 'An environment of sound with emphasis on the way it is perceived and understood by the individual, or by a society. It thus depends on the relationship between the individual and any such environment.'[127] Advancing the ideas of WSP, in the introduction to *The Soundscape of Modernity: Architectural Acoustics and the Culture of Listening in America, 1900–1933* (2002), Emily Thompson provides an elaboration on this definition:

> *Like a landscape, a soundscape is simultaneously a physical environment and a way of perceiving that environment; it is both a world and a culture constructed to make sense of that world ... A soundscape's cultural aspects incorporate scientific and aesthetic ways of listening, a listener's relationship to their environment, and the social circumstances that dictate who gets to hear what. A soundscape, like a landscape, ultimately has more to do with civilization than with nature, and as such, it is constantly under construction and always undergoing change.*[128]

Within the context of acoustic ecology soundwalking can simultaneously have a number of indivisible goals: pedagogical tool, qualitative fieldwork method and compositional practice. Composition was never far from the WSP concerns, which is unsurprising since Schafer, who is a seminal composer in his own right, had pulled his team from the Music faculty. In his *Handbook for Acoustic Ecology* (first published in 1978) Truax defines soundwalking as:

> *A form of active participation in the soundscape. Though the variations are many, the essential purpose of the soundwalk is to encourage the participant to listen discriminatively, and moreover, to make critical judgments about the sounds heard and their contribution to the balance or imbalance of the sonic environment.*[129]

The notion of a *balanced soundscape* is a founding tenant of acoustic ecology, with a concern for the relationship between the sounds of human society and the prevailing sonic environment. There is a clear link here with the burgeoning Green

---

127 Barry Truax, *Handbook for Acoustic Ecology* (Vancouver, 1999).
128 Emily Thompson, *The Soundscape of Modernity: Architectural Acoustics and the Culture of Listening in America, 1900–1933* (Cambridge, Mass., 2002), pp. 1–2.
129 Truax, *Handbook*.

movement of the 1970s and in particular the noise pollution agenda, however a positive stance is adopted, with a foregrounding of artist-based solutions, acknowledging that man has already been creating ideal soundscapes for the 'imagination and psychic reflection'.[130]

Schafer has differentiated between two types of soundwalking: a *listening walk* and a *soundwalk*:

- *Listening walk*: 'A listening walk is simply a walk with a concentration on listening.'[131] No talking is allowed for the duration of the walk.[132] The intention is that the collective mute experience raises the level of awareness to that of an attentive concert hall audience. It is practised in single file following a leader (a quasi-mute pied piper), leaving a wide enough gap between the participant in front so their footsteps are out of earshot. Of course if hard heels are worn and the terrain under foot is stone or concrete, then footsteps can provide a recurring motif, albeit modulated by the changing acoustics. Moreover, thanks to the proxemic gap 'a privacy for reflection is afforded'.[133]
- *Soundwalk*: 'an exploration of the soundscape of a given area using a score as a guide. This might also contain ear training exercises'[134] and sound-making tasks: 'In order to expand the listening experience, soundmaking may also become an important part of a soundwalk. Its purpose is to explore sounds that are related to the environment, and, on the other hand, to become aware of one's own sounds (voice, footsteps, etc.) in the environmental context.'[135]

Such an active role in the *soundwalk* shifts the participant from audience member to 'composer-performer'.[136]

WSP Soundwalks from the European Sound Diary

Whilst the WSP traversed Europe in a Volkswagen bus in 1975, en route to documenting the soundscape of five European villages presented in *Five Village*

---

130 Schafer, *Soundscape*, p. 4. For a full account of the underpinning concepts of acoustic ecology, see this text (first published in 1977 and republished in 1994) and Barry Truax's *Acoustic Communication* (first published in 1984 and republished in 2001).
131 Schafer, *Soundscape*, pp. 212–13.
132 I have witnessed Schafer's resistance to members of the audience recording and filming walks; by experiencing the work in an electronically mediatized route, they exclude themselves from the dedicated collective listening experience.
133 Schafer, *Soundscape*, p. 213.
134 Ibid. A series of tasks developed by Schafer to encourage focused and detailed listening to the soundscape.
135 Truax, *Handbook*.
136 Schafer, *Soundscape*, p. 213.

Soundscapes,[137] an unashamedly rural enterprise, they also visited a number of cities to undertake preparatory research. When they arrived in a new location they devised and carried out *listening walks* that consequently fed into the prescriptive mode of the *soundwalk*, that suggest modes of engagement with the environment. Some of these have been documented in the *European Sound Diary*.[138]

For example, the *Salzburg Soundwalk* calls for a level of interactive sound-making:

> *This is a soundwalk for baritone (and friend). The bells of the inner city form the framework for a walk, providing cues to move on from one place to another, on the quarter hours. A baritone voice is required in order to play with the eigentones found in the course of the walk. An eigentone is the resonant frequency of an enclosed space, and you will find it by humming continuously up and down until the one note is found which sounds louder than all the others do.*[139]

The *Paris Soundwalk*, located in the Louvre, eschews acoustic sounds, prompting the walker to 'LISTEN to these paintings? ... Let the genius of their execution speed your imaginations to provide the appropriate soundtrack.'[140]

The *London Soundwalk* asks for a contemplative overture, commencing at a Sunday morning Quaker meeting opposite Euston Station. On leaving the meeting it is expected that your 'aural facilities should [now] be well prepared',[141] challenging the walker to 'practice your aural flexibility by mentally closing out the traffic noise as you walk down the Euston Road toward [Regents] Park'.[142] Precise directions and tasks including directed listening are given (later on, some possible responses are given from their fieldwork of April 1975), for example:

> *Jets at fountain, north-central within Gardens [Queen Mary's Gardens in the centre of Regent's Park]. Consider here both kinds: water and airplanes. While considering the water jets, keep track of how many of the other kind, as well as propeller airplanes, you hear in a 10-minute period.*[143]

Continuing the theme of contrasts, the interface of the park and the street are highlighted: 'Leave the Park by the same route you came in, and note the THRESHOLD OF DISCOMFORT: the transition point where the sounds of the Park are once more buried by the sound of city traffic.'[144] This is in counterpoint to

---

137 R. Murray Schafer (ed.), *Five Village Soundscapes* (Vancouver, 1977).
138 R. Murray Schafer (ed.), *European Sound Diary* (Vancouver, 1977).
139 Ibid., p. 39.
140 Ibid., p. 86.
141 Ibid., p. 92.
142 Ibid.
143 Ibid., p. 93.
144 Ibid.

the 'THRESHOLD OF COMFORT' that the walker, it was anticipated, experienced on entering the park earlier.

Methods of soundwalking have recently been taken up as a valid *in situ* mode of participatory qualitative soundscape and environmental study, in particular this can been seen in the research of Jean-Paul Thibaud[145] and Mags Adams.[146]

Vicarious Soundwalking

Field recording offered an invaluable resource for documentation and analysis of the soundscape. In a desire to communicate their findings more widely, members of the WSP collected and edited recordings in order to create interpretative and pedagogic works for public broadcasts, resulting in the monumental ten one-hour radio series *Soundscapes of Canada* (1974). Hildegard Westerkamp continued this approach, beyond the winding down of the WSP in 1975, leading to such compositional projects as *Soundwalking* (1978–79), produced for Vancouver Co-operative Radio. She visited and explored a wide range of environments throughout Vancouver equipped with her microphone, and played back the everyday material on the radio. 'It brought community soundscape into the listeners' homes and simultaneously extended listeners' ears into the soundscape of the community.'[147] These were often presented without the obligatory voice-over, however sometimes she would provide a commentary, speaking from within the soundscape she was recording, 'forming a link between to the listener who is not physically present'.[148] Soundwalking has continued to provide a rich source of inspiration and material for soundscape/phonography-orientated composition, including work by Peter Cusack, Luc Ferrari, Sarah Peebles, Dallas Simpson and myself.

Conclusions

When I have led soundwalking (in Schafer's jargon, more correctly *listening walking*), at the end the participants are invited to verbalize what they got from the walk. I often find that initially there is a collective resistance to break the silence, not out of reticence but out of a desire to prolong the experience; once broken there is always much to share, and I am struck by the degrees to which each reading

---

145 Jean-Paul Thibaud, *La Méthode des parcours commentés*, in Michèle Grosjean and Jean-Paul Thibaud (eds) *L'espace urbain en méthodes* (Marseilles, 2001).

146 Mags Adams, 'On Soundwalking as Sensory Sociology', presented at *Beyond Text: Synaesthetic & Sensory Practices in Anthropology*, University of Manchester, 2007.

147 Hildegard Westerkamp, 'The Soundscape on Radio', in Dainer Augaitis and Dan Lander (eds) *Radio Rethink: Art, Sound and Transmission* (Banff, 1994), pp. 89–90.

148 Ibid., p. 90.

is unique and is often presented with a feeling of ownership: there is something uniquely empowering about soundwalking. Participants may have extant intimate knowledge of the sites, be that from a social, economic, ecological, political or architectural standpoint, but through such an ostensibly mundane procedure, unwittingly, new insight is acquired from a more phenomenologically situated stance: 'The feel of a place is registered in one's muscles and bones.'[149]

This approach can unconsciously engender a naivety of experience that experimental music culture has learnt to embrace, but is tacitly discounted as a valid form of research in the scientific community. Neurologist Oliver Sacks aptly writes, 'A piece of music will draw one in, teach one about its structure and secrets, whether one is listening consciously or not. Listening to music is not a passive process but intensely active, involving a stream of inferences, hypothesis, expectations, and anticipations.'[150]

Surely Sacks's evaluation of music can be applied to soundwalking as an arts practice: by providing a temporal and spatial frame for our ears to be open in the everyday, and open to the everyday, yet with a reverence of concert hall listening, knowledge, erstwhile habitually filtered out, may be unwittingly as well as consciously garnered of a soundscape's explicit and implicit structures.

In soundwalking in its many permutations, we find a social[151] art form that calls for active participation and in return offers a nuanced engagement with the everyday, where: all sounds are site-specific (autochthonous), *real time*, synchronized, diagetic[152] or (to borrow Luc Ferrari's term) *anecdotal*; fringe unspecified; and in a Cagean tradition, everyone is in the 'best seat'.[153]

---

149 Yi-Fu Tuan, *Space and Place: The Perspective of Experience* (Minneapolis, 1977), p. 184.
150 Oliver Sacks, Musicophilia: Tales of Music and the Brain (London, 2007), p. 211.
151 We walk because we are social beings, we are also social beings because we walk. Tim Ingold and Jo Lee Vergunts, (eds.) *Ways of Walking: Ethnography and Practice on Foot* (Ashgate, 2008), p. 2.
152 In film theory, diagetic refers to the 'narratively implied spatiotemporal world of the actions and characters'. Claudia Gorbman, 'Narrative Film Music', in Rick Altman (ed.), *Cinema/Sound*, Yale French Studies, No. 60, (1980): 183–203. The interesting question here, in regards to soundwalking, is implication, that is, how do we infer narrative?
153 Cage, *Silence*, p. 97.

'We have Eyes as well as Ears …': Experimental Music and the Visual Arts

David Ryan

Martin Creed conducting an 'orchestra' playing one note; Hayley Newman staging a choir that smokes cigarettes; and Anri Sala, so captivated by the detuned clash of two contrasting musical pieces on a radio, that he recreates it as a video performance in a gallery. Each of these pieces by contemporary artists not only reference sound as their basic material, but also question the social context, collective activity, and assumptions that surround the performance of those sounds. How do we differentiate these performance-based works from those of the 1960s and 1970s? And what is at stake when works become purely – or rather impurely – interdisciplinary? These are some of the questions that this chapter will raise and attempt at least some provisional answers. Needless to say, it will be necessary to view recent practices through the lens of both philosophical and historical debates in order to get some way to approaching those questions. Attempting a cross-disciplinary discussion is rife with its own problems, as in the 'and' of the title. It is one thing to put these two disciplines next to each other, but what does this 'and' signify: Cross-fertilization? Influence? Correspondence? Juxtaposition? Interpenetration? Obviously there are many different ways of reading this 'and': each will be relevant here, as will the issue of approaching a working definition of the 'experimental' common to both music and art.

A good deal of contemporary art embraces material other than the visual – sound being just one amongst many – so much so that there have been numerous cries against this turn toward the 'anti-visual' as it has been labelled.[1] Composers too have made use of collaborations with film, video, as well as performance art, sound or visual installations. Whether all this cross-disciplinary activity can still be called 'experimental' is a moot point. These 'experiments' have been with us now for half a century, and paradoxically, the 'experimental' is now a known tradition, and one

---

1   I have chosen to use 'visual art' predominantly here – which is useful when discussing different mediums; 'contemporary art' which is also used here and there, while more pliable in its denotation of media, is also perhaps too temporally restrictive.

that has slowly percolated through – at times unconsciously – into the mainstream of contemporary art practice. But, as in any discussion of the experimental in the arts, all roads seem to lead back to John Cage, the great 'permission giver' to a whole generation of artists, who will inform this discussion at various points.

1

An argument against the possibilities of interdisciplinarity or even cross-fertilization within the arts, and a well-thumbed critical reference point, is the rather trenchant position of aesthetic formalism, most brilliantly preached by the American critic Clement Greenberg. As far as he was concerned, the hopeless and idealistic yearning of 'media-scrambling' – a ghost of neurasthenic and symbolist art of the nineteenth century – was to be countered by concentrating on the qualities of the medium at hand. There is such a thing as a dominant art form, Greenberg asserted, and within modernism that was, for him, painting. 'The attempts to establish', he suggested, 'the differences between the various arts are not idle. There has been, is, and will be, such a thing as a confusion of the arts.'[2] And by honing the medium, by directly playing with its limitations, each art form could move away from this potential confusion, rationalizing and realizing its autonomy in the process, as well as bringing to bear a notion of aesthetic value derived from the direct perception of the work itself.[3] This resulted in an extreme form of art for art's sake, seemingly intransigent in laying down the gauntlet for what it conceived as 'high art': an almost pure experience of the medium, with no message, no interpretative content, and no depiction or illusion.[4] Modernist painting, from this formalist vantage point, saw a developmental procession of 'major' artists from Jackson Pollock, Mark Rothko, Barnett Newman in the 1950s, through to Morris Louis, Jules Olitski and Kenneth Noland in the 1960s. This was, in a nutshell, the Greenberg canon. Such was the power of the critic as the arbiter of 'quality' and 'relevance' that conceptualist Joseph Kosuth once said that the artist, under his regime, was reduced to firing clay pigeons for the critic to target and shoot down.

Needless to say, since the early 1950s other forces were at work while Greenberg was at his most powerful, including artists who didn't quite fit the formalist canon, and artists who were affected by Greenberg's *bête noire* – Marcel Duchamp. We

---

2   Clement Greenberg, 'Toward a Newer Laocoon', in Francis Frascina (ed.), *After Pollock* (London, 1985), pp. 35–46, at p. 35.

3   As a method, while empirical and intuitive, it is informed by Kant's *Critique of Judgement*.

4   There is widespread misunderstanding about Greenberg's denial of illusion and penchant for flatness in abstract painting. He suggests an optical space works best within the limitations of the medium, but it is still essentially a spatiality that is configured – as in Barnett Newman's paintings, which are as much about 'space' as a demonstration of flatness.

can include here a whole range of artists relevant to that 'experimental tradition' mentioned earlier – Robert Rauschenberg, Jasper Johns, and later, Minimalism, Allan Kaprow and 'Happenings', Fluxus, Conceptual Art and so on. And, of course, at the helm, Cage, the disciple of Duchamp, mentor of Rauschenberg and Johns amongst many others, and whose star had risen considerably in the 1960s. By 1982 – and reflecting back on the 1970s – in an interesting essay entitled 'Intermedia', Greenberg talks in war-like terms on the changes in art-making during that period:

> *The scene of visual art has been invaded more and more, lately, by other mediums than those of painting or sculpture. By 'scene' I mean galleries and museums and the art press. Now these welcome performance art, installation art, sound art, video, dance, mime; also words, written and spoken; and sundry ways of making poetical, political, informational, quasi-philosophical, quasi-psychological, quasi-sociological points.*[5]

Alluding to the 'happenings' of the early 1960s, he notes, 'They "happened" in the context of visual art, and most of the people taking part had to do mainly with visual art, yet they exhibited hardly anything that was visual art as such.'[6] Why is it, Greenberg asked, that the 'The printed page, the concert hall, the literary recital platform haven't been nearly so hospitable to the incursions of mediums not originally proper to themselves [?]'.[7] His answer is partly the fact that painting (central to his conception of modernism) had been at the forefront of experimentation since Manet, and provided a model for experimentation: 'None of the other arts had that early to dig into their own entrails. Certainly not sculpture, not music, not dance, not even literature.'[8] This made painting, and then only later the visual arts in general, as leaders 'in the matter of modernist newness'.[9] Greenberg's argument goes in a familiar turn, for those who know his later writings, with a lament concerning the decline of taste; but two additional facets are worth mentioning here: first, the issue of time-based work in galleries and museums, and second, the arrival of a new generation to whom innovation and newness become a second nature (for Greenberg this is mistaking 'effect' as an end in itself and appropriating a superficial conception of 'the new').

Concerning time, the model for Greenberg's conception of it within the visual arts is, again, that of painting: 'Drama, music, dance, literature, take place *over* time not just in it. Visual art is instantaneous, or almost so, in its proper experiencing, which is of its unity above and before anything else.'[10] When video or sound installations

---

5   Clement Greenberg, 'Intermedia', in Robert C. Morgan (ed.), *Clement Greenberg: Late Writings* (Minneapolis, 2003), pp. 93–8, at p. 93.
6   Ibid.
7   Ibid., p. 94.
8   Ibid.
9   Ibid., p. 95.
10 Ibid.

exist in a gallery, they bypass the conventions of the theatre, TV, the cinema, the auditorium – contexts where they must convince *over* time, whereas, in a gallery context a situation becomes apparent where time becomes arbitrary; where the audience can enter and exit at free will, and where a conceived 'wholeness' of the event might not be perceived at all. What Greenberg criticizes here is a culture that has jettisoned not only the particularity of experience framed by the specificity of medium, but also the lineage of works of 'quality' that that frame enables. But it could also be seen as (which he would dismiss) a situation where an experimental attitude dominates, resulting in a questioning of the relationship of time to form, of process to object and of fragmentation to wholeness.

Greenberg also points something else out here, which he recoils from analysing further, that of a 'new' audience, who experience a different sense of time, a changed sense of being alert. This is an audience (if we can generalize at all) who have a different and more eclectic cultural background from Greenberg and his generation, who reference a vast array of popular culture. This in itself was transformed in the 1960s from the manufactured mass entertainment of previous decades to include a chorus of critically active voices. It was also at this time, in the 1960s and during these cultural shifts and upheavals, that Greenberg's ideas of the purity of medium felt more and more embattled; certainly, in relation to what was actually happening in the galleries and museums. But, ever astute as he was even when discussing 'the enemy', it is possible to take three aspects from Greenberg's essay in relation to the cross-over of experimental music and visual art. First, it was the institutions of visual art – rather than other disciplines – that became hospitable to all sorts of media, performances and situations. Second, a marked change took place in the experiential nature of the artwork, with particular reference to how time is figured, and how space is articulated – in and outside the gallery or museum. Third, the consideration of the ever-changing cultural expectations and make-up of this 'new' audience, together with their infiltration of, and influence upon, the administration of arts organizations, and art educational institutions.

2

John Cage's huge retrospective exhibition of the mid-1990s is a perfect example of the kind of interdisciplinary event that might well have been Greenberg's worst nightmare. Having been planned before his death in 1992, and toured in 1994-95, *Rholywholyover* (the title appropriated from Joyce's Finnegans Wake) was described by curator Julie Lazar – who had worked closely with Cage on the project – as a 'composition for a museum'. The effect was rather like stepping inside Cage's chance methods, and if the exhibition was a self-portrait of sorts, one that brought together connections from the whole of Cage's career, then it was a de-centred one at that. Cage had long been critical of 'museum culture' with its hierarchies and linear structures, and rather like the late *Europeras* series of compositions, *Rolywholyover* was an attempt to work with antithetical material to his own interests, as in the medium of opera in the former case, and to see what could be done with these dislikes. When Lazar initially requested 'A major, but non-linear, exhibition that reflected both his artistic accomplishments and his wide-ranging interests', Cage responded and

> Recommended two things: that I make a preliminary selection of art objects, and then request permanent collection inventories from all modern museums in the country ... He wanted contents of the exhibition to be determined by performing chance operations on these lists, utilizing a computerized system based on the I Ching that he had employed in his compositions since the early 1950s. By departing from traditional organizational procedures in this way, Cage called into question the curator's role in defining artistic standards, and the museum's function in preserving them.[11]

With this procedure, we have two lists; one chosen by Cage of works by artists and musicians, the other effectively chosen by museums and the I Ching. Structure in Cage – if we can call it that – is a sort of absent structure, determined by an inventory or lexicographical procedure of determining the limits of the material that the computerized I Ching printouts bring into play at any given point. This is a procedure that informed his later music and later visual work produced at Crown Point Press in San Francisco. Cage was unique in being an artist who produced music, texts, visual work, allowing each to be informed by his chance methodology. 'Most people who believe that I'm interested in chance', he once stated, 'don't realize that I use it as a discipline – they think I use it – I don't know – as a way of giving up making choices. But my choices consist in choosing what questions to ask.'[12] If, in the context of *Rolywholyover*, the listing of objects and museum requests are taken as a pre-compositional plan so to speak, Cage's basic material was, for him, both known and unknown in one sense.

Exhibits were drawn from various artists' works, Cage's own visual work and the museum artefacts. The list of artworks included both eminent and lesser known figures connected to Cage's own output. From a truly immense list, in particular, we can pick out key associates of the 1950s and 1960s – Franz Kline, Willem de Kooning, Mark Rothko, Barnett Newman, Sol LeWitt, Ad Reinhardt, Robert Rauschenberg, Jasper Johns, Marcel Duchamp, Allan Kaprow, George Maciunas, Joseph Beuys – from a vast range of others. Their works were, during the duration of the exhibition, either stored on visible storage units or made 'live' by the chance operations. Three technicians rearranged the works daily, being given hourly printouts determining the placing or re-placing of works on the wall, floor (depending on their nature) and so on. So a Barnett Newman, for example, might be placed according to the printout instructions, only to be moved, say, a few hours later, by maybe only a few inches, or to a separate wall altogether, or taken back into storage, and so on and

---

11   Julie Lazar, 'Nothingtoseeness', in *John Cage Rolywholyover, A Circus,* (New York, 1994), unpaginated.

12   Robin White, 'Interview with John Cage', *View*, 1/1 (1978): 5.

so forth. As there was no coherent unifying eye level for the hang, works could be separated or clustered together at different heights. This resulted in, as Jill Johnston reviewing the exhibition for *Art in America* in 1994 pointed out, a situation where, 'the walls of the show are covered with eccentrically placed pictures – as though the works had been thrown onto the surface and later straightened'.[13]

In the 'Museumcircle' room, Cage included the artefacts from the invited museums; he had eventually limited the participation to museums within the local vicinity or county at each touring venue. In Los Angeles alone this amounted to 130 museums, and the particular room in that hang, as Johnston recalled, consisted of 'a Salvador Dali drawing [who Cage, incidentally, had very little time for], a bustier once owned by Ingrid Bergman, an Orange County land-use map, four manhole

Example 9.1   *'Rolywholyover: A Circus'*, curated by John Cage,
12 September–28 November 1993, The Museum of
Contemporary Art, Los Angeles

covers, a John Constable landscape, an elephant-seal skull, a Jacob Epstein portrait of G.B. Shaw, a woven basketry mask'.[14] No doubt Cage would have been delighted with these chance juxtapositions, of things 'speaking' to each other in new and different ways. It is also a reminder of the *operational* nature, literally, of the chance operation. Things appear to be transformed by chance, they can be seen afresh,

13   Jill Johnston, 'John Cage: Music for Museums', *Art in America* (January 1994): 72–2, at 75.
14   Ibid., p. 76.

in an alternative light, and in this way, chance operations can appear rather like a proto-deconstructive machine that reshuffles, re-orientates and allows endless new permutations. On seeing the exhibition at the now defunct Guggenheim SoHo in New York, the impact was one of a literal moveable feast, an exhibition that was moving in front of one's eyes, and an almost inexhaustible content of objects, art, documents, scores and other items. Cage had shown that his methodology had caught up, or even pre-empted, aspects of the curatorial practices of the late twentieth century. It is ironic that Cage's last major retrospective statement took place primarily in the field of visual art – as Johnston notes, 'Cage was given a chance to make his own imprint on such a [museum] space, something no comparable venue in music – his primary medium – ever allowed him.'[15] This, in many ways, leads us back to Greenberg's first point. Cage's ideas, after all, were taken up very early on by visual artists, and as readily, if not more so, than by musicians. It becomes a complex and reciprocal relationship, as Cage readily acknowledged, whereby his generation of composers, as he once said, found it necessary to formulate a 'reply' to the pre-war achievements of modernist artists such as Kandinsky, Klee or Mondrian (and equally, each of these painters were strongly influenced by music in formulating their own positions). *Rolywholyover* reinstated, quite clearly, Cage's milieu as one dominated by artists and their circles – Duchamp, Peggy Guggenheim, the Abstract Expressionists, for example. These connections, in fact, prefigure Cage and his New York circle of composers – Morton Feldman, Christian Wolff, David Tudor and Earle Brown. And Cage, we have to remember, was lacking any consistent means of livelihood during those earlier years – he was, as with the artists, disenfranchised from the academies, the universities and other normative means of earning a living. As a way of living and producing avant-garde art, the artists, no question, led the way. *Rolywholyover* as a visual installation, allowed a reflection on this historical moment.

It is peculiar in some ways to think of Cage as a fellow traveller with the Abstract Expressionists, but that is the case. He knew many of them well and worked with some of them – De Kooning and Franz Kline for example – at Black Mountain College, an experimental educational community in North Carolina in 1948. We can hardly equate Cage with the brusque machismo of some of these painters, but it provided a community, at least for a time. With their famous meeting places in New York, at a loft known as the 'the Club' on 8th Street – in its original location – and the Cedar Tavern, these artists set up an important creative dialogue and self-support system. De Kooning recalled its beginnings as primarily a social club – rather like the ones immigrant workers had set up in New York in the 1940s, and as an alternative to meeting in expensive cafes. Other significant members, besides participation by Newman, Rothko, Motherwell, Gottlieb *et al.*, included Willem's wife, Elaine de Kooning, Mercedes Matter – founder of the Studio School of Drawing, Painting and Sculpture, and who was to later employ Morton Feldman as Dean – as well as the sculptor Philip Pavia. Art historian Irving Sandler described the Club as 'Reacting against a public which, when not downright hostile to their

---

15   Ibid., p. 74.

work, was indifferent or misunderstanding, [therefore] vanguard artists created their own audience, mostly of other artists – their own artworld.'[16] It was this atmosphere of self-sufficiency that no doubt impressed Cage, along with Stephan Wolpe, Morton Feldman and Edgard Varèse, and an atmosphere would have a marked effect on their own dialogues and ideas, or at least the stimulation to ask new questions. Again, it was a set of complex, reciprocal relationships, but the Club and its discussions (Cage lectured there on several occasions) was an important incubator for many aspects of what we now know as experimental music. It was also an important audience for Cage's, and his colleagues', experiments. Earle Brown, who joined Cage in New York in 1952 later recalled

> We were conversant with all of them, they were the ones who came to our concerts; I mean, the musicians thought we were kooky, they thought we were nuts, they wouldn't even show up. I don't know if the painters liked our music either, but they showed up. We'd go every Saturday to their openings, you know, Guston or de Kooning or whoever. I felt it was a significant meeting of minds amongst the painters and composers – our group, that is, of composers.[17]

Neither group – the artists nor the composers grouped around Cage – saw themselves as a 'school' despite their lumping together of late as the 'New York Schools'. As Harold Rosenberg, an important participant in the Club and commentator on the work suggested, 'what they think in common is represented only by what they do separately'.[18] The same certainly could be said of the four composers now known as the 'New York School' – Cage, Brown, Feldman, Wolff and not forgetting David Tudor, the virtuoso pianist who made it all happen, and who later was to become a composer in his own right. But where was this 'significant meeting of minds'? Apart from a social support group, there were collectively addressed questions of form, of activity in and for itself, that were being transformed by these artists. Harold Rosenberg – someone who was a key influence in bringing debates around existentialism to these artists at the Club – in a now famous passage spoke of a situation where

> At a certain moment the canvas began to appear to one American painter after another as an arena in which to act – rather than as a space in which to reproduce, re-design, analyze, or 'express' an object, actual or imagined. What was to go on the canvas was not a picture but an event.[19]

---

16   Irving Sandler, 'The Club', in David and Cecile Shapiro (eds), *Abstract Expressionism – A Critical Record* (New York, 1990), pp. 48–58, at p. 51.

17   David Ryan, 'Y a-t-il une "école new-yorkaise"? – Entretien avec Earle Brown', *Dissonanz*, 52 (May 1997): 14–19.

18   Harold Rosenberg, 'The American Action Painters' (1952), reprinted in David and Cecile Shapiro, *Abstract Expressionism*, pp. 75–85, at p. 76.

19   Ibid.

As familiar as it is, this particular phrasing denoted nothing short of a revolutionary reading of the new painting (a misreading, and a dangerous one at that, to Greenberg's mind). Rosenberg suggested this was not an aesthetic re-orientation – that is, not one, 'In order to make room for perfect relations of space and colour.'[20] But rather, it denoted a new inclusiveness to the act of painting, of the event, 'The act-painting is of the same metaphysical substance as the artist's existence. The new painting has broken down every distinction between art and life.'[21] These issues – although framed in a very different way from Cage, who disliked the connotations of 'action painting' – would find resonance in the composers' struggles with new forms. Cage, himself, from the late 1930s on, had been concerned with structure and inclusiveness, a tension that had come to a head by 1950. A year earlier in a lecture given, incidentally, at the Club, Cage would write of structure, 'it is like a glass of milk ... we need the ... glass and we need ... the milk ... or again ... it is like an empty glass ... into which ... at any moment ... anything ... can be poured.'[22] Structure becomes a field of possibilities, and the moment is determined by the nature of the 'event' itself, exterior to Cage's mind and desires. Structure becomes a means of allowing certain things the possibility to happen or not – as in his empty durational structures given to participants in his various theatre pieces or 'circuses' – such as the seminal performance at Black Mountain College in 1952, with Cunningham, Rauschenberg *et al.*, or the *Theatre Piece* of 1960. But there is still a connection with all-overness or the symmetry of grid structures within painting in his abandonment of structure per se for *structured* process – both strategies giving the viewer more agile mobility in relation to the surface.

All-overness and the temporal aspect of painting – its seeming instantaneity – can also be translated into a model of time for composition, as Cage would demonstrate. This too concerned Morton Feldman, who like Cage – perhaps even more so – was affected by the discussions and the presence of both the painters and the paintings themselves. Clearly, both Feldman and Brown wanted to develop situations akin to the newfound physicality of the painters; Feldman suggested this in his oft-cited statement, 'The new painting made me desirous of a sound world more immediate, more physical than anything that had existed heretofore.'[23] And Brown formulated an equivalent statement in an early notebook entry of 1951-52, 'I want to get the time of composing closer to the time of performing.'[24] Both of these composers would demonstrate how aspects of painterly concerns could be translated into another medium, and convincingly so. Feldman was concerned with the creation of an 'aural surface' – one that is essentially static, even in the later massive compositions,

---

20   Ibid., p. 77.

21   Ibid., p. 78.

22   John Cage, 'Lecture on Nothing', *Silence: Lectures and Writings* (Middleton, Conn., 1961), pp. 109–27, at p. 110 [durational silences have been excluded from the quote].

23   Morton Feldman, 'Autobiography', in *Morton Feldman: Essays*, ed. Walter Zimmerman (Cologne, 1985), pp. 36–40, at p. 38.

24   Earle Brown, statement from a notebook 1951–52, Earle Brown Music Foundation, New York.

which retain this hovering and painterly quality; Brown's work, on the other hand, taking directly from Jackson Pollock's attempts to get 'inside the paintings', gives instructions to performers, for example, to bring 'an intensified sense of human and sonic presence and intuitive performance contact ... into an area of immediacy of action-reaction and flexibility' to a score's realization.[25] Passages of delicate graphism in certain works by Brown would be headed 'inarticulate'– an equivalent to residual, non-intentional marks that became part of the overall field of painting. Christian Wolff also developed a concept of 'zero time', an unmarked temporal space where the performer can take whatever time to realize a given task or event. And Brown's seminal graphic – or non-symbolically visual – score, probably the first totally 'indeterminate' piece in this respect, *December 1952*, which rejected a left–right reading of the page to initiate a situation where performers can enter and leave at any point (as in all-over painting). This is a piece that, in some ways, breaks the umbilical cord that attaches the score to the resulting sonic event, due to its 'ambiguity' in both corresponding interpretation and performance activity. Its continuous identity as a work lies, therefore, entirely in its visual manifestation, and not in any resulting audible realization.

The effect these experiments had on the conception and reception of music is, perhaps, taken for granted. It is a reminder of how much pre-war modern music was locked into a striated, counted time. By the late 1950s Wolff, commenting on new approaches to thinking time in experimental composition, could write,

> The music has a static character. It goes in no particular direction. There is no necessary concern with time as a measure of distance from a point in the past to a point in the future, with linear continuity alone. It is not a question of getting anywhere, of making progress, or having come from anywhere in particular.[26]

Wolff accepts that this is the source of, what he describes as, 'monotony and the irritation that accompanies it'. But he adds that this is, in fact, 'immobility in motion. And it alone, perhaps, is truly moving.'[27] In this way time becomes peculiarly spatial in these works. We get a sense of events occurring without the pre-given conventional narratives of how they should unfold *over* time. As with the painters who jettisoned composition in order to emphasize, in Rosenberg's terms, the canvas as an 'arena', it is a space where anything can happen. The white canvas becoming a void, or nothingness, against which the painter puts his or her mark, or existential trace, so to speak. Cage's conception of nothingness was perhaps the opposite of this anxiety that was rife in the artists' studios. Cage suggested a way, not of an aggressive act that stamps a trace upon the face of the world,

---

25   Earle Brown, from his performing instructions to *String Quartet* (1965), Earle Brown Music Foundation, New York.
26   Christian Wolff, 'New and Electronic Music', in *Cues, Writings and Conversations* (Cologne, 1999), pp. 24–37, at p. 36.
27   Ibid.

but of simply 'paying attention'. As artist Allan Kaprow pointed out, 'In Cage's cosmology (informed by Asiatic philosophy) the real world was perfect, if only we could hear, see it, understand it ... But if the world was perfect just as it is, neither terrible nor good, then it wasn't necessary to demand that it improve.'[28] Nor, we might add, make an existential commentary upon it. 'Things will happen and appear anyway', Cage seemed to be saying, as opposed to the weighted drama of *making* something happen.

The French philosopher Jean-François Lyotard discusses this 'making something happen', proposing that the act of musical composition is creating something 'audible' from the teeming mass of so-called inaudible sounds that form the backdrop to our perceptions. Music, he goes on, 'labours to give birth to what is audible in the inaudible breath. It strives to put it into phrases. Thus does it betray it, by giving it form' and that, 'Every sonorous phrase, even the simplest, announces that there will be another phrase, that it is not yet over, that the end of phrases is not yet to come to an end.'[29] And thus musical narratives mask a basic anxiety of 'nothing happening' which is where Lyotard's argument for a contemporary sublime comes into play – the situation whereby the inevitability of a safety net of knowing 'what happens next' is removed. Cage's 4'33" of 1952, the famous silent piece, as well as taking its inspiration from Robert Rauschenberg's white canvases of a year earlier, questions the very nature of gesture, of intervening as an author, composer or artist within what we take for granted – the 'invisible' or the 'inaudible' domains of listening or seeing. Both could be seen as 'empty' in relation to the expectation of something having to occur, and both curiously invert the natures of their respective mediums: Rauschenberg's white paintings allude to time – they make the viewer much more aware of the time of day, the specific lighting at that moment, the possibility, as Cage suggested, of the potential 'intrusion' of shadows within the viewing situation. Whereas Cage's 4'33" can be seen to accentuate the spatialization of sounds occurring within its time frames (this is my own experience of listening to realizations of the piece) and he certainly accentuates the visual aspect of performance, at least in its original context. Both these works have remained touchstones for avant-garde practices ever since, precisely because they have actively called into question the relation of the creation and reception of the art-event, but have also pointed to a fluidity, and called into question, the time and space considerations of their respective mediums.

The Abstract Expressionists, famously, as in the brooding iconic figure of Pollock, privileged an embodiment of male, rugged individuality.[30] Compatible with this inflation of the artist's ego was Rosenberg's suggestion that the artist becomes a

---

28   Allan Kaprow, 'Right Living', in *Essays on the Blurring of Art and Life* (Berkeley, 2003), pp. 223–5, at p. 225.

29   Jean François Lyotard, 'Music, Music', in *Postmodern Fables*, trans. Georges van den Abbeele (Minneapolis, 1997), pp. 217–33, at pp. 228–9.

30   That is, of course, the cliché: the participation and contribution of important women painters such as Elaine de Kooning, Grace Hartigan, Joan Mitchell and Lee Krasner amongst others, should also be pointed out here.

'cosmic I' – with a delimited, mythological sense of self – and that the 'Test of any of the new paintings is its seriousness – and the test of its seriousness is the degree to which the act on the canvas is an extension of the artist's total effort to make over his experience.'[31] Against this eulogy to the self and 'authenticity', shared by many of the painters, Cage's circle, including Rauschenberg at the time of the white paintings, sought a situation of *selflessness*. 'We should be free from the assertive, direct consequences of intention and effect', Christian Wolff suggested, 'because the intention would be merely one's own and circumscribed, while so many other forces are so obviously at work in the final effect'.[32]

While many might have been exasperated with Cage and his 'Lecture on Nothing' at the club – with its Zen acceptance of nothingness – for numerous others he offered a potentially new terrain for artists to mine in the later 1950s, including ones as diverse in outlook as Jasper Johns and Allan Kaprow. Cage's growing influence during that time corresponded with a renewed interest, a rediscovery even, in the ironic, detached and disinterested aesthetic of Marcel Duchamp, so much so that Irving Sandler could talk of a Cage/Duchamp aesthetic.[33] With its disavowal of personalized expression, its inclusiveness of noise and the everyday, Cage's analysis was moving toward a holistic reading of the event – accentuating the fact that the production of sound was actually embodied sonically, physically, socially and visually. 'Where do we go from here?' he asked in 1957. 'Towards theatre. That art more than music resembles nature. We have eyes as well as ears, and it is our business while we are alive to use them.'[34]

3

If Cage's statements about theatre threw down the gauntlet to visual artists, then, in certain quarters, it was taken up with gusto. And while the connection between Abstract Expressionism and the Experimental composers throws into relief certain methodological correspondences – such as the field, the event of gesture, trace or mark, or signs of residual materiality (drips, blots, splashes, extraneous or exterior sounds and so on), essentially both look in different directions in terms of their respective world views. It was in the embrace of Cage's notion of theatre, within Fluxus and the 'Happening', that an experimental approach to art-making – akin to Cage's work at least – appears. Many of the protagonists were his students at the classes in experimental music he gave at the New School for Social Research in New

---

31   Rosenberg, 'The American Action Painters', p. 81. Rosenberg here is alluding to a connection with Walt Whitman's notion of a 'Cosmic I' – one that has little to do with the biological, everyday notion of selfhood.

32   Christian Wolff, '… let the listeners be just as free as the players', in *Cues, Writings and Conversations*, pp. 78–86, at p. 82.

33   See Irving Sandler, *The New York School* (New York, 1978).

34   John Cage, 'Experimental Music' in *Silence*, pp. 7–12, at p. 12.

York: Al Hansen, Allan Kaprow, Dick Higgins, Jackson Maclow and George Brecht to mention but a few. Importantly Kaprow was to synthesize various concerns of Abstract Expressionism and Cage in order to develop the 'Happening'. As a serious contribution to the debates around action, performance and installation, 'Happenings' have been undermined by numerous take-offs and caricatures of 'far out art'. Kaprow, by 1967, was despairing at the chic and hip Sixties appropriation, commercial exploitation even, of the term, 'Happening'. It is only relatively recently that as a concept it has been revisited and has taken on a strange relevance for many contemporary practitioners, in the raw energy and attempts to cut across the boundaries of what is acceptable as 'art'. An early form – in their original incarnation – of non-narrative performance or theatre, as events they usually had a loose plan, score or script, and would consist of various activities, sounds, objects from everyday life, makeshift environments, props, audience participation and materials of virtually any sort. The photographic documents of these events show them generally, but not exclusively, taking place in artists' lofts, and attempting to break down the separation of artist, performer, participant and audience. The idea of them taking place in the artists' natural habitat of the loft was an important one, it meant taking a stand against the growing dominance of galleries, dealers and general commercialization that accompanied the acclaim of the American painting. Although one of Kaprow's early important works, *18 Happenings in 6 Parts*, took place in the Rueben Gallery, New York, in 1959, it was the grime and 'reality' of non-gallery spaces that attracted him. The chaotic, often chance-based activities were better suited to non-gallery or even non-art sites, which was Kaprow ultimately preferred. And, as with Cage, in most of these performances the unexpected, or unforeseen, was welcomed, as he states in 1961:

> *Visitors to a Happening are now and then not sure what has taken place, when it has ended, even when things have gone 'wrong.' For when something goes 'wrong' something far more 'right,' more revelatory, has many times emerged. This sort of sudden near-miracle presently seems to be made through chance procedures.*[35]

Kaprow's importance here is as a hinge between the diverse practices of Pollock and Cage. What he experienced in Pollock was an intensified ritual of action, one scarred with residues of the everyday, an almost uncontained space, which was to be translated into real space – an environmental space. In Kaprow's terms, Pollock had suggested an expansion to the artists' armoury, and an exploration of expanded materiality: 'not satisfied with the suggestion through paint of our other senses, we shall utilize the substances of sight, sound, movements, people, odours, touch. Objects of every sort are materials of the new art.'[36] Cage, on the other hand, pointed to the dual exploration of chance and non-art which spurned a new means

---

35   Ibid., p. 20.
36   Allan Kaprow, 'The Legacy of Jackson Pollock (1958)', in *Essays on the Blurring of Art and Life*, pp. 1–12, at pp. 7, 9.

of thinking across, or even fusing of art and music and, by implication, many other disciplines, as Kaprow explained:

> *It was apparent to everyone that these two moves in music could be systematically carried over to any of the other arts. But the more interesting prospect, as I saw it, was to follow the lead of these ideas well beyond the boundaries of the art genres themselves.*[37]

Kaprow was later to distinguish between sub-categories of happenings, 'Events' and 'Activities'. Events – most typically exemplified by the Fluxus group (which included George Maciunas, George Brecht, Al Hansen, Yoko Ono, Dick Higgins, Nam June Paik amongst a whole host of other temporary allegiances) were exemplified by 'disciplined attentiveness to small or normally unimportant phenomena'.[38] They tended to take place with a conventional performer/audience relationship, while Activities foregrounded the idea of participation in the given activity by abolishing, literally, the distinction between performer, participant and audience, in that everyone taking part in the Activity must *participate*.

It is here, in these two sub-categories of the happening, that the blurring of the boundaries of art and life, the examination of public and private spaces, and the possibility of operating as an *experimental* as opposed to an avant-garde artist are brought into focus. Cage had provided a clear exegesis on what constituted an experimental approach to music – it centred around process rather than the creation of objects, therefore impermanence was a characteristic, as was the embrace of the 'unforseen' in terms of what will actually occur; it focused on sounds themselves (and their production) freed from musical narrative structures, and shunned an aesthetic separation of art from life. 'Imagine', wrote Kaprow, 'something never done before, by a method never used, whose outcome is unforeseen. Modern art is not like this; it is always Art.'[39] This was the basis of his call for 'life-like art' rather 'art-like art'. The experimental artist was not sure what the activities he was involved in actually were. It was without any official legitimating constraints or codes of practice and therefore it had the freedom to explore for its own sake. As an example, a piece might be looked at such as *On/Off*, made in the 1990s for a workshop in experimental art. Here, as in other Activities, Kaprow simply initiated an activity that involved the immediate available surroundings:

> *We decided to play with the light switch. The idea was that anyone in the room could get up from where they were sitting and turn off the lights. How long it would take was unplanned. Then, anyone could turn it on. Then off. Then on, and so forth. Long periods of time followed. Although there were no*

---

37   Allan Kaprow, 'Right Living (1987)', p. 224.
38   Allan Kaprow, 'Pinpointing Happenings (1967)', in *Essays on the Blurring of Art and Life*, pp. 84–9, at p. 86.
39   Allan Kaprow, 'Experimental Art (1966)', in *Essays on the Blurring of Art and Life*, pp. 66–83, at p. 68.

guidelines about silence, no one spoke. You could hear people breathing. We peeked at one another, trying to anticipate who would make the next move. Sometimes we stared at someone, challenging them, to see who would wait the longest. People got up and played with the switch, flicking the light, or archly changing it back and forth, as if to convey some message. Equally there were 15 minutes more of doing nothing. The only advice given in advance was that anyone could leave the room when they had to. The experiment would end when no one remained. After about two and a half hours I had to give a talk elsewhere. There were nine in the room when I left. I went to the airport after the lecture and never heard when the room became empty.[40]

Anyone who has participated in musical improvisational activity will recognize that the same tensions, expectations and behavioural tics that take place in those situations are clearly apparent here. And for Kaprow, its status *as art* must be placed in doubt for it to qualify as a truly experimental event. George Brecht, another student of Cage's at the New School, also developed a focus on activities and prosaic events – especially in his early Events which gave laconic instructions to the performer, such as *Three Window Events* which consists of directions to 'open a closed window' and 'close an open window', or *Timetable Music* where a train timetable is appropriated as a musical score. As with some of La Monte Young's early event scores during his association with Fluxus, they need not even be realized at all, but simply imagined – and in turn question the need for the public domain at all. In connection with this, Henry Flynt, an associate of Young, recalls,

After I became involved in new music, I remember walking through Harvard Yard and seeing a man positioned at the corner of a dormitory, seeming attentive but not visibly doing anything. The thought occurred to me that he might be participating in a new music performance whose existence was unannounced.[41]

Such was the peculiar situation of the late 1950s, early 1960s with the introduction of Fluxus Events, Happenings and Activities. Flynt describes the above as a possible 'new music event', although such activities or events, as we have seen, could be by so-called experimental artists or non-musicians. Brecht, for example, was a professional chemist, and many involved in Fluxus, like Al Hansen or Wolff Vostell, were visual arts trained, despite the mores of music continually being spoofed or critically and humorously examined in their work. And Maciunas, the founder of Fluxus, had a deep antipathy towards 'career professional artists'.

Flynt's history is also interesting as a case study bringing to light some of these paradoxes that might be associated with the extremities of the experimental. With

---

40   Allan Kaprow, 'Just Doing', in *Essays on the Blurring of Art and Life*, pp. 247–52, at p. 248.

41   Henry Flynt, 'Cage and Fluxus', in Richard Kostelanetz (ed.) *Writings about John Cage* (Ann Arbor, 1993), pp. 279–82, at pp. 279–80.

a predisposition for the peripheral, and dipping into various activities at different times or simply attempting to be a thorn in the side of an avant-garde mainstream, Flynt remains an almost quintessential anti-art activist and something of an enigma. He demonstrated against 'culture' in general and against Stockhausen, twice, in 1964 – pre-empting a general disdain that grew amongst experimental composers for the German composer. His output questions consistency, the exploration of any particular medium or discipline, and the kind of relationship an artist (or musician) might forge with the world itslf, avoiding any of the pre-given legitimizing structures that ultimately mark and shape practices within the fields of art and music.

Flynt was originally a mathematician, who shifted to philosophy while at Harvard where he was a contemporary of Christian Wolff and the filmmaker and fellow Young associate Tony Conrad. It was Conrad who introduced him to Young's early music which remained extremely important to Flynt. In the early 1960s he developed 'Concept Art' (not to be confused with LeWitt's or Kosuth's later formulation of conceptual art). Flynt had militantly embraced popular music over the 'new music' – Delta blues, Bo Diddley and so on. In the late 1980s, for a short period, he revisited 'Concept Art' and – reluctantly entering a professional context – had several shows at the Emily Harvey Gallery in New York, and also a room at the Venice Biennale of 1990 entitled 'Logically impossible Space'. After 1993, Flynt went back to the hypotheses and treatises, with his 'personhood Theory' – a kind of empirical philosophy of the self, the world and their interrelationship.

What are we to make of all this? There are two ways of viewing Flynt's practice – as simply a way of living, with a reflective critical and ethical dimension, together with various forays into creativity unburdened by career constraints. Or, serving a critique of elitist, avant-garde practices which, in themselves, have become normative and uphold the status quo. Both could be seen as an experimental attitude to thinking about how one positions oneself within a dominant culture, a politicized experimentalism. Flynt asks questions about the nature of the 'career professional' in art, music and even philosophy, each of whom he would see as partaking in a distortion by a specialist mentality that is ultimately at the service of spurious social functions. Nor had Cage gone far enough, as he suggests,

> Cage's pronouncements in this period seemed to say that only listening and the environment were necessary for music, that composers and professional instrumentalists were passé. At the time, I took this to question the very legitimacy of art. Also Cage's juniors acknowledged and echoed these dicta. And yet Cage remained a professional composer, and his students became career professionals ... Seemingly extreme proclamations which are not acted upon (and in hindsight were not even meant) are troubling ... All the same, what are we to make of the presence of intimations of the end of art in the stance of career artists, intimations which turn out to be nothing of the sort?[42]

---

42   Ibid., pp. 280–81.

This is, of course, an extreme form of experimentation, demanding the liquidation of art as we know it. Cage's later works in the late 1980s and 1990s contradict any reading of him as simply a proto-Dadaist. And for all his pronouncements Flynt maintains a 'what is to be done next' attitude, one that ultimately betrays its avant-garde origins, as well as the requirement of a *public* face – that of the pamphlet, the radio broadcast, demonstration or even the conventional gallery context. If it doesn't have this communicative element, then it simply reverts to a solipsistic form of living, a self-induced 'silence'. But such issues were, and still are, relevant to the whole question of what it is to be an *experimental* artist. And Kaprow, Brecht, Flynt and many others brought this questioning into relief, with the private/public debate, interpersonal rather than expressive interfaces, the nature of work and its resistance to an increasingly commercialized mode of exchange and thought, and the question of how to operate in the world itself as an artist: which became nothing short of an experimental construction of subjectivity and its interrelationships.

4

Such discourses examine the nature of events with all their connotations: formal, social, political even, and seemed to gravitate naturally to the arena of the visual arts. Almost none of these debates were adequately discussed in music schools or conservatoires, where they might have been only briefly tolerated, impatiently at that. Think of English experimentalist Cornelius Cardew's marginalization as a teacher at the Royal Academy School of Music. Partly, the reason for this lies in changes that had been taking place not only in the tradition of avant-garde innovation but also in its relation to instruction and the traditions of teaching in the visual arts, which had changed beyond recognition if we compare it to music. The traditions of the Bauhaus and Black Mountain College with their implementation of empirical research and experimentation rather a notion of *techne*, pointed to the accommodation of experimental and even marginal attitudes. Robert Filliou, another Fluxus artist, suggested that art 'offers an immediate "right of asylum" to all deviant practices which cannot find a place in their natural bed'.[43] Also, it should be said, the philosophical basis of art had become a more public battleground – especially since the advent of modernism. Abstract Expressionism and Minimalism as movements existed as blank slates for critical discourse to excavate meaning and context. There appeared to be no *givens* here, in terms of interpretation or meaning, hence conflicting accounts of those movements, and very different directions for future practice being deduced from them. With the growth of conceptual and idea-based art within art schools, it was only natural that sound and performance in general would attract more attention. Even Greenberg would acknowledge that the basis of art was one that didn't lie, necessarily, in the production of an object:

---

43   Nicolas Bourriaud, *Relational Aesthetics* (Paris, 2002), p. 102.

The notion of art, put to the strictest test of experience, proves not to be skilful making (as the ancients defined it), but an act of mental distancing – an act that can be performed even without the help of sense perception. Any and everything can be subjected to such distancing, and thereby converted into something that takes effect as art. There turns out, accordingly, to be such a thing as art at large, art that is realized or realizable everywhere, even if for the most part inadvertently, momentarily, and solipsistically: art that is private, 'raw', and unformalized (which doesn't mean formless, of which there is no such thing.) And because this art can and does feed on anything within the realm of conceivability, it is virtually omnipresent among human beings.[44]

Cage's 4'33" could be considered as framing this 'raw art', as would Duchamp's ready-mades, such as the manufactured urinal *Fountain* or *Bottle Rack*, each drawing on 'anything within the realm of conceivability' as art. Greenberg, it has to be said, saw this position as extremely limited in its possibilities, outside the cultured constraints of high art, and 'sheltered from the pressure of expectation and demands' that those constraints bring with them. But it does point to the expanded field of investigation that informed visual arts practice in the 1960s and 1970s.

This also explains the very possibility of participation in art school teaching, during that period, by experimental composers. Cage, Brown, Feldman and Wolff were each invited to English art schools, Gavin Bryars taught, at the beginning of his career, almost exclusively in art schools, as did Michael Parsons at Portsmouth and the Slade School of Fine Art. Cornelius Cardew and pianist John Tilbury also taught at various art institutions. My own art school experiences at Coventry in the mid-1970s were coloured by another generation of musicians, the improvisers: Steve Beresford, Lol Coxhill, Peter Cusack and sound artist Max Eastley, amongst others. Certainly, all of these encounters shaped a variety of outcomes. Counted amongst these might be Cardew's experimental and anarchic collective, the Scratch Orchestra which owed much of its make-up to visual artists, and Bryars's Portsmouth Sinfonia – which in itself questioned the nature of skill and error in performance – and was a direct amalgamation of students and staff from the art school.

In America many artists in New York passed through the Studio School during Feldman's tenure as Dean there. Artist and critic Saul Ostrow, now Chair in Visual Arts at Cleveland Institute of the Arts, recalled,

I was a very arrogant student, and felt I knew more than, or at least as much as, my teachers. It was the sixties after all. Then I attended Feldman's classes – this was at the School of Visual Arts. I remember the first day of class there was Feldman in a rumpled suit, wearing thick glasses and smoking cigarettes that burnt down between his fingers – he read from note cards which he had

---

44 Clement Greenberg, 'Counter Avant-garde', in Morgan, *Clement Greenberg: Late Writings*, pp. 5–18, at p. 13.

to hold very close to his face, his eyesight being very bad. Feldman, though, was the instructor who made me realize that I didn't understand a thing about the avant-garde, or the important role that experimental music was playing in terms of what was happening at the time. That was an important realization![45]

Feldman provided an alternative view to the more extreme and politicized views of experimentalism. It was one that concentrated on the nature of material and how one positioned oneself within those materials in relation to process and technique. For Feldman, as with Lyotard, technique and convention tended to mask a fundamental anxiety that one needs to tap into in order to articulate a deeper experience of time and sound. A strong connection with the painters of Abstract Expressionism remained with Feldman, and we can note that his approach to sound was never abstract – as in Cage's or Wolff's notion of the performer 'choosing sounds' unspecified by the composers – Feldman always projected sound through the coloration of their *specified* instrumentation. David Reed, now an established painter in New York, and another student at The Studio School while Feldman was there, recalled Feldman's strong links to the original New York School of the early 1950s in his lectures and talks: 'In his talks he made many connections between the visual arts and music and told many stories about the painters – many of them pointed, but enigmatic.'[46] Students were in awe when Feldman would bring an artist from that generation in to speak, as he recalls:

Once he brought de Kooning into the school … A student asked: 'What made the breakthrough of the Abstract Expressionists possible?' De Kooning turned to Feldman, 'When was it Morty?' And they go back and forth with dates – and finally settle, I think, on the first week of June 1948. De Kooning: 'That was the week that no one could paint. We were all out walking in the streets. No one knew what a painting was anymore. And it was that one week of not knowing that made everything possible.'[47]

This process of forgetting was important to Feldman's practice as well as his view of the history of American modernism. It was a means of realigning oneself with material, but certainly didn't – as against Kaprow or Flynt – abolish or question the fundamental basis of art. While others were trying to move away from 'art', Feldman was trying to move his music closer to it. Music had become a form of entertainment as he saw it, while art still possessed that seriousness, that philosophical underpinning that Feldman required.

---

45 Email correspondence with the author, 2008.
46 Ibid.
47 Ibid.

5

If I have mapped two extremes, here, in the post-Cage activities of experimental art and music – with Kaprow and Flynt representing a philosophical and politicized reading of the thrust of experimental music in its translation into visual or performance-based activities, and Feldman viewing the relationship between the arts as a more subtle weaving of allusion and analogy informing ways of using methods and materials – then both these positions are still relevant and alive within current practice. In between there are, of course, many variants utilizing the visual and the sonic, either melding them together or each informing the other. Many practitioners of the 1960s and 1970s, directly affected by the first generation of experimental composers, are still active. Increased traffic has occurred between disciplines: Max Neuhaus migrated in the late 1960s from virtuoso percussionist to installation artist, while Phill Niblock, on the other hand, began his career as a filmmaker and began developing music by composing from taped sounds, in a manner similar to re-editing visual material. Often Niblock's drone pieces are simultaneously accompanied by his films of people engaged in manual work from footage shot across the world, each in their own way hypnotic.

Other artists have maintained multi-disciplinary approaches to their work, such as Charlemagne Palestine who from the early 1970s on has straddled installation, video, performance and music in his activities. Trained as a Cantor in New York, Palestine, whose works make use of either the voice or extended interference patterns on the piano, sees his work as an extension of the expressive depth of Rothko's or Newman's paintings. Atmosphere certainly prevails in his ritualistic approach, with low coloured lighting or ambience, and often with the appearance of fetishized stuffed toys embodying transitional objects in his performances. Sometimes these toys form installations and sculptures in their own right culminating in a cross-over with the work of artists Mike Kelley or Jeff Koons. Palestine's connection of sounds to a visceral sound-producing body resulted in performances where his own body would be subjected to physical strain in order to transform the sound. *Island Song* of 1976 might be a good example, where the small island of Saint Pierre Miquelon off the coast of Canada, apparently chosen at random from a globe, becomes the object of an audio mapping. Palestine, in this work, straps a video camera to his motorcycle and attempts to hold a single pitch for the duration of the cartographic excursion. Needless to say as the terrain became more difficult the sustained pitch distorts and involuntarily widens as the body is physically hurled about. Christian Marclay's video *Guitar Drag* (2000) inflicts similar damage to an inanimate guitar. Amplified, hooked up and tied by rope to a truck, it is dragged across terrain of San Antonio in Texas, during which it creates a variety of electronic screams, violent distortions and finally becomes a stringless battered resonating body. *Guitar Drag*, as Marclay himself suggested, is about references not only to cowboys and rodeos translated into a sonic 'road movie', but also violence, with a grisly starting point in a lynching. At the same time, the video also points to the destruction of instruments in iconic rebel rock concerts, and in Fluxus events (usually in that context, a piano or violin). This accumulation of different meanings, resonances and historical references is typical of contemporary practices. While *Guitar Drag*, as in Palestine's videos, takes the duration of an activity as its delimitation of form and process, it does not shy away from tapping into our memories of received sounds and images.

Both these examples use sound as a means of marking duration and space. Sound performs this territorialization of space in our day-to-day environments – think of alarms, church bells, mechanical, animal or bird sounds and so on. In Jean-François Augoyard and Henry Torgue's social analysis of everyday sonic experience, their starting point is the fact that, 'No sound event, musical or otherwise, can be isolated from the spatial and temporal conditions of its physical signal propagation.'[48] One striking aspect of Cage's *4'33"* was the accentuation of this perspectival aspect of sounds and their acoustical properties. Despite the rhetoric of sounds simply as sounds, Cage also leads to an analysis of production and place. And many recent works have followed suit in exploring this relationship to the spatiality of sounds and the perception of place. Max Neuhaus's early *Listen* (1966–76) was a 'lecture-demonstration' that consisted simply of the instruction to listen, while Neuhaus selected particular walks or sites particularly rich in their sonic material. These have included a power plant, with 'some spectacularly massive rumbling', or the underside of Brooklyn Bridge, 'with sounds of traffic moving across that bridge – the rich sound texture formed from hundreds of tires rolling along over the open grating of the road-bed – each with different speed and tread'.[49] Such focused listening and observation led to Neuhaus formulating architecture-specific sound environments and installations, placing sounds in particular architectural or exterior contexts. Sound becomes, here, a sculptural material that our physical presence enacts and bears witness to. Another variant is where artists might place specific sounds in various parts of a space acting as audible zones, but not necessarily site-specific. Bruce Nauman's *Raw Materials* (2004) installed in the Turbine Hall of the Tate Modern is a particularly dramatic example. Using 22 spoken texts – in the form of jokes, statements, propositions, emotional addresses or pleas – and organized in bands across the width of the Turbine Hall, the accumulative effect in the huge cavernous space of the Tate consisted of a disturbing cacophony of voices, which became particularized only as one moved around the space towards a given source. Often with manic repetition of phrases such as 'work, work, work, work...' or 'thank you, thank you, thank you, thank you...', the effect is one of a strange synthesis of the bleak comedic tragedy of Beckett combined with the relentlessness of early minimalism.

Similarly zonal in feel are Christina Kubisch's electromagnetic induction installations. Drawing on a wider array of sounds than Nauman, they bring together recordings of the sounds of nature, each resonant of particular landscapes or places, together with generated electronic sounds. Often, the only visual elements

48   Jean-François Augoyard and Henry Torgue (eds), *Sonic Experience: A Guide to Everyday Sounds* (Montreal 2005), p. 4.
49   Max Neuhaus, 'Listen', in Dan Lander and Micah Lexier (eds), *Sound by Artists* (Toronto, 1990), pp. 63–7, at pp. 63, 65.

in Kubisch's work are the actual means of sound production themselves – a series of cables that transmit the sound around which the public (wearing headphones that pick up the sound) walk – as well as the visual characteristics of the chosen spaces themselves, which are important: 'These sound zones', the artist has explained, 'are often created in the open air: in woodland glades for instance, or in buildings that were not constructed to act as concert halls, such as deserted factories, shipyards and cellars.'[50] In walking through Kubisch's sonic structures, the listener is able to mix 'impossible' relationships between zones – the sound of a jungle mingled with footsteps in a cobbled street and so on. Such installations also underline how these sounds suggest a corresponding visualization, and how one sense might trigger another.

Jack Goldstein's appropriation of sound-effect recordings in the 1970s explored the idea of utilizing sounds as *objets trouvés*, and acting as a sculptural reality. Sound as raw material – in itself – relates to *musique concrète* pioneer Pierre Schaeffer's formulation of the *acousmatic*; a notion that identifies the break between sound source and its sonic effect as one which, 'marks the perceptive reality of sound as such, as distinguished from the modes of its transmission and production'.[51] But sound effects are also naturally evocative of their causes, and again can lead to visualization, an imaginary filmic narrative. Creating such a narrative out of sounds themselves was central to Tacita Dean's early work *Foley Artist* (1996) in which she explores the work of 'foley artists' who find ingenious ways of emulating and replicating sounds for a film's post-production phase. This process of 'rendering' makes the sounds appear more convincingly *real* than they would if sourced from the actual location, and in doing so, creates an over-determination. This lends 'a double property to sound: not only do we believe that sound can "objectively" and single-handedly indicate its source but also that it evokes impressions linked to this source',[52] argues French composer Michel Chion. It is this double property – the pointing to a sound source, and the semiotic complexity of that connection – that has fascinated many contemporary artists. Dean's *Foley Artist* alludes to the almost palpable gloss that the *rendered* sound gives a filmic image. Only, in this instance, she is 'painting' her narrative with those sounds alone.

If each of these sound pieces put into effect a 'profound listening', one that is focused and developed, then this certainly due to the impact of Cage's 4'33", which has had almost legendary status amongst visual artists. Many examples could be given of an attempt to translate this piece into the visual. While working on *Rolywholyover* Cage asked curator Julie Lazar what she felt was the equivalent of silence in the visual arts. 'Nothingtoseeness' she replied. Numerous artists have risen to this challenge exploring such a blank emptiness, some perhaps independently of Cage, as in Yves Klein's *The Void* (1958) at the Iris Clert Gallery in Paris, where

50   Christina Kubisch, 'About my Installations', in Lander and Lexier, *Sound by Artists*, pp. 69–72, at p. 72.
51   Pierre Schaeffer, 'Acousmatics', in Christoph Cox and Daniel Warner (eds), *Audio Culture: Readings in Modern Music* (New York, 2004), pp. 76–81, at p. 77.
52   Michel Chion, *Audio Vision* (New York, 1994), p. 111.

the gallery was pristinely prepared but empty. In the late 1960s Robert Barry used electrical currents emitted by radios transmitters in a given space, and Michael Asher's *Air Sculptures* focused simply on air pressure, so one would *feel* a space. Others have positioned this 'nothingtoseeness' as a direct homage to Cage, as in Bruce Nauman's *Mapping the Studio (Fat Chance John Cage)* (2001). Nauman, who had used the empty studio as a foil for filmed and photographed activities in seminal works from the 1960s on, returned to this subject matter for this large-scale piece. Using infra-red cameras Nauman filmed the studio at night, completely empty, apart from its residua of half-finished or evacuated projects, and an infestation of field mice. Seven large video projections map the studio space from seven positions. Occasionally colours shift, or the viewer is aware of nocturnal movement, a moth or a mouse, but apart from this not much happens for a long duration. And yet, it has the effect of making the viewer more alert – and in looking for that thing that *will* happen, the tiniest of events become magnified in their significance. By surrounding the viewer with the projections, Nauman includes the likelihood that if this something does happen, then it could also be missed. Nauman's propensity for inactivity and duration could be traced back to the influence of both La Monte Young and Cage (although, for Clement Greenberg, this was expressed thus: 'the children of mid-century and after seem to have mutated into a tolerance, nay, appetite for boredom in the aesthetic realm that's unprecedented'[53]).

But what has changed? And what distinguishes contemporary practices that combine or integrate sound, performance and time within the visual arts from their antecedents? Marked transformations have occurred in cultural attitudes, including, despite Greenberg's barbed comments, duration and how it is figured as an element within the spaces of the visual, together with the whole issue of participation, and, on many different levels, the problematic of both repetition and appropriation. Most of these issues have clear roots in the practices of earlier experimental arts.

Critics and philosophers such as Frederic Jameson and Jean-François Lyotard discussed in the 1980s and 1990s a breakdown of temporal narratives at a cultural level. The increased use and accessibility of relatively new materials such as digital sound, video and computer handling within the visual arts have intensified a drive toward spatio-temporal dislocation that is also reflected in everyday culture. And on that level the experimental and avant-garde have been swallowed up by a popular mainstream, some might say recuperated by the very capitalist system that they appeared to resist or critique. Daniel Bell, in the 1970s, saw the process as, potentially, a negative one: the excesses and exponential democratic hedonism of modernism percolating through to a voracious consumer society, already out of control. Jacques Attali, writing at the same moment, saw these processes as a nascent but possibly liberating entropy that would transform itself into another cultural stage. It is a transition from a society deadlocked into the copy, the reproduction, the accumulated stockpile of dead artefacts: from a cultural phase

---

53   Greenberg, 'Intermedia', p. 96.

of *repetition* to one that foregrounds participation freely and individually – a phase of *composition*.

If we have moved from repetition to composition in Attali's terms, then the stockpile of reproduced, historical objects becomes raw material for new approaches. 'It gives voice', he suggests, 'to the fact that rhythms and sounds are the supreme mode of relation between bodies, once the screens of the symbolic, usage and exchange are shattered … An exchange between bodies – *through work, not through objects*.'[54] Attali sees music as prophetic of future social relations, and in using experimental music as a 'predictive reality' for this ideal of composing (a collective activity, that is, or composition as a 'bringing together' of diversity rather than an isolated activity), then he seems to have been accurate, to an extent. Certainly, more recent framings of practice, such as Nicolas Bourriaud's *Relational Aesthetics*, draw similar conclusions, although he stresses continuity rather than transition:

> The constitution of convivial relations has been an historical constant since the 1960s. The generation of the 1990s took up this set of issues, though it has been relieved of the matter of the definition of art, so pivotal in the 1960s and 1970s. The issue no longer resides in broadening the boundaries of art, but in experiencing art's capacities of resistance within the overall social arena.[55]

Social networks, conviviality and play – these might be seen as the hallmarks of experimental practices in the early stages of the new century. To this we might add humour and irony – perhaps one reason why Fluxus events have been revisited of late so often by contemporary artists. 'I get too claustrophobic when things get too analytical', Charlemagne Palestine once suggested, 'I need contradiction, irony, confusuion doubt. When I see a room full of these things I can relax.'[56] Salons and social gatherings have taken on a new import in the dissemination of creative work, new allegiances have been forged between composing, improvising and the inherited stockpile of images or sounds in the cultural memory bank. Christian Marclay's *Video Quartet* (2002) and Douglas Gordon's *Feature Film* (1999) both, in their very different ways, reflect a sense of re-composition of pre-existing audio-visual cinematic materials that is in alignment with Attali's sense of exploding the passive accumulation of the stockpile, and actively and creatively intervening within it.

If this is a kind of ecological position whereby artists are reusing materials, strategies, modes, objects and images, then is there not also the danger of a stagnation of the very notion of the experimental? If Martin Creed, to take one example, playfully addresses his doubts and attends to the question 'what do I do?' – an experimental approach if ever there was one – what do we make of the

---

54   Jacques Attali, *Noise: The Political Economy of Music* (Minneapolis, 1985), p. 143.
55   Bourriaud, *Relational Aesthetics*, pp. 30, 31.
56   'Looking for Mr Goodbear', Charlemagne Palestine interviewed by Mark Webber in *Resonance*, 7/1 (1998), pp. 26–30, at p. 29.

déjà vu that accompanies almost every piece that emerges in his response to that question? Is it a situation of creative exhaustion? Does everything now navigate to certain well-worn grooves? This is a pressing problem for composers, artists and those involved in intermedia. There is a thin line between replication and creative allusion, and being haunted by the objects of the past can gridlock cultural experimentation no matter how 'convivially' produced or addressed. There remains, however, to echo both Lyotard and Feldman, a potential indeterminacy within all fields of activity, including what we might see as 'old' media, that is essential to experimental practices. Surely this sense of an opening into the unknown is where the spirit of the experimental resides, harbouring within it 'an excess, a rapture, a potential of associations that overflows all the determinations of its "reception" and "production"'.[57]

---

57   Jean-François Lyotard, 'Critical Reflections', *Artforum*, 29/8 (1991), pp. 92–3.

PART II

Fourteen Musicians

James Saunders

I have always been interested in composer interview books. As a composer myself, I find the insight they provide into the working process invaluable, in addition to their essential documentation of composers' views on their work and the issues which surround them. They have informed much of my own development, helping to shape my views on music.[1] In 2003 I decided to start my own project with the aim of producing a book of interviews with composers, later expanding its remit to include improvisers. I considered doing face-to-face interviews but decided that this would be logistically quite difficult and would not necessarily produce the same depth of thought in the final texts. Having already conducted a series of email interviews in 1999 whilst running a website called *new music*, I felt this would again be the best way of producing the texts. One of the advantages of the correspondence format is that participants (ideally) have more time to consider their questions and responses, resulting, I hope, in a clearer view of their work. The trade-off is the lack of spontaneity perhaps: this is how they write, rather than how they speak. As it turned out, some of the interviews took many months to complete, whilst others involved a fairly rapid correspondence. It also became necessary to interview some of the participants orally, although these interviews, with the exception of Alvin Lucier, ended up taking place over the telephone.

The starting point was the desire to learn more about the working practices of musicians who interested me. The interviews primarily explore how the selected musicians work, focusing on the processes involved in developing their recent projects, set against more general aesthetic concerns. They aim to shed light on the disparate nature of some current work whilst seeking to find points of possible contact, representing a few streams within recent experimental music. Many of

---

1   There are many excellent interview books, but the ones which have informed this project are Geoff Smith and Nicola Walker Smith, *American Originals: Interviews with 25 Contemporary Composers* (London, 1994); Cole Gagne and Tracy Caras, *Soundpieces: Interviews with American Composers* (Metuchen, NJ, 1982); Andrew Ford, *Composer to Composer: Conversations About Contemporary Music* (London, 1993); William Furlong, *Audio Arts: Discourse and Practice in Contemporary Art* (London, 1994); Kevin Volans, *Summer Gardeners: Conversations with Composers* (Durban, 1985); and the literal transcriptions of composer interviews at Tim Parkinson's website www.untitledwebsite. com.

the practitioners are active in areas that span disciplines, such as notated music and improvisation, and the interviews explore the interaction of these activities in the context of their work. Unavoidably, certain trends emerged throughout the correspondences as a result of my own interests: modularity, reuse of material, duration, approaches to titling, notation, improvisation and involvement as performers, to name a few. I made a conscious decision to avoid biographical discussion, except where this related to the main subject matter. I also wanted to avoid where possible retelling their learned history: this is a particular problem with interviews and to an extent unavoidable. By concentrating on current work, I hoped they would have something new to add to existing writing.

The people I chose to interview have a number of different links both to me and to each other. Importantly I had met most of them, and knew some quite well. Some were at the heart of Nyman's 1974 study, whilst others were not born then. Some use the term experimental when describing their work, others feel less comfortable with some of its connotations. There is perhaps, though, a common interest in extremes, and in many cases radical approaches to making music, which unites them. Essentially, though, all the interviewees have created music which is important to me, and on that basis were chosen to be involved in the project. Their selection is therefore unashamedly subjective.

The clearest group comprises the four British composers Laurence Crane, Christopher Fox, Bryn Harrison and Tim Parkinson. They are, in very different ways, amongst the inheritors of the British experimental tradition. In their music there is a seriousness of purpose allied with, at times, a lightness of touch which is symptomatic of this approach. It is often an uncomfortable listening experience. They are not afraid to subvert some of the preconceptions shaping the ways in which composers should act: the surface of Fox's music is seldom the same from piece to piece; Crane almost exclusively uses a bare triadic harmony; Parkinson treats all material as available for use; Harrison presents a flattened sound world in which great richness resides.

The draw of this alternative canon for Christopher Fox as a young composer was its opening up of possibilities denied by various intransigent musical orthodoxies which surrounded him. Whilst at first listen the sound worlds of his subsequent compositions are somewhat disparate, in much of his music this is as a result of the collision of opposites: clarity and complexity, consonance and dissonance, rhythm and stasis, indeterminacy and fixation. It is this that binds his work at a deeper level alongside a sustained exploration of process in many guises, a strategy which underpins much experimental music. Indeed, there has been a marked shift in his recent work towards structural mobility and other indeterminate approaches to realizing material in particular, making this more explicit. His large-scale *Everything You Need To Know* (1999–2001) for up to ten players and voice(s) comprises 26 separately realizable compositions and can last from 5 to 85 minutes in performance. Whilst such modularity draws comparisons with the inauguration of modern experimentalism almost half a century earlier, Fox says these pieces offer order rather than anarchy, and it is perhaps that which sets them apart. I first became aware of his music in the early 1990s and was drawn to the sudden cuts between either subtly or extremely differentiated materials. The objectivity of this work was striking through its presentation of material in such a clear manner. Later, when he was my doctoral supervisor, the discussions we had helped shape my ideas on open form pieces at a time when we were both producing modular work, albeit in entirely different ways.

Conversely, whilst the exactitude of Bryn Harrison's music might seem to be the least overtly experimental presented here, the link with late Feldman is key. His primary interest is in our experience of time as listeners, and in particular the way we ascribe it with directionality. The moment is the focus in much of his recent work, played out against a cyclical repetition of events, sometimes exact, sometimes with almost imperceptible variation. Structural panels of rigorously controlled material are presented with a slower rate of change than is normally the case in Feldman: Harrison uses looping processes to independently determine the drift of individual elements rather than the clearer cuts formed by Feldman's gridded patterning. It is a music in which little happens and there is no sense of direction, even though it displays a constant, intricate motion. The scale of his music has changed considerably too, moving towards the much longer durations that allow this sense of immersion to emerge. As composers, we have grown up together. Both based in Yorkshire for most of our formative years, the relative distance from London provided by our location has perhaps formulated a sense of independence that would not have been afforded us were we to have moved south. We have tracked each other's development in post-concert discussions, long-distance car journeys and remote parts of eastern Europe for some 15 years and shared our first live experiences of the extended late music of Feldman. It is for me then no surprise that his music has started to find its place on a larger scale.

My first contact with Tim Parkinson, through Bryn, was via his work as a performer, notably at the series of concerts he programmed at the BMIC in its former Stratford Place home from 1997 to 2000. His industry in presenting music from composers who were new to me at the time, alongside my own pieces, was a galvanizing force. The associations we made through those events have led to many subsequent projects, including this book. Although I came to know his music well at this time, it was the later experience of working with Tim as a performer that led me to a clearer understanding of his work as a composer. We began playing together as a duo, Parkinson Saunders, in 2003, working on mostly indeterminate repertoire which uses any sound-producing means, seated at two tables. The kinds of strategies he uses to realize the music we find interesting reflects his tendencies as a composer: there is a meandering mix of randomness and extreme control, with one often subverting the other with surprising results. The multiplicity that appears in so much of his music confronts our notion of compatibility as a defining factor in a piece's identity. There is an indirect connection between elements which only becomes apparent through our experience of them, and the way we make the links ourselves as listeners. So whilst found or pre-fabricated material is at the heart of his music, part of a need to look outside of himself to begin work, it is the often bare presentation of these tightly crafted moments which allows their natural beauty to project.

Laurence Crane, also regularly performed by Tim in his concert series, makes the link himself to previous work through Scratch Orchestra founder Howard Skempton, emphasizing the importance of simplicity and clarity in his music. Crane's material is resolutely abstract, and despite the superficial references to a classical tradition, his harmony has little sense of teleology. Tonal constructions are hinted at, but mutated through a studied use of unbalanced and extended repetitions. His approach to titling is important too: descriptions of the ensemble, as with Feldman, form a large proportion of his catalogue, as do names (which make passing references to the music's original performers). The Skempton connection can also be heard through his general preference for miniatures and movements. Although more recent work has explored longer spans, much of Crane's music deals with economy. When I first encountered Laurence's music, my interest was in extreme miniaturization, and his exquisitely constructed, poised compositions made a deep impact on me, both through their own beauty and in the way they made me readdress the assumptions I had grown to have about the way music could (should?) be. It has been interesting to see the way in which his music has changed since then: principally the sound world has expanded in some pieces, often looking away from pitch to define material. The focus and reduction is still apparent though, with a carefully selected palette of sounds distilled from the objects used to make them.

Objects and their sonic properties are more overtly central to Jennifer Walshe's music however. The terms of reference for her work are wide and draw in the world around her: everything has potential as material, whether it is found text from food packaging, old answer machine messages, skateboarding or the texture of ribbons. There is a voracity to her collection of sounds and exploration of ways to elicit them from performers, exemplified by pieces such as *Hostess-in-a-Jiffy® Brings You Cooking With Stone: 4 Five-Minute Dishes* (2004) which presents instructions for sonic cooking, or *elephant* (2004) with its unique scoring of 'harp, gun'. The manner in which sounds are made is perhaps every bit as important as their audible result. Instructions in her scores typically indicate the necessary attitude required to make sounds as a primary focus, or differing forms of documentation are used to enable performers to triangulate her intentions when working with objects. This consideration of the physical situation of performing is a constant in her work, drawing on her own experience as an improviser and a concern with what it feels like to make sounds. Often this involves recontextualizing her material, stripping away some of its inherent meaning so that it can be used as a building block to construct new identities, finding a natural extension in her recent installation, stage and intermedia work. All of this was present in the first piece of hers that I heard at the Darmstadt Ferienkurse in 2000, her astonishing duo for violin and voice *as mo chéann* (2000), which she also performed. This piece helped me begin to expand the palette of my own work and its impact on an unsuspecting audience was startling, as was her follow-up lecture there two years later, which mostly used kick-boxing as a presentation medium.

I also came across Manfred Werder's music for the first time in 2000, following up encouraging comments made by others about his work and that of the Edition

Wandelweiser composers with whom he is associated, eventually meeting him whilst he was on a residency in London later that year. These composers, centred on Antoine Beuger's publishing company, create an uncompromising music: it deals with extremes and archetypes, is generally very quiet and silence has a large share of the often extended performance durations. The presentation of sound material is very clear: gridded structures and the establishment of spaces in which sounds might be placed are common traits. Werder's music comprises a number of different ongoing series. His *ausführende* writing project (1999–) is a set of compositions for between one and nine performers. Each of these pieces contains a series of 160,000 time units, each lasting 12 seconds and consisting of six seconds of sound, followed by six seconds of silence. The scores are performed in succession, with the next performance starting at the action following the final one of the previous instalment. In his recent dated pieces, however, Werder specifies a gradually reducing number of conditions for the presentation of sounds and actions, from the trio *stück 2003*'s instruction for two of the performers to play a common pitch lasting three to seven seconds once during the performance, to the more open requirement of *2005*[1]: place/ time// (sounds). The precision and subtlety of his exploration of modes of performative action can be seen when comparing this with the later *2006*[2], which specifies: places// a time/// (sounds). Werder's music questions our place in the world as both participants and observers.

This is a sentiment shared by Antoine Beuger, whose assertion that the subject of music is the pervasive noise of the world and that its form is cut from this infinite diversity is perhaps surprising for a sounding result that is permanently on the verge of disappearing. The extreme dilution of sound emphasizes both its savoured value and the importance of space as its receptacle. Calm inaction is the norm, with sound and momentary action the exception. Listening to performances of his music, it is easy to forget what is being experienced: when sounds reappear after a long period of silence, they have an impact which is born only of necessity. Sounds also rarely appear together intentionally, almost always in isolation to further reinforce their identity: this is music of the utmost clarity. Yet within each sound Beuger suggests there are infinite possibilities, so that everything can be contained in the brief moments of activity which characterize his work. Structurally, his music from the 1990s is either rigorously ordered with a grid at its heart or very open, with the minimum necessary instructions as to how to project sounds. These approaches are linked: freedom out of precision, and precision out of freedom. More recently he has begun exploring the ontology of ensemble size in a series of pieces for specified numbers of players, such as *dedekind duos* (2003) in which two performers play specified pitches as long quiet tones, separated by enough time to breathe, or much longer, carefully listening to each other. From these pieces fundamental questions concerning the nature of separation and togetherness emerge, as does the serendipity of coincidence, focusing on how people interact with each other and project sound in performance. I was introduced to Beuger's work by Manfred Werder, and we finally met up in Witten in April 2002 in a hotel breakfast room surrounded by most of the German contemporary music establishment, in town for the Neue Musiktage. Antoine showed me some scores, producing them from a beautiful well-used leather briefcase, and we had an interesting morning discussing each other's work. I have been fascinated by his music ever since: for me it is a benchmark to which other music must be compared. The interplay of action and inaction, of sound and silence in carefully weighted and understated amounts continually makes me evaluate my own practice, and the ideas behind his work cut to the heart of the nature of music and making art.

The meticulous placement and balancing of sound is also of note in Bernhard Günter's work, whether electroacoustically composed or, more recently, improvised. Whilst he points out its wide dynamic range, it is essentially a quiet music, one which seeks to draw us in as listeners. The body of work for which he is perhaps best known – the series of recordings beginning with his 1993 release *Un peu de neige salie* – explores a reduced palette of glitch sounds, working with highly detailed textures which have an innate complexity. Günter's approach foregrounds aspects of sounds that otherwise go unnoticed, whether due to existing on the border of sound and silence, or their perceived ancillary status as musical material. Whilst he is at pains to point out that he does not consider his music experimental, given it is ostensibly result- rather than process-oriented, this particular concern has much in common with other practitioners in the field. His processing of sampled sounds strips them of their more conventional meanings, allowing him to work more closely with them as abstract sonic materials. His recent improvisation projects have continued to explore this reduced sound world, working first with Mark Wastell and Graham Halliwell as +minus, and later with Gary Smith as Klangstaub. Here too a slow, breath-paced layering of gradually changing drones allows the material's detail to emerge over time.

It is arguably a similar process in Phill Niblock's music. Although the dynamic level is very different – he generally requires at least 110dB in contrast to Bernhard Günter's near silence – the immersive nature of both composers' work is a vital part of our experience of it as listeners. Niblock has been developing his layered drone pieces for nearly forty years, working with multi-tracked sampled recordings of solo instruments that combine to produce a vibrant beating of fractionally detuned difference and sum tones. Heard live, the physical impact of his work is powerful: the chaotic richness found within the wall of sound he presents takes time to emerge, but once attuned to reveals an interweaving of dense oscillating counterpoint. The scale of his pieces is important too in this regard: most average around 20 minutes, a duration which is essential for this attuning process. I first heard Niblock's live performance in Ostrava in 2001. He was midway through his annual European concert tour and spent a morning playing five pieces accompanied by his films of people working. Although I had heard some of his music on CD previously, this had not prepared me for its live performance. As with my early encounters with the work of many of the people interviewed here, it was an experience which changed how I thought about music.

I also initially met both Alvin Lucier and Christian Wolff in Ostrava at the first New Music Days, organized by Peter Kotik. Both composers' work had fascinated me for some time, so it was a great opportunity to find out more in person. Lucier has been central to developments in experimental electronic music since the 1960s, with a focus on acoustic phenomena as the material and subject matter for much of his earlier work. From pieces like *I am sitting in a room* (1969) in which the continual playback and recording of a text in the same space reinforces the room's overtones to create a throbbing harmonic drone, to *Still Lives* (2003), which sets piano notes against slow sliding sine tones to create variable beating patterns, their audibility is framed by his compositional approach. Subsequent work has tended to draw on these techniques and instrumentalize them to various degrees, such as with *Diamonds* (1999) for three orchestras where the violins replace the sine waves. Whilst in Lucier's work processes are articulated with extreme clarity, it is music which constantly confounds expectations. It is of course possible to read his scores and gain an understanding of the principles involved, but it is only through the acoustic reality of the sounding result that the music emerges. One of the questions posed by the work of all the interviewees here is a consideration of how we listen, and this is in many ways most clearly exemplified by Lucier.

Christian Wolff's work addresses the way musicians interact with each other, and with material. In much of his work the contingency of the relationships he prescribes between people leads to a vibrant provisionality in the resultant music. In pieces like *Looking North* from the *Prose Collection* (1968–71) or the fourth part of *Burdocks* (1970–71) performers are, in differing ways, asked to attempt to synchronize their actions with those of others. The performance energy set up by these simple constraints can only be achieved by players listening and responding to each other in this manner: any attempt to capture this activity through more conventional forms of notation would be pointless. It is no surprise that Wolff has worked for a long time as an improviser: the spontaneity in his notated work draws on this experience whilst at the same time formalizing it. Performers are sometimes asked to make decisions during performance. Whilst these are not necessarily improvisatory actions, there is a freedom of movement granted through his use of optionality: time brackets, multiple transpositions of the same material or the gravitational pull of heterophony. The result is a social music, in which participation is a rich and rewarding experience. In his recent work, it has been interesting to see how he has revisited the varied strategies employed over the course of his career, whether contingent or more determinate. There is a compendium-like summary of ideas in these pieces, whereby disparate fragments are presented together to form longer spans, such as with the hour-long *Long Piano (Peace March 11)* (2004–2005) or the piece for three orchestras *Ordinary Matter* (2001). This admission of personal history is unusual amongst composers, for whom the pressure to move forwards is constant, and it is indicative of the inclusive approach to his work.

Whilst Wolff has been extremely active as an improviser, improvisation is central to the work of Evan Parker. Known for his fluid development of multiphonic aggregates to produce a constantly changing patterning, Parker has evolved an instantly recognizable sound. Despite the flux of the music's surface, he talks of his recent exploration of limited interval types to underpin his improvisations, emphasizing the reduced nature of his approach. Here practice and memorization are important, allowing the development of sequence-building methods which inform subsequent performances. The impact of group work is also of note: specific developments in his technique arose from the necessity of responding to the musicians around him, leading to the possibility of working as a soloist. Recently, his exploratory work with different groupings of musicians, taking on 'the specifics of time and space', has allowed the further development of the research ethos that lies at the heart of improvisation. Finding new things in new or old situations is central to experimentation. There are moments which leave an indelible mark on your memory, and hearing Parker perform live for the first time was, for me, one of these. At the beginning of a workshop in Huddersfield whilst I was a student, he talked a little about what he did, and then played for five minutes: I was completely unprepared for the complexity of the sound, and the shape of the resultant performance, and it has stayed with me since then.

The work of the group of the younger genertion of improvisers subsequently labelled New London Silence has also been important to my own development as a composer. Their interest in quiet, carefully placed sounds came at a time when I was beginning to engage with similar material in my own notated work, and this was reinforced by knowing Rhodri Davies from his time as a postgraduate in Huddersfield in the mid-1990s. His interest in improvisation developed from around then – I was at his first improvised performance – and grew into a music which has been extremely influential over the last decade. His response to the prevailing conditions was to do the opposite, initially looking to small gestures and silence as a way of reassessing conventions, but more recently exploring a wider palette of sounds, expanding the scope of his instrumental preparations. He describes this as a gradual process, one which developed organically: it is mirrored by his approach to group work, where his strategy is to challenge himself to work against the grain. This is not to say he is deliberately reactionary: these trajectories are creatively necessary to stimulate change. Davies also works regularly with notated music, and has commissioned much new work for the harp. He draws a clear line between his work as an improviser and his expectation of notated music written for him however. The music's identity must not be reliant on a mining of his resources as an improviser, a view echoed by other practitioners concerned about the appropriation of their work by composers.

Whilst improvisation also forms a component of Philip Jeck's music, he considers it as much arranging given his use of records as its material. His work in performance, recording and installation is linked by the equipment he uses, but is in other ways very different. In his performances, making decisions about the deployment of material can be altered by the inconsistent response of his ageing record players and well-played records, necessitating the readjustment of ideas when something unexpected occurs. The installation work uses domestic time switches to control grouped banks of players set with a prepared tone arm tied to create loops, or the use of locked grooves. Over time, these too degrade and produce slippage: the time switches drift chaotically out of phase, and the arm and groove preparations become worn. Here the equipment defines the detail of the resultant music, taking its own course within Jeck's prescribed boundaries. Both these approaches contrast with his recorded work, surprisingly created by mostly cutting and pasting minidisc recordings of live performances. The opportunity to audit the results of this process allows for more precision, although he notes the importance of surprise here as well, with a dislocation between his memory of a performance and its newfound context as sample informing his decisions. It is perhaps no surprise that collage is a common theme through all this work, given that his material is derived from locked physical objects in which sound resides. It is testament to his skill at manipulating them, though, that subverts the music's construction in the sounding result.

*

Despite the remove from their normal practice, I would hope that the process of engaging in discussion about their work has been a creative act for the participants. Whilst at times I am sure it has been a disruptive activity, they have patiently allowed me to question their working methods and learn more about their approaches to music. I am extremely grateful to all the participants for their commitment to the project, and the time they have taken from their busy schedules to correspond with me in the preparation of these texts. From their initial involvement through to final editing, it has been a revealing experience, and I hope provides a snapshot of experimental musical practices at the beginning of the twenty-first century.

Antoine Beuger

I am interested in your notion of music being a cut into what you call the 'timeless noise, which consists of everything that sounds',[1] in the same way that sculpture relates to stone and the possibility that it might contain all sculpture. How does this relate to your own work?

The main attraction of taking 'timeless noise' or 'the world' to be the matter of music is its infinity. So, instead of assuming music to have some finite number of basic elements to start with, I am suggesting the opposite: the matter of music is 'all that is (sounding)'. The form of a specific music, then, is the way it cuts into this infinitely dense continuum. This suggests that, in creating music, one is not, as it were, going into the continuum to look for or to discover certain definite things to be taken out and to be used as elements of a composition. There is no way of entering the continuum: because of its density, there is no place to walk around. It seems more appropriate to think of creating music as cutting into this infinity, knowing that even the smallest slice one carves out, again, contains an infinite number of elements. So, asking someone to play an 'a' of a certain duration, a certain volume and a certain tone colour is like asking him to write the number pi: he'll do something more or less approaching something else, which is more or less close to something else again, etc.

As you may see, I am trying to argue against the idea of reduction in music. Quite often my (our?) music has been called reductionist: reducing music to its basic elements. I am completely opposed to that view. Music is not made up from basic – material or formal – elements. Whatever musical thing you are hearing, be it a tone or a phrase or a chord or a piece, is an infinity in itself. Difference is everywhere. Sounding always means: sounding different. According to Leibniz there is no repetition in nature: no two leaves are exactly alike.[2] This means to me: composing is not about creating or inventing differences or concatenations of differences. Each sound is going to be different anyway. I like the idea of a piece of music being just a few sounds, of performing music as just playing a few sounds.

---

1   Antoine Beuger, 'Grundsätzliche Entscheidungen', *Edition Wandelweiser*, http://www.wandelweiser.de/beuger/ABTexte.html (30 May 2006).

2   The original source for this can be found in paragraph 9 of *The Monadology* (see Gottfried Wilhelm Leibniz, *The Monadology and Other Philosophical Writings*, trans. Robert Latta (London, 1971), p. 222).

Composing seems to me to be about making a few basic decisions, that open up a specific, still infinite world of differences: just a few sounds.

So when you place relatively isolated sounds in your music, to what extent is there an implication that we listen beyond the note/event level, that we hear these sounds as infinitely variable complexes of microtonal, rhythmic and timbral fluctuations with their own internal structure?

I am tempted to say that we probably never or only very seldom hear 'a note' or 'a sound' and by implication always hear beyond the note/event level. The situations, in which we would say, that we hear a sound, I think, are those where we are afraid, don't know, what is really going on. In normal circumstances we hear things that happen: we hear a car drive by, or someone screaming, or someone open a door. We even hear him open the door very carefully or hastily. We hear that it is Sandra who opens the door, because we know that is exactly the way she always opens the door. We may even hear that it is Sandra opening the door being a bit impatient today, trying not to show it, ad infinitum. A description of what we hear will never end, especially since we never hear just one thing. Even sounds put in isolation in a piece of music always appear in a certain environment, they are part of an atmosphere, which, of course, they also help to create.

So, in a musical performance, I would say, we do not hear 'sounds' with certain acoustic qualities. We do hear people play sounds (on instruments, usually) and upon hearing them, we immediately know lots of things about what is going on with them, how concentrated they are, how sensitive they play, how attentively they listen to each other, whether they are nervous, whether they are serious about what they do, etc. We hear that it is two people who are playing, and the way they relate; or three people, four, the way their activities/sounds get mixed and fused…

All these levels and innumerably many more are essential to a musical situation, to the experience of playing or listening to a piece of music. Listening, we immediately grasp the atmosphere, which is a conglomerate of an endless number of minute perceptions on all kinds of levels, most of them not conscious. If we are confused or don't feel comfortable in the situation we will either try to find our way into it (using the experience we had with (similar) music before – or in other situations), or we may refuse it and stay outside. In order for a musical situation to develop, I think, someone just has to play a few sounds. A composer may have set the frame for it. I am convinced that composing has nothing to do with inventing (concatenations of) differences, and that composers focusing on that level are very superficial.

This issue of the particular relationship between people in a piece seems to be important for you, and this is perhaps most keenly observed in a solo or duo, of which there are a relatively high proportion in your list of pieces. For you, what is a solo, or a duo? How do you view the different types of relationship which might exist within them?

You are right. The number of performers is a very essential issue to me. I am strongly convinced that there is something so to say ontologically different about a solo, duo etc. situation: it has to do with being alone, being 'zu zweit' (I don't know how to say this in English. there doesn't seem to be a word for it, maybe just 'being two'?). Three again is a very different situation. When you go higher up differences seem to become more gradual and less ontological.

So I think solo music at its best is revealing something about solitude, about seclusion. *calme étendue* (1996–97) in all its different versions to me is an exploration of this situation: someone sitting there, either performing a regular activity on his instrument or just sitting quietly, doing nothing. Silence all around him. No communication, no showing, no presentation of differences to an audience. Just sitting there, all by himself, sometimes doing something, sometimes not.

ins ungebundene (1998), and in a slightly different form *tout à fait solitaire* (1998), takes it one step further. The player is basically sitting in silence, very rarely playing one single very soft, rather short sound. Somewhere between 10 and 40 minutes into the piece the sound stops appearing. Silence remains. The piece ends somewhere between 60 and 90 minutes after it started. This piece is revealing something about disappearance. The way the sound appears (very rarely, very soft, rather short) is already very much a form of disappearing: the moment it is there, it is already gone. Then, at some point, it has disappeared altogether and doesn't return. What remains is what was already there: silence, but now without the rare occurrence of the sound. A silence coloured as it were by the absence of the sound: the sound has gone, isn't there anymore. The concept, or better the experience of 'not anymore' as the strongest possibility for us to relate to emptiness or the void has been the focus of my attention for many years. This focus on emptiness and silence, I feel, is absolutely connected to the idea of solo music. Today I would, axiomatically, say that the content of a solo is the void.

The content of a duo is something different. I started exploring this in *aus dem garten* (1998). Two players playing the 'same' tone (again: very soft, rather short). In ten-minute sections they alternately play the tone once. So somewhere during the first ten minutes the first player plays the sound once, somewhere during the next ten minutes the second player plays the sound once, etc. A player may also decide not to play the sound. So what is at stake here is the experience of separation: they can never come together, since they are separated in time. They can come very close, if one player plays near the end of his time and the other player plays at the beginning of his time. But this nearness has renewed distance as a prize: only after nearly 20 minutes another situation of nearness may be established. So a very subtle 'communication' based on separation takes place. Or, in other words, being separated is established as the basis of a relationship, of 'two-ness'.

ein ton. eher kurz. sehr leise (1998) is similar: 30 second sections this time and the additional rule that the decision not to play the sound during a section implies not playing it anymore for the rest of the performance: it means leaving the other player alone. This very much reflects a love relationship: two people are together (which means: are in a situation of being separated) for a while (I am tempted to write: twogether). Ultimately they are separated forever, by parting or by death.

Three again is very different. Here neither void nor separation is the issue. It has elements of these, but sharing, fusion, mixing, having things in common, and connecting also seem to enter the stage.

My counting for a long time has been: one, two, many (a group of people). Next step would be a mass of people. Musically: solo, duo, ensemble, orchestra. If you follow this line the limit is everything, which in sonic terms is white noise. Here we are back at where we started talking…

Recently I discovered a possible way to differentiate between three and four etc. with the help of the concept of ordinal number as defined in Cantorian set theory.[3] Counting, here, starts out with zero, not with one. One, therefore, is not something given as basic unit. Set theory doesn't accept basic units of count.

Zero is equivalent to the empty set: the set which has no elements at all. Let us write: 0. One now can be constructed as the set which has 0 as its only element: (0). This set is clearly different from 0, since it does have an element, whereas 0 doesn't. Two is (0, (0)): the set which contains both 0 and 1. What is interesting here is that the elements of this set (0 and 1) have nothing in common, pure separation, or disjunction. Three is: (0, (0), (0, (0))): the set, which contains 0, 1 and 2. Here two of the elements have something in common: (0) and (0,(0)) both contain 0. So we have both sharing and separation. In four (the set containing 0, 1, 2 and 3) there is even more sharing: 1, 2 and 3 have 0 in common, 2 and 3 have 1 in common. Only 0 has nothing in common with the other elements. Sharing grows, of course, when you go higher up the scale. Void and separation, although always included, become more and more marginal. Also, the number of possible combinations of elements (subsets) grows, exponentially. In this language I see a clear difference between three and four: Gemeinsamkeit (sharing), emerging in three, is becoming the main thing in four, then, of course, even more in five, six etc.

In *cantor quartets* (2003) I am musically exploring what happens when you go from one to two to three to four. A quartet's score has four lines, seven notes on each line. The tones are long to very long, very soft and there is time between the tones. They are all notated within one octave (upward from middle C on the piano), but each may be played in any octave.

Four phases:

1. solo: one player plays line 1.
2. duo: after finishing he plays line 2, another player, simultaneously, plays line 1
3. trio: after both players finished their lines, they move down one line (to line 2 and 3), a third player now plays line 1.
4. quartet: after they finished, they move down another line (to 2, 3 and 4), the fourth player plays line 1.

---

3   The text Beuger used as a reference whilst developing this approach was Alain Badiou, *L'être et l'événement* (Paris, 1988), published in English as Alain Badiou, *Being and Event*, trans. Oliver Feltham (London, 2006).

It is amazing what happens in a performance of these pieces: each step is a step into a completely different world, from a solo-world to a duo-world. The trio-world, then, works as a somewhat hybrid situation, still somewhat reminiscent of the duo-world, but no longer being it. The quartet-world really is a world of mixture, fusion, sharing.

Well, these were some thoughts on number and how I feel it impacts a musical situation.

Although you seem to indicate that sharing is impossible in a duo under these circumstances, could you envisage a situation where this might be possible in your work? The duo section of cantor quartets *seems to imply this for instance, if only in a transitory way as part of the movement from isolation towards sharing.*

That is a very interesting question, indeed. Of course it is possible to have a duo music in which the aspect of separation, or, as I would say, of two-ness, is not or not primarily realized. Just as in life not every relation of two people is a love relationship (e.g. two people working together, two people being friends or sharing a train compartment, etc.), in music not every duo is automatically reflecting the intrinsic or ontological structure of 'two', which is disjunction. In these cases it might be more appropriate to speak about 'with-ness', the basic experience being with someone else, not being separated from someone else, as in a love situation. Probably most duo music is doing just that: two people being/playing together for a while.

Number, in these cases, doesn't really matter, and is basically a question of density: how many 'ones' are brought together: three is a bit denser than two and so forth, but not structurally different. When I write for duo situations, I want to learn about what is specific for 'two' as opposed to 'one' or 'three'. In other words: writing a duo, I want to learn about separation, not about sharing; about love, not about friendship, etc. On the other hand, if I want to find something revealed about sharing, why should I write a duo?

The interesting thing playing the *cantor quartets* is that the four phases are really separate stages. There is no building up, no reaching the next stage. The next stage is not reached, it is entered by stepping into it. It is a new beginning, each time. Discrete steps, no continuity. So I wouldn't say that there is a 'movement from isolation towards sharing'. The four worlds are not contiguous, there is a between each time. So the first stage is a real solo situation, there is nothing the other three players contribute. They are in a way just part of the audience. It completely depends on the soloist, what happens, how long it lasts (theoretically, it could take hours). Only after he has *finished* his line the duo world may be entered. So there is a cut one thing *ends*, something else *begins*, not a transition. Upon its start, then, the duo world is immediately there. For it to start, though, the solo world must have ended. And so on.

You haven't asked me, but I would like to add a few thoughts on Emily Dickinson. Her work has fascinated me for a very long time and in 2001/2002 I focused on composing a series of nine pieces on Dickinson poems.[4] Each of the pieces lasts 100 minutes, is for two performers (one speaking voice, one instrument) and is basically a syllabic reading of the underlying text. Most of the texts are fairly short, so the syllables read are surrounded by vast silences. Also the ('accompanying') instrument plays very few tones. Sounds of speaker and instrument never occur simultaneously. The syllables are read the way you read when you write a word and simultaneously say it: a very introverted sound, shaped by the writing movement, not aimed at communication. The pieces may be performed either individually (as duo pieces) or all together (19 speakers, 19 instruments).

I think Emily Dickinson's poems, i.e. her writing, must be seen as (writing) letters. She wrote over 10,000 letters, most of them extremely poetic by themselves or containing poems she copied by hand for the addressee. It was her way of publishing. Absence, separation is the basis of communicating by letters: when the letter is written, the addressee is absent; when the letter is read by the addressee, the writer is absent. The time of the writing always is different from the time of the reading. This was the way Emily Dickinson wanted her relations with other people to be. With the people she really wanted to be close to, she refused to sit together and talk. To her, doing this would mean a form of betrayal to the relation. It is told, that on the rare occasions a friend visited her, she would sit in one room, the visitor in another, the door ajar. Even with her beloved sister-in-law, with whom she certainly had her most confidential relationship and who lived with her family in a house on the other side of the Dickinson mansion's garden, she used to communicate by writing letters. She never attended lectures or society meetings. To me this means she wanted all her relationships to have the intensity of a love relationship. She avoided sharing, she forced separation. Two was her number.[5]

Therefore I cannot see how Dickinson's poetry could be recited without destroying it. You don't recite letters in front of an audience. For it, declamation seems to be completely out of place. Let alone musical settings… My Dickinson pieces try to be faithful to the 'two-ness' implied in her poetry. I hope they reveal something about it in a very subtle, non-spectacular way. I tried to find a voice for the poems, which stays as close as possible to the hand-writing and is not searching for communication. Could this be the way a hand writing a letter sounds? As you see, Emily Dickinson has taught me most I think to know about 'two'.

The parallel with this form of duo discussion is clear of course, as the separation in time and place leads to a curiously disjointed approach. In working on these interviews we are sucked back into their world when new messages arrive, and our thoughts naturally change over the course of their writing, whereas in face-to-face interviews there is perhaps more of a sense of belonging to one time and place.

The Emily Dickinson piece brings me to a question I wanted to ask you about the regular appearance of related series of pieces in your recent work. As well as landscapes of absence

---

4   *landscapes of absence* (2) (2001–2002).
5   Beuger cites Cynthia Griffin Wolff, *Emily Dickinson* (New York, 1986) as his main source on Dickinson.

(2) (2001–2002), there are other striking examples of this approach, notably another text-based piece calme étendue *(1996–97), and also* place *(1996–97) and* sound *(1997). Could you explain your interest in series, and the relationship between the experience of separate and complete performances of their component parts?*

You are right, there are many series to be found in my worklist.

(1) *first/second etc. music for marcia hafif* (1994). These titles mark pieces which represent significant changes or accomplishments (as I perceive them) in my work. Marcia Hafif is a monochrome painter.[6] Her work develops in series. Meanwhile there are maybe about 18 series, some of them finished, some of them still going on. The first series consists of thousands of drawings, in which she drew small vertical lines, starting at the left top of the page, going from left to right until she reached the right bottom of the page. All drawings are very similar, all are different. She did the same thing over and over again for several years. What came out were all these differences. Another series she called *the extended grey series*, grey paintings, each of them a different grey. As she couldn't find another shade of grey, the series was finished (108 paintings). In the series of *black paintings* she goes back to the old (Renaissance) techniques of creating the colour black. The paintings present these different mixes of colour supposed to look black. In yet another series she takes two colours plus white, mixing the colours anew for each stroke, of course never reaching exactly the same result. Her work and her thinking has been a great help to me ever since I saw it for the first time.

(2) *calme étendue* (1996–97) was my project for a number of years. The structure of the piece stays the same in all versions: minimal duration of a performance 45 minutes, maximal duration nine hours; sounding phases alternating with silent ones according to a chance generated structure; in the sounding phases one sound every eight seconds, usually three seconds long, leaving five seconds of silence until the next sound. My task in composing versions for different instruments then was to find an activity on the instrument, say on the cello, which reveals something about what it is to play cello. An activity, in other words, which could be really fulfilling and satisfying for a cello player to be involved in for many hours. I used to meet with the player and just watch him play his instrument, noticing what is going on, sometimes suggesting things, trying things out until we found this one activity, which turned out to be the most revealing and satisfying. These years were in a way another study of instrumentation for me, the focus not being to find out what variety of sounds may be produced on a cello, but to find one single activity, which is really about playing cello, rather than violin or viola or a wind instrument etc. The activity was the focus, the sound resulting from the activity its natural result: this is how this activity sounds.

I continued working on *calme étendue* until I got stuck. The end of 1997, beginning of 1998 was a real crisis for me. The structure of the piece: some sounds in regular

---

6   For more information on Marcia Hafif, see her website at www.marciahafif.com. Beuger particularly recommends the text *Beginning Again*, originally published in *Artforum* (September 1978).

intervals – silence – some more sounds – silence – some more sounds – silence, etc. had turned into a real problem for me. I found out that what really interested me was what happened when a phase ended: when something was over, not there anymore, and how I could turn the experience of 'not anymore', of 'something gone' into the main thing, the 'event' of a piece. In *place and sound* (ten-minute pieces which are derived from the *calme étendue*-series) the sound, once it has stopped does not come back. The difference between them is: in *place* there is some silence, some sound, some silence again; in *sound* there is some sound, then silence. The number of sounds for a performance of these pieces is determined by a chance operation and may vary between one and 55 sounds. These pieces radicalized the structure of *calme étendue*: sound gone is sound gone, there is no restart, no return.

(3) *ins ungebundene, tout à fait solitaire, ein ton. eher kurz. sehr leise* and *aus dem garten* (all 1998) in fact constitute another series, in which I did away with both sound variety, which was still important in *calme étendue*, and with regularity, which had been a dominant feature of my music for some years. The focus is completely on (dis)appearance, on 'not anymore'.

(4) the colour 'series', *cadmiumgelb, saftgrün, coelinblau, cadmiumscharlachrot, marsgelb, cyaninblau, gebrannte siena, antwerpener blau, carthamrosa* (2001–), is different. I was asked to take part in an art project: some 20 artists from different disciplines were asked to contribute 50 individual pieces (drawings, paintings, poems, music scores, etc.) each on a sheet of A4 format paper. The result was 50 boxes. Each box contained one of the pieces of each artists. I decided to create 50 title pages for non-existent pieces. As titles I took colour names (in fact I took them from a Marcia Hafif catalogue: she used to name her paintings after the colour the painting is made of). To each title comes a (chance generated) combination of instruments. I then was so fascinated by reading these title pages, that I started to get curious as to how these pieces might sound. So I started composing them. The first one I did, *cadmiumgelb* for double bass, basically belongs to the *ins ungebundene* etc. series of pieces. But from *saftgrün* onwards, the colour pieces started to develop a very new character: repetition started to play a major role (first time in my music), also a completely different way of playing together (no counting, no stopwatch etc., a feeling of – very slow – 'groove' instead). So in this series, there is no common structural idea given. What is given, very unusual to me, is the instrumentation and the name (although in some cases I combined a name with a different instrumentation).

As this series developed (and it still is), new ways of looking at silence, at (dis)appearance etc. started to reveal themselves to me. Stillness maybe is describing best what I started focusing on. Instead of silence occurring as the effect of an (irreversible) cut/event, which had been prevailing in my music, I now started thinking of silence as stillness, as a place, which is just 'place' without something 'taking place'. Repetition seemed to be closest to such a place: when something repeats, nothing (else) happens. Of course in such a situation difference is taking place all the time, but it is a non-intentional difference, being there because in our world being is difference: to be = to be different.

(5) At about the same time I started the Emily Dickinson series (*landscapes of absence*). All the things I have been talking about seem to be reflected in her work,

which I had been reading for years. Now I wanted to find a voice, a sound for this poetry. I wanted to create situations in which the poems might be read (both silently, by the audience, which has a copy of the text; and aloud, by the speaker, who is reading the text without reciting it or representing it). I decided to select about 20 poems and to create a 100-minute piece or situation for each of the poems. At first I thought they all should be for speaking voice and piano, done by one player (like a singer accompanying himself on the piano). After I performed the first piece (*ein einz'ger vogel um halb vier/at half past three, a single bird*) I discovered that it should be done by two performers, that it really is music for two. I also decided that I wanted to have German translations of the poems, so in Germany the pieces could be done in German. A 70-year-old German lady,[7] who had grown up bilingually in Canada and who had sent me her translation of *four trees upon a solitary acre* which I found brilliant, translated the poems for me. Even if she isn't a professional translator, I think her translations are the best to be found for Dickinson's poetry in German.

I wanted each of the pieces to be based on the same set of basic decisions (one poem, 100 minutes, syllabic reading, very few sounds, voice and instrument never coinciding), still having a distinct individual atmosphere. At the same time, unlike other series I had been working on, I wanted to envisage the option of playing all pieces simultaneously. The idea being that in such a simultaneous performance all distinct characters of the individual pieces would disappear, still, so to say 'undercover' would determine the atmosphere of the amalgamated piece. This type of disappearance I would like to call 'disappearing into containment': the individual pieces and characters are now contained in the amalgamation, without being presented as something by themselves. I speculated a 'Dickinson-world' would emerge comparable to a late summer meadow with its specific overall sound, in which the individual occurrences are contained. This is exactly what happened, when we did a performance of it last year (*landscapes of absence 3*).

(6) *que le lieu* (2001) is another series slowly developing: the core part of each of these pieces is an extended unison phase, which lasts at least 2/3 of the total duration: nothing is taking place but place itself. This unison is the result of the first part of the piece, in which it is gradually approached. At the end the unison is left again: going to a place, staying there, leaving the place.

(7) *ce qui passe* (2002) is a series of pieces for instruments that can produce non-decaying sounds (winds, strings). They all have the same structure: 70 tones structured as a very slow melody (each tone a quiet breath or bow; some silence between two tones); one of the tones is repeated 34 times, one of them 21 times, one of them 13 times, one of them eight times; four of them five times, five of them four times; six of them three times; seven of them two times. To this series I can add as many pieces as I want: I just have to apply the chance procedures generating the intervals, and the ones identifying the tones to be repeated. In these pieces there is a sense of melody (going on), which turns into stillness time and again (repetition).

(8) the *dedekind duos* and the *cantor quartets* (both 2003–) are the series I am currently most involved in.

---

7   Edith Kloss, although her translations remain unpublished.

My answer turned out to be very long. I thought the best way to answer your question would be to look at the individual series. In each case the working process seems to be different, although I think in all cases it has to do with staying with an idea, testing the consequences of it, trying it out until I get stuck or just leave it. I think there is a lot of similarity to Marcia Hafif's method in painting.

I was interested in your comment about repetition appearing for the first time in your work in the colour pieces, and later in ce qui passé. *Whilst you seem to be referring to repetitions of sounds (and the implication of difference that this creates), the repetition of structures seems to have been present for a longer time (in* calme étendue *for instance). I particularly like the way you test structures many times to see what they might reveal through making different cuts into the mass of potential sounds available. It's all too easy to finish a piece and think everything has been said in relation to a particular idea without really exploring some (all?) of the other possibilities. It's an experimental approach, and a particularly exhaustive and rigorous one at that.*

For me repetition also implies a concern with scale and duration (repetition denies oneness), and I was hoping you could say something about the relatively long duration of some of your pieces?

You are saying some interesting things about repetition. While I referred to it in relation to sounds being repeated, you are certainly right, that it is possible to think of repetition as something staying the same, not changing: a structure is repeated, like in *calme étendue* (three seconds of sound, five seconds of silence; sounding parts alternating with silent parts). Even if the sounds involved may be different from each other, the structure is staying the same.

In such a situation what you are listening to is the concrete sounds and their differences, not the structural intricacies of a composition. What is going on is immediately clear, so you can concentrate on listening to what is really sounding. That, of course, is not at all clear (in terms of structural comprehensibility), since now you are facing a world of singularities, of differences, of ultimate non-repetition. Maybe it is more a world of similarity than of sameness. And similarity means difference. What is similar cannot be the same. I think similarity is a very interesting concept as it locates itself somewhere between sameness and difference. It also plays an important role in thinking about series. A series of pieces is not just a collection. It is not about addition, it is more, as you say, about exploring and has to do with the idea of exhaustion. Do you know Deleuze's text about Beckett in which he differentiates exhaustion from fatigue?[8] It is very inspiring. Exhaustion means all possibilities have been explored, there are no more options left. Fatigue means one doesn't have the (physical) power to continue, even if exploration hasn't yet come to an end. Involving oneself in a series to me really means staying with an idea, exploring the different ways it can go, observe the changes taking place

---

8   Gilles Deleuze, 'The Exhausted', in *Essays Critical and Clinical*, trans. Daniel W. Smith and Michael A. Greco (Minneapolis, 1997), pp. 152–74.

from piece to piece. Not just applying the same concept over and over, generating an increasing number of pieces.

In the Dickinson series I wanted each piece to have a very definite, singular atmosphere. They shouldn't be the same piece in different forms. On the other hand, they shouldn't be just different pieces. They are similar. Similarity connotates both sameness and difference. And similarity cannot really be planned or constructed or generated. It is more something to be found. The image of exploring (unknown territory) seems very adequate. Being involved in a series is very much like exploring unknown territory, of coming to places, where you haven't been before, of finding out about things rather than inventing them. And it is something done stepwise: you go from here to there and on and on. You have to go through one place to come to the next one. Of course, it is hard to say, when such a journey has come to an end. Usually it just finishes by decision: it is enough. But I think one should not stop too early, even more so because one inevitably will stop too early. Basically such explorations are infinite, so you'll never arrive. The job is never done. So leaving a job for another one or getting engaged in a new relationship should be based on a wise decision.

Duration very often has been my first inspiration for a piece. My first thought would be: I want to do a piece for one singer, which is two hours long. Or in the case of *calme étendue*: what about a nine-hour piece? At first, the idea of long durations had to do with a piece being identical with a concert, instead of being included in a concert. When you go to the theatre, it is very unlikely, that you are going to see two or more pieces being performed. Instead, you are going to see *Hamlet* or *Waiting for Godot*. In music you are going to hear a concert by the London Symphony playing this, that and that. I wanted a music performance to be more like in the theatre: one thing, one experience.

So my idea has always been that as a composer you don't just write pieces which then are performed in concerts, if you are lucky. What you really (should) do is to invent situations in which people are coming together to hear music. The music then is the centre of the situation and not just included. In case of the very long durations, it is necessary to think of the whole context: people should feel free to leave the concert hall for a while, so there should be a nice, inviting place for them to stay, when they want to take a break, something to drink, to eat maybe. At the same time the stillness of the concert room should be guaranteed, you may want to think about how people are going to be seated etc. So in thinking about the piece, you are really thinking about what the experience is going to be like. And the piece is not just the score or the notes or the sounds, it is the whole context of its performance. Another aspect which I like about long durations is that they give you so much time. It is an extremely generous way to deal with time: we just take ourselves four hours or nine. No economical concerns ('isn't it taking too long, doesn't it cost a lot of time'). Sheer generosity. You don't have to be rich to spend time. Time is no one's property.

The interview was conducted by email between 1 December 2003 and 12 March 2004.

Laurence Crane

For a lot of listeners the first contact they have with your work is through the title of course, and you seem to have a clear approach to titling pieces, whether they draw on practical descriptions of the instrumentation, or names of people and what they do. There often seems to be unstated relationships between the choices, such as the nationality of people or the number of letters in their names (or both). Could you explain how you choose titles, and what role they have for you in relation to the music?

I think the first thing I want to say about this is that all my instrumental pieces are, without exception, completely abstract. For me, there is no such thing as extra-musical 'inspiration'. With pieces which have titles which state, as it were, the bare facts (for example *Four Pieces for Alto and Bass Flutes (1996)*, *Two Movements for Small Harp (2002)* and *Seven Short Pieces (2004)*, among others), this abstraction is very clear in the title choice. With pieces which have titles which at first appear to be more descriptive in an extra-musical sense I think my intention is to give the piece some sort of extra identity but the actual music is no less abstract than in the pieces with purely functional titles. The titles that I use often include names, sometimes of the performer for whom the piece is written, sometimes of the dedicatee, or sometimes just a name that I happen to like the sound of. Or they refer to the performer or dedicatee in a more oblique way, for example Raimondas Rumsas is a Lithuanian racing cyclist with a great name. *Raimondas Rumsas (2002)*, my piece for solo cello, is written for Anton Lukoszevieze, who is of Lithuanian descent. I also like using names of places for titles, which again sometimes have some real or imagined relationship with the dedicatee and/or performer.

I'm sometimes asked to provide a title for publicity purposes well in advance of starting the piece. This is actually quite a good discipline. It means that if I decide that I am going to write a set of four short pieces entitled *Four Short Pieces* then I should endeavour as much as possible to stick to that scheme so as not to contradict the pre-concert publicity! This tends to narrow down the possibilities and therefore concentrates the mind on the task in hand. My choosing of titles is more often than not based on this sort of decision. If a title suggests itself then all well and good. If not, then I will have a purely functional title. The sort of title I would go out of my way to avoid would be overtly poetic ones. Although I do accept that there is a kind of poetry in people's names and names of places.

But again, I must emphasize, whatever kind of title I use, I think of the music as a purely abstract creation.

For me this is also apparent in the way your use of tonal materials is undermined by the avoidance of functional tonal harmony. The harmonic pull of tonal music is often absent and, when allied with your use of short repetitive phrases, the music has a tendency to float free of such tensions. To what extent do you feel your musical language reinforces this abstractness?

It's certainly true that static structures appear to create more of an abstract work than goal-directed or developmental structures, although I realize that in both cases there are exceptions to this. In my case you are right to focus on my preference for avoiding functional tonality and developmental thinking as part of my desire to compose in an abstract way. I can relate this very strongly to the music which has influenced me the most in my work, music by composers in the various American and English experimental 'schools' of the 1950s, 1960s and 1970s. I can't emphasize enough how important this music was to me at a crucial time (the early 1980s, when I was studying at Nottingham University). I made a decision to follow what they were doing and reject the methods, techniques and language of the more mainstream composers of that time. The close relationship of the experimentalists and various groups of abstract, minimalist or systemic painters is well documented and, while I do not have a particularly close working association with any visual artists (although I like to follow what is going on in that world), I do feel a great empathy with the way those worlds relate, and in particular with the sort of parallels drawn between a piece of experimental music and a piece of abstract sculpture or a painting. Although music is a time-based art form, use of static materials and static musical structures definitely can push it towards existing like a piece of visual art. Often in my work, a piece will consist of simply a number of different statements of the same material, sometimes different from each other, sometimes the same but never ever in a state of what would generally be thought of as development. The analogy with viewing an object from a number of different angles has been used many times before when talking about the minimalists/experimentalists and in a way it almost now sounds like a bit of an old cliché, but like most clichés it has a strong element of truth. I like to think of the materials that I work with in my music as objects of some sort or other, familiar objects maybe, but extracted from their previously familiar situations and placed into a different context. I want to present them and view them but I don't want to develop them or force them into areas to which they don't necessarily belong. The material that I work with is very carefully chosen. I can spend weeks deciding on what that material should be. In an article written several years ago Howard Skempton points to the very clear difference between experimental and mainstream composers in their approach. He says that experimental composers talk of 'material' while mainstream composers talk of their 'ideas'. I think this is an interesting distinction; I always think of working with material and I completely reject the notion of inspiration.

What for you is material?

The surface of my music is very stark, bald and simple and the basic material reflects this. The material is the essence of the particular piece, normally one or more separate musical objects on which the whole piece is based. If there is more than one of these objects they may or may not be related to each other in some way. When I start a new piece I never feel that I am starting with a completely blank sheet of paper, as there is a pool of almost archetypal material that I'm constantly exploring. When I start a piece I know that there are certain practical things to take into consideration; instrumentation, where it's going to be played, who's going to play it and duration being some of these considerations. I'll also think long and hard about the type of material I will work with and how I will structure the whole in relation to its content. I might also take something from a previous piece, perhaps some very small aspect of it, and decide to explore that particular aspect in a more detailed way, focusing on something that was perhaps quite peripheral in the previous work. For example, in *Seven Short Pieces*, which I wrote in 2004, there's a slightly off-beat thing in the piano where there's a chord on the main beat and then there's an off-beat triplet crotchet and I took that basic idea as my starting point for writing the second movement of *Ullrich 1 and 2*, the piece I wrote for Orkest de Volharding in 2005–2006. In some cases I'll literally explore the same material in a different way, in a different context, as a different way of looking at it, a process I generally regard as very removed from re-arrangement or re-scoring.

To summarize this – and also referring back to part of my answer to the previous question – the best analogy I can make is the one commonly made within experimental music or the sort of music we're talking about: the similarity with objects, a piece of sculpture or a painting, and looking at the object or objects from different perspectives. The materials I'm working with are objects which I try and place alongside each other and I also try and place them in different contexts to try and view them from different angles.

I feel the type of material you are using has perhaps changed over the last three or four years. Listening to recent pieces it is perhaps fair to say you are moving away from harmonic/melodic/pitch-based material to incorporate more noise-based materials and I wondered perhaps why that is?

It's absolutely true to say that noise or timbral-based material has started to play a part in my recent work. It starts in two works from 2003; firstly *John White in Berlin*, written for Apartment House in the spring of that year, then *Four Miniatures*, written for Noszferatu a couple of months later. And continues in a handful of works since then. In all these there is a usage of unpitched or noise-based timbral resources that was previously absent from my work as a whole, which up to that point had been more or less dominated by vertical harmony. But I can't remember making a conscious decision about this and I think it's actually the result of a direct influence of composers around me, some sort of response to fellow composers' work. I think really one is always responding to other people's work. I'm not sure whether my current interest in this new sort of material will prove to be a major element in my work or just a temporary diversion, I'm not in the habit of making plans as to the direction that my work should go, it's a case of moving from work to work and following what interests me at the time or whatever is appropriate for that particular work.

Do you see any difference between the way you work compositionally with your pitch material and with the more recent noise materials? Has your approach changed for dealing with those in any way?

No, I don't think it has changed my approach. I would say that the most important change of approach in my music in recent years has been the gravitation to longer pieces, to larger formal structures. The longer pieces that I've done so far have all been composed in the last five to ten years. When I was younger I wrote exclusively short pieces, they would be maybe three or four minutes each, and then perhaps a longer work would consist of a collection of those, a series of short pieces. It's only in the last five to ten years that I've started to try to make longer single movement structures. But it doesn't mean that I'm now developing the material. Again it means that I'm still viewing it from different directions.

When you are starting a new piece, how do you normally begin?

It usually takes me ages to actually get to a point where I can start writing bar by bar. Even with the shortest piece I really am very slow. But my starting point is always all the basic practical considerations; instrumentation, venue, performers, duration. I suppose once I've taken all those things into account it's a question of how many movements, then the character of the piece and then I'll think for ages about the actual raw material. All that practical information listed above would be the starting point, from which I would derive an idea of the sort of piece I want to write, the sort of material I want to use and how I would employ the resources.

But I'm now trying to think further back to a previous question of yours; how it came about that I started using more noise material in recent works. I think it's definitely a response to those around me. I don't know if you can put this in your own book, but you, Markus Trunk, Joanna Bailie, Christopher Fox, Matthew Shlomowitz, Bryn Harrison and Tim Parkinson, among others, have, through their own work, all actually alerted me to some possibilities and I wanted to explore these in my own way. I think that in the case of the *Four Miniatures* for the ensemble Noszferatu what I aimed to do in those was to base all four pieces on a different drone. I had already decided that they would be one or two minutes each. Each piece would be based on a drone from a different instrument. A percussionist was a member of that particular ensemble and the logical thing was to make a non-pitched drone, which in its most basic form is a bass drum roll, and it sort of went from there I think.

For my first experience of that piece. I didn't have the programme in front of me and it took a while to recognize it as your piece. But then I realized very quickly once the structure started to make sense that just the material was very different.

In another recent piece *Come back to the old specimen cabinet John Vigani, John Vigani part 3* (2007) there was a loose non-abstract programme covering the whole project. It was a commission from Queens' College Cambridge, who commissioned 12 composers over a three-year period to write pieces to be performed in the vicinity of Queens'. The brief was that you should loosely or not so loosely base your pieces on this thing called Vigani's Cabinet, which is this remarkable cabinet of scientific curiosities and objects, all sorts of odd things, collected by John Vigani, who was the first professor of chemistry at Cambridge in the eighteenth century and a fellow of Queens' College. There was a practical consideration to make in that the piece had to be got together very quickly in Cambridge and it had to involve some students and rather than write for them playing conventional instruments I wanted to explore a music for non-instruments; plastic bags and tin cans, beach stones and newspapers; 'found objects' really. My idea was to create a collection of my own objects, which might be found in my own cabinet, as it were, and then I extended that to the idea of found objects, the instruments themselves, so then once I'd collected the instruments for their noise producing quality I then worked on the piece. Even though, as you say in reference to the *Four Miniatures* and your experience of hearing them for the first time, the material is in some way slightly different because of the noise elements, I think it was structured in my characteristic way in this piece too.

You mentioned earlier when we were talking about starting your pieces that there was a period between deciding on the practicalities and starting to write out the bars that took a long time, and what is it in particular that you focus on in that period before you start to write out the piece or deal with the detail of the piece?

Generally it's the quality or the nature of the material that I'm working with. It's got to be just right and I try and refine everything so that I'm just working with the most basic elements and it's just a question of working away at those and making sure that they're definitely going to stand the test of time.

So say you are working with tonal materials, is that trying the right chords, planning melodies, finding the right structure. Is it that sort of thing, or is it more general than that?

It is that sort of thing, yes absolutely. There is a piece of mine that I wrote for the Ives Ensemble in 2003 – *Movement for 10 Musicians* – that is fundamentally based on two elements. A sequence of three rising triads, which merge, and then this repeating two chord sequence where only one note changes between the two chords. I just took ages trying to get those elements absolutely as I wanted them. And that's what takes me ages. Writing the bulk of the piece takes ages too because you're presented as you go on with a myriad of choices, an array of things one can do and what I'm trying to acheive is to do as little as possible with the material. I'm concentrating on these things in extreme close up and I'm trying to eliminate multiple possibilities. So I have to be absolutely sure that it's the right material because you don't want to get three months down the line and then suddenly think 'Oh no!'

There's a famous story about the American composer Carl Ruggles sitting at his piano hammering the same chord out time and time again because he wanted to make sure it sounded as good the 150th time as it did the first time. I can certainly relate to that!

When you are at that stage are you planning structure and working out patternings of bars or repetition schemes?

Yes I am, definitely. I think my procedure is first of all to establish the integrity and quality of the material, as I say that takes a long time. At the same time I'm getting an idea of the overall structure of the whole piece, how many sections relate to each other, what is the overall shape, that sort of thing, but I don't necessarily adhere to a scheme very strictly. I'll have a rough idea of what it's going to be and I will try at each stage of writing to be absolutely sure that I can justify each step but if I do set up any sort of system or structure I'm then quite happy to break the rigour of it if I think it's going to be more interesting to go off in a certain direction. With the Ives Ensemble piece that I mentioned earlier I think when I got that initial material I probably planned about two-thirds of the piece – maybe a bit less – in how the material was going to present itself. But the last main section I wasn't sure about at all and I only really worked that out properly when I actually got to that section when writing out the score. I couldn't decide about it and I left it until I had to properly do something about it. Deadlines are very important to me. Given no deadline I would just procrastinate so if I have a deadline I have to think 'well by this date I really should start actually working on the score' and then when I've started writing the score it means that I will then work out these problems which previously I could not work out in the more abstract way, I have to then just get on with it and write it!

Obviously in your work there is quite a lot of repetition of material, and often unusual numbers of repetitions (it is not balanced in that sense) and I wondered how you deal with repetition and what function you feel it has in your music?

I mentioned very exact repetition earlier but I'm also more and more interested in slightly differing repetition as well. A lot of the music I've been interested in throughout my life has employed a lot of repetition; I am thinking most obviously of the American minimalists here, but also rock and pop music. Repetition has an important function in my work because the harmonic rhythm in my music is intentionally extremely slow and the music is very static. Repetition obviously enables that harmonic rhythm to be slowed right down and it helps real stasis to occur. Another function of repetition in my work would be to enable me to focus microscopically on a small fragment of material. I think that repetition enhances the material and it has a sort of ritual to it too, which I find very elegant.

I often feel frustrated with the way some music of our time is always restless, always seemingly trying to get onto the next thing, always on the go. And also the way that some of it seems to try and make big emotional statements. I have to say I find this overbearing and self-importance very irritating. It's as though this way of 'being' is forced upon the listener. Use of repetition is for me one way of creating an antidote to that approach; letting the material sit there for a while and inviting the listener in to experience it.

I think it's interesting what you said earlier in relation to that pre-compositional period where you're spending a lot of time getting the material exactly right. So presumably that sets you up for repeating it and using it in those sorts of structures, because you've done the work almost?

Yes indeed. I'm working on a brand new piece for the Ives Ensemble at the moment and I'm in that phase of having found the material and refining it and now I'm about to start writing the score. There is going to be a lot of repetition in this new piece. I know I keep referring to my earlier Ives Ensemble work – *Movement for 10 Musicians* – as I feel it's one of the pieces I'm most happy with. In that piece the repetitions are very 4-4-4-4, that sort of thing, but here, in the new piece, I'm planning to do more irregular repetition.

How are you planning that? I mean obviously if it's a regular repeat it's self-defining perhaps, but in this sort of situation where you are working with irregular repetitions, how are you deciding on how to do that?

Well it's just a matter of going through it again and again. Sitting there at a keyboard and trying things and seeing how they work against each other, you know, one following the next, how many times to repeat. I'm very aware of the pacing of the piece, balancing textures against each other. In larger works, where there are more instrumental resources on hand, instrumentation and register become very important structural elements. I'll be thinking very much about how the sections are different in approach.

An important part of the process is imposing various rules upon myself; it's vital for me to impose restrictions on what I am allowed to do at all sorts of levels in the piece.

You mentioned in the course of that reply trying things out at the piano. Do you tend to work at an instrument, normally a piano, when you are working?

It's split between piano and desk. My practical resources at home are very limited, which I think in many ways is a good thing. Practical limitations are important in determining some musical restrictions. I've got a 20-year-old Yamaha DX7 keyboard from 1988 (now on its last legs!) and I would say my compositional process was probably about 20 per cent spent at a keyboard and 80 per cent at the desk. I have a basic schedule, which I generally follow for most pieces. I will think for a good few weeks about the nature of the piece I am to write, taking all the practical considerations mentioned earlier into account. I do not have an acoustic piano so I actually rent a little practice room for a few sessions when I'm starting the piece in earnest in order to try to focus on the material away from my normal environment, as it were. By that point I have a general idea of the nature of my material and I then almost try and 'mine' the material from there, sitting at the keyboard, having an idea of the character of it and trying to find what I'm looking for and then I'll spend a few sessions trying to refine it. Then I'll use my keyboard at home, my knackered old DX7, to check things, play things through, perhaps expand on things but once I've done that initial phase in the practice studio I will spend much more time at the desk writing from there.

Is the stage of composing of writing out the score an important part of the process for you?

Definitely, yes. I don't ever envisage myself notating my scores on computer as for me the job of writing out scores by hand is a very important part of the process and it's where I make a lot of decisions about the detail of the work. But also, the physical process of working at a desk with the full score, actually physically writing the notes on paper is a vital part of it all, definitely. I find that working this way makes you really think hard about each note because deleting stuff on a handwritten score is a pain! I also find that I can do vast amounts of pre-planning in sketches but that I am more likely to make crucial decisions when faced with the reality of the full score.

We've talked a little bit about structure already and about the sorts of pieces you tend to write, but I wondered why you perhaps in different pieces err more towards multiple movements or a single movement piece? What is it about those two approaches which attracts you?

I think practicalities again come into play. How long does the commissioner want the piece to be, you know, that kind of thing? They usually specify something so you start to think how best to do this. So that's one factor. As I said earlier, I've only become interested in using longer single movement forms in recent years. I think my first one really was *Riis* in 1996, for clarinet, cello and electric organ, for Apartment House; it's about 10 minutes long. Previous to that nearly all my pieces were miniatures and I think the nature of my material initially dictated the brevity of these pieces. But in 1996 when writing *Riis* I wanted to find out how to make a longer span of music using deliberately limited, very static material. I wanted to find out whether it was possible for me to make a longer movement out of this sort of material. I've continued to explore that in other pieces such as *John White in Berlin* (2003), *Movement for 10 Musicians* (2003), *Ullrich 1 and 2* (2006) and *West Sussex Folk Material* (2006), among others. To make the larger structures work well requires modifying your approach to the material but I definitely don't want to change my fundamental relationship with it.

One of the other things which interests me about your work, which relates to that, is the idea of a one-idea piece, which is very focused. We've talked about focusing material a little bit already but is the one-idea piece, of which a lot of different composers have written a lot of different examples, something which is central to how you work?

Yes, it is.

Something which sets something up and just does it?

Yes, that sort of single-minded approach is absolutely central to my work so far.

Because there are some pieces, I'm thinking of pieces like Ullrich 1 and 2 *where there are quite different types of material in it as well, where that's not so much the case?*

I think in *Ullrich 1 and 2* it's different types of material in different movements. I would still think of them very much as single-minded movements. With *Movement for 10 Musicians*, for the Ives Ensemble, I've got those two chordal objects, which are similar; they integrate with each other and I definitely see that piece as a very single-minded sort of work, even with the interludes, which are pitched in a slightly different tonal centre. The interludes – for want of a better word – are really there to offset the main material. This is the same in *John White in Berlin*. In *West Sussex Folk Material*, my orchestral piece, there are two sorts of material, one rising and one falling, but really they are cut from the same cloth. I'm really mentioning all my larger structures as it almost goes without saying that the single-idea concept applies more or less throughout my shorter pieces.

A friend who heard one of my recent pieces described it to me as kind of music in extreme close-up, like using a microscope on certain little elements. I do want to pare everything away and try to make it as stripped down as possible. So far in the new Ives Ensemble piece I am working with many repetitions of a single chord, and the opening of the work is fixated with this chord for nearly three minutes.

So as a final question, obviously an adjective which is used in relation to your work is simplicity *and I was wondering what your feeling towards that was and also perhaps the use of humour and how you feel about those two areas?*

When thinking about simplicity in music I always refer back to the impact that Howard Skempton's work had on me when I was still a teenager and student; it was a revelation. I didn't know that music like that existed until in the autumn of 1980 I heard a fellow student play some of Howard's piano pieces from the very early Faber volume of his work and it was really that experience that sent me in the direction I've gone I think, and it's not one I want to leave. I want to keep exploring music of extreme simplicity, there's still a lot more work to be done!

Of course my aim is to make pieces which are unique in themselves while retaining a connection to my output as a whole, that is to say stylistic identity is extremely important to me. I also want to continue to try to explore different ways of structuring pieces but I want the surface of my music to remain essentially extremely simple, with very basic material at its heart, even if sometimes the textures might become a bit more rich and colourful, as in some recent works. Simplicity is to me essential and fundamental and I am totally and utterly committed to that aesthetic.

I suppose in a different way like with Feldman, it is not simple music, because it is pared down as you say it has its own complexity which results from that.

I think so. Yes I think so, so in a way I think simplicity is maybe the wrong word?

I think clarity is a better one perhaps.

Clarity is a much better word I agree. As regards humour, well, I mean I don't know what to say about that really. Sometimes what one finds very funny, other people find very painful.

The interview was conducted by telephone on 14 June 2007.

Rhodri Davies

Given that the harp is your instrument, I thought I'd begin by asking about its role in your work as an improviser. Do you feel, as Derek Bailey said, 'the instrument is man's best friend, both a tool and a helper, a collaborator', or that it intrudes 'between the player and the music'?[1]

Derek mentions in his book two distinct attitudes to the instrument amongst improvisers: pro- and anti-instrument. He later states that the division between the two views is not as distinct as they might seem at first, and says, 'at one time or another most players investigate both the pro- and the anti-instrument approaches. Some oscillate continuously between them and some contrive to hold both views at once so there is no clear division into two groups of musicians'.[2] That is closer to how I view things – that there is oscillation or constant flux between the instrument as friend and as something that comes between the player and the music. There is no one solidified stance. Furthermore, I play different kinds of harps, and it's worth discussing them individually because they propose different challenges. I play a 47-string pedal harp, 32-string lever harp and a 26-string electro-acoustic harp. I also build Aeolian harps that are suspended via strings attached to trees and I suspend various harp parts to the walls and ceilings of buildings.

In relation to that, what pushes you one way or the other? You say you oscillate between the two positions: is there something that drives you more towards the instrument or more towards the point where the instrument gets in the way almost?

Perhaps this idea of oscillating between two poles is ultimately unhelpful: it's better to think of it as a multitude of approaches. Often a specific instrument presents explicit limitations. For example, to facilitate travel I perform with my small lever harp. And of course this instrument imposes different restrictions to what the larger pedal harp would. There are fewer strings, individual levers on each note instead of pedals, and it has a quieter dynamic range. The lever harp presents limitations, which for me, being used to playing the pedal harp for so long, makes it difficult to improvise. These constraints eventually push me into discovering other harp

---

1   Derek Bailey, *Improvisation* (London, 1992), pp. 98–9.
2   Ibid., p. 102.

sounds that I wouldn't necessarily have found if I only performed on the pedal harp.

So the instrument was really a helper in that sense?

Yes, but at the same time it is an obstruction and a difficulty to surmount. When I go back to play the pedal harp I find it somehow easier because it has a louder dynamic range and deeper resonance. This renews my playing and my approach to the instrument. Recently I've started playing a small electric harp, which I place horizontally on a table. Placing it on a table challenges my technique and the electric harp opens up a wider dynamic potential. It immediately requires another approach to the standard harp technique.

Do you make a clear decision to move from one harp to another for a particular concert to put yourself at a particular starting point?

I'm always weighing up which set up would be most appropriate for each situation. And by appropriate I mean what I find appropriate to stretch me artistically. For instance, one of the loudest concerts I have participated in was Otomo Yoshihide's group Core Anode at the ICA Theatre as part of the London Musicians Collective festival in 2006. While it would make sense and seem more appropriate to take my electro-acoustic harp to such a context, I felt it was more of a challenge to try and play acoustically. And as a result, I was surprised by my response, which was to essentially scrape my harp strings with Mark Sanders's cymbal as this was the loudest sound I could produce on the acoustic harp for a sustained period of time. I doubt many people heard my sounds amongst the intense barrage of noise in the room. It became a very performative action – though I didn't set out for it to be.

You mentioned the electric harp, and technology has become part of your set-up recently. I wondered how that links to your harp playing firstly, but also how you've developed a set-up with electronics?

It's an extension of my harp playing and I approach both in the same manner. The combination of experimentation and playfulness that I apply to the acoustic instrument carries through to the electronics. In the same way, I explore what happens when I put a preparation in different places on a harp string. It is rather akin to the differences between saxophones such as soprano, tenor, alto, etc. Certain techniques can be carried through and played on each instrument and then each instrument has techniques that relate only to that individual instrument and suggest unique approaches. I try to keep my electronics stripped down, so I'll use an electric harp, pre-recorded harp sounds and lo-fi electronics. My pre-recorded harp sounds are now mostly made up of close mic'd harp, e-bowed harp or Aeolian harp sounds, and the rest of the material consists of field recordings relating to a concert space or day-to-day sounds around me.

Following that on one stage further, do you ever play without a harp?

I have done a couple of performances and recordings using only electronics, which I found liberating, but at the same time I felt slightly vulnerable. Pushing myself into uncomfortable or exposed situations is an aspect I've been working on in my performance for some time, going back to the All Angels concerts that I co-organized with Mark Wastell. Back then, I was working with the harp and positioning percussion instruments around the floor of the space. This was a way of confronting a situation where I sometimes felt tempted to hide behind the harp. It could come between the audience and me, and I felt the need to push myself to get away from behind the harp, and minimize the barrier between the audience and me.

Obviously you've done a lot of solo concerts as well as playing in groups and I was wondering how your approach changes between those two situations? How do you adapt what you do?

It completely depends on who, and how many people, I'm playing with. If I'm playing with a large ensemble I'm less inclined to play very much as I think it's very easy to overplay in that context. But it all depends on the circumstances, the room, and the audience. I can only say that I use my solo work to explore a very personal space which references and cross-references my previous solo work. In my ensemble work the challenge is to work with or against the other musicians whilst listening.

The quantity of what you play differs in larger groups, but does the quality of what you do change in any way? Do you deliberately do different things when you do make sounds?

Part of what I enjoy is exploring the unexpected. So in very simplistic terms, when I share a space with a loud instrument, I tend to explore quiet areas, and vice versa. There's a multitude of strategies I employ depending on how interesting or relevant I feel it is at the time.

Could you perhaps give some examples of what those strategies might be, or the sorts of approaches you might take?

This example is less of an approach and more of an obsession. I got quite fixated for a few years with the precise placement of a harmonic in time. This particular type of harmonic was difficult to achieve and was produced by holding the edge of an eraser against a top octave string and plucking the string with a plectrum. I would force myself to find what felt like the absolute right time to play the harmonic and it had to be articulated cleanly. Perhaps this was the result of exhaustion from too much touring! One strategy I use is to discard certain preparations from my palette and this affects my habits and sounds. There are many preparations that dominate an improviser's palette such as bows, e-bow, wire wool, fans and crocodile clips.

255

I often get sick of hearing a certain sound and this will affect my approach and I will drop the offending preparation out of my palette, or sometimes, I will continue working with it for this very fact.

Going back to playing in groups, what differences do you find when you're starting to play with somebody new for the first time? Obviously it's going to be somewhat different, but does it change how you work at all?

There is a potential for openness in the first meeting but it can also be prone to a tiptoeing politeness when players don't know each other. And I don't particularly enjoy rehearsing improvisation. There is something about performing with an audience that I value. However, when I started I used to rehearse in duo with Phil Durrant and Mark Sanders and I used to record everything and listen back to it and that was an immensely valuable experience. When I was starting out especially it was important to analyse and revisit a playing situation.

I suppose the flip side of that is for the people you have worked with for a long time, how do you keep those relationships fresh musically?

I'm in three or four long-term groups including Cranc, The Sealed Knot and Broken Consort. We're all living in different places: I'm currently in Newcastle upon Tyne, Mark Wastell and Angharad Davies are in London, Burkhard Beins is in Berlin, Nikos Veliotis is in Athens, and we probably only get to play as groups once or twice a year and that in itself actually keeps things fresh. We might be doing a six date tour for instance, but with a year between playing, and we come back refreshed and have all possibly moved on into different areas. Obviously within a tour it is not always easy, but that depends on so many variables, on the venues, acoustics, PA and basic factors like how tiring the work is.

In those situations do you ever discuss what you're doing?

I tend to gravitate to improvisers who do discuss what they are doing, such as the Berlin musicians, Burkhard Beins, Michael Renkel, Andrea Neumann and Annette Krebs, who I first met in 1996. And from England, Robin Hayward, Matt Davis and John Butcher, who are all very articulate in discussing the music. Generally when I first moved to London, I got the impression that musicians would rarely discuss the music. Maybe they'd come up and say 'well done' after a gig if they really liked it. However, a small group of musicians would discuss what the music could be before we played which was a change from what had been the trend on the London scene. I got the impression that it was almost considered contrary to the spirit of improvisation to discuss the music in advance. And of course there is a strong argument that there is no need to talk about the music, as it is all being worked out in the medium of sound.

I suppose you're also talking about previous generations of players and how improvising works for them and I was wondering what your view was on guided improvisation and compositions which have a degree of indeterminacy in them, particularly given that you also play composed music as well?

I've been commissioning solo harp pieces for the last three or four years and I'm interested in composition that takes me to areas that I wouldn't necessarily arrive at if I were left to my own devices. I'm not interested in pieces that get me to improvise freely because I do that already. I'm very open to compositions that include indeterminacy and certain elements of improvisation. I also think a composition should have a certain identity and not borrow too heavily from my own vocabulary and improvising palette.

Where do you draw the line there though? If someone's heard you play and wants to write a piece for you, what sort of things specifically do you not want them to write for you?

If I feel that a composer is being naïve or lazy, by simply giving me a text that gets me to improvise, or perhaps offering too loose a framework, then I feel I may as well improvise my own music without the composer claiming credit for the work. However, if we look at a piece like *Tea Ceremony* by Catherine Kontz, she uses graphic notations of around 52 different little sections and it remains heavily improvisatory but within clear parameters. When I perform her piece I get a sense that it has an identity of its own, and I like that.

Does playing composed music affect how you improvise, or the other way round for that matter?

I can become very attached to the sounds that I make and throwing them out of my vocabulary can be a wrenching act. I might be happy to introduce a composer to some of my techniques that I've developed over the years when I no longer feel I have any use for them. I'm happy to pass on that knowledge so that other people can use the techniques in a different way and in a different context. And by passing those techniques on, it exorcises them out of my vocabulary because once they have another life, I feel I don't have to go back and use those techniques again. In a way I'm renewing and renegotiating familiar techniques and the vocabulary evolves in a continual process. I've found that commissioning new pieces can be a way of invigorating my playing. For example, I asked Fluxus artists Mieko Shiomi and Yasuano Tone to write pieces for harp, and they obviously approach the harp completely differently to how a composer would or I would.

It's interesting you've said that, and earlier you were talking about changing instruments or performance setup as a way of refreshing things. Are there any other ways you find you can reinvigorate your own playing, as an improviser particularly?

Yes, by playing with other people. It is possible to learn such a lot from listening to other musicians whilst improvising together. Such a lot of information can be gleaned from listening to other people's approaches and strategies in the moment.

We talked a bit about your previous playing, and when you first started to become known as an improviser it was in relation to very quiet, reduced ways of playing and you've moved away from that now. I just wondered if you could say a bit about the process of moving from one style of playing to another one, that movement of reinvigoration if you like?

I don't see it as moving consciously from one style to another but rather as adopting a whole host of approaches. I don't wake up one morning as a reductionist and then the next day I'm a noise artist: the change – if there is one – is slow and organic. Regarding reductionism in London, in the late 1990s I was working with Mark Wastell, Matt Davis, Robin Hayward and Phil Durrant. We were all searching for something, which was not necessarily the same thing, and we didn't know exactly what we were looking for. It was a messy actuality and we were all playing in different contexts and not necessarily in a reductionist way all the time. There was something there to be explored that caught my attention. It was challenging the unspoken value systems that were held by improvising musicians, and more importantly it was challenging my own value system. I view reductionism as a form of reassessing and critiquing improvised music itself. I think it's a healthy critique. And of course this has been happening throughout its history. If you look at people like Steve Beresford who came along after people like Evan Parker and Derek Bailey and said if I'm free then I'm free to play tunes and cut and paste and cut and paste melodies and to get away from virtuosic improvisation.

I'm just trying to keep things interesting and I've moved into other areas like the electric harp and amplifying the acoustic harp, building wind harps, setting fire to harps and all that kind of thing! I'm working with Aeolian harps, where I suspend a harp soundboard or sound box and attach the strings to various parts of buildings or trees and get the elements to activate the strings. This is an attempt to distance myself from my playing. This is an investigation into random occurrences. There are many random factors in my playing and many things outside of my control and it's an acceptance of this and an investigation of the unknown, which I try to pursue to different extremes.

Linked to that, do you ever feel constrained by your previous work?

No, no. I think if anything I'm constrained by all these different labels: Welsh harpist, improviser, composer, reductionist, etc. and when people have a fixed idea of how music should be or how a musician should perform.

You've already said about how you don't like to rehearse in the context of a group, but on your own, what do you do away from a concert situation? Do you do any sort of work on your harp; is there any sort of sense of technical development in what you do? Do you try and hone sounds outside of the performance situation?

Of course I work on my material. I have been lucky to be invited to a few residencies recently, at Westwerk, Hamburg, Q-02 in Brussels, and then a week with contact dance improvisers and Zolt Sores in Budapest. I used that time to woodshed and work on my electric harp and the wind harp. It's good to have that focused time away from everything else. When I get the time back home I'll do the same, but obviously not in such a long block of concentrated time.

What do you do when you have that time to work on your own? What are your aims?

I'll explore and experiment with unknown things as well as reappraise things. I investigate technical and practical aspects such as 'what does this do and how is the sound affected if I change a certain parameter'. Also a lot of the bigger jumps in what I've done come from art, film or literature, away from the harp.

Where do you see your work progressing at the moment and what's coming up?

I'm excited because I'm living in Newcastle-upon-Tyne at the moment and this is a real opportunity to focus on my work. It's not so easy to pop down to London to do a door money gig. In the past the financial implications and difficulties of living in London for 12 years meant that I had to accept work that I was sometimes at odds with artistically. Hopefully I'm reaching a stage where I can pick and choose a little more and work more on my own projects. But perhaps this is just wishful thinking!

The interview was conducted by telephone on 9 October 2007.

Christopher Fox

Some of your work seems to place an emphasis on recognizable structures and audible processes, and I wondered whether these served as a starting point for a piece, or if the material tended to appear first?

I would like to think that some pieces work in quite mysterious ways – but I am drawn to things, both in life and art, which seem to define themselves quite clearly at some level or other. The paradox, however, is that often something which appears straightforward will turn out to be quite complicated, and vice versa. It might even be worth risking a generalization and saying that things which have a consistent degree of simplicity or complexity will usually turn out be less interesting than those which work in different ways at different levels. I'm thinking for instance of the role of mountains in landscapes: the ones we can immediately recognize and name have very strong profiles but the detail of that landscape will include many forms which one does not see at first glance. The best pieces of Xenakis, or Feldman, or Beuys work like that. Equally there is that delight when one works through the initial complexity of a work to discover it is full of quite straightforwardly comprehensible individual elements. I'm just reading Joyce's *Ulysses* properly for the first time and finding enormous pleasure in changing the focus of my attention – here the vocabulary, here the syntax, here the stylistic play – from section to section.

In my work I always start at the point where I have a sense of what it will be like to hear the whole of a piece. If structure and process are there in particular pieces it is because that it was I heard. I would also argue quite strenuously against a separation of 'material' from 'structures and processes'. For me there is no such distinction: all musical material has structural implications and the processes I want to use evolve out of the character of the materials I choose to work with. Everything in *an der Schattengrenze* (2001–2002), for example, radiates out from the way in which the piano is played; similarly in *Canonic Breaks* (2002–2003) the sorts of rhythmic development I wanted to explore necessitated a collection of instruments in which timbral distinctiveness was much more important than any other consideration.

I would certainly agree with the lack of distinction between material and process or structure, but you seem to be saying at least that it's the material that primarily governs the way a piece develops. For me one of the interesting things then is the nature of the material you use, which varies to quite a large degree. Could you say a little about how you find and develop material, and whether there is something common to what on the surface seems quite disparate?

I agree that it can seem as if I write many different sorts of music and earlier in my career critics would say that this indicated that I had yet to 'find my voice'. I would argue that there are some fundamental ideas about music that inform everything I do. The paradoxical relationship between clarity and complexity would be one. Another would be the co-existence of consonant and dissonant harmony. In the 1970s when I was a student the notion of some sort of historical imperative that meant that dissonance was more advanced than consonance was still very much in the air and in Darmstadt in the 1980s it still defined one of the main aesthetic battle grounds over which we fought. I have been interested in developing ways of using both and this happens in most of the things I write.

But there are also many different sorts of music that I want to write and I don't believe that they can always all be drawn together within single spans of music. Indeed that sort of integration of materials implies a sort of homogeneity which I find at odds with the world in which I live. So some pieces are microtonal, for example, and others aren't; some have a powerful rhythmic impetus, others deliberately dislocate any sense of forward movement.

I would also say that the finding and developing of material happens at the same moment. The ways in which material will unfold must, for me, be immanent in the material itself, so that in a sense the material only defines itself in my head at the point when I know what will happen to it. That discovery is in turn the result of a process that begins when I know what the piece as a whole will be, or, more accurately, when I know what it will be like to have experienced the piece. Once I know that I simply have to find what the stuff of the piece is made of. To a certain extent this is also determined by circumstances such as the dimensions of the piece and the nature of the performers and performance. As an extreme example from my recent work, a seven minute piece to be played in a mixed programme by Noszferatu[1] is (for me at least) probably going to be very different from a 25 minute piece for Apartment House[2] and I have to say that I revel in the challenge to my creativity that such different opportunities present.

I'm interested in how this works in pieces such as your Generic Compositions[3] *where the results are more open-ended. Although the structure of events in each piece is fixed, the synchronization and resultant sounds will always be different. How did you go about developing the material, and structure, for these pieces?*

---

1   *KK* (2002) for alto saxophone and five cow bells.
2   *ZONE (Zeit-Ort-Name)* (2002–2004) for clarinet, trombone, tuba, accordion. electric guitar, violin, viola, cello, double bass and pre-recorded electronic drones.
3   The eight *Generic Compositions* are components of *Everything You Need To Know* (1999–2001) written for the Ives Ensemble and Barbara Hannigan (soprano) and premiered by them in de MuziekCentrum, 's-Heertogenbosch on 13 May 2001. It consists of a series of component works which may also be combined or performed separately.

The recurrent element in all these pieces is the isolation of aspects of instrumental behaviour. This is something I do in virtually every piece anyway but in the 'Generics' it became the foreground. So each *Generic* has a very clear technical focus – for example, clusters in two, bow rhythms in four, unstable fingerings in seven – and what we listen to is the interaction between the playing technique and the acoustic structure of the instrument. I used self-similarity as the main way of organizing material, deliberately leaving the formal organization of each piece as 'cool' as possible so that the listener's attention will go to the sounds rather than to the architecture. This coolness also makes it possible to overlay different *Generics* – they're all sufficiently transparent to avoid getting in one another's way. In quite a few of them there are also opportunities for players to pause so that they too can listen to what other players are doing in multiple-layer performances.

On the other hand there are quite wide differences across the set (originally seven, then I wrote an eighth for Anton Lukoszevieze's BachBogen[4] and there is still the possibility of adding a few more). The first (percussion), second (keyboard), third (plucked), fourth (bowed) and sixth (valve instrument) will always tend to be immediately recognizable because they have quite clear pitch or rhythmic identities. Five (sliding), seven (woodwind) and eight (multiple sustaining strings) leave the player free to translate notations which specify the shape of events but not the sounds which constitute those events. The difference between a trombone version of 5 and a double bass version of the same score can be very different.

Self-similarity is a feature of much of your recent work. Could you explain how it operates here, and its role in your music in general?

I discovered the potential of self-similarity through Tom Johnson's music and, most helpfully, when one of my MA students (Mary Wilson) did some analytical work on mathematical applications in his work. I liked the level of complexity that self-similarity produced in his rhythmic and melodic construction – one's ear can detect some sort of rule-based pattern-making but the patterns resist immediate aural analysis, which seemed to me to offer some kind of halfway point between chance operations and minimalist systems. I think the *Everything You Need To Know* (2000–2002) pieces were the first to use self-similarity and it's become a regular part of my compositional arsenal ever since, with *Canonic Break* providing probably its most sustained and (deliberately) audible use in my music so far. Like Tom Johnson I use it as a technique to produce rhythmic and melodic proliferation, usually starting with a group of two elements (one rhythmic value and another shorter value, or one upward interval and one downward interval) and then finding a simple formula to make the relationship between them proliferate. In the violin piece[5] I'm writing at present I am working with a set of self-similar rhythms which evolve out of the

---

4   The BACH.Bogen is a curved bow. The high arch of the bow allows full, sustained chords to be played and there is a lever mechanism that affects the tension and release of the bow hairs. It enables string players to play one, two, three and four strings.

5   *Iridescence* (2005).

rhythmic grouping 1 2 1 2 2 (1 = quaver, 2 = crotchet), a bit of found material (a rumba, I think). Using the principle that, as the pattern proliferates, 1 becomes 2, and then 2 becomes 1+2, the next generation of the rhythm is 2 1+2 2 1+2 1+2, and the one after that is 1+2 2 1+2 1+2 2 1+2 2 1+2. It's hard to describe in words but it's quite easy to see evidence of it, if not to detect exactly how it's working, in lots of the recent music.

To what extent do you intervene in such processes: once the formula is established, how do you deal with the end results? I'm thinking of how with someone like Tom Johnson, the process becomes the piece.

As you say, Tom Johnson tends to use such patterns in a very rigorous way; I use them more as material to be placed within the overall composition, often using chance operations to cut across them. I'm quite comfortable with this because by their nature these materials are self-similar so that interrupting them won't necessarily sound like an interruption and also, because the generations of the chains which I tend to favour are the longer ones, it's quite hard to hold them in the memory for long enough for anomalies to be apparent.

The analogy occurred to me last week during the EXAUDI recording sessions when I had to listen to a lot of my music from across 25 years, that I seem to work in a way not dissimilar to that of a sculptor like Antony Caro, who talks in terms of bringing together a collection of materials that he feels somehow belong together in the piece he is thinking of making. The creative process then is about finding ways of getting these materials into relationships which relate to the ideas behind that particular piece. Of course at the end part of the satisfaction is discovering not only that lots of the material remains unused but also that the piece has become something different from those first intentions.

You mentioned found material, and its use has been a feature of much of your work (particularly where the provenance is explicit). How important are intra-musical links in your work?

I think there are two aspects to this in what I do. On the one hand I have often made my music out of bits of other people's music; on the other hand, even when I am not using specific pieces of existing music, I often take some element of an existing musical practice as a compositional starting point. Often these practices are, as it were, 'given' by the medium or, more particularly, by what previous musicians have done with that medium. Richard Rijnvos recently suggested to me that one of the things that makes me relatively unusual within the world of art music composers is that, according to him, I write music that very clearly acknowledges the possibility of there being different genres and I am certainly interested in responding to generic ideas about different musical situations.

One of the clearest examples is *Themes and Variations (1992–96)*, the set of six ensemble pieces I wrote in the mid-1990s for the Ives Ensemble. There is no explicit found material in the sense of music borrowed from other sources but each movement offers a radical reconstruction of the possibilities of the available instruments, starting very obviously with the first piece, 'memento', in the world of the late nineteenth-century piano quartet and gradually moving to something very remote in 'string quartet', the last piece. Appropriately the instrumentation for this last piece is not the normal string quartet but violin, viola, cello and double bass. My method in a situation like this, where I wanted 'memento' to sound familiar, is not to attempt pastiche or quotation but to create music out my own memories of what the Schumann or Faure piano quartets sound like.

In other pieces I have made much more direct use of existing music, although I do this a lot less frequently than I did when I was younger. Then I used to spend hours in music libraries transcribing bits of useful material before transforming them into my own music. Gradually I've come to realize that it's the transformational process that interests me most, not the identity of the sources. It's more important that listeners should be aware, however vaguely, of some sort of generic link from my music to something they already know, than that they should be able to give a specific name to that connection.

Why do I do this? I have always been interested in the way in which part of the act of listening involves finding a personal context for the music one is hearing and I am interested in playing my own compositional role in fixing that context. Also, and without wanting to be falsely modest, I think the world already has so many fascinating ways of making music that it's just as interesting for a composer to make his own use of things that already exist as it is to attempt to invent new ones. There are lots of models for this, of course, amongst the work of composers who have had a big influence on me. Stravinsky and Kagel are obvious examples of composers who borrow and recycle but I love pieces like Cage's *Hymns and Variations* (1979) too and I was delighted to discover that when Christian Wolff began writing his wonderful *Exercises* (1973) he was attempting to respond to early minimalist pieces like the Riley *Keyboard Studies* (1967–68) which Cardew had introduced him to.

This is certainly the case with your electroacoustic pieces, particularly the Three Constructions (after Kurt Schwitters) *(1993/1998), where the sampling is clearly more overt. What differences of method do you find working in this medium, as opposed to acoustic music?*

The collaging of materials in the Schwitters pieces was itself a given really, since his method of working was centred on found materials. But what drew me to him in the first place was, I suppose, in part this similarity in our ways of working. I'm not sure I have a particular modus operandi in the studio though. *MERZsonata* is like it is in part because I had to make the piece very quickly in an unfamiliar BBC Radiophonic studio and so I based the piece around the sampling capabilities I found there, coupled with the archival resources of the BBC library.

In other pieces which use studio technology I've worked in quite different ways, using sequenced synth pre-sets in the first part of *More things in the air than are visible* (1993–94) and unedited real-time field recordings in the third part of the same piece (found materials again, however). In *ZONE* (2002–2004) I've used very precisely tuned sine waves, while *klaxonik* from *Alarmed and Dangerous* (1996) and the version of *chant suspendu* (1997–98) with CD both used granular synthesis to stretch acoustic sounds. The one feature throughout though is the avoidance of what one might call orthodox electroacoustic transformation of sounds. I avoid this for the same reason that I don't use the gestural language of mainstream 'new music' – I just don't find them interesting and I don't know why their use persists when the best pieces using that vocabulary and syntax were made 40 years ago.

I should also say that I like the social dimension of music-making. I like best the time spent in rehearsal with musicians making my music come alive – it's what I look forward to most when I am at my desk alone. Consequently it's perhaps no surprise that I have made a number of my studio pieces with other people sitting alongside me and in many instances taking quite significant creative decisions of their own. *Alarmed and Dangerous* owes a lot to the brilliant radio producer Alan Hall, who effectively directed the whole project. Also, in *klaxonik* the computer transformations behind the trumpet were created by Jo Thomas – I gave her the source material, told her how I wanted it to sound and sat beside her when we mixed it, but it was she who gave the piece its wonderful texture. Similarly in *The Grain of Abstraction* (1997–99) Rob Scorah did things to my source sounds which were much more radical than I had imagined but were eventually intrinsic to that work's peculiar strangeness! Arguably, this is yet another sort of found material: responding to the set-up of a particular studio, or the predilections of a colleague, is like coming to terms with the nature of a particular instrument or ensemble. A lot of the music I like best from the last 50 years is the product of similar accommodations: Miles Davis putting musicians together in a studio with just fragments of material, the Beatles working around the limitations of the Abbey Road four-track, Stockhausen making *Telemusik* in an unfamiliar Japanese studio.

In his profile of your work[6] *Ian Pace describes it as having a 'latent narrative', and I wondered to what extent you agreed with this statement, particularly given this emphasis on collage and block construction in much of your work (not that these deny narrative)?*

I think there are narratives latent in everything that human beings do. Certainly I am very conscious when I make music that it is above all a time-based medium and that whatever my music does it will be interlocking (or not) with other human beings' attentions. I have always seen it as my principal compositional aim to leave my listeners in a different state from that in which they began – anything less would seem to be a waste of all our time. How to make this difference? That varies from piece to piece but here are three very different examples.

In *BLANK* (2002) the music has an intensity that comes from the absence of pauses (it's made up of long, continuous tones), registral focus (it's in a narrow pitch band) and purity of intonation (it uses just intonation). It seems to spend a long time doing the same sort of thing before beginning to change quite near the end. For me it's a piece which ends on the verge of catastrophe, about to fly

---

6   Ian Pace, 'Northern Light', *The Musical Times*,139/1863 (Summer 1998): 33–44.

apart, and its form means that that catastrophe can only happen in the listener's imagination – it's a narrative that they must finish for themselves.

In *Prime Site* (1997) there are seven sections which don't obviously relate to one another in a moment to moment sense but whose interrelationship may be understood after the piece has finished, if the listener chooses to think about it. This is perhaps less a narrative and more a way of viewing a multi-dimensional object. It's a version of what elsewhere I have called my 'compendium' form – a collection of possibly quite diverse sorts of music organized around a central subject which may be stated but often isn't.

The recent choir piece *Open the gate* (2004) has a more conventionally 'musical' narrative in which accretions are gradually stripped away from the underlying plainsong melody – reverse variations, a form I like very much.

At the heart of all this though is my belief in form as something which should be expressive, both of changing emotional states and ideas. This it seems to me is true of all good music, a belief which marks me out as an unreconstructed modernist I suppose.

Could you explain how you work on a practical level?

I work any time, anywhere and I work every day. If I don't I quickly become quite bad tempered – writing music is what I do and it's really my primary indicator of how I am.

I work primarily on paper at a desk (or on a table, or on a train, or wherever I am). Occasionally I play fragments of pieces at a piano, mostly to reassure myself that the sense of pitch relationships in my inner ear is still working and to enjoy the sensation of real acoustic sound. I really don't play the piano well and one of the key influences on my early musical development, the harpichordist Virginia Black, suggested that if I tried to write at the piano it would inhibit my imagination. I also use the piano in what I suppose is a deliberately alienating way, often playing passages in the wrong octave to avoid any confusion with how the piano sounds and how the music will really sound.

Until last year I always copied everything by hand in ink onto transparent paper, designing the page layout myself and using a photocopier to make the finished score. I still use this method for some pieces but where it's possible (i.e. if the notational demands are sufficiently conventional) I now use Sibelius software. I don't compose at the computer and I don't use playback, both of which I am convinced are the enemies of musical imagination! Like Feldman I believe in hand-made music.

Of course, none of this says anything important about how each piece is written. The process of composition for me is, I think, about discovering the piece I want to hear in a particular setting and then creating the means (usually a written score) by which this can happen. The current piece, for example, is for solo violin. I don't know the playing of Farran Scott, the violinist who will play it first, but I do know the occasion, part of a day of new music all commissioned by Queens' College, Cambridge to relate to an early eighteenth-century cabinet of scientific curiosities in the College, Vigani's Cabinet. The cabinet has many things in it but the drawers of pigments are particularly striking, still wonderfully vivid, and my piece is called 'iridescence'. So, in a way I started with three found objects, the solo violin (Farran is the College's Musician in Residence), a tray of brilliant colours and the context of an afternoon of new pieces, most of them probably quite short, so that the audience has the opportunity to move between different venues in the College and re-hear pieces if they want.

I wanted to write music that might be heard as refractive, so there is a recurrent set of pitch relationships (which proliferates, once again through the use of self-similarity) and a rhythmic cantus firmus (more or less a rumba rhythm!) which underpins everything. Each is heard through the other and each changes slightly all the time. The result (and the piece is nearly finished) is music that uses formations quite familiar from older music but which never coalesces into anything that really is familiar.

The context for Iridescence *suggests it is to some extent a site-specific piece (although it might be argued that all pieces where we know the details of the first performance are to an extent site-specific). You've produced some installation work in the past, and I wondered how this aspect of your work has developed?*

I think I would like to suggest that for me all first performances are site-specific works and all performances are installations. If I know the circumstances in which a new piece will be performed (and I almost always do) – musicians, venue, occasion – then that inevitably colours my approach to the work of creating it. Similarly, I always enjoy the process of taking over a space and preparing it for a performance, even when that consists of no more than moving chairs, music stands and lights, and plotting entrances and exits. On the other hand I don't think I have a piece that is literally site-specific – everything I've written can be done in virtually any space. The installation pieces I've done, like *Liquid Architecture* (1998) and *Everything You Need To Know*, consist of materials which can be realized in very different ways in different spaces.

It seems that increasingly composers are referring to themselves as sound artists (when they are still really composers). How do you view yourself and the work you have produced?

I am a composer. Terminology is interesting – for example, the fact that the Arts Council of England thinks there is a sphere of musical activity that could be called 'contemporary classical' demonstrates their lack of understanding about what is happening in music these days. I compose, because I see my work within a tradition based around notation, using that notation (in whatever form it might take) as a means of abstracting musical ideas. Today I think notation is more diverse than ever before, from jazz charts, to graphic scores, to detailed note event notations, to graphic interfaces on computer, but as soon as you use notation you are making a separation between the thing itself – sounds – and the ways you can think about that thing. The end result of this process of abstraction and mediation may not be aurally distinct from what a sound artist or an improviser might produce but it can be and in my work I try to exploit the potential that this process offers me. In particular I think that composing music enables ways of organizing sophisticated large-scale musical relationships which perhaps no other form of music-making allows.

The interview was conducted by email from 5 November 2004 to 7 November 2005.

Bernhard Günter

You've talked about an interest in sounds that question our perception, and in general work with very quiet sounds. Could you explain how you see them fulfilling this function, particularly in relation to the range of listening environments in which we might experience them?

I think that generally speaking our perception is tied to a sort of 'internal description' of the phenomena perceived that works by reference/comparison to prior perceptions. I believe that this internal description of perceived phenomena we perform in our minds is also strongly tied to language as a means of definition. On a little less abstract level let's say when I hear a dog barking, my mind registers 'a dog is barking', the perceptive input is thus identified, classified, and in most cases this will be the end of processing it. It is also possible, though, that I listen to the dog barking (as opposed to simply hearing it), and maybe draw conclusions about the dog: it sounds like a big or small dog, an excited, happy or aggressive dog, and so forth. The least used perceptive option is that I listen to the dog's barking as simply sound, i.e. without connecting it to my memories/concepts regarding dogs, and thus make it an abstract sound event perceived in its own terms, so to speak.

If we now replace the dog's barking by music we approach the meaning of my statement about 'sounds that question our perception'. When I listen to, say, a piano playing, this perceptive input triggers references to a large amount of information regarding the piano, the musical tradition(s) it is used in, various piano players and their playing style, etc. stored in memory – this is my cultural knowledge of 'The Piano'. This cultural knowledge will even make me hear 'a piano' when the piano is coming from a cheap portable FM radio (or low resolution MP3 file, for that matter), even though what is coming from the little radio's speaker is quite different from the sound a piano actually produces. It is interesting to note that Morton Feldman spoke of a 'deceptive likeness'[1] (to themselves) of musical instruments, and the danger of listening to the concept of the piano, rather than to the piano. He made it very clear that he needed to hear what the piano really sounded like when he was composing on and for it.

---

1   Morton Feldman, 'A Compositional Problem', *Give My Regards to Eighth Street: Collected Writings of Morton Feldman*, ed. B.H. Friedman (Cambridge, Mass., 2000), pp. 109–11, at p. 109.

What really interests me as a musician is to make use of the third option described above – if I let go of my cultural knowledge, even listening to a grand piano played right in front of me will become listening to a number of abstract sound events I can perceive in their own terms. My inclination towards Zen Buddhism may be in part responsible for my strong tendency towards this kind of experience, the goal of Zen being to get rid of all attachments to words, concepts and descriptions, in order to intuitively perceive what Western (German) philosophy has termed 'das Ding an sich', 'the thing as itself', and, contrary to Zen, concluded that we cannot perceive. I have, however, often experienced moments in which all prior knowledge about music fell away and I felt becoming one with the music I was listening to or playing (yes, Satori is at hand even playing guitar in a rock band!). I believe that this kind of experience, for me first and foremost linked to music, determined my wish to become a musician.

From what I have pointed out above it is quite logical that it is easier to achieve a direct experience of a musical work if it uses sounds that are not yet classified and filed away as part of our cultural knowledge. Sometimes members of the audience told me after a concert that at first they were trying to guess what the sound material I was using was, and, finding this impossible, let go and 'felt like they were using their ears for the first time' (this is a comment I got more than once). As a side note I might add that this is of course a race one can never win – after a while my unidentified sound will become a 'Günter sound' – but at least there is still a little less cultural ballast involved with that kind of sound material…

The last and maybe most important aspect in creating a potential direct experience of sound is *Attention*. If as a composer or performer I want the listeners to reach this kind of experience I will first have to try and ensure that they pay attention to what I have to offer. Now attention is becoming a rare thing in the modern societies of our days – a never ending stream of stimuli is directed at us by those who want to make us consume their products, stimuli that must become ever stronger because they all wear off after a while as we are becoming very skilled at not paying attention to them. Our sonic environment is polluted by all kinds of noise to a point it is actually making large parts of our populations ill (scientific data regarding the stress caused by constant noise are readily available, but no consequences drawn from them, as apparently no profit is to be made from them – which is actually not true because relaxed people not working under stress will be more productive). In consequence what I'm trying to do is to create sound work that invites people to pay attention instead of aggressing them, something they can lean into, rather than recoil from it. Of course when I have a sound source that approaches me softly, I will lean forward towards it, feel that it is something I might want to perceive, and that is more pleasant than 120 decibels thrown at me with no means to escape. Hence my tendency to create my work from rather low volume sounds, and to underline tiny details that invite the listener to explore them. I believe this kind of music can make a person more aware of the hearing process, and essentially sharpen one's perception/awareness. As a musician I pay more attention to more sonic events than the average person (scientific research has shown that the areas concerned are actually larger than usual in the brains of musicians), and picking up photography as a hobby about three years ago I have found that I now see things I did not pay attention (sic!) to before – tiny red berries and dark green leaves have become objects worth noticing and looking at closely (and taking a photo of).

There is another topic that merits our attention within this context, namely dynamics. Dynamics, quite like attention, are a great loser of our modern life: all recordings and transmissions of various popular music styles are dynamically compressed to the point that a whisper is as loud as a shout, making one of the most essential parameters of music a rare animal threatened by a mighty predator: the digital multi-band compressor. Contemporary studios are using a compressor on each channel of a multi-track recording, then during the mastering process everything is compressed again. When music is transmitted by radio and TV it is compressed one more time to fit the bandwidth. I probably do not have to mention that when mastering my own, or other artists' work for release on my label *trente oiseaux* I use no compression at all. My own music is not 'low volume music' (as it is often called), but dynamic music, and you will often find that the peak volume of one of my pieces is actually at 0db, while most of it may be around –20 to –40db. Since digital sound is not neutral in terms of volume, changing volume makes a big difference in terms of how a recording will sound, and I feel that finding the right volume for a part of a composition or the final master is quite similar to manually focusing a camera. As composers we should pay attention to keeping dynamics alive as an important means of musical expression (or at least contrast in case expression sounds too old fashioned).

I take it from your question that I should shortly discuss the various environments we experience music in. Without any doubt headphones have become an important means of listening to (especially quiet) music, and I have actually become very fond of using earphones, preferably in the dark of the early morning or late at night. Although I first shared the general reservations about spatial listening with head- and earphones I have come to enjoy the feeling of 'being alone with the music' that almost plays in my head – it can be a very intimate experience, and, in the form of a good quality portable CD player with the best quality head/earphones available, is also a quite affordable way for most anybody to get close to the music. A stereo set and a pair of speakers capable of reproducing music at similar quality is many times more expensive. To make sure that my label's releases are compatible to this kind of listening I check each master on my portable CD player – I like to call this my contribution to musical democracy. The most impressive way of experiencing music is of course in a live concert situation where ideally an atmosphere of collective attention is enhancing the experience. Unfortunately, concerts can also be far from an ideal listening experience, bad room acoustics, bad sound systems, impolite audiences and a lack of attention from the audience can make one wish to be back home with one's headphones, but one should take the risk as the reward is often quite wonderful.

I've always been attracted to the pacing of your music and the way, as you mentioned in relation to attention and dynamics, it is non-intrusive. Events seem to evolve at their own pace, they aren't forced. When you are working on a piece, how do you deal with the time domain?

It seems clear that if I want myself (and my potential listeners) to be able to directly experience the sound of my (largely non-referential) sound materials I need to give each sound the time to present itself, to have, so to speak, a right to its own life span, the time to arise, last, decay and finally disappear. This becomes even more essential when we look at the combination of sounds, their interaction over time (sic!) and the developing relationships between them. Once each individual sound material has been chosen, it demands a certain time, so that the compositional choice left to me in terms of timing finds itself within certain limits. This actually is quite an advantage, rather than a drawback, as there is nothing more frustrating than having infinite possibilities and no clue as to which of them will work. Before I started to work in this fashion I experienced 'writer's blocks' that lasted for weeks, sometimes for months, simply because I wanted to shape my material into something that was within its potential. Respecting the material's own terms liberated me from this form of self-torture. I feel that this also applies to the possible combinations of sounds, and the possible formal structures to be used, which is why I like to say that my compositions kind of grow like plants do. My role is to help my material to unfold its potential. This is also how I approach my work as an improvising musician which I have recently become again after many years of inactivity in that respect (it seems evident to me that composition and improvisation are doing the same thing on a different time scale, the same decisions have to be taken, but in improvisation one has to take them in a split second rather than having a week to think about them).

Other than the timing proposed by the sound material itself, I use my own slow breathing as the measure for the overall timing and rhythmic flow of my pieces: a silence, for example, may last five deep breaths. Considering my slow breathing as the beat gives me the means to add slight variations – a silence or the attack of the next sonic event a little before or after the next breath can play the role of playing forward, straight or laid back play in Blues, Jazz and Rock music. If I can manage to make the listener pick up this breathing rhythm during the piece, he/she will feel the slight slowing or accelerating of it as slightly relaxing or creating a small amount of tension. This phenomenon becomes clearly perceptible when one of my concerts is successful – the whole audience is breathing at the same rate after some time, which creates a very intimate, almost magic, atmosphere of collective attention. I like to call this my 'magic moments', and these magic moments are what I try to create at each concert – they are a singular experience that cannot be recreated when listening alone at home. Hence the importance concerts have for me, and, as a side note, why it is perfectly admissible in my opinion to 'just play CDs' at a performance (and there is quite a bit more to it than just playing them – it is serious work that demands one's full concentration and intuition). I have been asked more than once after a concert how it could be that my absolutely abstract music could sound so 'organic' – I think the above answers the question.

Music is essentially a time-based art form, so the importance of the time flow in a piece cannot be overestimated. I have a recording of Morton Feldman doing a workshop in Frankfurt, and at one point he says: 'All we composers have to work with is time and sound', pauses to think, giggles, and says: 'and I'm not so sure about sound', followed by his laughter. This anecdote reminds me of a Zen Koan, it sounds absurd, but has a deeper sense.

Another thing that merits our attention is the difference between chronometrical time, and the time we experience through works of art, be it a piece of music, a painting, a ballet, a book and so forth – this experience of time is that of living time, not the ticking off of seconds: each work of art needs to be 'read' (even though a painting has a sort of direct impact, our eyes need time to scan it, our mind takes time to assemble it into a unified object, and the same is true for all other art forms). The living time of an experience of art is a paradigm entirely different from that of chronometrical time, and probably much more becoming to humans than mechanically ticking off seconds. Our whole physical, mental and spiritual being is an immensely complex polyrhythm of organic processes, very unlike a clockwork, and very different for each individual person. Nevertheless our modern societies subject us to the pressure of uncountable clockworks, our personal feeling of time and personal vital cycles are in no way respected, and so it is in the experience of art we find what we should find in our entire daily life. Art is presenting us with an alternative way of *living* time, and in this aspect, too, has a definite relevance in socio-political terms. Imagine for a moment that all humans decided that they wished to live according to their own biological cycles and stood up to fight for it – it would be a revolution to dwarf all other revolutions in human history, and imply a complete reorganization of our societies. This is why I like to say that art, by its very nature, will always be subversive to a certain degree (even though a Mark Rothko painting is part of the art market and costs millions in whatever currency, this cannot take away its intrinsic quality of giving one a unique experience – the art market can only destroy art in so far as artists sell *themselves* to it, instead of their art).

I have often found that people are incapable of estimating the duration of my pieces. I talked about this with an artist I had shared a concert in London with, and asked him to estimate what the durations of the three pieces I played during the concert had been. He said he didn't really know, but they were all about the same length. I smiled, and replied that one was 9 minutes, one 15 minutes, and the last 21 minutes long. He was as amazed as I was at how differently we perceive time in such situations. I found that a live performance of Feldman's String Quartet II (1983) lasting over five hours wasn't too long, yet have found much shorter concerts endless, an experience I think anybody reading this has known.

It becomes clear from the above why I have always hated the displays on CD players counting the seconds of a piece playing, and am lucky enough to have one that lets me switch off the display. Giving the duration of my works on CD covers has always bothered me, so at one point I devised a different time unit. I had learned that neurologic research had found that our perception of 'now', the 'present moment', was a kind of time window of three seconds. Anything outside this time window would thus have to be defined as either memory or anticipation. I decided to use this 'present moment' time window as the time unit for my compositions, and called it DIM ('durée ici/maintenant', 'duration here/now' in English).

The DIM unit described how many times during one of my pieces the present moment was updated by the listener, and so, I felt, referred more to human perception than to the chronometrical time derived from the time the earth takes to revolve around itself and the sun. To my utter dismay going public on this concept only resulted in time-consuming and useless (would-be) philosophical discussions (except for some feedback from people writing me saying they really liked the idea). The concept seemed to serve most people only to display their academic education in human sciences or philosophy. Being a rather pragmatic person (I like to call myself a 'pragmatic idealist'), an artistic autodidact, and only interested in theory when it helps me advancing my work, theory for theory's sake is definitely not for me, and I was thus quite frustrated with the resonance my concept found. After a while I decided that the best time unit for music was none at all, stopped giving any duration for my works, and now advocate masking CD players' display with black tape.

You seem to imply here that sounds might evolve into complete pieces, or at least large sections of pieces, as a result of giving them the time they require to grow and develop (rather than impose your own more explicitly). Would you be able to explain your working method when developing a sound from the initial sample into its final form in relation to this?

I am afraid there is nothing much exciting to report regarding my way of treating, editing and developing sounds – I am only using the most basic sound design operations, i.e. equalizing, pitch transposing and some time stretching every once in a while. I generally stay away from treatments like granular synthesis, morphing and frequency, phase or ring modulation because they appear too 'evident' to me, meaning that they are too easily identified by the listener. My main strategy is to transpose samples, then listen to them to find out which of their sonic properties have changed, or become more apparent, and to then 'underline' or 'highlight' these new aspects by means of equalization. This process is repeated numerous times until it can be likened to getting an ever closer microscopic view of the material. It is near incredible how much can be found in a single sample patiently working this way.

I'm still using the Digidesign Sound Designer II, a software that most people I know think of as antediluvian, but I know this tool inside out from years of using it and so can arrive at results that nobody would expect from it. A good example is using the parametric EQ to build multiple resonant filters by applying it to the same sample several times. I also like the way it sounds, a little rough, that to my ears gives the sound a bit more 'bite', making it more 'palpable' than most more evolved software tools that seem to create spectra sounding a bit 'farther away', less concrete. My generous use of quotation marks hints at the fact that these are quite subtle nuances, hard to describe because more of a certain 'feel' than a clearly defined impression. Very probably an acquired taste…

Another thing I frequently do I learned from the Ensoniq samplers I first used for sampling: the back/forward loop that I imitate by reversing a sample and splicing it with the original. This works best when starting with the reverse sample, as with most samples this kind of creates an automatic fade in/fade out effect with the volume peak of the sound in the middle. It needs some patience and experience to arrive at not having the splice click or pop. I'm not above using reverse samples either (and still have an idiosyncratic love affair with backward guitar loops dating from my guitarist past). With some samples one cannot really tell they are going backwards, they just sound a little uncommon, and I like that.

Sound design is basically a combination of three tools for me: a digital sample editor, my ears and my intuition that tells me what might be hidden in a given sample material. I prefer to have one basic tool I know how to use to having a number of powerful tools I cannot really work with in a controlled manner. There is a new generation of sound design tools around that it would literally take decades, if not centuries, to explore all possibilities of, and I sometimes wonder how many people will ever make use of something other than their factory presets.

As is my habit I'd like to add a few quotes regarding the importance of sound in creating music. Feldman reportedly said to another composer (whose name I forgot) that once he had determined the instrumentation for a work, the rest was only detail work. The other composer said: 'You can't really mean to say that when you have made choice of instruments the composition is almost done?' Feldman said: 'For me it is.' Paul Bley, a great improvising musician, when asked how he went about improvising his music, said: 'Well, even on a great piano there are only a few perfect notes. I find out which ones they are, and then play with them.' Feldman also said that he hated to admit it, but that he had a wonderful Steinway grand piano in his home, and that it was slightly out of tune. He never had it tuned because he preferred the way it sounded (Feldman always composed at the piano and I really like his saying that composing without a piano was 'like going on a honeymoon without a wife'). (Please note that all quotes are from memory and are probably not textual.)

Clearly whilst composing you are working outside of the performance time of the music, and this precise approach to the magnification of sound is therefore possible. You've recently begun improvising again though, and I was wondering how this related to your composing? Does the cellotar[2] replace the sample editor in your sound design set-up, and how do you deal with the need to shape sounds in time whilst performing?

Now that I have developed the final version of my amplification system for the electric cellotar I can really say that it kind of replaces the sample editor in my sound design: the system presents the cellotar as if magnified by a microscope, and

---

2   The cellotar is a five-string baritone guitar played with a cello bow.

as I'm monitoring my playing with headphones it feels as if my head was inside the instrument. Scraping the bridge with my thumbnail sounds quite close to a kind of electroacoustic music, for instance, and sometimes I have to lower the volume to just dare to play – all playing noises are amplified to an incredible degree, making it sometimes difficult to control the instrument, but this 'magnification' also provides me with an (at least for the moment) unfathomable number of possibilities.

I have just recorded with Graham Halliwell for three days using this set-up for the first time, and it was very different from the times when I was still using a microphone and a guitar amplifier. These recordings resulted in a kind of music I had never played (and never heard) before. As a side note: it is quite strange to me as a rather proficient guitar player to play with an instrument I have no fixed (and thus limited) vocabulary for – while creating extremely detailed sounds on it I could not even play a simple folk tune on it to save my life. It is as if a person became a cello player only playing Helmut Lachenmann without even once practising a C major scale. On the other hand the absence of a defined (and thus limited) vocabulary for the instrument opens all the doors for me that the electric guitar never did, simply because near everything possible had already been done with an electric guitar.

The timescale of improvising vs. composing does not really pose a problem; for one thing the pace of our improvisation is far from the intensive and hectic Free Jazz playing of the past, and the years of working by myself on my Macintosh have trained my intuition (even though this statement may seem strange, it is true) so that I am now able to direct towards the musicians I am playing with. The inspirational input is of course much higher from fellow musicians than from a Macintosh, and I am of course highly susceptible and sensitive to it after my long 'lone wolf' period. I should also point out that my fellow musicians and I are not purist improvising musicians – with Graham for instance I recorded duos as well as trios and quartets, one trio with a piece of mine as the basis track, and another one we played as a duo with another piece of mine as basic track, erased the basis track, and overdubbed another duo. This latter piece turned out to be particularly interesting and really special. I will edit, mix and finally master our recordings during the coming weeks. Editing in this context not only means getting rid of playing mistakes, but also taking out parts or phrases by one of us that do not further the piece as a whole (everything is recorded onto separate tracks so this can be done). This implies 're-composing' the pieces to a certain degree, and of course my experience as an electroacoustic composer will be quite helpful in handling the task.

As you can see, the membrane between composition and improvisation is becoming quite porous in this osmotic process. There are musicians in improvised music who regard recordings strictly as documents of live playing (thus in some way giving the poïesis of a work more importance than the work itself), while I tend to think that a live concert and a tone carrier are two quite different things: while a playing mistake or a piece formally failing are quickly forgotten in a live playing situation, they can be repeated infinite times listening to recordings. Given the aspect of virtually infinite repetitions I believe one should give listeners music fit to stand the test of repeated listening. This conflict is mirrored in photography by photographers who consider cropping and editing photos as a mortal sin and the end of photography as an art form on one hand, and those who believe that all means should be used to provide the best possible result on the other hand. I adhere to the pragmatic school of thought that the best possible result should be obtained by all appropriate means. I do think, however, that the edited result should still reflect the essence of what was improvised, not stray too far from its sources, so that the inherent qualities of improvisation, the spontaneous communication and intuition put into each moment by the players remain intact.

I think the analogy of photography is an interesting one, and reminds me of Laszlo Moholy-Nagy's assertion that '"photography" [consists of] all the results which can be achieved with photographic means with camera or without; all the reaction of the photo-sensitive media to chemicals, to light, heat, cold, pressure etc.'[3] So using an instrument as a complete configuration, potentially bypassing its designed mode of operation as you suggest with your approach to performance. This implies an experimental attitude, with open-ended results of course, where predictability is perhaps lower than in more controlled situations. Given your emphasis on editing when recording improvisations, what happens in a purely live situation, where no editing after the event is possible? As a composer used to extremely precise control over the finished music, how do you react to this situation?

I designed the instrument by myself and for myself; there is no repertoire for it that would define a 'designed mode of operation' other than the one I define for it by developing a musical vocabulary for it. I happen to dislike the term 'experimental' very much when it is applied to my work – the term, in my view, can be employed for work in which the process of its genesis itself has priority over the result of said process. This is basically never the case with my work. More concretely, my approach to improvisation is result-oriented, rather than process-oriented – the result I/we try to obtain is rather clear in our minds, though not in technical terms, but rather in terms of a certain atmosphere, a certain mood and so forth. There is a predictability of a certain field of possibilities/options we will choose during an improvisation that you might describe as our musical vocabulary and language. This may be described as knowing what one will say without knowing the exact words and sentences, yet, while language and vocabulary are already defined – the situation I find myself in when I start answering one of your questions, for example. The language will be English, I will use a certain vocabulary, and write in a certain way that is my personal way of using the English language (my 'writing style'). I am, in a way, improvising my answer, and like in a musical improvisation situation I might use a new combination of words, a way of putting something I have not employed before. It is not 100 per cent predictable for me what I will finally write, but I have a defined idea of what I will have to express, and a certain self-confidence that I will be able to do it successfully. This nicely describes the way I approach improvising.

---

3   Laszlo Moholy-Nagy, *Visions in Motion* (Chicago, 1947).

When it comes to editing recordings as I have described earlier you must not think that this is a kind of 'composition after the fact' approach – most of it is eliminating unwanted playing noises (like a string plucked when it was not intended, or in Graham's case, a saxophone feedback getting out of control and distorting the recording). These little incidents are far less important in a live situation, and quickly forgotten. An example for a more substantial way of editing I'd like to use is that at a certain moment in one piece I tried playing an arpeggio on the cellotar, this worked well, and after a short pause I played a series of arpeggios that sound very nice, but in retrospect make the first (test balloon) arpeggio sound out of place. I will thus edit out this first lone arpeggio, and leave the others in. I may also delete a too hesitant beginning, or an unnecessary second ending when there was a perfect one before. This is the structural way of editing, and about as far as I will go in modifying the original material. The things I correct in the recordings are perfectly acceptable in a live situation, they are a part of that particular situation, and I have no problem accepting this. My concerts using pre-recorded material sometimes fail to function, too, be it because of the sound system, the lack of attention from the audience or maybe a street with lots of traffic right outside the concert space. I think the question of presenting composed or improvised music in a live situation is only one of the factors that make or break a concert – I have played many concerts under conditions reaching from 'perfect' to 'plain ridiculous' and the risk of failure is something a live performing musician has to be able to handle. I feel the chance of playing a wonderful concert that makes both audience and artist(s) happy is well worth taking the risk of failure. I am a confessing perfectionist, but my definition of perfection is being perfect in one's own terms, i.e. doing the very best one is capable of doing – it is quite clear to me that as a performer I will never reach the perfection of, say, Zakir Hussein, simply because I am not single-minded enough to only play tabla all day all my life, and I will never become Morton Feldman (but then, who will?).

A lesser degree of perfection is acceptable for me in exchange for a larger variety of things to explore (I cannot compose while taking photos, for instance, nor can I compose on my Macintosh while touring as an improvising musician, reading books, visiting art exhibitions, etc.) and I believe that at the end of the day all these 'distractions' make my life and work more rich and interesting. Likewise trading in a bit of control for the intuitive exchange and interaction with my fellow musicians, for the inspired moments that happen, strikes me as a pretty good deal – I am perfectly persuaded that in the long run improvising will make my compositions better and vice versa. When asked to choose between walnut and cinnamon ice cream I tend to choose both, and then ask for some more flavours.

Postscript: the state of things – August 2008

After +minus, the trio with Graham Halliwell and Mark Wastell, disbanded, I began collaborating with Heribert Friedl, Vienna, who plays the Hackbrett (a hammered dulcimer) in a number of creative ways. I played the electric cellotar and various bamboo flutes, some of them self-made; all of the collaboration was done through the mail. We have published two CDs, *Ataraxia* released on trente oiseaux and *~trans*, a single long piece based on a field recording, on Heribert's non-visual objects (nvo) label.

Some time later I was asked to contribute a track to an album of re-mixes of solo improvisation work by guitarist Gary Smith, London, which led to my publishing my first guitar track after 30-plus years of playing the electric guitar, and to Gary and I agreeing to try and work together on more music. The first result of this collaboration was a set of six short pieces created by means of exchanging sound files by mail and in which I played clarinet, bamboo flutes and an Indian Esraj (that served as a percussion instrument).

Gary and I finally met to play and record together in 2007, and eventually formed a duo named Klangstaub. Klangstaub recorded a body of improvised work in July and November 2007, and March 2008; our first concert was at the no.signal@ Wire 25 festival – AvantJazz in London on 17 November 2007. We also created a web label (klangstaub musik) to distribute both our solo and duo work, as well as collaborations with other artists. A collaboration with Michael Vorfeld, Berlin, has already resulted in an EP titled *Mellom Paradis og Helleviga*, and we plan meeting again in autumn 2008 to further develop our musical work. Klangstaub's website is now online at www.klangstaub.com.

By now my instruments include clarinet, alto clarinet, pocket trumpet, duduk and bass duduk, acoustic baritone guitar and five string fretless-bass, all played combined with live looping and mixing. Not all of these instruments have found their place in Klangstaub's work yet, although I hope they eventually will. My latest acquisition is a cheap classical guitar that I made fretless, stringed and tuned like an Oud (Arabic lute), and currently use in learning the Maqamat (the Arabic system of modes) while saving up for an actual Oud. I take a vivid interest in Arabic music and really want to get into playing it.

I also played and recorded with the French improvisation ensemble SAP(e) and Sylvian Chevaux in Montpellier in February 2008. We plan to release a CD and a DVD of our collaboration (SAP(e) are currently working on this) and to do a promotion tour for them in France next year. I have also been involved in a number of projects concerned with electroacoustic music that I cannot describe in detail here, and am currently thinking about beginning a rather particular electroacoustic composition – after quite a while away from the computer I seem to be coming back to this sort of work again, too.

The interview was conducted by email between 2 January and 10 February 2004, with the postscript being added in August 2008.

Bryn Harrison

When listening to your music I'm always struck by the way time seems to be suspended, or at least slowed down, and I wanted to start by asking you how you use repetition and change in your work?

Well, I'm fascinated by the whole notion of time in music and, in particular, by the ways in which repetition and change may occur when one shifts one's attention away from a dialectical time (in which sounds have intentionality) towards a less goal-orientated way of construction. I would say that, in a post-Cageian (or post-Feldman) world it is possible to view musical time as something other than a device which provides directionality or rhythmic impetus (and all the other rhetorical devices that this implies). For me, time can be viewed on a moment-to-moment basis as a space in which to contain musical material. I would say that my whole motivation to compose and the subsequent working methods that I've chosen to use have come directly from my response to that situation. If time seems suspended, or at least slowed down in my music, as you suggest, then this may be to do with the way in which I'm trying to place the material into a sort of time-continuum in which the repeated figures can be expanded, contracted or subtly varied from one moment to the next. I try to work with material that will allow for a degree of flexibility or manipulation. Working with rhythmic and melodic cycles has been the natural consequence of this approach. I try to make each cycle have an internal logic (i.e. simple repeating intervals) that is clear to the ear but then manipulate the patterns in a way which is disorientating to the listener. Here, I think, there is a sense of implied motion within the cycles but not of musical progress. There is more a feeling of going round in circles, literally.

This seems to imply an interest in process at various levels in your work. Could you explain how such cycles operate, and whether there are any links between individual moments in a piece and its overall structure?

My use of pitch and rhythm is entirely process-based although I tend to take a 'looser' approach to other parameters such as timbre, dynamics or the overall structure of a piece. When working on a new piece, I usually begin with pitch and often test out certain pre-structured intervallic patterns at the piano, most often to determine issues of registration or rates of harmonic change. Once I have a fragment of material defined sonically I can usually deduce, what I feel to be, an appropriate tempo and level of rhythmic activity. I then tend to work away from an instrument, expanding on the material and developing rhythmic cycles that can be coupled with the chains of pitches. I try to work with pitch and rhythmic cycles that are of slightly different lengths in order to generate longer sections of music or to subvert a sense of the music repeating in exactly the same way (or both). In earlier pieces such as *Open 2* (2001) and *Four Parts to Centre* (2002), I tended to focus on a very limited number of pitches (typically between five and seven chromatically-adjacent pitch classes) to create a feeling of harmonic stasis or of very gradual change. In these pieces I tried to maintain a level of musical interest by constantly altering the registral, timbral or rhythmic aspects of the music or, in the case of slightly larger ensemble pieces such as *the ground* (2000) or *low time patterns [#1–5]* (2002) by dividing the ensemble into smaller groupings, each playing cyclical material within a particular harmonic range.

Whilst these techniques are still intrinsic to the way I work, I feel the more recent pieces operate in a slightly different way. In pieces such as *rise* (2003), *Octet* (2004), *six symmetries* (2004) and the piece that I completed recently for the London Sinfonietta, *four cycles* (2002–2005), I've been working with longer chains of notes which move through an entire octave before reaching their starting point. This developed from an interest in exploring the ways in which our perception of time passing is governed by harmonic change, metre and rhythm – i.e. what happens if the rate of harmonic change is slowed down whilst the level of rhythmic activity is accelerated or vice versa? I found that focusing more specifically on harmonic rhythm necessitated a broader note range and pitch cycles of much more variable lengths. At the moment I have only explored this area tentatively but have found myself utilizing different ways of organizing pitch such as the very straightforward use of a chromatic scale which, until recently, I always found too obvious to use. This is particularly noticeable in the pieces *rise* and the second movement of *four cycles* in which continually rising glissandi in the strings are pitted against the more harmonically stable sound world of the rest of the ensemble. The effect is wholly disorientating and gives the effect of something which is always moving whilst at the same time remaining largely unchanging (analogous, maybe, to that of a river or waterfall).

In answer to the second part of your question, since what I'm aiming to achieve is purely experiential at the moment of it taking place and, since the music is largely non-developmental, I don't tend to concern myself very much with how the micro-structure of the music will be perceived in relation to the whole. Unlike in traditional performance practice (where a piece will ordinarily have a sense of a beginning, middle and end) I do not feel it necessary for the performer to consider how their approach to a particular note or phrase will impact upon the piece as a whole as I don't think this will be of consequence to the listener. There are, however, internal relationships in tempo or regulated levels of stasis/activity in the music which provide me with some kind of system to work with. The resulting flexibilities in sound structure are then presented as a variation on what has gone before or as the presentation of the same pitch series in a different way or as part of a gradual shift from one place to another. These slightly different approaches have seemed to result in pieces that fall into two different categories: those in which the material is presented in sections (or movements), rather like 'panels', in which the music goes on largely undeveloped until it stops and something else takes its place (*etre-temps* (2002), *low time patterns [#1–5]* or *six symmetries*) or those where a piece very gradually grows organically out of itself (*Four Parts to Centre*, *Octet*, *rise*). As I begin to work on a piece it becomes apparent quite quickly whether the material has the potential for an Escher-like metamorphosis or whether it is better suited to smaller degrees of variation. In the first movement of *six symmetries*, for instance, the rhythmic contours seemed to pull away from each other and then fold neatly in on themselves. The pitch cycle I was using was, coincidentally, of the same length so the whole section neatly resolved itself without change or the need for any development. In these kinds of instances I tend to 'frame' the material by putting repeat marks around it and allowing the material to be heard several times. I might then expand or contact the material subtly and then allow this to be repeated to a slightly greater or lesser extent than the previous 'frame'. At some point I would like to explore much longer durations, to explore material much more fully and to take the listener on a much longer journey into different musical territories without a sense that we've really gone anywhere. I particularly like the American playwright Richard Foreman's comment on Philip Glass's early music expressing that 'the work of art as primarily a structure articulating its mode of being-present'.[1] I think, through the use of cyclical processes, that that's what I'm trying to articulate as well.

One of the interesting things about both these approaches to structure is that they are almost infinitely scalable: regardless of whether there are more panels or you use a longer process, it does not radically affect how the piece operates. Whilst the panel approach alludes to Stockhausen's moment form, the latter resembles Jonathan Kramer's notion of vertical time, where a single moment becomes the entire piece.[2] Given that, I'm interested in how you might go about articulating longer spans, particularly given your interest in late Feldman and his concern with time/memory structures?

I like Jonathan Kramer's description of a music which adopts the requirements of stasis as its entire essence and there are some good examples of pieces which operate successfully in this way (the late so-called 'number series' pieces by John Cage for example). I think that, for me, approaching the material from the perspective of issuing forth a very gradual change could lead to a longer, infinitely scalable structure. However, I'm not sure that it would be possible to use the panel approach indefinitely as I think it would, beyond a certain point, affect the way the piece operates. Jonathan Kramer's notion of a vertical time refers to an immobile, undifferentiated sound world which is, of itself, the piece. For me, I'm trying to set up clear internal relationships between one panel and the next. This is why I tend

---

1   Richard Foreman, 'Glass and Snow (1970)', in Richard Kostelanetz (ed.), *Writings on Glass* (New York, 1997), pp. 80–86, at p. 80.
2   Jonathan Kramer, *The Time of Music* (New York, 1988), p. 55.

to leave gaps between each panel and present them more as individual movements than moment by moment sections. Hopefully this will give the listener time to observe these relationships more clearly than if the sections followed each other without a pause. For instance, in *low time patterns* and *six symmetries* there are very clear structural relationships in tempo, pitch organization and levels of rhythmic activity between one section and the next. Typically, each section is relatively short in relation to the overall piece (2–4 minutes in a 15–20 minute piece). I think adding more and more panels in this way might deter from the overall structure and could appear monotonous. Feldman successfully avoids this by simply replacing one moment with another to create one continuous experience. At first, to my ear, these changes from one moment to the next can seem quite abrupt and, at times, even dramatic but the persistent presence of the material ensures that we very quickly forget what we were listening to before.

My interest in writing much longer music comes from thinking primarily of a piece that would be in a constant state of growth or metamorphosis. What I have accumulated over the last few years are these various techniques, these various ways of doing things and the idea would be to set myself the challenge of getting from one place to another, drawing on these different techniques as I do so. It would be interesting, I feel, to return to previously used material but by a different route rather like in an Escher woodcut. I have been working on ways of modulating from one pitch area to another, of moving between modal and chromatic note series and of moving from counterpoint to static chords. I am thinking perhaps of a continuous solo piano piece but without a commission and time available this material might remain as sketches for some time to come.

Ironically, the solo piano piece *Flowers Fall* (2004) lasts only one minute. I was asked by the Guildford Festival to write a miniature for Clive Williamson as part of the One Minute Wonders project. My response was to take a purely deductive approach by writing an entirely process-based piece. The piece begins modally with a seven-pitch cycle and builds chromatically to a twelve-pitch cycle with the addition of one new note in each bar until it returns to a seven-note cycle in a different key. The whole piece goes just once through the entire cycle. There is a succinct coherence and logic to the music that feels, to my mind, structurally right despite the brevity of the piece. The only difficulty I have with musical coherence and logic is that it ensues a sense of closure which is something which I want to avoid musically. Another route that I considered was just the opposite – to offer a brief glimpse into a potentially longer piece – a vista into a larger world, although this seemed, in some ways, too conceptual an idea. Perhaps it will only be through writing a much longer piece that I resolve some of these issues concerning time and perception. For the moment, most of my pieces seem to be coming out at about 20 minutes which, of course, prohibits me from entering most composition competitions or calls for pieces!

There is a particularly fine degree of rhythmic differentiation in your music and I wanted to ask you how you develop this aspect of your work with regards to metre and the duration of notes.

Prior to about 1999 I would experiment with different ways of creating rhythmic patterns and often found myself using a technique of creating durational values from simple generative number sequences. As I became more involved in this process I began to look at ways of generating bigger numbers to create more finite rhythms. This necessitated a working method that would allow me to determine more precisely the exact rhythmic placement of notes within the bar. Around this time I also re-read both Morton Feldman's essay 'Crippled Symmetry'[3] and Brian Ferneyhough's essay 'Duration and Rhythm as Compositional Resources'[4] and was subsequently reminded of their individual and idiosyncratic approaches to, what Feldman refers to as, 'containing' material within the bar. I became interested in looking for a way of being able to create small temporal shifts by leaving the original rhythm in place and instead altering its relationship to the bar. What I eventually arrived at was a method in which I would begin with a time-space version of these rhythms and then trace the resulting points into grids containing beats and bar lines. From there I could deduce (and subsequently convey through conventional notation) the exact placement of notes in relation to a particular beat or the whole bar. Tracing these same points into a grid of a slightly different size enabled me to stretch or contract the figure whilst preserving the original relationships between the note values (a method not dissimilar to that used by a figurative painter copying from a photograph in which the original image is divided into a grid and all the details then copied into a magnified version of the same grid so that the scale changes but the details remain in proportion to one another) By putting the emphasis on the size of the bar, the use of these frames led me towards a more regulated system of time signatures. The same material could be repeated but within an ever-changing metre. I began to see each bar almost as an area of compression, in which I could subtly contract, expand or in some way distort the rhythms. I would then overlay, combine or link material into longer chains of note values to form whole sections of music or even entire pieces.

Over the last few years I have used the number sequences with less frequency but have retained the use of the time frame. I am constantly looking for new ways of plotting material. At the moment I use about ten different time frames and tend to determine the placement of points either by overlaying acetates of a particular rhythmic pattern or by creating simple geometric contours based on a sixth of a circle (a method adopted from the British artist Bridget Riley). In both instances I trace directly onto the frames themselves and then translate into standard (but sometimes quite complex) rhythmic notation. The piano piece *I–V* (2003) illustrates the former technique and *six symmetries* the latter. What both techniques allow for

---

3   Walter Zimmerman (ed.), *Morton Feldman: Essays* (Kerpen, 1985), pp. 124–37.
4   James Boros and Richard Toop (eds), *Brian Ferneyhough: Collected Writings* (Amsterdam, 1995), pp. 51–65.

is the same unifying temporal aspect to a piece that the number sequences provide. Rhythmic unity seems to be an important part of my working process – a way of allowing a piece to proceed from a limited starting point that is coherent and logical but with twists and turns developing along the way. Both the acetates and geometric curves still have their origins in simple numerical sequences and I am drawn by the fact that, as in Renaissance and Baroque music, there is a silent system of number and proportion underneath the surface of the music. It is irrelevant to me whether the listener is able to perceive the precision of these slight rhythmic changes but it seems important that the player is able to convey a sense of exactitude and poise through performance in order to make these small differences 'visible'. Despite the lack of any discernable pulse in much of my music, the rhythms still seem to have a bodily effect on the listener and both musicians and non-musicians alike have commented on the resultant gravitational pull as material is expanded and contracted. Of course, all this is experimentation and I am still trying to determine the exact degree that these figures can be manipulated. If the changes are too small then the results can be imperceptible or simply uninteresting and if the material is expanded too far then the results can appear as a novelty to the listener.

One of the things I find interesting when listening to your work is the paradox of it being a densely textural music yet one where linearity, and to an extent counterpoint, is the driving force. How does the ensemble size affect the approach you take to an individual piece in this respect, and how important are the particular sounds you use? Are they simply ways of articulating the material, or do they have a more important structural role?

I think my approach is largely the same, regardless of the number of instruments that I am writing for, as I see the use of linearity and counterpoint simply as devices to articulate the given material. The rhythms come mainly from the time frames and can be used to explore the different contrapuntal possibilities for an instrument with homophonic capabilities (i.e. the piano, guitar or keyboard percussion) or as a way of creating hockets between several different instruments. What appears to differ, however, is the resultant focus of the music. In other words, the way in which we perceive the linearity or counterpoint in my music seems to be different when listening to a large ensemble piece to that of a piece for duo or a solo instrument even though the music has been created in much the same way. For example, in the opening section of *six symmetries*, with its 17-part counterpoint, the perceived result, to my mind, is of a combined or contained mass of sound that shifts around as a series of quietly oscillating canons. Here, I find myself listening to the ensemble as if it were one large instrument. This comes partly from the fact that I chose not to concern myself with the colouristic possibilities of the different timbres available and thus avoided individual instruments drawing attention to themselves. In the flurries of activity, one can still perceive a high degree of rhythmic articulation taking place but it becomes impossible to identify what any individual player is playing at any given moment.

In other pieces, however, written for, say, 5–8 players, such as *the ground* or *low time patterns* the resultant focus tends to be more on the ways in which the material is layered or intertwined both melodically and rhythmically. With both of these pieces much of the material is created from different rhythmic cycles that are superimposed to create more rhythmic complexity. The individual timbres of the instruments then present the listener with different points of focus. At times I feel myself drawn to a particular line, let's say played by a viola, and at other moments find myself focusing on the harmonies resulting from the combination of these lines sounding simultaneously.

Obviously, with the solo piano pieces (*etre-temps*, *I–V* and *Flowers Fall*) or the recent solo electric guitar piece *Return* (2005) where there are fewer simultaneous events taking place, the counterpoint becomes a point of focus in its own right. So, depending on how many instruments I have to write for, it is really a question of scaling up or down and in the process considering what effect this will have on the listener. If the piece is large then the rhythms will appear more inwardly mobile whereas if the piece is small then the rhythms will feel more articulated or projected. I am interested in exploring these different levels of material density and the phenomenological responses that arise from working with ensembles of varying sizes. I very often write 'tutti' throughout, regardless of the scale of a work, to give the piece an 'all-over' textural density somehow akin to abstract visual art. A large ensemble piece, to my mind, is rather like looking at an object from afar whereas a smaller ensemble piece is more like looking at the same object close up.

Hockets and counterpoint can also have the effect of breaking up the surface area by splitting events into different registers or timbres. There seems to be a tendency in my compositions to let the music flow through you and I sometimes feel a need to counterbalance this with a tension that runs contrary to notions of relaxation. I am interested in making the surface more detailed, 'grainy' and occasionally unpredictable. What I'm trying to do seems to be about maintaining a balance between flow and resistance – to create transitions that are smooth but at the same time slightly unsettling.

You've recently completed a few collaborations with artists in other fields and cite the paintings and writings of Bridget Riley as an important influence on the development of your compositional technique. Could you explain how your interest in visual art in particular has impacted on your work?

My interest in modern abstract painting goes back several years and I have found inspiration in the work of a number of artists coming mainly from the Minimalist and Abstract Expressionist traditions. I feel the artists that have had the biggest influence on my working methods are those who are able to engage the viewer in a kind of kinetic stasis. I am thinking primarily of the British painters Bridget Riley, James Hugonin and Mike Walker (with whom I have collaborated on several occasions) as well as American artists such as Brice Marden and Agnes Martin. I am drawn to the idea that painting, as an immobile art form, can convey movement and conversely, that music, as a temporal art, might be able to convey stasis. In the work of all these artists (and Marden is perhaps the loosest) there is a certain organizing principle in which the process of variation can only occur through a counterbalance with regularity and symmetry. The grid in particular, in Hugonin's and Martin's work, creates a dialogue of shifting sensations which sustains the visual experience as the eye is drawn continually across the canvas. In the work of Bridget Riley, the picture plane is divided into music's most primary elements – tonal values and rhythmic gradations and it is often the way that these forces interact that maintains both the painting's dynamism and equilibrium. A detailed survey of the paintings often reveals rhythmic and tonal repetitions that are derived from simple number sequences being superimposed on top of each other – a process not dissimilar to that of the isorhythm in music.

When writing *six symmetries* I made a careful analytical study of how Bridget Riley uses the curve. I wanted to be able to convey in musical terms the same sense of transition and oscillation that occurs in the paintings of the mid-seventies. The result was a series of rhythmic canons that I coupled to pitch cycles, running these backwards or permutating the rhythmic sequences to create the variations in the piece. In *Rise* and the second movement of *four cycles* I also use the influence of the curve to create a series of trajectories to plot the upwards movement of continually rising glissandi played by the strings. There is something analogous here I feel to the upwards motion in Bridget Riley's work in which the eye is taken from bottom left of the painting to top right. Riley herself has spoken of the sensations that arise when clusters flow into each other along the twists of a curve.[5] In musical terms, this can be achieved by the superimposition of melodic and rhythmic cycles. I think this creates a type of art that is situational – it is not about creating the results but the things that make up the result.

Over the last few years I have had the privilege of finding out about many of the techniques under discussion through the collaborative work that I have undertaken with painter and printmaker Mike Walker, which has culminated in several projects for different gallery spaces. In particular, Mike's unique approach to over-layering in his linocuts has made me think differently about how different layers of music can be superimposed. The beautiful *Linden Sequences* is a perfect example of how a sense of continuity and variation can be achieved within one singular set of prints through the superimposition of a limited number of templates. Similarly, in the highly reductive *Music for a Light Room, Music for a Dark Room* one is reminded of how much dynamic and tonal variation is available from very economical means. Here, in a complete environment, our vision becomes focused not just on one painting but on how each relates to the others. Perception becomes not just the act of looking at a singular object but allows for a degree of contextualization. In a lot of visual artists there seems to be an interest in building a large body of work that utilizes the same procedures, processes and structures. There is much more of a sense of continuity as there isn't always the need to start anew each time. Through working with Mike and the interest I have developed in abstract painting in general, I have come to see my music as the continuation of one or just a few ideas and of setting up frames of material that can exist as musical objects. I feel that I am always

---

5   Bridget Riley, *The Eye's Mind* (London, 1999), p. 99.

looking at the same thing from lots of different angles and yet, at the same time, as time progresses, I am aware of a very gradual shift into new areas.

I have also been involved in another project recently, *passage*, with John McDowall who is an artist working mainly with books. From a set of 25 pages of images (the magnified holes and tracts of bookworm taken from a secondhand novel) I and four other composers were invited to translate these marks into a musical score. One of the interesting aspects of working with an artist from a different medium is that it makes you have to look at what you do in a different way. This project in particular has made me consider how I organize material on the page and the consequential impact that this has upon the performer. It has also made me take greater care in the presentation of my finished scores. I now feel also that there is a strong link between my interest in visual art and my idiosyncratic approach to musical notation. Hand-copying my scores is a laborious task. Like each of the paintings by James Hugonin, developed slowly and methodically over the course of a year or so, it allows me to look carefully at each aspect of the composition in detail.

Do you feel then that notation and the writing of scores are integral parts of your compositional method?

Yes, absolutely, because the specific use of notation and the final copying of the score itself are essential parts of the actual working process. For me, composition is very much a process of discovery and notation plays an intrinsic role in throwing up possibilities that I can explore further. I think there is a great deal of difference between the traditional role of notation as a means of transcription and a more experimental approach in which notation can act as a compositional tool. For me, the way I use notation to organize material on the page has a very direct consequence on the spatial and durational aspect of the music itself as well as helping to preserve a sense of continuity to the whole piece. For example, when defining the exact placement of notes within the time frames I may, for example, find myself using irrational ratios 5:4, 7:6 and 3:2. I may then limit myself to only using these particular ratios for the rest of the piece – thus setting up a kind of rhythmic design. This is just one simple example, but my approach is always to work with strategies that will allow the piece to come into being. The most important thing for me is to try to get a balance between how I want to hear something and how this might be in some way slightly tempered by a system that runs counter to my intuition. I am not interested in a so-called 'paper composition' approach to writing music since I am primarily concerned with the sonic result. It is of no real interest to me whether the listener is able to read a score or relate in any way to these strategies. I feel this approach has more to do with allowing me to become an observer by giving me the opportunity to step back slightly from the material that I am using. Perhaps I have a certain mistrust in the notion that the composer can, in some ways, control the experience itself. The experience, for me, is what results from the active and mutual engagement between the composer, performer and listener.

The methods of organization that I employ always seem to be slightly different for each piece thus providing each particular score with a certain 'look' as well as a certain sound and intention. Some pieces seem to require more involvement with spatial organization than others. It all depends how the material is to function within the piece. In the solo piano piece *etre-temps* I was dealing with a very limited number of pitches, often presented within a sparse context. So here, I began by setting up certain systems to ensure that the temporal aspects of the music became the main feature. I set up each page as a metric grid – a series of self-contained organizational units into which I could place the rhythmic figures that I was working with. Each page is characterized by having the same pattern of time signatures running vertically down each page. This then becomes an organizational tool, helping to regulate the degrees of compression as well as helping to define the precise lengths of the pauses between events. Subsequently this has an impact upon the actual way in which these phrases and silences will be interpreted by the performer.[6]

Another example of the use of notation as a compositional tool is illustrated by the II, IV and VI movements of *six symmetries*. The vertical contours that were used to create the tightly regulated canons for the other three movements are here magnified and presented in a looser way to provide wave-like patterns running down the page. Although the listener may not be able to visualize the precise shape of these patterns the effect of an oscillating wave is immediately discernable. Indeed, after the premiere of this piece several people asked me if I had a strong interest in or connection with the visual arts. Of course, if I was to use computer software to write my music then none of this would come into being. Even if I was to make a rough copy of the score and then typeset the information onto computer then this would require having to present the score exactly as it appears in the hand-written copy. One could argue that, even then, some of the intention would be missing. In a technological age which promises more and more time-effective ways of documentation, copying by hand slows one down and requires a certain level of patience and commitment. It is also an approach in which, to get to know the material I am working with, I require a certain scrutiny. I often find myself making important changes at the point that I copy up the score and, as this can take several months, a piece may go through several fundamental changes along the way before I arrive at the final result. As mentioned previously, it all gets back to how I'm trying to deal with time really.

The interview was conducted by email between 5 January 2005 and 16 August 2006.

---

6   A more extensive survey of how the performer engages with this material can be found in Eric Clarke, Nicholas Cook, Bryn Harrison and Philip Thomas, 'Interpretation and Performance in Bryn Harrison's *être temps*', *Musicae Scienitae* 9 (2005): 31–74.

Philip Jeck

I thought we'd begin by talking about the overall sound of your music. What is it about record players and vinyl which interests you in particular?

My background is in visual art and I've always had an interest – my first love in the arts is really music, and for me I found music is the strongest and most immediate of all the forms. But if I had any sort of talent at anything when I was younger it was at drawing and painting and stuff so I ended up doing quite well at A Level art and then going on to art college. But I learnt a little bit of guitar and stuff when I was younger in my teens, but what I could do on a guitar just didn't satisfy me, I felt frustrated because what I could do on it wasn't enough for me to feel like it was what was in my head, so to speak, and when I listened to other people playing guitar, it just sounded terrible I suppose, you know people that I like. So my way in was for the late 70s, I went to New York in 1979 and went to some clubs and stuff. It was good to go to discos and stuff and see people play records but it was the first time I'd seen people you know really mixing records, and not so much the hip-hop stuff like Grandmaster Flash, although that's something that I also enjoy, but what particularly got me were people like Larry Levan and Walter Gibbons. They would like extend just parts of records that were interesting to them. Also it was all completely dance based so it was pretty well all round 4/4, you know four to the floor stuff, but I bought some twelve inches and stuff in New York that had been mixed by these people and bought them home then started hearing stuff anyway here in clubs and went out and bought a little mixer and another turntable and started off like trying to copy, I suppose, those people and so that was the way in. That was how I sort of started using record players, and I did stuff with friends, but at that time I was living in London and the people that I was associated with were people that were involved in performance art and dance and also like music people around the LMC [London Musicians Collective] so I wanted to find a way of like what I did would work within that sphere. I was also doing performance work myself at that time which was an extension of my visual background, and trying to incorporate sound and stuff into it and I bought a couple of old record players to use. But also at that time I was working with a dance tour, this is the early 80s, and I worked with him right up until about 1990 I suppose, sort of just afterwards was the last time I worked. He had like management in Europe and we got loads and loads of gigs, loads and loads of work and he then sort of had a company that did work with us, and this was Laurie Booth, and so I sort of just played on the road.

I mean I spent just three or four years just … well it was just fantastic, I was being paid to learn what I do you know and like find out what was possible. Also being in the circumstance of it being a performance and stuff it wasn't geared to, you know, getting everybody up to dance, you know playing, keeping the beat going or whatever, so it gradually in a way I suppose developed my own language. Also one of the things that really kicked me then to using old record players was that I had some 78s that I wanted to use and I found one in a junk shop, an old record player that played 78s and had like a tape out so I knew I could put it through a mixer. But in a way the thing that was then really interesting to me wasn't the 78 it was the 16 rpm, the really sloooow, and as soon as I started playing around with records at that speed it, it was one of those moments, you know 'oh my god, that's, how amazing is that?', you know, that in a way the expansion of the detail of the sound even though it was very lo-fi. You know when you play a record at that speed (I think they were probably all to do with speech, learning language type records) because the fidelity is so low when they speak, but it just somehow to me opened up the sound that I could get into even further, you know, what I was playing around with. So yes, working on the road with Laurie and also meeting up with other musicians and stuff in London and sort of playing around with them and still continuing some of my own performed work and things which I incorporated the record players into. Yeah, it's over a fair amount of time, I think in a way I became quite separate. I mean, I'd seen Christian Marclay and I knew other people and stuff that were working, doing what became known as turntablism, but in a way I think I was quite separate from a lot of that a lot of the time and was actually working more in the theatre or performance or visual field rather than in music although I knew of stuff and so probably developed on my own. I feel I've developed my own way of working on this, my own language that I'm working with, the way that I use records and record players. You know what the sound that is interesting to me is you know is the stuff that I can find in the records and I pretty well feel that almost any record that I use, I mean the records that I use are, on the whole, they sort of come at me at random in that there may be a whole bunch that I pick up from a junk shop or people have given them to me but there's always something in each record that I feel that I'm able to pick up on or use. It might only be a slight little bit, but generally I only use very small parts of records anyway.

Just to pick up on the performance side of your work, when you are actually performing is it fully improvised or do you plan aspects of it in advance, do you have an idea of the sorts of things you might do in a performance?

Yeah, improvisation is certainly within it but I can't say that it's all improvised because generally the records that I've got with me I know, so I know most of the material I have with me. So in a way it's like, I feel it's arranging it in a way rather than completely arriving at new things, but in the nature of the stuff that I use, the old record players that I use, and the scratched up old records and stuff, that you know they do things that I don't quite expect quite often like the record player I say is 16 rpm and 33, and 45 and 78, but I think if you actually really measured them they vary quite a lot in between them. I know I mean the two record players that I'm working with at the moment I can just by eyesight tell that the 33 rpm on both record players are different. One is definitely running way slower than the other one. Yeah, because it's these old late 50s early 60s things, so you know they've had a long life and so they are a bit worn out, so those things happen and so I am surprised by the things that happen with it. So in a way that forces me to improvise around those things that happen. So I mean it varies from performance to performance, sometimes I will really just go off on a tangent, find something and then just go somewhere else and then maybe that's like 70 per cent or 75 percent even like improvised, but you know to be honest I think it's 50–50 on the whole and sometimes it could almost be the other way round, certainly 25 per cent improvised and 75 per cent is what's already known to me but I feel I know that works and then it does. Although that's the surprising thing, sometimes there's something that I've done several times and has always felt really good and then I'll do it again and it just sounds completely flat. I'm not 100 per cent sure whether that's because my connection is not strong enough or that I'm picking up on what the audience are feeling about it. You know all those things come into it, you know you can certainly sometimes feel when people are really listening and attentive and into what you are doing. That is, obviously, it makes playing really easy because you can like float on it and then there's other times when people are unsure, or there are not many audiences that are downright hostile but, you know, less than enthused let's say. Then you feel like you work really hard to establish something that can be a connection between you and the audience. I mean it's good to have those times – I wouldn't want every show to be like that! You'd just feel, completely, I'd want double the fee! You feel absolutely drained when it's like that. Yeah, but the other times when you feel people are really into what you're doing it can make it possible for you to really fly in a way.

When you are selecting your records, do you pick a handful, or do you make very specific choices – 'I need that one, that one and that one for this show'?

I mean I used to take lots and lots of records with me and then in a show I probably only use about ten different records, sometimes more and sometimes even less. But I used to take, I'd have a huge boxful, but I thought it's crazy carrying all these things around and so over the last four or five years I've gradually thinned it down so I pretty well only take away about twenty records now, maybe 25, and I know probably, as I say, I'm only going to use half of those, sometimes even less, and that group of records that I take with me evolves I think over time. You know, using records like that over a long time they actually get completely worn out and so all that you end up with is just like *kghkghkghkghk* you know, just in the end the actual original music of the record pretty well just disappears and the styluses have been running round them so many times, so many times. You know these are really old-fashioned styluses, really heavy, so they really do cut their way through the records. It pretty well makes it a groove without any waves in it so it's just one *kgh* sound you know. So then when they get like that then they get binned really, and so some new ones come in. But every now and again, I mean I think about where I'm going to as well, I mean that does affect what I take and there might be references that I want to take to a particular festival that's about something in a particular place or whatever. Not always, and also the other thing maybe, the other, if it's in a festival as I say the other people on the festival make, you know, references or whatever. It may be a bit oblique but that's something that I think about when I'm selecting them. I mean I suppose that I go through periods of favourite records that I use a lot and then they gradually fade away. At the moment there's probably four or five for each show that I go to I always pick up and take with me.

What are they?

I won't name him, I think he's dead but the record company probably have still got the rights to everything, but there's a country and western guitarist who did like instrumental albums and he played on Kitty West albums and stuff like that. He's actually a really fantastic pedal steel guitarist, his solo records I really like and so at the moment I've been using him a real lot. Well I've just got one album that I use, I mean I also have all his stuff on CD that I listen to at home but there's a vinyl album that I use a lot. I've been using that for well over a year and a half now and I'm still finding new things in it that I really like. And there's certainly a couple of Indian classical records, not sitar but sarod. I just like that deep sound of the sarod. And a couple of, or one particular tone record that's just simple tones at different Hertz which is you know, I find to make like some sort of thing to hang all the other sounds on is nice to have behind and also it's always really good to sample that. You can get some clear movements of sound and I definitely always take, and they really vary, but some records that have some particular bits of percussion in it. You know I've recently been using some Turkish singles and stuff, but I also have stuff from reggae or whatever, and funk records.

When you are working on stage, what are you doing to manipulate the records, how do you work?

Well to start with the records themselves, one of the things that I do which I picked up off of Christian Marclay, was like, you know to put a sticker on the record, equivalent to like a little round price sticker in a way, which is the simplest way of making like a loop. What happens is the stylus just sticks in one groove as it goes round, and sometimes it will flip back two, but you know then you get a really simple loop. Then at different speeds, obviously 16, 33, 45 and 78, I can manipulate records between those speeds and also I'll put my hand on it to stop or slow, make the record flip backwards or whatever. But then the process after that, they go into my mixer and in the mixer there are like effects in the mixer like reverb, and delay, and it's got 99 effects, most of which aren't very interesting, but the simple reverb and delay are actually quite nice. And there's like a pitch thing, so you can like lower it or make it go up in divisions of a scale and that can be nice because then you have the original then you have it like played a fifth higher or whatever. Also there are several phasing things in there but there's one that to me sounds quite good, the others sound a bit too cheesy. And then also the other effect that I have is a guitar pedal which is a delay pedal which goes from a very short delay right to a very long one, and also you can reverse it. The delay that comes back is backwards. I think it's a Boss pedal, a guitar delay pedal. Then the other major processing part of what I do is the Casio SK1 which is like a very simple sampling keyboard. So the sound that's going through my mixer goes into the sampler so as I'm playing I can sample anything that's happening, any individual record, or the whole sound or whatever. That I think is just about a second and a half, the length of it when you play it back at the original pitch, and what I like about it is that again it's very simple to use. You press one button to do it, and then press another button to loop it or whatever, and it's not a clean sample, it does affect the sound and I think it's actually really in keeping with the record players. It's really lo-fi sampling and I think that to me it's like a little magic keyboard which they stopped making quite a long time ago. That's one thing that I've sort of collected off of Ebay because I've got two and then about a year ago one broke down. The record players I can fix, I mean you look inside, I mean it's just this big printed circuit and it's just a total mystery to me, but the record players are quite simple mechanics so on the whole I can usually just repair them if they don't work. So I'd feel really a bit lost if I'd completely run out of Casios, so I've got about six or seven now which I've bought off of Ebay, and I always carry two with me in case one breaks. Since I've been carrying two, actually, touch wood, one hasn't broken down but you know, I'm sure it will again but at least I'll have a back-up.

What is it that attracts you to that lo-fi sound world in particular?

I don't know, I think it's something about being that little bit removed or whatever. I mean one of the things that I think that happens when I'm playing records and stuff it's like I'm playing with sounds – they are sort of little memory things the records. Imprinted in those grooves are these recordings of all these sounds and I feel like I have the whole bloody history of music. Everything that is part of the history of music is somewhere, it's on vinyl somewhere, and so there's all these things, collections of stuff, and when it's sort of affected in some way and it's at some remove so it's not immediate thing, that's the Beatles' so and so or that's Mozart's whatever. I think there's still like some sort of recognition or some connection with it, and I like that sort of slight mystery or distance, and maybe even slight nostalgia sometimes, for that thing that you can't quite put your finger on anymore. And in a way the Casio samplers also almost do that as well. As soon as I first used one it was for me like a really 'oh what a fantastic keyboard'.

It's interesting what you say about the whole history of music being there. Obviously there are fewer vinyl releases now than there would have been 20 or 30 years ago. How do you see that affecting your work?

Vinyl is still being pressed and in a way I think there's been a slight bit of a revival in a way and so the stuff is available, and stuff still keeps arriving to me. You know people give me, sometimes when I play locally or play in Manchester, people come up to me and give me like a carrier bag full of records which is very nice stuff, even though sometimes I have a limit of what I can carry anyway, but I'd never be rude enough to say 'oh, no, no, no, don't, I can't … no more'. Because I mean I just have boxes and boxes of stuff at home. Stuff that probably, you know, I might never ever get around to using, there's so much of it. And so, there is just, even just in my house, there is so much material that as I say I probably won't, even if I work until I'm 90, I can't see me getting through it all, so the material that is there will be there. But I suppose stuff that's more contemporary – it's like that most of the more recent stuff that I use, the stuff that's been recorded as of late, it mostly would be like twelve inches stuff that is more to do with club stuff that I get. I haven't got too many contemporary vinyl records that are you know classical or recent classical, more recent modern discs you know. I mean I have recordings of stuff like that but I mostly have that on CD, thinking of people like Adams or Arvo Pärt or whatever, I mean I don't know even if that stuff is on vinyl, I've only ever seen it on CD. There may be specialists that do it I don't know. So mostly the stuff that I do see more are in the pop or club world, the only bits of vinyl that I've bought recently, and also people that are doing electronica and stuff as well. My next release will be on vinyl, it should be vinyl only in fact.

Do you practise?

Occasionally I do, yeah. In a way I tend to do quite a lot of shows so it's sort of, you know, that's sort of my practice and stuff but yeah occasionally. We're fortunate we've got quite a nice big house and there's like a top third floor which my gear is pretty well always set up in so I can just go and do something if I want, you know, without having to worry about setting it up and just basically just turn everything on and play around with stuff for however long I feel like. I mean I can go quite a long time without doing anything at home actually and then sometimes I really get the urge and then maybe like every day I'll be up there for a couple of hours. I'm never really quite sure why that's so but sometimes I really feel I need to and other times I'm glad to not to. I feel maybe I'm making myself stale by doing it every day.

Which areas of your playing are you working on at the moment? What do you feel you want to work on in particular?

My main concern at the moment is I'll be releasing a new CD before the end of the year on Touch and it's like been three years since the last one and so for me it's really important that to me it's really good. I've been working on it quite a bit already so this is a time at the moment, I mean I haven't done anything on it today but I certainly was working on something yesterday. One of the ways that I produce the stuff for release for CDs is most concerts that I do I get recorded and so I work with them, rework them, edit them and maybe one track that ends up on a CD might incorporate up to six parts of six different concerts you know. Also then

I might add some stuff at home, some links, or even occasionally overdubbing, but I don't often do much overdubbing because it's busy enough as it is. I might layer stuff that's the same, like from the same recording, where I just lay some different parts of the same recording over each other, but I don't often play over the top. I have done but I don't often, so that's the most important thing. It's like if I can really get to grips, you know feeling like I'm getting to grips with it and so one of the things I do is I make stuff and then I'll put it away and maybe I'll be doing some other stuff then I'll come back maybe two or three weeks later to listen to the stuff that I thought I'd finished before. Then I'll listen to it and usually, sometimes, I think 'oh actually that is good, that is fine and I don't need to do anything' but usually I always say 'well that's too long, that could be shorter', and so I sort of get the virtual snipping shears out and cut lumps out and listen to it again. And then sometimes I feel I have to put stuff back and then I might put it away again and come back to it another time. I mean that could go on forever, but usually there's some point where I feel, no, I feel good about that now, that's something that's better than it was you know. I mean when I spoke to you at the Faster Than Sound, one thing that is always in my head is the thing of like stepping up every time I do something, whether it's a live show or working at home. All the time I want to step up, just get it better each time that I'm working on something and that's purely for me and of course I think that will translate into people who listen to it. I hope that it will also for them, obviously they wouldn't know the thing that I'm stepping up from, no, but I want it to be for me, it's like this has got to be really seriously the best I can do at this very moment and which is different to playing live because it is then in the moment and CDs aren't in the moment. People listen to them at any time at home and you might have six tracks on there and they listen to them in any order and they might actually fast forward through a track to go to the next. I know I do that with stuff and so it's a completely different control. The listener at home is in control of the order and the way it gets listened to. When you're playing in a venue as a performer you have most control because, I mean not always that – sometimes the sound system is not quite what you want or something goes wayward – but on the whole you control the volume and you control the order of the sounds that people listen to and then the audience's choice is then to listen or not to listen. But obviously with a CD at home it's very different, a very different thing.

Are there types of sound that attract you, and what tends to work well in your pieces?

There certainly is. Usually I find some part of a record that's interesting, but maybe a lot of the record no, it just doesn't work, and whether that's because it's too busy or I don't know. I think I like sounds that have some sort of, to me, resonance or ring to them. I love the sound of the pedal steel guitar or whatever. And the other records that I use sometimes are records that have bells in them, like hand bells and things like that and also the sarod is in a way similar to pedal steel guitar with slides and that sort of thing. Sort of metallic ringing sounds, and sort of clear percussion is a simple element, and guitar, I like electric and acoustic guitar sounds. Brass I suppose, I probably would lean more to a trombone sound rather than a trumpet, although I love listening to trumpet, but to work with somehow a mellow trombone sound is maybe for me an easier thing to work with. So if there is a preference, I mean I'm just going through my head what are the last records that I've been using and there probably is something that in a way, like Chuck Berry said 'plays guitar like a ringing bell'.[1] It's something that resonates for me and often it's maybe instruments like that or sounds that are like that, although sometimes when you slow a particular instrument down it actually then starts reverberating in a very different way, then lower, it gets more bassy and then you almost feel like the sound waves, especially if you slow something down to 16 rpm, you really get this *wooo-wooo* sound that comes out.

When you are making your pieces, how many layers do you tend to have in a texture, how thick do they go? Do you ever thin it back to just one?

Let me think. Probably the usual maximum is about five, maybe four or five layers. And usually there's probably, I'd say, usually it's less than that because there's, you know, the source material with which I work there's quite a lot of distortion in all the things, when you multiply it a lot of times then in the end you are only listening to distortion rather than to what it's distorting. But if you're using very simple things then actually the layers can be more, or there are layers of different parts of the same record, in theory I suppose it should work together but it doesn't necessarily always do so. You know I've worked in the past with lots more layers than that on top of that, when in the past I've done the things with the multiple record players and that was sort of almost an acoustic sort of like an unplugged thing, that's just a sound that's there is only the sound that comes out of it's own internal speaker, each record player. *Vinyl Requiem* was the biggest one of those with 180 record players although making it actually, I discovered in the making of it once I got above about 35, 40 record players at once, no matter what you played the sound started to sound the same. It's just that mass of sound that actually started to be the same so actually in the *Vinyl Requiem* piece in the end there were only two moments when all the record players were going, and that was just a big noise basically. Maybe just occasionally you could distinguish some things in it so it was more to do with shifting the sounds around the different record players, like having a certain spatial thing was happening. But rather than all these 'I'm going to have 180 record players all playing at once' because actually whatever you play it doesn't make any difference.

You've said a little bit about making the pieces from concert recordings, so I'm assuming you do that on a computer?

No I don't do that on a computer. No, I do it a couple of ways. I have like quite an old now, like a Fostex four-track hard disk recorder, so I can put stuff there, but actually I do do pretty like the equivalent of snipping stuff like when it used to

---

1   Chuck Berry, *Johnny B. Goode*, Chess, 1691 (1958).

be reel-to-reel, but I do that on minidisc, just edit and switch stuff around, on the minidisc, inside the minidisc player, so just maybe take 30 seconds out here and shift it to somewhere else or just drop it out altogether or then just butt something against something else, so yeah, jump cuts in a way, quite severe cuts although I've never known that people have ever really noticed it, but quite a lot of the editing I do is like that. But otherwise I put it to the Fostex recorder and then that can crossfade between stuff.

So you basically take your concert recordings and other records, record those onto minidisk and then edit and bounce them?

Well sometimes the concert has been recorded straight to minidisk anyway. Then I just do a copy of it and start editing on that, just listen, I just sit upstairs here and just listen to it and then just take bits out and listen to it again, and what's nice about minidisk you can put it back again if it's wrong.

And then that's layered up on the Fostex?

Yeah, sometimes yes, and sometimes the only editing I do on some tracks is just on the minidisk and so all the bits are edited together.

That's amazing, I would have never have guessed that. So I'm assuming you don't plan pieces in advance in that sense? It's about auditing the material you've got in a more intuitive way?

Yeah, listening through, although I do have memories of stuff, like one concert, and so when I'm starting on something and I'm thinking 'oh, I think I remember the concert I did in Amsterdam earlier this year, there's something there I think will really go with this' then I'll listen to it and sometimes it does, sometimes it doesn't. But often once I've started it starts triggering off memories of other stuff that might be appropriate with it, so it's not completely at random. I mean I certainly start with part of a recording that I really like. There's something at one concert I did that I really like and that's my beginning and then if there are other things in the same concert that I really like and then sometimes I will go to another concert recording which maybe was dealing with the same material but in a way I'd done it in another way and so it's another variation on the same thing that I was doing at that one, but because it was done a month later or a month earlier, whatever, it has a different feel so it shifts the whole feel of the piece somewhere else.

You've obviously over the course of your performance and composition work, and installations, you've produced pieces which have a variety of durations and I wondered if you feel if there's an optimal scale for your work? Is there a minimum duration past which it needs to be?

Yeah, I don't feel that I'm particularly good at doing stuff that's very short. I wish I could sometimes, I mean I feel maybe I don't get to the point quick enough although I think I am being a little bit more brutal with the editing and stuff now. I always feel like I need to establish over at least a couple of minutes anyway to begin with to actually make it like something that then I can expand on. So I don't know what the usual length of the tracks, I mean they do vary but certainly between five and ten minutes is probably a more optimum length for many of the tracks, and then obviously if it's a live thing then it's anything between 20 and 40 minutes long.

What changes between those two durations, from 5–10 and 20–40 minutes?

I don't know, it's something about being really in the world, in its world, establishing its world, and I mean that's what I really admire sometimes when I listen to great pop music. It's so brilliant at establishing a world absolutely instantly, like Tamla Motown stuff, like you are instantly in it, which I think is a great ability to do that. But for me I'm slower about arriving and stuff and even like the stuff that that is part of a concert that's really strong and then so I edit that out and I can start with that. It actually doesn't sound so good without all of the stuff that's gone before because there's a reason for it suddenly and so I'll maybe shorten the introduction. Certainly I'm always shortening the intros when I come to doing the editing at home, but it still always needs some introduction into that world, like an overture I suppose. You know, this is the world that this sound is inhabiting then maybe it can really fly later.

I just wanted to move on to talking about how you play with other people because we've talked a lot about solo work and obviously a lot of your playing is with others. I just wondered how you feel what you do changes when you start to collaborate with other people?

It depends who I play with. So if I take an example playing with Jah Wobble, I mean obviously there is always a drummer there with Jah and so pretty well I drop out most of the beat things that I play or the drum parts of records, the percussion things, because there is a bass player and a drummer there that in a way that's playing that. So I feel what I'm doing then is creating some sort of soundscape that they can rest on. And I suppose it's true it's this rock solid rhythmic development going on I can sort of fly over the top of it as well. Yeah, so certainly my playing in that context is different, very different to my own, otherwise I'm using similar stuff, and then if there's other players in the band and stuff in a way not using stuff that's really going to conflict with their particular instruments or whatever. Although sometimes as a comment I might put, if there's a flute, I might have a flute record but that's very tricky because if the flute player is listening on the monitors then there's this other flute in a completely different key playing it can send somebody mad, probably, or make it very difficult for themselves to play in the right key. The rest of the musicians are all playing in G or E or whatever, and all playing to a set rhythm, but I'm the person who has the luxury of not having to do any of that, just in a way react to what they're doing or then introduce stuff over or in amongst what they do. For me that's really just listening to what's going on and also being prepared in the sense of knowing what sort of stuff is likely to happen with that playing, and perhaps selecting what I think are records, or parts of records, that I'm going to be able to work in amongst it. So playing with Jah Wobble I wouldn't take any reggae records.

Then playing say in a very different thing is playing for Gavin Bryars, then it's just possible to put some like rhythmic things in or depending on the piece. Like for *The Sinking of the Titanic*, I sort of see the themes and stuff that the other musicians are playing to do with hymns from the time and stuff, the gradual degradation of the overall sound which in a way is sort of what happens with my sound a bit anyway, stuff that gets degraded or disappears into the ether. So I just dug out of my collection of stuff sort of contemporary pieces of music and stuff, music hall songs and the stuff that mostly I already had lying around in my boxes and used that. But then for the commission that he did for Steve Reich's 70th birthday at the Barbican, and that was playing with four singers and a string quartet, and it was a new piece of music so I didn't get to hear that before. I mean I was offered that I could be sent the score, but anyway I don't read music so it wouldn't have made any difference to me. So I was quite nervous about that because I thought 'oh god, you know you've got a couple of days' rehearsal and then you've got to play it' so I actually took, this is one of the few times when I did take a lot of records with me. I feel like I was going to cover all the bases, although Gavin sort of emailed and spoke to me about the feel of it and everything and also the instructions that I had as part of the score, where I should play and where I shouldn't and so I sort of knew all those things. I just found out that the best things to use in the rehearsal time and actually a couple of things that I thought might work actually did, and a couple of things didn't, and so I found that out very quickly so in the end that was fine. There was a couple of rhythmic things that I put in there and also stuff that was pretty way out of tune in their sense, and I know at some points that it was like a struggle for the musicians because I was playing against what they were doing. They'd each learned this piece and then somebody else comes along and starts playing something completely different loudly over, not loudly but you know in their heads. But in a way it's quite interesting how it affects how the playing works. So that's sort of quite different, and then occasionally I just, maybe there's like improvised stuff that I do with other electronic musicians where there'll be other turntablists or laptop or whatever and then it's obviously, you play less than when you're playing on your own because maybe there's two or three other people. I'm thinking maybe generally when I play there's probably a maximum of four or five layers, and then maybe if I'm playing with a couple of other electronic musicians and they've got their four or five layers or whatever as well then actually … it can be interesting for a few moments if it's like that, but generally for me it's like feeling when somebody is actually, what one of the individuals has really picked up on something and in a way then you step back then and let them expand on that and then when you feel that maybe it's been resolved or something then interject with your own. And if they're also people who really listen and stuff then they will let you have a little bit more. Everybody, hopefully, is really listening as well as they can.

The last thing I wanted to touch on, and you mentioned it earlier with Vinyl Requiem, *was the installation work that you've been involved with and I just wondered how you went about determining the set-up for each installation, how many players you choose, the sort of vinyl choice, placement in space and the time structures that you use?*

When it's a pure installation for a gallery the record players, I mean they are set off by timers, those simple timers that you can buy to plug in to turn your lights on and off at home when you are away. If I have loads of those, not one for each player, but one for three or four players, and maybe three or four players that are in different places within the installation, where they're all stacked up vertically or laid on the floor or whatever circumstances they're in, and so they're basically on for like ten minutes and then off for ten minutes. But if you have lots and the starting times are all a few seconds or a minute in between, you just have this gradually shifting pattern of sound across the whole mass of record players. And then the records, the way that they play, again they're either, not with a sticker because if you use that for an installation for a few weeks in the end it will bust its way through the sticker, so what I do then is use some very fine wire to just hold the arm in one place and it actually might just skip slightly but then it's not going to break the wire. But the other thing that I do is actually, those record players what you used to be able to do was stack up a bunch of 45s and when it got to the end the arm will reject and then the next record would drop down. But what you can do is you can doctor that mechanism by just getting in underneath the arm so you can actually make the arm drop at any distance on the record. But usually the old ones have a set drop at either 12 inches, 10 inches or 7 inches, but you can make it drop anywhere in the record player by just turning one screw actually. Also the other thing I do is just to jam the mechanism so in a way the rejection process is constantly on, so what happens is that it will go and drop like on the part of the record that I've turned the screw to make it drop on the arm and also whatever speed I've set it at, so it would drop on there and stay there maybe for, depending on the speed. If it's slow it will stay there for three of four seconds, if it's at 45 or 78 it will stop there for maybe a second or whatever so it just drops on one part of the record. So you just get a *doo-da-do-do ... um-ck-ck/doo-da-do-do ... um-ck-ck* like that. And if you have like maybe five or six record players all doing that and all doing it with the same record, you know you get just these phased bunches of sound that are related because of the same record, and that's obviously on or off with the timers. And also as I said quite often in installations I might use 10 or 15 copies of the same record, but just playing different parts of the record, so again you get like this gradual shift across. It's not just in the sound, but also the way the record players are placed obviously and then the sound is just coming out of its speakers. There's a spatial shift of sound as well and then there's the one installation I did around the room three different banks of speakers so it really did go surround sound around the room and here in Liverpool I actually built three walls that you basically walked into a room and the walls were all record players, a small room.

The interview was conducted by telephone on 13 June 2007.

Alvin Lucier

To what extent do you still feel your pieces are experiments in the sense that the activities and the compositions that result from that are a means of testing something?

Many of my new pieces are not really experimental because I am making them for instrumentalists. I'm making pieces that explore acoustic phenomena but not in the way that the early electronic pieces did. My early electronic works lent themselves to that description because I used test oscillators and test equipment, but when you use a clarinet, a viola or a violin, then you're more in the realm of sound producing objects that already have well known acoustical properties. I usually respond when somebody asks me to make them a piece. I accept the offer if I get a good idea but it's not so much a test or an exploration as making a piece that works as chamber music.

How much do your previous pieces inform your current work?

Many of them are about audible beating which I use as structural material. A solo piece called *Charles Curtis* (2002), which I wrote for the cellist Charles Curtis, uses oscillator sweeps against which the cellist plays double stops causing beating patterns to occur. The work is in two identical sections. In each, two pure waves draw the letter C. Starting from Middle C one wave moves slowly up an octave, the other down an octave. After a pause, the same gesture is repeated exactly. The double stops were composed to cause simultaneous slowing down and speeding up of the beating patterns. One tone of a double stop, for example, may start in unison with a semitone along a sweeping wave causing the beating pattern to start at zero and speed up. (The farther the distance the faster the beating.) The other may start above or below a sweeping wave and, as the sweep approaches unison with the tone, the beating is caused to slow down. So you get a double counterpoint thing going, one pattern speeding up, the other slowing down. I worked very hard to find intervals that accomplished that. The double stops in each half of the piece are different, producing different beating patterns. I had really old fashioned compositional problems of getting the intervals right, making them varied, and making sure that each one causes the beating patterns to speed up or slow down at the same time. In that sense it's more of a conventional composition, but what happens is you hear acoustic phenomena and the little artifacts that result from that activity.

In the sine wave pieces there's often a visual image that is a starting point for the sweeps, and I was wondering how you go about choosing the pitches and the timings of events against them?

There are three pitches you can use to make audible beating against a sine wave, or any other more or less pure wave for that matter. One is the near unison, the second is the near octave below, which has a strong second harmonic, and the third is the octave and a fifth below which has a weaker but still usable third harmonic. So for every semitone along a sweep there are three choices. Sometimes I choose them by ear according to a personal sense of voice leading, more contrary motion, less parallel and oblique. Sometimes I use a simple numbering system that helps me choose among the three. The three possibilities are given to me.

It's interesting that you mention counterpoint in that you've almost developed your own set of rules which you have to follow. I mean you're obviously bound by those because they are acoustical realities of the pieces.

Sometimes I go against conventional rules of counterpoint. I use parallel octaves and unisons in certain ways, and I enjoy doing that. One thing I loved in music school was writing sixteenth-century counterpoint.

With reference to working with instrumentalists more than perhaps you did previously, how do you feel that has changed your music?

It's not a complete departure because I'm still focused on acoustics and not on musical gestures. There are no musical gestures in these pieces. I was concerned about the concert on Monday night[1] because so many of the pieces are similar in that they use repetitive or long tones. In *Fideliotrio* (1987) the strings sweep up and down as the piano plays single tones against them, and in *Sestina* (2000) for low instruments there are no musical gestures, only long tones separated by silences in various combinations. I worry about audiences' attention spans with this kind of music. For that reason I don't let these pieces go on too long. There's an interview with Feldman and Cage, and Feldman says what the world doesn't need is another twenty-minute piece. Then John Cage said he was a thirty-minute composer because at that time he was writing pieces about that long. I'm a twelve- or sixteen-minute composer. When I write for chamber ensembles, I'm very careful about making them just long enough so that they do what I want them to do and no more. I have no reason for making *Fideliotrio* longer than it is. Twelve minutes is short enough to be put on a concert with other pieces. It's a practical matter and an aesthetic matter too. If I needed them to be long they would be. For example, I recently wrote a tuba piece for Robin Hayward[2] that turns out to be close to 50 minutes long, but I say

---

1   The interview took place during a short festival of Lucier's music at Dartington College of Arts on 14 November 2007.
2   *Coda Variations* (2007).

in the directions to the score that you don't have to play the whole thing. It's a set of seven permutations of 63 tones each but you can stop at the end of any phrase. Robin plays it for about 24 minutes (four phrases) which I thought would still be too long for an audience. (It's a solo tuba piece.) But when he played it in Ostrava and Berlin everyone was focused on it. For the recording he played the entire seven phrases. Listeners have changed.

In a good way?

In a good way. People listen to this music more attentively. I watched the young students at the concert on the Monday night and they were extremely attentive. They didn't get impatient. They might have been less attentive twenty years ago.

When you're working with players do you feel the material you use has transformed as a result of that? In addition to the duration and practical aspects, do you feel the actual material of your work is different now?

Well, I am using instrumental sounds. I don't use extended techniques. I want to hear the natural sounds of the instruments. I love to listen to long, medium loud string sounds lasting for a bow length of eight or ten seconds, then a change of bow direction causing a natural phase reversal; or wind instruments simply blown, producing pure sounds. In a sense they're like oscillators.

Have they replaced oscillators?

Sometimes I make pieces with oscillators, sometimes without.

How do you deal with the notation of your work? What's your view on how you present your music to performers in terms of notation?

I'm starting to notate my music conventionally as long as it conveys my intentions to the performer. A long time ago we thought we could develop new ways of notation that players would be willing to accommodate. Players learn conventional notation, in school, they're very comfortable with it, and if you can write music that's as close to what they have learned then it makes performance easier. John Cage had all these ideas about making the performer noble – he said that once – giving them certain freedoms and so forth. I don't think that he accomplished it entirely. If you give them something they know and they feel comfortable with, then they'll perform well. I usually use black or white round (neutral) noteheads. Black ones indicate semitones along glissandi, white ones indicate instrumental tones of various length. In *Still Lives* (1995) the white noteheads are written directly under the semitones along the oscillator sweeps but the player is free to play a little earlier or a little later causing variations in the resulting beating patterns. He or she doesn't have to be exact. The player is not bothered by overly notated music, he or she just sees white notes that can be any length. And if you have the pedal down, on a piano for example, as in *Music for Piano* (1992) and *Still Lives,* that takes care of the length of the tones.

Because that's in contrast to your work from the 1960s and 70s where you used text notation quite a lot?

I use texts when it seems to me to be appropriate. The score of the bass drum piece[3] consists of a set of instructions and a drawing of the set up. There's no way to notate that piece with conventional notation. A young fellow recently realized a version of this piece and he got it pretty accurately from my score except that he had to use smaller bass drums. Four 36' bass drums, even in large cities, are hard to find. The problem with playing experimental music now is that players will often revert to those techniques they already know. They think they're adding to the work by doing something that they have experienced from other music. Percussion players who are used to changing mallets, for reasons of contrast, think that's a virtue whereas in most of my pieces contrast is not an issue at all, there's no reason for it. Perhaps they want to participate in the creation of the work in some way.

There's a little spoken piece that the students are performing[4] here in which they make vocal sounds into found resonant objects. They're performing it in a room that has a balcony, so they decided they wanted to go up in the balcony. They wouldn't have thought of it if it weren't there. They also wanted to perform it in the dark. There's nothing wrong with that, I suppose, but then the audience won't see the objects. If an audience can't see performers, it gives them an eerie feeling, so I had to persuade them to come down and stand up in front of the audience. They were embarrassed about doing that, which is the reason they went up in the balcony and put out the lights in the first place. So while it's not wrong, it's something added on to the performance. They loved doing it because it was their idea.

And the piece is about simply presenting that situation.

I think so, yes. There's a performance practice issue that's getting dangerous. A few years ago a performance group in California recorded a Feldman piece. They were having problems recording it softly so they simply played it loudly and played the recording back softly. That's just wrong acoustically. Feldman wanted his music to be *played* softly. Music sounds very different when played softly. And if they didn't understand that – and they were intelligent players – then that's frightening. There is a recording of Christian Wolff's *For 1, 2, or 3 People* (1964) in which the players planned it out in advance so it sounds like spectacular *avant garde* European music. Much of Christian's early work is about uncertainty and professional players don't want to sound uncertain. They did it because they wanted the recording to be sure and successful. They were well meaning, but...

---

3   *Music for Pure Waves, Bass Drums, and Acoustic Pendulums* (1980).
4   *I Remember* (1997).

...it misses the point somewhat. What are you working on at the moment?

I just received a commission from the Mozarteum in Salzburg. It's a reconstruction of the *Requiem* of Mozart. In Salzburg they play the *Requiem* every year and ask a composer to interact with it in some way. For example, George Friedrich Haas composed interludes between some of the movements. I chose the nine movements that Mozart didn't finish. I put together excerpts from each movement forming a three minute suite. The orchestra, soloists and chorus will play it once, then sit quietly and listen as the sounds are recycled into the space using the *I am Sitting in a Room* (1970) technique. The missing parts will be filled in by the resonances of the room. The title is *Music with Missing Parts*.

And recently? You've said a little bit about moving away from the initial ideas you had in the 1960-90s and I wondered what direction you feel your current work is taking?

I suppose I could say that I simply ran out of ideas of what to do with electronics, although it's not inconceivable that if somebody asked me to compose an electronic work I'd do it. But the real reason is that performers keep asking me for pieces. I was thinking about it last night because several visual artists were at my concert and I think that they were more interested in my earlier works than the newer insrumental ones. You can see why. I don't relate to computer-generated sound although my oscillator sweeps are made with computer. Now if somebody asked me to make an installation for a gallery I would surely come up with an idea. It seems to me electronics goes with installations.

In fact I'm working with the Italian artist Maurizio Mochetti for an exhibition at the National Gallery of Art in Rome. He's going to make some sculptures and I will supply sound. Recently I've been working with a technique called impulse response (convolution). You simply record a spike of sound in a space (I use balloon pops), then load it into a computer program (Altiverb). Any sound you feed into that program will sound as if it is in that recorded space. When Mochetti's objects are finished I plan to pop balloons around them and use the recordings as virtual spaces in which to recycle sounds. I've collaborated with Sol LeWitt using this procedure, as accompaniment to his massive *Curved Wall*, first in Graz and again a few years later at Wesleyan. First I recorded the ambient sound of the gallery in which the wall was installed. Then I popped balloons at six points along the wall. Then I recycled the ambient recording into these virtual spaces until the resonances of the room at those points were revealed. One of the conditions is that there's an instrumental ensemble associated with the Rome project, so I have to write music for their ensemble (Alter Ego). That's not the first thing I would have thought of doing but I will accept their wishes.

So will the impulse images you create process the ensemble, and is it a piece with live electronics in that sense?

I'm not so sure about that yet. I've got to figure out where to place the loudspeakers because I don't want to violate Mochetti's visual space. There are so many beautiful small loudspeakers now coming out of computer technology. I'll just have to see how large his objects are. I'm going over to Rome in March to visit him.

I just finished a piece called *Canon* for the Bang on a Can All Stars in New York, for electric guitar, cello, clarinet, piano, vibraphone, and double bass. The cello, bass and guitar – I put an E-Bow on the B string – sweep up an down while the other instruments play single long tones. I'm currently writing a piece for an ensemble in Norway.

So if that's a piece you're thinking about a the moment, could you say a bit about the stages you've gone through with it so far in terms of making it?

The name of the ensemble is asamisimasa. First I looked at the letters in the name and transcribed them roughly into musical pitches as: ABAEABA. The ensemble consists of piano, quarter tone marimba, clarinet and guitar. The electric guitar will sweep through the pitches in four measure segments. The form will be a palindrome using those pitches as signposts. Since the piano and marimba cannot sweep continuously they will step up through the pitches. For example, the piano repeats A for two measures, then alternates A with A# for the next two until it finally arrives at A# by the fifth measure. The marimba will have a similar stepping motion except that it steps twice as fast because it has to move though quarter tones instead of semitones. I designed a simple number system to ensure that the repetitions among the two players were unsynchronized. The clarinet sustains long tones throughout at pitches that produce its own set of beating patterns. I compose by going to the piano and playing two or three notes, then I go away. I think about it until the idea gels. Somehow it's working in my mind even when I'm not thinking about it conscously. I don't sit and work at it for long periods of time. Pretty soon I'm able to see what the notation looks like, and once I get it blocked out on music paper it's just a question of writing it down.

How do you see the status of a recording of your work?

I love to make recordings. They are a different from performances. I work with sound engineer Tom Hamilton. He knows what I want and we make beautiful recordings at Systems Two, a studio in Brooklyn. We spend a great deal of time editing, and that part's enjoyable for me. Tom has a wonderful ear and makes wonderful decisions. I love it when a recording is clean with no noises and the effects are vivid.

In some of your pieces where the contingency of the performance is more important than in others, I wondered how you felt about the fixed nature of a recording in relation to that?

In a performance small errors and mistakes can be OK. But in a recording which people listen to over and over again, those things are not as interesting as you thought they were. So we try to make our recordings as perfect as we can.

Looking to the future, where do you want to go with your music?

I just follow my nose. I asked my friend artist Richard Tuttle, how he gets new ideas. He said, "I just follow my nose". People like to pin you down. I make a spaghetti sauce at home, it's totally simple, even simple-minded perhaps. No salt, no pepper, no herbs, just organic tomatoes – from a can no less. If there's a bay leaf in it I take it out. I want to taste the organic tomatoes. People don't like me to change the recipe. If I add capers or olives they say that they like it out of politeness but prefer the original. Often people don't like you to change, they think you've violated something, but of course you want to keep moving on. Stravinsky did, Cage did certainly, so did Feldman with his extremely long works. I'm 76, not 40. I'm a different person, times change and I am open to different inspirations.

What I'd like to do is to get my scores in order. They're kind of messy and it's stressful because people want scores and I have to find them and xerox them, dub a CD and go to the post office. It's time-consuming and that's a problem for me. I do have a small publisher in Frankfurt, *materialpress*. More and more they are taking over these duties.

I don't answer my emails quickly enough. I'm terrible about that. I get irritated by receiving so many. I should make peace with them. I simply keep going, making pieces for ensembles. I enjoy that a lot. It has been enjoyable to work with the Barton Workshop. They're good friends, great players. They want to do one's music right and they work hard and their performances are wonderful. That's enough for me.

I'm inspired by Christian Wolff. He makes one piece after another, one chamber work after another, hundreds it seems, for any conveivable combination--piccolo and tuba, whatever. As a result his pieces get played all over the place.

Several years ago I visited the Percy Grainger Museum in Melbourne. You may know that Grainger invented electronic instruments, they're in that museum. They're extremely interesting but they never entered the mainstream of music. I wrote my early works not thinking much about being in the mainstream, but they are being played more and more now because a lot of young musicians love technical challenges. Several of them are even making versions of David Behrman's analogue music on computers. I never thought our pieces were going to go anywhere. But they are because of young performers, sound hackers. You never know what's going to happen.

The interview took place at Dartington College of Arts on 14 November 2007.

Phill Niblock

I thought to begin perhaps we could talk a bit about the overall sound of your music, and I wondered what is it about drones and sustained textures which interest you as a composer in particular?

It's about sound and recording I think. I began to really listen to music in 1948 and to listen to recordings and to collect records and in the early 50s. It was exactly the time when LPs came out in 1950 and it was possible to have home hi-fi systems and everything seemed to work together. Tape also, the first tape recorders from the late 40s – so that sound began to be almost immediately much more like the sound you hear when you go to concerts, I mean much more realistic and less canned sounding, and so that was all a big influence on sound. I built my first hi-fi speaker system in 1953 which is still functioning in New York (it sounds great!) My first tape recorder, the first fairly cheap amateur tape recorders came out around about '53 and so I actually began to work with tape and recording at that time. So the whole business of sound and the reproduction of sound, because my music is very much about reproducing sound in the space which sounds and … well I mean there isn't really a live sound of my music. It is reproduced sound basically because it comes from recording. That's the whole idea for me – being able to record sound and to play it back in a way which makes it sound bigger and fuller than it does if it were played live.

What was it about recorded sound and use of that technology which really led to you working with drones? Was it something to do with the layering of sound perhaps?

I guess the initial idea was to work with this thing of using tones that are close together in pitch to produce other harmonic variations and that only works very well with drones I think. So I'm not sure which came first, the drones or the idea. But it all comes from sound of course and reproducing sound.

One of the things I want to talk about is how you make a piece, and perhaps as a starting point for that could you explain how you go about choosing instruments or how that happens in terms of how you work?

Well the thing about using different instruments is that each instrument has a different timbre and so that creates a whole different set of overtone patterns and that's probably the most major difference between one piece and another piece since they're all drones and all using microtones. There are some internal changes of structure in the course of the piece, but a big part of it is the fact of these instruments having different timbres, and sometimes even the nuances of recording change that immensely. There's a piece for acoustic guitars played with e-bows[1] which we recorded with a single microphone very close to the guitar and the sound that results was certainly extremely pure, and had a very sine wave kind of quality almost, and so there were an incredible number of beat patterns which occur just because of the purity of the tone. There's another recording of a piano[2] and it's recorded very close up but there's sort of no fundamental there – no sort of sine wavy fundamental – so that the tone that's produced is so sharp edged and varied that even when you make microtones close to each other it doesn't really produce any difference tones. I mean it sounds great but it doesn't work well in terms of being a piece of mine with microtones. That's just two examples.

Do you tend to aim for lower range sounds in general due to the need for a strong fundamental?

Well I think that depends on the instrument because for instance in the piano piece we were using an imperial Bosendorfer so we had lots of low sounds and it makes this really marvelously full clangorous sound. I mean I also work with flutes and stuff which don't have low sounds. I made a piece recently for soprano saxophone[3] and I actually pitched the sound one and two octaves down so there's a real bass tone but all of the sound comes from the soprano but it's all a manufactured two octave down sound (made in Pro Tools with pitch shift) which makes the piece sound strange but there's these bass notes and then floating over that there's much higher pitched soprano saxophone sounds.

What is it in particular which attracts you to certain sounds? Do you approach instrumentalists because you want to write a piece that uses saxophone for example, or is it more the other way round with people coming to you, and you finding projects which are interesting?

I guess part of it starts with the musician. When I find people that I'm interested to work with and then I tend to make pieces with them because I know they're going to sort of work out. For instance I've made six pieces with Ulrich Krieger from Berlin playing saxophone and didgeridoo and that's just an amazing idea to make that many pieces for one musician. I did make probably that many pieces at least, for David Gibson the cellist, from the mid-70s until the mid-80s. The cello is just an amazing instrument, and he is an incredibly good player for me. He knew

---

1   *Sethwork* (2003).
2   *Pan Fried 11, 27.5* and *70* (2001/3).
3   *Zrost* (2004).

very much what to do, what to produce and so that's part of the thing that's just working with different musicians. I mean I've now pretty much exhausted most of the range of instruments so what else to do?

When you are working with a player how do you decide which sounds to use, which pitches for example, but more importantly which sorts of timbral quality do you look for in the sound of an instrument?

I tend to talk to them about what notes are particularly resonant on the instrument and on some instruments, like cello, that really varies from cello to cello. And then pick some notes which use that resonance and then probably a small cluster around it. I tend to work quite a lot with three half-tone intervals particularly in recent years. So that's sort of basically it, just talking to them and finding out what's going to make the instrument sound good.

So you want the instrument to have a good resonant quality to it essentially?

Yes. Because the resonance is the richest overtones.

When you have actually recoded your samples, what's your next stage? Do you use everything that you have recorded or do you edit it at all? How do you take it from that point to make a piece?

OK, I guess I'll talk through the stages then. I go to a recording studio, which can also be quite a small studio. For instance the last set of pieces I did with Ulrich Krieger we recorded in his apartment and he lives in the top of a building and it has a very broken panelled ceiling that's peaked in various places and so that it turned out that it was a very good sound space and the sound we got using just a single mono condenser microphone was really very nice for those pieces. So part of it then is the recording studio, the recording medium and who is engineering, if anyone is. I just made a recording which I'm actually looking at, listening to right now, with a church organ, a baroque organ in a town outside of Krems, Austria, and the sound was very good. I was using one large diaphragm AKG microphone to record it and going directly onto the hard drive from Pro Tools so it's a very direct recording. So after I've recorded the material, I start to edit. I would delete samples that did not work. I would take out some clicks and pops if they occur or if there is a splutter at the beginning of the tone I might just fade it in. There's normally quite a bit of difference in level between the sound samples, so I might try to even out the levels by raising some and lowering others and then normally after all that editing is done I bounce to disk. I rerecord the material with the edits intact. Then from that material I begin to create the regions (the sort of tones that I use) and then I make a list of those and then I'll start manufacturing some pitch shifts in the computer itself.

How long are the sample tones that you tend to take? Is there a duration you aim for, or is it variable?

Most wind instruments can hold a note for about 15 seconds and strings if they're playing fairly slowly between 10 and say 12 seconds or something like that, before a bow change.

So really it's as long as you can with a sustained sound?

But what I tend to do with strings is to record say a minute or so and leave the bow changes in, and if they are fairly smooth then that works out quite well. So if I were recording a wind instrument I might record say ten examples of one note. I would edit out the samples that were with errors, and trim others. In addition, I take out the breathing spaces between samples, leaving the trail-offs and the attacks. After the editing, I would have one to three minutes of each note, and that becomes a named 'region'.

Once I've got the regions set up I just start to think about the whole structure of the piece. By that time I've listened to the material and I have an idea of what might really sound good and what maybe doesn't sound so good. There's a piece for hurdy gurdy,[4] with Jim O'Rourke playing and the hurdy gurdy had been somewhat damaged so there was a clunk every turn of the wheel and I recorded a whole bunch of material and I thought I wouldn't be able to use it because it was so marred by these clunks. Then I found one note which really sounded good and I did some octave changes and a lot of pitch shifts and so I constructed the piece from that one note for the first nine minutes and then I just threw everything else in at the end for six minutes! And it's a piece which, considering I didn't think I was going to be able to finish the piece with that material, that piece I admire very much and I tend to play it a lot particularly at the beginning of a concert. It's a very good first piece to play.

How long does it take you to make a piece, start to finish, once you've recorded your sounds?

It can be a couple of days. One phase is recording the sound material/samples. That's usually a session of two to three hours – but then it takes maybe a day normally to do the editing to get the regions all in shape and then another day or two to put it together. It depends what else is happening (in life) so it's difficult to put an exact time. The guitar piece[5] went slower just because I had this technical difficulty and I kept stopping and working on it and coming back to it and trying to figure out what I was doing wrong and then I realized I was only nine days from the performance of it and it was really going slow! Then I really speeded up and

---

4   *Hurdy Hurry* (1999).
5   *Stosspeng* (2007).

solved the problem and put the piece together. There's no set answer as to how long it takes.

So after you have edited the material, does the structure emerge at that point in the process of writing or do you ever plan it in advance?

It's mostly a matter of listening to the material and deciding what's really interesting and then trying to figure a structure around that. I just finished a piece[6] that was for me extremely long, it was 59 minutes and it really did make a huge difference in the way that the structure of the piece went internally. I normally make pieces which are about 20 minutes long. I like very much that time length as it allows me to play several pieces in a concert. If I play for an hour and a half I can play four pieces for instance, which is good, then it gives quite a different sound quality for those four pieces. And so a 59-minute piece, well that's pretty much a concert!

How did the structure of that piece differ from your other pieces? Perhaps as a preface to that question could you say how the structures tend to work in your 20–25 minute piece? I'm always aware of the comment Feldman made[7] about his generation being hung up on the 20–25 minute piece and it became their clock in the way that they managed to always articulate that length of time, and I'm interested in the fact that most of your pieces are around that sort of duration.

And he also says something about longer pieces – that it really changes your whole sense of form and there was a very interesting statement that he made and I've forgotten the terms that he used! I really like the 20-minute piece so I'm quite satisfied with that and a lot of it has to do with simply being able to play several pieces in a concert and I'm mostly doing solo concerts. I very seldom play a piece within a concert of four different composers.

How do you tend to articulate a 20-minute span?

I try to make it different each time! Sometimes it isn't much different except for the timbral qualities of the particular instrument.

I think there's a very clear difference in pacing often and I wondered how you went about doing it? Is it an intuitive thing or is it more planned?

Well hmm … I guess I could say something about this 59-minute piece. There are several things interesting about it. I recorded two guitars in stereo and they remained in stereo so that one guitar is always on the left, the other guitar is always on the right and the chord is three half-tone intervals so that the left guitar gets the lowest note and the middle note and the right guitar gets the middle note and the

---

6   Stosspeng (2007).
7   Universal Edition, *Morton Feldman* (Wien, 1998), p. 3.

highest note. And we recorded a number of octaves of each note as well. I started the piece with the central note which was an F and it goes for say ten minutes before any other note enters and without too many pitch bends so that it's sort of gently rolling and phasing but there's not a lot of variation in that first ten minutes and then the first lower note comes in and it's a half-tone interval that beats really very fast with the F and so then I start making a lot of pitch bends right after that so that the beat isn't a constant beating and it becomes very much modified by the other microtones that are happening. So it becomes a very varied tempo (beating pattern) instead of a very singular one. At 20 minutes it becomes quite thinner in sound and fewer tracks are utilized and then it becomes only the outside notes so that each channel has a different note so that the left channel is playing E and the other is playing an F#. So we even hear these two different notes staying completely separated in the stereo, then it gradually begins to mix in the other, central note and it manages to continue changing every few minutes considerably. When you're playing this thing in Pro Tools you can stop it and then advance say five minutes and start it again very quickly which you can't do with a CD because I didn't put any programme numbers in which would make that possible. Probably if it comes out as a recording I would do that – I would put in programme numbers so that you can advance through the piece, and if you do that and play, say, every five minutes the difference in sound is incredible. I was amazed how much it changes because when you are listening to it as a continuum it sounds like drones and you may think that, well, it must sound different from other periods of time, but the actual difference in the sound quality is quite amazing.

That's something I've always liked about your music. The moment you are in seems fairly stable but as you say when you jump a minute ahead or a minute behind it's enormously different but the changes are so slow, subtle and gradual.

You also just mentioned using Pro Tools and I wondered how using the computer affects how you write? Obviously it's your tool for making your piece – I think I read previously you used tape technology and I wondered whether that's actually changed the way you work in any way or even just made you more prolific perhaps?

I think it changes a lot. It particularly makes it much faster to work, except for this guitar piece where I had some technical difficulties because of the stereo. I'd never actually made a piece using separated stereo recordings of samples, it was always mono, and I was having some trouble mixing this stuff down because it kept going to mono and it turns out that some of the pans were slightly off and they were converting the stereo files to mono. But then once I solved the problem, it was a matter of very few days to actually finish the piece.

I began working, in the beginning, in the 1960s, with a stereo tape recorder. In fact, the first piece was recorded with a mono full track machine. And then I managed to get a quite good Revox stereo machine and so I was dubbing stuff back and forth to build up tapes from different tape recorders. I began to work not too long after that on multi-track recorders. Actually I had access to a 16-track Ampex in Boston in the early 70s and made a number of pieces. I would simply go to Boston and spend the weekend, just go in to the studio on a Friday night when nobody was using it and stay up for about two days and work and sleep on the floor if I had to sleep. So that was amazing to be able to really use a multi-track machine which sounded very good. Then I went through a succession of four-track and eight-track Teac machines. Some time in the mid-80s or so I pretty much stopped making music for several years and started again in the very early 90s, so there was a period of about five years which was sort of blank of compositions. And then I was working more with computers but having someone else actually do the technology so I would make a score, I would record the material, edit the material and make a score, then they would sort of build the piece from that score. But in '98 or so I began actually working in Pro Tools myself and then it was just very fast work. And it was also possible, instead of recording the micro-tonal intervals, to manufacture them in Pro Tools. And they sound quite good, so in the end the piece sounds good. I mean the digital recording process is amazingly different.

So was there a difference between the pieces pre-1998 where you had to give the information about the structure of the piece to somebody else, to how you work now? Were they slightly more planned perhaps before that point?

Well I obviously had to finish the score before building the piece. In the original tape recording pieces/multi-track pieces – I actually made a score for the multi-track set before I began working with tape and then when I did work with the tape I simply dubbed the material from mono onto one track of the multi-track and just built the whole tape. So I never listened to the stuff and changed the material as I was building the recording. I made the score and I just manufactured the tape, then I listened to it as the mix. So one thing about Pro Tools is it's very easy to do a little bit and then listen to some and then do some more and then listen to some. I'm not sure how much it really affects how I work. I think it has more to do with just the ease of working in Pro Tools and putting things in and also getting so many more tracks because the material is so much more thick than it was when I was working with multi-track. Building the piece in Pro Tools is simultaneous with making the score – the score appears before your eyes as you work!

How many tracks do you usually use?

Usually it's 32 now, and in this recent piece it was 16 stereo tracks.

Do you think the reason also you are perhaps working more intuitively is because you have a clearer understanding of what you are trying to do in your pieces now than you might have done 20 years ago?

Yes. But I think basically I'm working pretty much in the same fashion that I worked even at the very beginning before I began working in multi-track. I mean, basically there's a piece for tenor saxophone[8] from like '69 or '70 made by dubbing tapes back and forth and technically it sounds remarkably the same as now, I think.

Obviously you just mentioned about producing sketches, notation, plans for your pieces – do you still do that at all, or is Pro Tools the only score you need?

The Pro Tools score, the actual Pro Tools edit window, is the score which occurs as I'm making it so the same kind of decisions I would have made on paper are now just made in front of my eyes on the screen.

So there's never a need for any sort of other realization of the piece in that sense?

In terms of the score, no.

That brings us on to the performance aspect of your work and obviously you have quite a busy programme of concert tours going around the world playing your pieces. I wondered, given that it's a recorded music, why it's important to you to play your music live?

You can't really hear my music the way it should be except in a concert and you can't really do that concert without me! So I mean even I make some decisions during the concert set-up which are strange but there's usually a reason for it, but really what you hire in having me come to do a concert is having the right sound of the music (or as close as I can get, under the conditions). You can buy the CDs – the same CDs I play from sometimes – but no one has the kind of system at home usually, except maybe for me, with which you can get the kind of sound that the music is all about. So when you buy a CD and play it on your home sound system it isn't at all the music that I intend.

Do you see that as a problem?

Well sure it's a problem. It's the one reason why I never wanted to do recordings in the first place. In the 70s for instance it was because LPs never really sounded that good for my music. But it's a problem that when I didn't do records I simply wasn't known. It's always nice to have a couple of CDs out!

When a composer is heavily involved in the performance of their work it always creates a problem for the long-term presentation of their music. Have you thought about building up a performance practice around what you do – is that something which concerns you at all? How do you ensure future performances of your work are correct?

I don't! Even if you did something like a DVD. Actually an interesting DVD of a performance situation and the only documentation that ever worked I think, was

---

8   *Tenor* (1969).

done by Jim Staley at Roulette in New York.[9] He is doing a whole series of studio things that were eventually published on DVD and you can actually get many of them from him. There are pieces by Pauline Oliveros and I think Lucier and many different people from the improvising world as well. And they were all half hour shows and we did it in a studio. We were actually projecting my video on a large screen. There were three musicians playing guitars with ebows and I'm sitting at a desk with my computer also playing a part and the music is in the room but also then they could cut to the film direct (so not from the studio camera but directly from the video source) and they could light the musicians well enough so you could see the musicians and see what was happening and it was an amazing idea. You could see it and hear it. But I don't see how that would help gain the right kind of sound for me even. I mean how do you specify that somebody has to listen to the sound quality making it loud enough but making sure the speakers are working and all of that stuff. But I don't know, I don't see any way to do it.

Talking a bit more about the whole set-up of your performances in a live environment, is there an ideal space for your music to work in? What is it that works well, and have you been in rooms that don't work particularly well?

I mean I've worked in so many different kinds of situations – with either rooms that weren't very appropriate or sound systems that weren't very good, but sometimes the sound system can be mediocre and the room can be great and it sounds really good, and sometimes it sounds horrible. I tried to play in Budapest last week, this new guitar piece, and it was in a very small room with a lot of soundproofing and there were big speakers, and you really heard the speakers instead of the acoustic/architectural aspects of the space. You didn't hear the room sound because there wasn't any room sound. It was completely dead. But the ceiling was very low and it had metal panels with fans and and everything rattled – you couldn't hear the piece because the whole room was rattling. I simply had to fade that piece out and fade in another piece and play a completely different programme. I did a sound check and I thought maybe it was going to be OK, but then the actual performance simply wasn't OK.

What sort of normal set-up do you go for with speakers – how many, placement, that sort of thing?

Well I always ask for speakers in the four corners of the space, and big speakers. It's frequently a problem that there isn't enough power available because the sound is so continuous that there's no chance for the amps to take a break. Where you have something with a heavy beat there's space in between that beat for the most part

---

9   Billy Bang/Phill Niblock, *Roulette TV Vol. 5*, RouletteTV05 (2000). Previously two individual VHS programmes from the Live at Roulette Cable TV broadcast, reissued on DVD, and now archived at http://www.ubu.com/film/roulette_niblock_2000.html (accessed August 2008).

and I've had amplifiers that just got too hot and just cut out for several seconds and would come back in and cut out again later. And I did a concert recently where the speakers were quite good, it was in a church, it was quite a big church, and usually the church is really good because the reverb of the space is so good that the music sounds great even if the sound level isn't quite so loud. But the speakers simply distorted when I got the right level, so strange.

What is the right level for most of your music?

I'm setting things peaking at about between 110 and 115 dB and I normally set up the sound system with a sound level meter so I'm listening but I'm also pushing it up to that level and then seeing how it goes. In some rooms, the room is simply too tight. I think in Budapest for instance because you really heard the speakers and they were right in front of you that it was simply too loud, so I probably was maybe 5 dB less loud. But it still was quite loud generally!

And that's obviously so you can hear the overtones and the beating and differenct tones?

You really hear a completely different overtone pattern at the louder levels. There's one piece[10] in particular, from 1974, and for cello, and it's only eight channels and not all eight channels are on all the time either. When it's loud enough you hear the overtones and you lose the cello completely and when you turn it down you just hear cello. It's just the best example of what happens with different loudness levels.

Often in the performances, certainly the ones I've seen, you also use a live musician playing the same instrument as on the recording and I just wondered what you felt was the purpose of that in a performance situation?

It probably has more to do with simply satisfying the audience! Playing back a recording, I think that it's harder to convince the audience if they just hear a tape that it's a valid performance somehow. Generally what happens if there aren't musicians is that I play a computer part myself, so I sit at the table on stage and I play an additional eight channels and I change the pitch. So I'm sitting there and interacting with the music or appearing to interact, but if I turn my part completely down (and leave the recording level up) and continue to sit there and play or do email or something it doesn't make any difference really in the sound because it's whatever is there in the recording that counts.

Is it important in that sense to be able to hear what the live player is doing? Are they affecting the sounds in any way or is it just literally for the visual aspect?

In general they do affect what's happening and they affect it especially in areas close to where they are in the space, and if they're not (amplified) in the mix itself.

---

10   *3 to 7 – 196* (1974).

So that it does work. I mean there is a reason for their being there and they do make a difference and that's very interesting so I shouldn't pooh-pooh it too much! And some players are very sensitive to what they are doing and what the effect is in the space. I have the pleasure of working with many musicians over a long period of time (from 1975, for instance), and that is a special pleasure for me.

What do you ask them to play?

Generally I work with people who know the music or the piece that they are playing so that tends to work more intuitively. But if I work with people who don't, then I ask them to play the tones that they hear in the recording and be slightly off so they can themselves hear the beats and tell what's happening with the overtones.

Then again you wouldn't ever specify you know '1'36 – start playing'?

In general no…

Is that because you want more of a free relationship with the recorded version?

I don't know that I have a good answer for that!

Do you prefer an intuitive approach from performers in that case? You don't want them to learn the piece?

Anybody who was interested in the music wouldn't play it the same way twice anyway so I don't think that's a problem.

I suppose just speaking from my own experience when we did that concert in Huddersfield[11] last year. It was the first time that I'd played the piece and I felt that I had to listen through it quite a few times trying to work out where the pitch changes happened and trying to have that as a rough guide to the shape of the piece I suppose. But with that in mind, are there incorrect ways of playing the piece if it starts with a single tone, presumably you want that single tone or very near tunings of it to be the only things that you can hear. Is that fair enough?

Yes that sounds good, I mean certainly there are many bad ways to play my music and I've had some horrible experiences where there wasn't enough rehearsal or where people simply didn't get it so they didn't understand what they had to do and they'd start improvising whatever they want to on top of the piece. They consider it a sound piece they should improvise over. This happened very recently with someone in the US and we arrived late at the gig and there simply wasn't time to rehearse and she played and I was amazed that she had a complete

---

11   Electric Spring, University of Huddersfield, 26 March 2006, UK premiere of *Sethwork*.

misunderstanding of what she should do. She did exactly that, she was just improvising over the piece.

In general you would prefer them to follow the structure of the piece and actually try to match the pitches they are selecting in particular?

Yes, and especially not to either play other notes or to play too fast (not to play the tones with a long duration). The idea is to stay with that sort of steady long tone process stuff. I always find it hard to explain that to musicians. I think, being not a musician myself, that the musicians who are really good just hear the music and they really have a sense of what they should do and they do a great job.

Let me say one more thing about the last section, which is sort of implied, but I never really made the statement. I think that this (my) music sounds incredibly different in every different performance situation and so it's not canned – it's recorded yes, but it's not canned because every aspect of the performance situation – the acoustics of the space, how big it is, how reverberant it is, plus the sound system, even where you (the audience) sit in the space. I mean there are many places in the space where it sounds so different than other places in the space that it's just amazing and if everybody wandered around (during the concert) which audiences generally don't like to do, especially if there are films on, it would be a much richer experience in terms of sensing the differences that occur. So it's very much architectural/acoustic music that's occurring and it changes really drastically with every performance space/situation.

I suppose that brings us on to the issue of writing just for live performers, which you've done certainly with the orchestra piece Disseminate (1998), *and I wondered how your approach changes when you are working with musicians purely in a live situation?*

In some sense the score of course exists in the same manner as the old multi-track tape scores, so that instead of my realizing it by dubbing a tape together, the orchestra is realizing it by playing it. It's a problem of working with musicians who have a sense of what my music is. One aspect of playing this music in Ostrava was that the orchestra is used to playing Dvorak and, I think, they really didn't much like the contemporary stuff, not even really where it was sounding more like classical music. They didn't know how to deal with dynamics and stuff and they tended to want to make more swells. If you listen to the recordings of *Three Orchids* (2003), a piece for three orchestras, the difference the musicians make is very obvious. There are four recordings of performances: the original premier in Ostrava; another in Ostrava a year later; one from the MaerzMusik Festival in Berlin; and one from Merkin Hall in New York. The first three were played by the Janacek Philharmonic of Ostrava. The last with a smaller number of New York professional musicians who play all kinds of music and they were amazing because they all know exactly what should happen in my music and they really played super, with an incredibly small amount of rehearsal and we got actually a seven channel surround sound recording from that concert. I hope that it will be on a DVD at some point as surround sound. The MaerzMusik/Berlin recording was with three orchestras and with three conductors, which Petr Kotik, one of the conductors and the producer, was really objecting to. All other performances were with Petr conducting all three orchestras, alone. There are all these swells and dynamic changes, so it's interesting to listen to the two versions with such a different result.

So what do you actually give the players in terms of notation?

There is a score, in standard notation, for all the orchestra pieces and there are now four of them. The microtones are indicated next to the note figure, with arrows pointing up or down, showing the range of sharpness or flatness.

One of the problems that I've always had is that Petr Kotik (the conductor and producer of the orchestra pieces) doesn't rehearse enough. He always says that the musicians will get too tired and they can't go on to the next rehearsal etc. if they play continuously for a long time. But I think that he doesn't rehearse enough for them to really get a sense of what it should sound like and he should go through the whole piece at least once because it isn't about reading the notes it's about sensing how one deals with it within the orchestra. The last recording on the CD I gave you is the piece written for two orchestras and what Kotik did that year (2005), the third time that the festival occurred, was to bring a bunch of musicians from elsewhere and to essentially form another orchestra. The core musicians were the ones he plays with in New York and the other musicians come from various other countries and they're all very together – they're really hip and so it works very much better than using the Janacek Philharmonic. The concertmeister of that group, the Ostrava Banda, had played all three of my orchestra pieces within that year! So he was amazingly practised in my music.

In terms of the notation you give them, do they have a stopwatch or do you give them particular frequencies?

Kotik uses a technique that I think came from Cage,[12] where he lifts his arms over his head and then gradually brings one or the other arm down to his thigh, over one minute. He has a stopwatch but the orchestra only watches him and he tends to vary the duration a little bit. One of the instructions they have is not to change the note immediately at the end of the minute but to feather it so that different people start to do note changes at different times, so that there is a continuity, rather than a sudden change of note every minute.

So the score is actually fairly fixed, so that is very different to the situation with your concerts where you perform and have a live musician playing with the recorded sound. And in the orchestra pieces they are given a score essentially?

---

12   In the conductor part from the *Concert for Piano and Orchestra* (1957–58).

They are given a score but in a way it's the same – that if they don't understand the context they won't play it well. And that was the always the problem. It was great to do those pieces, but when they were played in Ostrava generally it was not played perfectly. And in the case of *Three Orchids*, when it was played in New York it was played by people who know how to play it and even without much rehearsal it sounded really great.

Does the music still work at what I am presuming is a lower volume level, and with mixed timbres as well?

Well yes and no. It's more of a spectacle to have a big orchestra! No wonder those guys (those orchestral composers) always wanted to have a big orchestra! It's much more subtle – in fact probably the recording (if it's done well) sounds better than the live thing (because it can be played louder). And of course where it sounds best is in the front and middle of the orchestra, where the microphones are normally placed. The audience is too far away and cannot hear the music as well as the microphones.

Have you tried repeating your normal concert situation of you playing your CD recorded version with a live instrument, doing that with the orchestra, so you have a recorded sound with the orchestra to get that level of sound, the volume level you require?

Well if you made the recorded sound at all louder than the orchestra you wouldn't hear the orchestra anyway I think. So it seems like it should be the purity of the orchestra or not. There are a number of instances where quite a few musicians have played with the recorded sound and especially if they are amplified that's always interesting. And there are some other pieces for smaller ensembles made in the 80s where the musicians basically were tuned by listening with headphones to a four-channel tape which has tuning sine waves on it. They were only playing four notes, but on the other hand they would be separated on the stage. The few who were playing the same note, the same tuning, would be separated and they would probably not play the same note anyway since each one would tune somewhat differently to the tuning tones! It only worked when there were at least a dozen musicians, otherwise it wasn't loud enough. There was a piece for quartet and stroke rods (especially tuned, long, aluminium rods, about 0.5 inches in diameter, and many of them, played by rubbing along their length with resined fingers) which was Dean Drummond, and New Band was the name of the group. There simply weren't enough people to attain an effective volume of sound. The recording didn't sound so bad but the live, acoustic quartet and the stroke rods didn't sound particularly interesting at all.

Is that an area you want to explore, working with live musicians?

Yeah, but I probably wouldn't go back to that same thing. I mean the orchestra pieces are interesting to do but the smaller ensembles are not so interesting to do.

I think one of the best pieces of mine is basically done the same way. It's the *Five or More String Quartets* (1991) and it's made with the musicians tuning to a four-channel tape with headphones so that each one hears a different tone – except that there were five different four-channel tapes! That is, five string quartets on 20 tracks of tape, and all made in five continuous, acoustic recordings of 25 minutes. And so in the multi-track recording, all of which was made in a studio with the four musicians playing at the same time but miked separately enough that they're pretty much separated, the piece really sounds great I think. And when you play that recording fairly loud then you really hear all of that micro-tonal interaction. But it's also a piece that when you don't play it so loud you can still hear a lot of the overtone patterns. It's one piece where you can play it at less volume than I would ever think of as concert volume and it does really sound remarkably good.

Does it open up the possibility of a quiet Phill Niblock piece?

Well I wouldn't say quiet! Not so loud! Do you have a recording of that? It might be interesting to try it at a different volumes.

I will do that. I always try and see what my stereo will go up to and what my neighbours will let me play, which are normally not the same thing.

Five or More String Quartets was constructed very much like an orchestra piece, scored in a different way, but meant to be played in a continuous time, acoustically. The structure of that piece became the structure of the first orchestra piece, *Disseminate*.

Several of the orchestra pieces have now been played and recorded by small ensembles reading the scores and using multi-track recording to build up an orchestra sound, in a fashion very similar to *Five or More String Quartets*. In a live performance, the recording is played at a volume to match the acoustic sound level of the instruments, which are being played live. Or more likely, the live instruments are being amplified to match the sound level of the recording playback, which gives the volume necessary to produce the overtone richness.

Just to finish with, obviously I've not mentioned any of your work as a filmmaker but I know that you started working with film before you worked as a composer. I just wondered how you see the relationship between the way you work as a filmmaker and the way you work as a composer in the first instance?

That's an oft asked question which I think maybe in recent years I've had a slightly better answer for. Normally I'd just say 'oh, there's no relationship – you figure it out!' But essentially it's a very minimalist approach to both and it's easier to see in the music. As the music is so abstract that you take out the melody, rhythm and, you know, harmonic progression, and you're left with that very simple music with a lot of internal life. Whereas in the film I'm also the stripping out a lot of the typical structure of the film. The shots are all quite long so that there's no cutting, editing time imposed, no montage, and there are relatively few sequences – it mostly goes from one shot to another – completely different place or different activity etc. so I've really cut much of the normal structure of film out. Obviously there's no narrative but on the other hand there's hardly any of the typical faces of people – I mean documentary filmmakers usually hate it!

Is it in a sense you are just framing events whether they are sounds or images, and just presenting them in a quite bare way I suppose?

Yeah, this bareness, simplicity, starkness, is one thing and I never use really any effects. I only move the camera if something is moving in the frame I'm following. I mean zooms are really, urgh, awful! I used to teach film and the first thing I would do was to tell them that they couldn't make zooms! I couldn't stand to watch them!

Thinking more recently do you make the films with knowledge that they are going to be used as part of your music performance? Does that affect how you make the films in any way or are they completely independent?

I don't make those films any more. That's a series of films from 1973 until 1991, which is already getting close to 20 years ago. I simply stopped making them. I had a lot of material and I was spending a lot of time and having to raise a lot of money. It was also the time when the funding completely dried up in the United States. I was getting quite good funding from the late 60s until 1990 and after that – phttt – nothing! And so it was very much harder to go out and shoot the films. I did start shooting video which was much cheaper but the travel costs weren't that much cheaper.

Have you ever used any other visual imagery with your music in performance other than the films of people working?

There's a series of pieces using very high contrast black and white photographs which I did from roughly 1986 until '92 or '93 and they are either used as slides and they dissolve with slide projectors or in recent years they are in the computer and they simply dissolve. I do quite a few installations with that material. There's one running now in a suburb of Chicago and sometimes I've done those with the music but for the most part I was never interested in using music with that material. I did one very long installation with three of those images in a very big room – they were 6 feet wide images – and I used the string quartets which I thought worked as well as anything with those pieces. So it was running as an installation all day long, day after day. But the staff kept turning down the volume of the music.

Just one more question – what's next? What have you got coming up and what do you feel you still want to explore in your music in the next few years?

In about four days time I've finished this 59-minute piece for two guitars. While it was being rehearsed, I did a lot of work on the score for a new piece for Ostrava which is for solo baritone voice, chorus and orchestra. The day after the premiere of the guitar piece, I recorded material for an organ piece. I didn't make any pieces in 2006 because I made too many pieces in 2003, '04 and '05: there were 13 new pieces and I just thought it was time I took a break. I did make one sound collage piece[13] but I didn't make any music. So this guitar piece is actually the first piece since 2005 that I have finished.

Do you think that break has caused you to have a late-Feldman phase and all the pieces are going to be very long now?

Naagh! I can't imagine the organ piece is going to be more than 20 minutes![14]

The interview was conducted by telephone on 11 May 2007.

---

13   *Bells & Timps* (2006).
14   He later added: 'it turned out to be exactly 20 minutes, not a second over!'

Evan Parker

There is a clear identity to your playing which makes it instantly recognizable, and I wanted to begin by asking you how you have worked with this definition over time. Do you see the language you have developed as a positive constraint?

The idea of having a 'sound' has always been a key part of the work but in free improvisation everything is up for re-negotiation including the notion of everything being up for re-negotiation! In other words there are situations in which my 'sound' would not be the best contribution I could make, but there are others where it is the only thing that is needed. Maybe the key to it is to have a 'bag' (another venerable jazz term) from which you can pull the right stuff at the right time. Some players you meet don't want to negotiate much, others are very mutable; it really is 'site-specific' work as our fine art colleagues put it.

How do you tend to respond in those situations where your sound is not what is needed?

A glib response would be – 'improvise'. Some people emphasize the etymology of the word in the notion of the 'unforeseen' and might anyway have the view that it is only such situations that are truly conducive to improvisation. In practice it is extremely rare to find myself in a situation where no aspect of 'my sound' can fit, so it really becomes a question of deciding when to lead when to follow, when to determine an approach and when to accept one that has been determined elsewhere. Given that all of this happens at the speed of thought or – even better – intuition and is not really subject to rational analysis until after the event, there is a danger of the theorizing running away with itself.

How does this work with musicians with whom you have a long history of playing together, potentially where your sound might fit too well? Clearly each encounter will be different, but there are, I expect, shared experiences which inform a practical knowledge of each other's approaches. Do you have a way of addressing this situation, if indeed it is a problem, or is it just intuitive?

If an analogy is made with a conversation with old friends then several questions arise. Why are we still friends? Have we discussed this subject before? Where were we? Is there any mileage left in that old topic? and so on. Since the topic 'improvised music: what is it? how's it done?' is the subject under discussion, as with philosophy, religion, politics, education, the state of the world, read any good books lately? – in such conversations, many points and topics will be approached over and over with the same vigour, rigour or sometimes rigor mortis then there will be much that is redundant when seen from the vantage point of a lone composer working with notation and all the options of revision, changes of mind and the chance to scrap everything and start again. What comes instead is a sense of immediacy, of collective effort and a unique music made for a particular time, place and people. Each particular occasion will, like each new day, have much in common with the one that went before. There are two important considerations, each of which is a partial reflection of the other: from the listeners' points of view it may not matter how the music arrived at its specific acoustic reality, it just has to be a worthwhile listening experience but it is nevertheless clearly not appropriate to expect to find the formal qualities of fugue, gagaku or serial music in collectively improvised music. The two polar mistakes are therefore: on the one hand to think that because it is improvised there can be no qualitative estimation and on the other that a background in formal musics of one kind or another is the sole requirement for understanding improvised music.

Personally I don't see repetition in this context as redundant and agree with your comment on immediacy: much of the music I find interesting, whether it be notated or improvised, deals with site specificity, and the fact that aspects (often major ones) are not predetermined or are somehow provisional. I like your comparison with daily rates of change in this regard. Have you found that changes in your own playing happen very gradually, or have there been sudden epiphanies which open up new ground for you?

There seem to be layerings of different rates for different elements. Crucial factors are the frequency and intervals at which a particular combination of players works. There is a marked feeling of starting where you left off, even if the interval between is measured in years in some cases. There is also a ritualized aspect to identity-building where a certain shared set of assumptions about what a group stands for act both as guide lines and as traces to be kicked over. One group might work very much with the idea that the group has no clearly defined modus operandi but that becomes a meta-modus operandi as soon as it is articulated. In solo improvisation then the rates of change are determined more by the work pattern. The best circumstances for development are in a concentrated series of concerts or of practice in periods without concerts. These will only arise if I plan ahead and for the moment my approach is to take things as they come. Until I have solved some technical problems to do with learning the characteristics of a new kind of synthetic reed I will not have many 'epiphanies'. This is my plan for the next fallow period.

Given the variety of ensemble situations in which you have worked and the kinds of networks of relations which inevitably emerge from this, have any particular combinations of players or ensemble formats encouraged specific developments in your playing?

This is really a very interesting question and one to which a short answer can only scratch the surface. I have often cited the example of working with Hugh Davies and Derek Bailey in the co-operative group Music Improvisation Company. Their use of controlled feedback in order to sustain pitches indefinitely made it essential for me to develop the circular breathing technique. Once I had this technique under control it led to the approach which made solo playing attractive. Other examples would be working with John Stevens in the early SME [Spontaneous Music Ensemble] made it necessary for me to learn how to play at a quiet level appropriate for a group with unamplified double bass, John was emphatic about the need for everyone to hear everything at all times. Playing with Peter Brötzmann made it necessary for me to learn how to play louder, in Peter's bands the bass players had to fend for themselves! Working with Misha Mengelberg encouraged me to think about what the thinking behind my playing was, Misha was very nervous about what he called 'mood music' – I'm still not sure that I have solved that one. Playing with Schlippenbach and Lovens has given me the opportunity to revisit the same combination year on year for 35 years now. The question of when repeating tropes and patterns passes from investigation into ritual and/or redundancy is a constant in a group of such long standing. The almost equally long-standing trio with Barry Guy and Paul Lytton raises similar issues but results often in completely different music. The chance to play once a month at the Vortex with groups of my choosing is an opportunity to try different combinations in the same space. This has something in common with research where one element is constant while others vary. There is a whole book to be written in response to this question.

I'm interested in the analogy you make here with research. Do you view your work in that way? This is perhaps a central question within all experimental music.

The fact that the final outcome is a performance in real time in a particular place for a specific audience has relevance. The ideal of going somewhere new is always there but it is shaped by the sense of what is appropriate in a given time and place for a given set of listeners.

If all is going particularly well the sense of limitations/possiblities imposed/ suggested by these elements disappears and you are in a place where only the musical imperatives exist – a kind of 'transport of delights'. It is not a simple act of technique, wishing or wanting that gets you to that place. Steve Lake has spoken of 'the higher magic' alluding to this I think. Magic may very well be the right word. But as the Sufi dictum has it, 'Trust in God, but first tether your camel'. This amounts to being in shape, the way to Carnegie Hall, etc. Practice for an improviser must consist in part of research.

Could you explain how you practise, and how this fits in with the patterns of your work?

I am slowly memorizing the tunes of Thelonious Monk. This is in part a result of thinking about Steve Lacy's work with that material stretching right back to the early 60s and partly to do with Schlippenbach's more recent 'Complete Monk' concerts where they play all the tunes in three long sets. I had known a few of the tunes for years but now I try to be more analytical about the specific structures. There seems to be a concern on Monk's part with limiting the interval types in many of them.

In fact everything else I do is also about memorization and analysis too. I think I wasted a lot of time learning to play written etude material fast when I should have been working from memory more slowly. I am developing a system of pattern and note sequence building that relates to the Slonimsky-type patterns but develops on an additive or you could say catenary method. Note sequences based on only two interval types and so on. I don't practise much in the investigation of multiphonics although I do have some notebooks full of fingerings from the time when I did do that and I sometimes poke around in old notebooks. The *Top Tones*[1] book by Sigurd Raschèr is a constant stimulus. It is not completely clear how all this feeds back into performance but I am sure it helps.

How does this patterned note-sequence construction work in practice? Could you give an example of how you use it when playing?

There needs to be an equivalent of the 'Chinese Wall', in banking parlance, between material consciously memorized in practice and the state of mind aimed at while improvising. The risk otherwise is that it will sound like running memorized patterns. George Lewis told me that the older players he met when in the Count Basie band referred to such things as 'riff books'. There is a short recording between tunes on one of the Charlie Parker recordings made by Jimmy Knepper where he plays such a pattern and someone asks him where's that from and he says Rudy Wiedoeft. I think Wiedoeft was a popular saxophonist who had a 'riff book' on the market at that time. Obviously Parker made a very clear demarcation between practice and performance. The aim of my practice is to run pathways that would otherwise be unused and consequently unfamiliar to my brain and fingers with a view to making the line from my imagination more fluent. The obvious place to look is when the music slows down and then there are often passages which are clearly based on the kinds of interval sequences I've described but by the same token when the music is moving slower there is time to embed and disguise such sequences. I have used the analogy of a sculptor's use of an armature to support an otherwise unstable structure.

So how do you erect this wall? How do you effect the separation between technical preparation and performance: is it something that you consciously attempt, or does it just happen?

It is something like a moral imperative, 'Thou shalt not play out of the riff book'. Where things get really complicated is that there is, especially in solo improvising, an element of something like practice going on, in the sense that you return over and over to the same situation, problem, problematique, challenge, namely: 'I'm

---

1   Sigurd M. Raschèr, *Top Tones for Saxophone*, 3rd edn (New York, 1994).

here to give a concert of improvised music.' The sense of own voice, own language, own style, a responsibility to make sense of own past through coherent, logical, consequent, satisfying, communicable efforts connected to previous attempts at the same self-imposed task is filtered through a tangled mass of memories, habits, weaknesses. The dialogue with the past is presented in a permanently unfinished state which nevertheless seeks to arrive at a sense of statement however provisional it is in reality.

It is unlike the attempt in notated music to deal with a particular set of issues, themes, etc. and then write *Fin*, close the book, give it an opus number and send it out into the world. The distinction between improvisation and notation as compositional methods is not always so neat. There is a statement by Busoni about the essential musical idea starting in the imagination and whether it is written down or played directly on an instrument is secondary, something to that effect – I'm afraid I don't have time to look it up.[2] For the improviser there remains an aesthetic necessity for music to reflect, sound of, adequately its philosophical foundation. Why improvise? Music is time-based and sequential, it has that much in common with life itself; to seek to 'fix' music in a permanent form, the opus number, is to deny time's arrow. An improviser could be said to 'go with the (Heraclitean) flow'.

If it were to be seen in the way you outline in your question it would be like the injunction, 'Don't think about an egg.' In other words I don't think I can answer this question!

For me, all of your first paragraph is applicable to composing. Even though the score is notionally permanent (regardless of the relative indeterminacy of the performed results), it is only provisional from the perspective of the composer's ongoing attempt to make the same statement. You write the piece and move on; you improvise and move on. Everything else is a trace of those acts, as Busoni says. How do you feel about recordings in relation to this?

In your question you use 'composing' and 'improvising' as if distinct methods – perhaps a slip, perhaps a provocation or a test of my resolve! I repeat: my whole argument is that this is bound to lead to apparent contradictions – or even false analogies at the other end of the spectrum. Since both notation and improvisation involve turning the mind to the construction of a sequence of sounds, notes, rhythms, pitches or other imagined events (what we can perhaps agree to call 'composing') there will be an overlap in the techniques used to order the material.

Using an instrument designed to play the chromatic scale in tempered intonation offers the improvising instrumentalist the choice of working with the patterns derived from that gamut. There is also the option of dealing only with extended techniques or unconventional ways of playing that render such materials irrelevant. I am of course interested in such possibilities but also in the conventional materials that a conventional instrument, saxophone, was designed to produce.

---

2   See Ferruccio Busoni, *Entwurf einer neuen Ästhetik der Tonkunst* (Leipzig, 1911), p. 11.

There are clearly fundamental differences between the two methods. The possibility of revision, the possibility of writing works on a scale that means they may never be performed or of a complexity that means they will never be accurately realized are all distinct qualities of notated music. Improvised music that seeks to take on specifics of time and place nevertheless has much in common from performance to performance by a given group or individual.

On recording: Celibidache refused to make records of his performances saying that, 'The Holy Mystery of music cannot be pressed into the form of a pancake', however since he died they have issued dozens of his recordings originally made for radio broadcast only.

For me the question of surviving as a performer and making recordings are inextricably linked. There is no doubt in my mind that because I made records as soon as it was practically possible I have survived as a performing musician. With the repeated listening that a recording makes possible comes the learning of a musical language and the kind of analysis that makes qualitative assessment possible. This was true for my musical 'education' and it is quite evident that recordings of improvised music have made for the rapid expansion of the community of both players and listeners. The idea that recording somehow contradicts the ethos of free improvisation carries no weight for me. It is simply a time shifting device in the first instance and the purist is welcome to listen to a recording just once.

The interview was conducted by email between 24 February 2007 and 4 August 2008.

Tim Parkinson

I thought we could begin by talking about how you incorporate found materials into your work. Could you say a little about what you're looking for in potential material, and how you go about finding it?

I don't incorporate found materials at all, except in so far as I feel that all the notes available to use are the same notes and intervals that any other composer has ever used. So I have at the start a certain objectivity in working with what I present myself with. What I want beforehand for myself is a large and unforeseen diversity of pitches and intervals – randomness, patterns, shapes – and of course there are countless ways to generate pitches. Writing the detail is often more subjective, but sometimes not exclusively. The whole writing of the piece takes place between these objective and subjective positions. I am uncomfortable being all one or all the other.

Sometimes, in the end, people have asked if I quote other composers, but I don't. I'm quite inclusive about what pitches or intervals are presented – I like consonance and dissonance – so sometimes a sequence of notes might be reminiscent of other music, and of course it might not be reminiscent of anything to me, but it might to others. In one piece someone once heard Verdi and Chopin in a piece all the melodies of which had been derived from the curves of tree branches. So everyone has their own references. I have certainly toyed with the idea of direct quotation sometimes, but ultimately I feel that is a completely different thing altogether, and it's something in which I'm not interested at all. But you see the opening of Beethoven's Fifth is only a major third and there's countless different ways a major third has been used, and so this is why I think of these notes and intervals in general as found objects. The G and the E flat in the middle register. Used by everyone, but in different contexts. So I use these same old well-worn intervals, but treating them with a preciousness. Like a Joseph Cornell. And for me, instead of making a whole piece out of one gesture, like Beethoven's major third, I use a whole mass of diverse little sculpted things to make the piece, collecting together a hoard of moments and presenting them all at once in a chaotic environment, which for me is like everyday experience.

I like this idea of tiny crafted moments somehow multiplying out to create a finely crafted whole by implication (however chaotic that might be). When sculpting these little ideas, do they exist in the abstract in relation to possible pieces though, or do you work on them with the idea of belonging to one piece, or even to a particular point in the piece? I mean, do you make them and have an idea this is an ending event or whatever, or does that come to you later when you have a pool of ideas?

I work on them with the idea of them belonging to the piece I'm working on, but they might not at that time necessarily belong to any point within the piece. When I write, I think of each one as I come to it, just as a thing in itself, there and then, very moment to moment, as a closed self-contained unit, not in relation to what's been or what follows or what's around.

Often I have used the page as a structural unit, like a movement or a panel, and allowed the players to choose their own order of pages for a performance. Moments work differently in different places on different occasions. The landscape of the piece can be experienced from another angle. Beginnings and endings are often natural events anyway, without my having to announce them in the piece. Switch on the radio, for example, and you start listening from that point, whatever's playing. And anyway, my pieces are not narrative or illustrative. They are more frames of time within which things happen, rather than a specific discourse or something.

Sometimes I do have an idea that something would be good as an ending event, but this is just vanity, and if I fix it as an ending I'm denying that moment, which I fancy as sounding valedictory, any opportunity of working equally well and potentially more extraordinarily within the rest of the piece.

No, I don't just write the individual moments and have lots of them stored up somewhere for use sometime, which is more like how you work, isn't it? For me, I feel the piece – almost I suppose in counterbalance to how much I feel the material to be inclusively heterogeneous or even discursive – is unified in a very general sense, from my point of view, by my initial image of the piece and by my having worked from and on this over a specific period of time. A collection of work within a frame of time. That as well as the frame of time which is the piece itself.

Certainly I see each fragment of material as a module which might be contextualized differently in each performance, so in that sense it's different to you. I tend to make new modules very much with their initial context in mind however. It's only later when they are reused that the dislocation happens: they might be placed against entirely different types of material and in doing so change considerably in character. The material also often suggests structural functions, at least initially, and is presented with this in mind. In subsequent performances I tend to try to subvert this by deliberately placing modules so as not to repeat their original structural role, so if I start one version with some quiet, sparse violin harmonics, they might be part of a middle section in a thicker texture with other similar sounds in another version. But that's a conscious decision I would say.

In your pieces, given that the pages are often reordered so that fragments aren't heard in any kind of predictable or prescribed sequence or combination, and if each of these fragments is a self-contained moment, what's stopping material from previous or succeeding pieces bleeding into each other? Is there anything tying them to one piece specifically, apart from practical things like instrumentation? I suppose it's a question of whether you draw notional boundaries between the material and its presentation as 'a piece' or not.

Yes, I think for me, the fragments of material are definitely more local to a specific piece. So the recontextualization within every performance is only amongst a fixed set of things. It's subsequently interesting how things can be shuffled about within a piece, and it still remaining recognizable as that piece. Also, as I said, the piece is partly a gathering together of things over a period of time of work. Like a collection – yet part of a continuity – localized by time and instrumentation.

But I also change elements of the way I work from piece to piece. Pieces are all different, of course, and have different needs.

But the material in your #[unassigned] project must be evolving now? When you write a new module, are there significant differences to what you might have written two years ago?

Absolutely, and I think that's where the recontextualization is most striking. There are still a few older modules which I regularly reuse, but the role they have in versions has changed quite a lot. For example, there's a high violin glissando module which I began using in early 2001 and it's since been adapted for other string instruments and occasionally stretched to about ten times its original length, as well as appearing in its original form. Sometimes it is used very much as foreground material, but at other times it is less gestural in its use, normally because it's combines with other instances played by other instruments. So in some cases this works well (in that there is a closer relationship with later material), but in other cases I might have written a module which has only a single use because it is tied to a particular performance practicality (e.g. a specific instrument), or it's used only a few times because of the kinds of relationships between sounds I was interested in at the time. These have changed quite a lot over three years of course, and it's this which tends to govern whether modules have a longer life.

Could you say a little about the currents constraints time and instrumentation are imposing on your work, or in other words, what are you working on at the moment?

My new piece is for percussion.[1] What's been interesting for me during the working process is that I've just come back to the mobile structure again, but my arrival at that decision was as if I'd never done it before, as if I'd just come up with the idea for the first time, like a surprising revelation. But yet that structure was in the last piece. I start afresh every time and I seem to work very close to the page, then step back and see what's emerged.

When you do this, do you find you reject much material, or do you readily accept everything that has emerged during this period of working as part of the piece? Does this close focus stop you seeing a (preconceived?) larger picture, or does it allow a more interesting one to emerge do you think?

---

1   two cardboard boxes (2003).

A mixture. I think I am keen to be inclusive of material, but sometimes for some reason something might not be right in some way, so I do throw things out as well. The close focus I think is more interesting for me in my day-to-day working process. I don't pre-plan anything in the piece but I have a general sense of what I want the piece to be, and work with that image in mind.

Could you say a little about the working process so far? Do you compose each moment at a separate session for example, or do they take longer? What sort of pattern do you find yourself adopting when working on a piece?

The general image of the entire thing is certainly always at the back of my head, to a degree, when working on the piece. I imagine it's the same as other people where some times the working momentum is going well and other times days go by, for whatever reason, just trying to do one thing. Walking or traveling is a good catalyst for me of turning over thoughts. The trombone and piano piece[2] I wrote over the summer was written in the West Midlands, Wales, London and Catalonia, with some parts of it written on trains.

Some days more than others it excites me very much how the world is a collage, or composite. When I see very clearly the separateness of each and every thing. Just glancing at things in my room now I can see a piano, five rocks from a beach, a carpet, a box, a teaspoon, a calculator... What actually have they all got to do with each other? Apart from a conceptual umbrella of all belonging to me, or of them all being in the same general space. Put two things next to each other and it's a juxtaposition, but add more and a general specificity might begin to emerge from the jumble.

When watching TV also the various images on the screen are actually a sequence of very diverse and changing images, which of course we connect together in our minds and form a narrative (if one is not already given, which is very seldom.) Then, simultaneously, there's the stream of thoughts going through one's head, affected and sometimes not affected by what's being seen and heard, and sometimes self generated, like an impulse to switch it off, or make a cup of tea or something. Add that to the plethora of objects, sounds and images, the mass of things constantly coming in through our senses. And of course in the face of this, the separateness of each thing is forgotten because one's brain orders it all into degrees of importance, into categories, seeks patterns, reasons and so forth. But seen in the light of being without any preconceptual ordering, suddenly it's perceived as a mess.

And people are part of this. I have always liked watching people in a queue, or sitting next to each other on the tube; again, their separateness, individuality, their independent being, their movements. I remember being captivated by watching two people in back-to-back adjoining phone boxes standing next to each other having separate conversations. And also in that context when someone is on the phone, half of them is also somewhere else.

---

2   *trombone and piano piece* (2003).

To return to the question, I feel my actual writing of the piece is composite also because we are not the same person every day, but are always changing. So I come back to my thoughts about the piece being a collection of work over a period of time, and there are other concerns and interests as well.

This reminds me of your programme notes, where you say things like "lots of different stuff things I don't like also no point in any of it all at once with no consequence as if it was just something happening the weirdness and incredulity of actuality", and also the analogy you make between your music and a party, which is certainly apt, and mirror my experience as a listener. I was wondering how you see non-intention as being part of this: what is the point of it, and are there consequences?

Well, the party is an immediate easy analogy for such a structure. That was an old programme note which I don't use anymore – it was good at one time for some things but soon fell apart as a neat way of explaining everything, of giving the 'artist statement' that is required by people sometimes. The pointlessness was meant just in the context of being both a way of beginning for myself, to disarm and humble myself, and also in that during the course of the piece there is no narrative structure. In the light of expecting a traditional development or discourse, there might appear to some to be no 'point' to the consequence of events, no fulfillment to the expectation that the piece should 'go somewhere'. I'm not interested in that, so I start with that supposed negative quality of 'pointlessness' and work upwards. The actuality, or suchness, of what's there is what I'm wanting to provide a space for, and considering this is to think in other ways than consequential thinking; to say that things lead to other things in a developmental way, and to make a piece the direction of which appears to be completely aimless, which is at home in every moment within itself and doesn't need to justify itself by aiming at something else.

Then I suppose this suchness of the individual moments is often complicated by the multiplicity of these things going on. And I suppose ultimately I'm thinking of a situation which, rather than being 'a piece of music' or 'work of art', is more like some kind of natural experience, which for me is my preferred experience above all, which is full of this actuality, but which mostly is elusive because one is often too preoccupied and distracted with one's thoughts all the time.

I expect this goes some way to explaining the use of titles in your pieces, which tend to be fairly undemonstrative and factual, for example viola piece *or* ten brass. *You also use the prefix 'untitled' in some pieces, as in* untitled winter 2002, *or* untitled cello and piano (2002). *Is this part of a desire to distance yourself from any unnecessary poetic meaning or inference, and how do you feel about the association it makes with other music or visual art practices?*

Two hundred years ago it seems there was less of a problem. I remember seeing a list of C.P.E.Bach's output and seeing Sonata after Sonata. The actual substance of the music was the whole focus, and the title as convenient extremely general descriptive stuck-on label. Possibly they didn't even ask what the piece was called each time, but it was always 'new work' or 'new sonata'. The experience of the music becomes a little more forefront. And then of course as a direct result of that, people end up giving nicknames to the list of Haydn Symphonies, like 'The Hen' or something, because somebody thought that something sounded like a hen in the piece, which was very probably never in Haydn's mind at the time he wrote it, which nonetheless ends up in a catalogue and programme note, and which in this case ruins the piece for everyone else then because we end up listening out for this hen and miss everything else.

When writing a piece, in terms of titles, I often just think of what it is. I do consider a number of things, for example considering whether the 'trombone and piano piece' should be *untitled trombone and piano*. But my titles aren't as blank as yours are, or Richard Ayres'. When listening to a new CD, without thinking I often end up never looking at the titles, unless I have to talk to someone about something on the CD. On one's CD player, everything is just Track 1, Track 2 and so on anyway. Along these lines I remember going to an exhibition of new paintings by Cy Twombly, and everything was *Untitled*, and all very similar and exactly the same size.

A title is just a label to put on the experience you're about to have, or the memory of an experience you have had. A title for a piece of mine full of 'poetic meaning or inference' as you say would just frustrate me, and to my mind, limits the expectation and perhaps experience of the listener in some way, which is diametrically opposed to what I'm wanting. So at the moment I tend to give pieces some kind of unrevealing title, so that the memory of the piece itself becomes the image held in mind.

The interview was conducted by email between 3 November – 9 December 2003.

Jennifer Walshe

One of the features of your work which has always interested me is the provenance of the sounds. They always seem to have an interesting story behind them, can you begin by saying how you go about finding sounds, and what types of sound interest you?

I like to use a wide range of different sounds, and I'm often particularly taken with 'dirty' sounds – sounds we might commonly regard as flawed, or as by-products of normal techniques of playing an instrument, or even as by-products of life, rather than objects worthy of attention. I use a lot of extended techniques in my work, and so I really enjoy digging around on an instrument to find things I haven't heard before, whether it's blowing into the soundhole of a violin, using different types of pressure on a drum head, or using an instrument like the trumpet as a resonator/amplifier rather than in the normal way. I am also interested in whatever sounds I can find outside of the vocal/instrumental world – the crunch of porridge in a plastic bag, the creak and split of ice in a puddle, as well as field recordings, found sounds and old recordings. This often means that performers of my music find themselves having to play, for example, bags, stones, tape recorders and wool as well as their instrument. I wrote a piece in 2007 for voice and percussion quartet called *Physics for the Girl in the Street*, and that was such a joy – percussionists expect to be asked to play anything, and they will develop a technique to get it right.

Sometimes the sounds which end up in my pieces are versions of sounds which have significance for me; for example, when I was a child I was home sick from school, alone in the house one day, and I looked out on the empty road we lived on, and I could hear the wind blowing through the vents and pipes of the house, making a roiling, blustery, metallic sound. I've used this sound in lots of pieces; it always manifests itself in different ways and through different instrumentation. Other times I'll have an idea for a sound, and then try and recreate that sound with instruments or find it. Like the sound of a brush scrubbing wet tiles. A lot of the times the sounds might be described as the foley sounds in a film – when I watch films I am always very interested in the sound design, in how light bulbs sound as they flicker on, a dog's nails clipping on lino. It's especially interesting knowing that what you are hearing from a foley track probably wasn't made with the implements you see. If you watch a foley track being made the disconnect between the objects they use to make the sounds and what you see on the screen is quite wonderful. This appeals to me hugely because the way I think about sound can be very visual, and it's nice to twist that a bit. Often I find myself writing a piece which is basically the foley track of a film I can see very clearly in my head.

Still other times the sounds I use are either the sonic equivalent of or products of certain physical situations – like holding your arms out over a table, parallel to the ground, and tensing them until the muscles start to tremble and quiver, which induces this certain feeling of focus and tension, and then you can hold shoelaces in your hand so they dance and jump as you are shaking and the tips flick off the table. I'm also very interested in sounds which have dominant visual aspects – I wrote *My Extensive Relationship with Mr. Stephen Patrick M.* (2007) for the Schömerhaus in Klosterneuburg, a venue with an internal atrium and four storeys of balconies. At certain points in the piece the performers poured feathers and packing peanuts off the balconies of the upper stories – they came pouring down in huge, very quiet drifts.

My connection with the types of sounds I use is quite visceral. When I write a new piece often I draw up a sort of a mood-board, the way a lot of fashion designers would, beforehand, where I think about colours, textures, smells, anything. And the sounds will often grow out of this – so choosing beige, off-white, dirty cream and pastel milky blue colours, with felt, greasy metal and shaved suede textures, chalk stinging your nostrils and dust mites blinking in dry light, thinking about crackling and spitting and sounds which create tiny clouds of dust, sounds like a lighter bristling into flame or spray cans of water articulating irritated text or vitamins fizzing in water with radio static beside them.

In the past I've also worked with sounds which are imaginary, sounds which function as conceptual descriptions. A lot of the time this involves textual notation, just pure text with no standard musical notation involved. I did a series of 'cooking' pieces which described sounds in highly detailed imaginative terms. The performer, for example, might be required to imagine the inside of their body as the interior of a mountain full of mines, feel the blood moving through their veins as tiny carts carrying diamonds to and fro through a tunnel system, and then tip these tiny imaginary diamonds into their lungs to prepare for creating a sound. The audience of course can't 'see' the performer creating blasts of white light in their lungs to pulverize the diamonds they just tipped into them. But my intention is that all this preparation and delicate attention means that when the performer emits a vocal sound which atomizes the diamond dust, creating a crystalline mist through the air, there's a quality to the sound which comes from these imaginings. Preparing these scores for performance is a complicated experience which requires a lot of thought and meditation on the part of the performers. The cooking scores have been performed in a wide variety of places, probably the most special for me was during a Deep Listening workshop with Pauline Oliveros in Switzerland in 2004 – the performers had spent the entire week listening, meditating, doing Tai Chi and generally fine-tuning their ears and bodies. Their sensitivity and thinking about sound was heightened in a way that only a week of healthy living and getting up at 6 am in the Swiss Alps can produce, and you could hear this clearly in the sounds they produced.

Do the sounds ever act as a catalyst for a piece though, or do you always start from the perspective of developing a conceptual sound world then populating it? I imagine you have a few archived sounds waiting to appear in pieces and wonder if they ever become starting points for future compositions.

It works in different ways depending on the piece. A lot of the time I find sounds which I think are really beautiful, and then I archive them away or note them, or just keeping making them obsessively, and they get processed and understood over time. For me it's very important to make the sounds a lot and listen to them, think about them, live with them, until you begin to understand things about them. In that case, its like the opposite of the first process – you create this piece, and you keep listening and stripping things away until at the end of the piece you have formed the conceptual sound world, instead of creating that first. My mother is a writer, she always says you have to kill your darlings, and that's very true of music too, you need to keep listening to what the sounds need or demand and be willing to take a knife to those beautiful bell sounds you found in a German mountain town and have imposed on the piece. Sometimes it's a matter of scanning the sounds I have collected or been struck by, when I need a certain sound, like trying to find something in your wardrobe that matches. When I worked on my sci-fi opera *set phasers on KILL!* (2004), the music functioned as sound design in a film would. In one section I wanted sounds that were very sparse and dusty and had these recordings I had made of all these different central grooves of records, and that was great because it fitted perfectly what I wanted and I could then work with and expand on them.

Is the stripping away of information something that is also important to you when deciding how to recontextualize sounds within a piece?

Yes, it is. I don't want to leave all the information out there. Part of the process involves stripping away old contexts and building new ones around the sounds. You can take a sound from a Britney Spears song, where she does a glottal groan moving into a throaty note, something which in context is highly sexualized and provocative, and get rid of everything except the glottal groan, string it out for minutes at a time, and surround it with banal answering machine messages about getting rid of flies and the sound of ice cubes plonking and cracking into glasses of water.

Of course, everyone listens to the sounds and hears completely different things, depending on how 'stripped-down' the sounds are, and what sounds are next to them, and also on the listener themselves, what music they like, how sound has played a role in their life, what they had for breakfast, whether they are in a good mood. I strip the sounds down as much as I can because it is impossible to be able to get them to the point where they are semiotically neutral – instead, I just want to confuse things a bit and make things less clear. But one person's 'clear' is another person's 'muddy' so you can never absolutely know. And I think one of the problems in contemporary music is that, from some points of view, there is this idea that something should be absolute – the meaning of the piece should be very specific and unalterable, everyone should get a very clear point that the composer is making very clearly and absolutely – you go to concerts where the programme notes describe how the piece is based on the behaviour of fractals or something like that. And so if you can't 'hear' the behaviour of fractals, you haven't listened to the piece the right way. I don't like this thinking. And when I work with these types of sounds, there are lots of different ways people hear them, and quite often the way they interpret sounds has a lot to do with their life, their experiences, and when people talk to me about what they heard in a piece of mine I am always very interested, because it tends to show a lot about them, often very personal things. Sort of like inkblot tests. I agree with Roland Barthes about the death of the author, and so I understand that people are going to form their own listening of the piece, and I actually like this idea that there is a space where people ultimately hear the sounds for themselves. This can result in quite beautiful stories from listeners about what they heard in the piece, but it also leaves you open to less-pleasant experiences. When I was lecturing at Darmstadt in 2002, I was talking about this topic, and I played one of my pieces and one of the students, a man, commented aggressively 'That piece was in the structure of a male orgasm!' He felt this because the piece had a climax. I don't have the medical training to outline the extremely similar climactic structures of the male and female orgasm here; suffice to say that for me, the male student's making that sort of ridiculous comment told me a lot more about his feelings about women composers, gender and sexuality than his musical thinking.

Is this also true of the performers in your imaginary sound pieces? There's always a degree of degradation or alteration of an initial idea in the composer–performer–listener chain and, given your last comment, I wanted to know how far you feel you can stretch this as a composer whilst still feeling comfortable with the end result?

I think that me sitting in a room on my own, being the composer is one aspect of the process. I perfect the sounds in my head, but they are really a very specific version of the sounds. In that version, I have the best seat in the house for the piece, and I can hear everything perfectly, and in the case of my vocal pieces, can make the sounds perfectly. But then there's always a loss when you give these sounds to other performers, and that's to be expected and its okay, because now different people make these sounds and even if you are incredibly-specific/verging-on-completely-anal in the way you notate things, as I often am, some things will always change, when the sounds are in space, moving around, being played by other living, breathing human beings. And you could drive yourself insane rehearsing for 400 hours with each performer, trying to get it to be so completely specific, miking every instrument with 17 mics instead of one, using four conductors and synchronized stopwatches and so forth but in new music there's often not enough money for two rehearsals and life is too short. I understand there'll be some change, some deterioration as you put it, but I don't think of it as deterioration. And in fact, sometimes, the sounds can change for the better. But I enjoy that experience, in my room, working on my private bag of sounds and trying to put together this perfect little puzzle, and when I show other people the pieces I know they'll chip them a little bit or the paint will rub off on their coat, but it's still my puzzle.

The degree of deterioration which occurs before the sounds hit the listener is even more problematic, I think, because mostly we forget that listeners are also human beings, and (similar to performers) the way they hear a piece will be affected by their mood, their back, their knees, the temperature of the hall, the day, what they had for dinner, whether they had dinner, whether the person they came to the concert with is their long-lost childhood sweetheart who they found on the internet and are trying to impress by bringing them to a contemporary music concert on their first date in 25 years. My mother has tinnitus and is deaf in one ear, and so she always has a different impression of concerts than other people do; the same goes for where somebody is sitting. And there's no way you can control this unless you had a masseuse, chef, psychiatrist, hearing specialist, etc. on call before a concert. What you can do is, where possible, frame the piece well, pick a great space for the concert, programme it interestingly, use the seating imaginatively, so that the odds are with you. I curated a concert in Schloss Solitude in Stuttgart with Apartment House where every piece was in a different location – it kicked off with Ellen Aagaard doing Cathy Berberian's *Stripsody* under the arcade of the Schloss, then I did *Ursonate* by Kurt Schwitters up in a tree, then we had pieces in the chapel, in the ballroom; we finished with Alvin Lucier's *I am Sitting in a Room*, which we did in the vestibule under the Schloss. The vestibule is an open-air space – you have a view over the whole of Stuttgart, sitting tucked under a Baroque pleasure palace. We timed it so that we performed the Lucier during sunset, the generations unfolding as the light faded over the city, and we had benches and mattresses out. And people's attention was so focused in this concert, and I think a lot of it was the moving around – each time they moved, they got their blood circulating again, and the change of place kept their senses from shutting down. This, for me, was the ideal situation, and of course it's not easily emulated again, but I want to do so.

You perform in a lot of your pieces, as a vocalist, or violinist, or playing other instruments, and I wondered how you feel this has shaped aspects of your work as a composer?

This has shaped how I think tremendously. From a practical standpoint, there are many benefits to playing in your own pieces – firstly, you can take part in the piece, and there's the sheer enjoyment of playing, and playing with other musicians. You can write things which you know you can do, which other people might not be able to do, or which might otherwise be extremely difficult to notate, and you know how to do them, how to interpret the notation. It shapes how you think in so many ways. Probably the first thing that is affected is notation, because you can use shorthand, or leave things a little free, and its hardwired into your brain how you want it to sound – this is especially useful with the voice, when notation can be so problematic, and you are dealing with so many parameters that to leave a few a little loose allows you to finish writing the piece ... that said, though, I often push myself to notate everything as accurately as possible, as if I were writing for other people, which I suppose is the conservatory training, because through the festivals and masterclasses and whatnot I've found there is this real feeling for a lot of contemporary composers that other people should be able to play it/sing it, that it should be notated in such a way that they can, and if you've written something that only you can perform, then it shouldn't be considered a 'real' piece of music, worthy of merit or discussion in such arenas. And this sort of idea of notational accessibility is quite amusing at times when you consider, relatively, how few people perform or listen to a great deal of contemporary music ... but that's a shame, I think, because if you start performing in your own pieces, often you vastly open up the range of sounds available to you as a composer, and sometimes these sounds are easily done by other performers, and sometimes not, but you should be able to use all of them anyway, and notate them however you want. When I started improvising, that really forced me to rethink all aspects of performance and notation because I started to build huge vocabularies of sounds which would be extremely difficult to notate, and was using them in conjunction with other musicians in extremely flexible ways, and I realized that in the context of free improvisation, we could build pieces which were 'valid' in the classical sense, which were structured and elegant, but they did not need to involve a score. I could write pieces for both other musicians and myself that could have improvisational aspects, and these could work in different ways but still be the piece. Especially I found with writing pieces for myself as solo performer, the pieces became part of a sort of an oral tradition with hints; I could create maps and guidelines as scores, and let them have some space to breathe and come alive on the page and in performance.

I think this is part of the problem of being 'trained professionally' as a composer, like you can take a poet and send them to poet school and then they know how to write poetry. Preferably in rhyming couplets ... young composers are told that they should notate their pieces so that everyone can perform them, and they spend a lot of time doing this, and then ... not very many people perform them. It's not that I'm against the idea of learning to notate sound, I highly support that because I think it's important to understand what you want transmitted, what you want to be understood about your music and the sounds you use, and how this is presented to other people. Plus, I have synaesthesia so I have an interest in how information is presented visually from an intellectual standpoint, and I will always spend time choosing my method of notation and presentation. The other part of the problem is that young composers are told that the path to success is winning competitions and getting performances by big-name ensembles. So they trawl through Gaudeamus Foundation news or whatever, and all that is available to them are competitions for pieces which are 10–12 minutes long, for flute, oboe, violin and piano or some such ensemble, and everyone knows that if you were to submit a non-traditional score you would not have a hope. My recipe pieces are text scores, printed on pastel-coloured recipe cards, all individually hand-stamped, and they come in limited-edition envelopes. My skate-boarding piece is an embroidered transfer on a T-shirt.

So if you're writing a piece in which you are not performing, how do you approach notation, particularly given the timbral precision required by the sounds you use? Do you tend to notate sounds or actions (or a combination of both)?

It depends on the situation. I strongly believe the method of notation should reflect the overall philosophy of the piece – you should learn something about the piece just by looking at the way the information is organized notationally. I also believe that one of the most important technical skills as a composer is to learn how to organize this information as clearly and simply as possible. Some pieces I notate in a way which is incredibly complex and highly specific – I want a particular sound and so I notate it as accurately and in as much detail as I possibly can. Anyone can perform it, because the notation locks everything down. This can involve developing my own notational methods which build on standard techniques, augmenting the normal systems we use, such as the five-line stave – in *passenger* (2006), a piece for string orchestra, I used a large number of different clefs which allowed me to turn the stave into a continuum which indicates positions on the fingerboard, horizontal cross-sections of the instruments and points along the body of the instrument and bow. The performers' parts retain the standard look of musical notation; the clefs open up what the staves mean.

Other systems of notation are quite complex and explode the individual part into multiple information streams – in pieces like *your name here* (1998) which is a piece for solo vocalist, where there are six or seven streams of information, covering all aspects of sound, and *they could laugh smile* (1999) for solo trombonist, where there are also multiple streams of information, I was challenging myself to see how particular I could be, in a way that was digital, being so precise. Other pieces are notated more freely – for example, in pieces such as the recipes to cook with sound (*#112: dear hero imprison'd*; *#132 the leather runs smooth on the passenger seat* (2004)), I know that the basic actions will stay the same globally, however timing and sounds will change locally depending on performer, but I welcome this because you get very interesting things from it. Sometimes I notate actions, because that is easier for the performers to deal with than trying to notate the sounds in traditional terms – in *a sensitive number for the laydeez* (2004), it was easier to insert photographs of actions in the score, of things the pianist and percussionist did with shoelaces, of the positioning of card between the strings of the viola; the performers will pick it up instantly from the image.

Over the past few years you've worked on many large-scale projects, most notoriously your Barbie opera XXX_LIVE_NUDE_GIRLS!!! (2003). Could you explain how this piece developed?

The Barbie opera developed out of several different impulses. I don't like most modern opera. Robert Ashley's work I love, but I am not interested in hearing someone walk around the stage singing in a standard word-setting style. I grew up with TV and film and MTV and that sort of work doesn't make any sense to me anymore. As a composer who works in the contemporary music sphere, you continually find yourself confronted with these genres which many say are dead – the symphony, the opera – and you have to negotiate your place in relation to them.

And I had been thinking about opera, because I do love the theatrical, visual element of performance – on one level I consider everything I've ever written music theatre – and I was considering whether it would even be possible for me to write an opera. Part of this was the financial aspect – most modern productions are incredibly expensive, both to stage and to see. One day I was reading about Mozart and Haydn's marionette operas and this low-cost aspect was very interesting to me, and in thinking about updating it I instantly fell on Barbie dolls. That led to a lengthy meditation on Barbie dolls, and to a lot of research about them, including talking to many people, most importantly a lot of kids, about their views on Barbie dolls. I wasn't interested in making points about whether Barbie dolls are 'good' or 'bad' – this is the focus of most research and writing about the dolls. I was interested in how people used them. When I was a child and we played with dolls, they were embroiled in very complex storylines which involved very adult themes, and I found that to be the same when I talked to other women and men, and also to the kids. All the things that the dolls go through over the course of the opera are storylines that you can easily see if you look closely at the way little girls play with the dolls. Or indeed the way little boys play with GI Joes. Traditionally little girls are viewed as taking part in innocent and passive play, usually sequestered in their bedroom, and in fact their play is sophisticated, intelligent, often very violent and in my view, sees them implementing all sorts of social situations they don't understand and are trying to figure out in their play, producing quite sensational and bizarre storylines in the process – one group of kids I talked to, for example, loved marrying their Barbies over and over. And when I asked them if they divorced the dolls after the wedding so they could have more marriages, they answered 'oh no, the husband gets drunk and the police come and kill him. Then the Barbie can get married again.' In the universe their dolls inhabit, Barbie gets pregnant unknowingly, gives birth and leaves the undesired baby on the kitchen table then goes to the disco; Barbie's legs are both broken by a nasty fall and the doctors don't believe her so she has to crawl around trying to find someone who will treat her; Barbie will marry a horse or a 4-year-old boy because 'there are no men left'. This universe seemed like a very interesting and suitable place to set an opera.

How did you translate these ideas into a music-theatre context? All of your work has a strong visual impact in any case, and I was interested in the more overt staging of the opera, and how it relates to the music.

The basic visual idea of how the opera would work – the house with the two video screens and the musicians spread around it – was there right from the very beginning. I really liked the idea of having a stage which was so tightly focused on the house, and that the audience would be able to see the movements and actions of the dolls blown up on the video screens, so that everything would be extremely clear. Using the videos meant that in a tight close-up, a doll's head could be 5' tall, which is a very bizarre way to see a doll, and meant that there were a lot more visual details made explicit than would be a standard opera stage working just with people. The puppeteers move the dolls, whilst listening to the recorded libretto on their headphones, so the movements of the dolls function as a silent film, and the music is then layered on this, pushing and pulling against it.

The interview was conducted by email between 10 May and 5 December 2004, and edited in September 2008.

Manfred Werder

In the preface to the score of stück 1998 you write the phrase 'für sich, klar und sachlich. einfach' (to itself, clear and objective. simple). This seems like both a performance indication and an aesthetic statement which defines your work in general. In practice, how does this statement relate to the way your music operates, and your aims as a composer?

That's a very interesting point to start. The phrase 'für sich, klar und sachlich. einfach' replaced all further indications on dynamics, sound qualities, etc. since 1997. In general I wanted to write a music where the used material – sound and absence of sound – were just there as material (and not as an author's composed preferences). The used material could be seen then more precisely as context specific material (the accidental qualities of performers, instruments, the site), as general conditions in a world, and itself as part of the world. In this sense every sound bears its precise dynamic and quality through its context.

I thought all indications would lead to representation only, so I decided to describe (more literally than poetically) a general and essential attitude aimed at letting the 'world' emerge from its context specific potential. I think all my work operates in relation to our complex situation of being the world, and at the same time observing the world.

For me one of the interesting things about the piece is the disparity between the extremely tight control of pitch and duration, and the relative openness of the sounding result (as a consequence of unspecified instrumentation, or uncontrollable sound production within certain boundaries for example). So when looking at the score or listening to the first few events in performance it seems to be completely about the structure (a repeating pattern of a sound lasting six seconds followed by silence for a further six seconds, with only the pitch and register specified). Gradually though the timbral fluctuations that result from sustaining these events for long periods of time reveal themselves and I find my listening focus gets drawn into the sounds: a note becomes a complex of micro-events. Given your comment about the importance of context, do you feel your music operates at this level primarily, or at the more immediately obvious level of the event?

In *stück 1998* I think the framework still generates contextual questions relating primarily to 'music' and 'composition', and I agree with your description of a note becoming a complex of micro-events. Although it may strongly depend on the performance: you describe with 'extremely tight control of pitch and duration, and the relative openness of the sounding result' a framework which may also lead to a performance of some ten minutes of silence by using an instrument with a small pitch range.

There's a fundamental disparity between the score and a performance. I see the score as a specific section of the world, a performance as a specific section of the score (and also the world), and context as the support of a possible event. Both, context and event, are essentially inseparable, and arise everywhere (in our experience and perception). A performance proposes and creates a specific intersection of articulation, context and the listener's experience and perception in a heterogeneous mutuality. The more balanced the meeting of all parts, the more challenging an event may emerge.

Later then in *for one or a few performers* (2001–) I propose a framework focusing rather on an acoustic exploration of the surroundings. And there I think the sound events operate primarily as articulations affecting the listener's quality of perception of the surroundings.

Presumably this is a consequence of the more unpredictable placing of sounds: the only direction in the score is 'a lot of time. a few sounds. for itself simple.' I would hope that musicians contemplating a performance of this piece would be sensitive to your approach, but to what extent is the range of possible performances acceptable to you? A 'lot of time' and 'a few sounds' might mean many different things to different people.

One of the things which I find intriguing about your work, and that of Antoine Beuger and Jürg Frey, is the tension created by relatively little sound in a listening environment: you're almost torn between two parallel existences. So picking up on your previous comment, do you intend an active exploration of the surroundings by the listeners and/or performers, or do you feel that the articulated events are the listening focus?

I wanted this score to become 'a function of truth'. It's essential to get a performer to the point where he advances into fields where he and his risk are not backed up by a structure, however far this structure would go in the composition. If I see a performer not willing to collaborate in this sense, it hardly is acceptable to me, so I locate this question rather there. But still, that direction of four lines is literally the score which prescribes a very clear and intrinsic situation. I think this score comments on 'precision' and its omnipresent impact, especially in occidental culture, and hopefully generates some experiences towards an other 'economy of precision'.

The two parallel existences are the human condition: being nature and (consciously) observing nature. The absence of articulated events brings about a heightened experience of being more and more dissolved into this whole environment of sounds, of nature, and in happy moments we experience just 'being', or 'being nature'. Then, in the very moment of an articulated event, as a moment of awareness of oneself observing this articulation, emerges the space of consciousness of the human being's condition.

Maybe experiencing this space again and again is already enough. But how to get 'composition' to that level? And knowing that 'composition' is only one of the 'involved parts' of such a moment.

What then is your role as a composer, and to what extent do you feel you can intervene in this relationship?

A composer not backing up his work against the risk of its disappearance will find himself exploring the potential of his work's own effectiveness.

I think all composers would view that in a different way: notation is always a compromise. For me notation should be efficient, meaning it should serve its purpose without containing redundant information, even if a lack of explicit direction in some areas creates particular contingencies in its realization (looking at what composers don't notate is always revealing). I think your notation is efficient in this way, and its role in your work is a very interesting one. I'd like to ask you about how it relates to your working method. Whilst some of your scores involve quite a lot of material (the 4,000 pages of stück 1998, *for example), others are more conceptual. Could you explain how you work?*

An important part of how I work is observing, sensing the world and nature of the involved parts of this performance moment. The performance as a moment where people meet and where all incidences may coincide, where the possible (*das Mögliche*) may become the real (*das Wirkliche*). I observe and sense this moment of coincidence and interaction in order to refine my propositions towards such a moment. I'd say the most important and beautiful part is observing and sensing how I personally coincide with the world's very sound. Often I just listen for hours. Then I try to think what it is that I did when I listened. So I look at the world wherein I see myself interacting. There I see my possibilities to be effective.

What appears in a score in a certain way is what a composer (still) may consider worth mentioning (the same would stand for an interview), bringing us back to the question of an economy of precision. We live with a tremendous excess of the explicit. Conceptually I wouldn't separate too much scores like *stück 1998* or *ein(e) ausführende(r)* (2002–) with their 4,000 pages from later prose scores including only a few words. I'd rather think that a certain idea or layout for a composition proposes a certain ideal form of the score.

There are some quite fine distinctions between your pieces and particularly between versions of pieces (such as ein klang und eine stille, *or* stück 2003*), where sometimes there is only one word different in the score, but the impact of this change is often very large. They seem to hint at trying to isolate performance archetypes, particularly in relation to listening and observation as you have mentioned, but also relationships between performers. Is this questioning of how people interact important for you?*

Beyond a cultural extinction through what has been called 'the society of the spectacle' a richness of expression does obviously exist, and personally I feel a fundamental necessity to deconstruct the complex 'wickerwork' of elements and parameters involved in musical composition and its performance situation. This 'wickerwork' is actually mirroring our entire culture. So I try to isolate basic questions. In this sense I aim at focusing on 'that people interact' before questioning 'how people interact'.

Where do we localize the essential impact of a performance of one performer in relation to a performance of two performers, or three performers? Where do we localize the essential impact of no articulated sound in relation to one articulated sound, to two or even three articulated sounds which already seem to be much closer to infinity? Elementary numerical relationships, especially within the numbers zero, one and two, and the ideas of the infinite reveal quite some questions on 'composition' and its 'constitution', finally on being.

In the scores I claim these questions to be the compositional questions (and there I aim at omitting to work on all questions I consider being contextual in order to avoid their dominant presence). The performances then materialize these questions, and a whole contextual situation emerges where the compositional questions and their materialization should maintain a transparent balance.

At the end I hope the richness of being and expressing to become a palpable experience.

Some of your pieces are performed in succession, continuing in the score from where the previous performance finished. You've also organized series of daily performances of your pieces in a particular space. This seems closely linked to your idea of being and observing the world, perhaps mirroring the structure of the pieces on a larger scale. Why do you present your work in this way, and how do you view the boundaries of both a piece and its performance?

The presentation is always an invitation for people to meet. A performance lets a whole range of human beings' sensations emerge, and the more we care for these sensations' quality, the more we need to care for the presentation as well, which actually opens a new field of compositional decisions.

There is an essential relation between the what and the how of a proposition. I aim at bringing forth a flat as possible hierarchy within all the incidences coinciding, and its quality is then the listener's possibility to live his own experience. With the performance succession I intend to balance 'performance moment' and 'non-performance moment', finally to balance the performance moment and life.

Incidences demand a general and certain awareness of care and attention otherwise they get lost in mere representation. I intend to conceive how 'the world' appears as 'world' in a performance.

I conceived a more general layout (for example in *stück 1998*) in order to continue to refine a layout as one complex: all pieces then intend to refine this complex. I need to reduce the focus on both an inner-compositional field of possibilities of 'attraction' and a linear process of a work as a succession of 'autonomous compositions' in order to let appear the mere world as a field of incidences.

So I conceived these scores which are performed in succession: each new, both easily recognizable and essentially different succession may so draw our attention to the situation's 'material' as an exact moment of 'world'.

Maybe the boundaries of both a piece or a performance are the boundaries of its potentiality as thought, or as information. Intuitively I would ask for a centre, or centres of a piece and its performance. The centres of a performance could be what I called before a heterogeneous mutuality.

The interview was conducted by email between 1 and 10 February 2004.

Christian Wolff

A lot of your work explores the nature of social interaction in music, and I wanted to begin by asking you what draws you to such contingent processes as opposed to specifying more fixed relationships between sounds?

OK, here goes – I'm afraid I'm a bit longwinded. Your question does go to the heart of a matter. And I can't think how to answer properly without some history. Also, in advance, apologies for overlap and repetition of what I've said on other occasions, or written – at this point, at the moment, I just plunge in not worrying about that – though I'm starting to get haunted by my *deja-dit*.

I first thought of devising 'contingent processes' as a way of dealing with what we came to call at the time indeterminacy. It was in the air. Cage's looking for a way to find detachment, in the Eastern way, through chance operations. Feldman making the graph pieces, to put himself on an edge, and because he wanted to work directly with sound as weight (varying and shifting), not part of a system of pitch arrangements. We were all looking for new ways of making music, starting, if possible, from scratch – i.e. rethinking what music might be. Why? Because of a sense of general bankruptcy of the music being made around us.

Some time in 1950 I made a piece for three (unspecified) voices which was through composed except for the pitches. The notation was a single line, the notes on, above or below it, indicating melodic direction, but not the intervals or any reference pitch. These were chosen freely by the singers individually. I did this because I didn't (in this case) want to deal with pitch systems. Also I wanted the piece to be flexible – for any kind of singer, for various skills. More positively, I shifted the focus. Singers usually worry about getting pitches right, rhythm, dynamics, etc. come second, or are done more *ad hoc*. Here it's the other way around. Though it's not as though one area is more or less important, it's just that different kinds of attention are involved.

My next, more thorough going try at contingent processes came about out of practical necessity. (I tell this story often.) I had committed to making a two piano piece for Frederic Rzewski and myself to play. At the time (1957) I was writing complex, entirely through-composed music, and I thought I'd be doing more of the same. It turned out I couldn't find the time to write like that, and even if I had, we wouldn't have had time to learn to play the music. So Frederic and I worked out a scheme – time spaces with variably usable material to play in them, each of us proceeding independently except that the totals of each of our time spaces (they were determined by a Cagean square root rhythmic structure) were the same. So we started and ended together (stopwatches were used). What we had was a through-composed scaffolding or structure within which we made individual choices, from preset material. So a shift of focus to performance, somewhere in between improvisation and following prescriptions. Preparing the piece we found that, of course, it changed all the time, which made rehearsals (and performances) really interesting. I also noticed that, though I might have prepared certain things – made preliminary choices from the material – in the actual playing my choices were inevitably affected and altered by what Frederic happened, at any given moment, to have decided to play, and the same, reciprocally, for him.

After that, for quite a while (years!), everything I wrote involved such processes, variously elaborated. There was still a pragmatic motivation. I was trying to make a music that could be performed under the circumstances of the time – for my work very limited performance opportunities, my own involvement in performances in spite of my quite limited playing skills, the involvement of others, usually non-professional, who were not virtuosos (some of course definitely were, like Frederic and David Tudor).

There was also musical motivation. My indeterminate procedures could produce a kind of rhythm that I couldn't think how else to do – caused, for instance, by playing freely within variably fixed time frames, in spaces not along a linear grid of pulse; and by requirements of coordination (the business, for example, of player one plays a sound of free duration, player two must play the moment she hears the sound stop, not knowing when that will be). These procedures were also occasions or incentives for the performers to be inventive about sound itself. Often instruments were not specified (again, more practical), but certain ways of playing were, for instance the requirement to change the colour of a sound three times as it sounds, or the use of a noise element to be devised by the player with his instrument, or not.

I had the notion, and still do, that the music should be exploratory, experimental, partly to get out from under the enormous weight of traditional Western classical music (though it's a music I know well, and to much of which I am quite attached), partly because I can't think of – or haven't the skills for – anything else.

While at school in New York my friends and I used to go hear Dixieland jazz, which I liked a lot. I think the use of the fixed structural elements – eight-bar units, alternation of chorus and solo, unrelenting pulse, standard instrumental framework, underlying given tunes – combined with improvisation, exploration of instrumental possibilities (well beyond anything I'd heard in classical or, then, 'new' music) and, especially, a kind of free heterophonic playing by several or more players: all that, though I didn't reflect particularly on it at the time, made a great impression.

As for 'social interaction in music', you could say I stumbled on it. The conditions for getting my work out, making it social – to my mind the only way that music exists at all – drew me to these kinds of pragmatic solutions. That the ways to them were experimental (indeterminacy etc.) has come to be a social, and political, matter too. The techniques of coordination, interaction and interdependency, all players being equal (really, the normal thing in chamber music), and the sharing out of musical independence between composer and performers – that can have a metaphorical or exemplary force: social democracy. That doesn't mean, by the way, that when making a piece of music everything is driven by what it should mean politically (which could be a musical disaster, and so also a political one). When making music I just make music. But in all ways possible – how the making is set up (this could be musical-technical or social), realized, how presented, how you work with the musicians, how relate to an audience, for instances – I hope to stay always aware of good democratic principles.

I used to object to the notion of experimental music having something tentative about it (it's only an experiment, not something properly established like 'fixed relationships between sounds'). Now I don't mind so much. The state of the world is alarmingly tentative, seems more than ever on the brink. Can music be anything else? Not that it has simply to reflect this. Some expression of hope, however unjustified, is still in order. But doesn't it also have to have some 'realism', has to avoid mystification? The notion of experiment, contingent processes, matters because I think it represents an image and attitude which allow for the possibility of change (for the better).

Although you are clearly still working with such processes, you seem to be implying a widening of your practice to include (or return to) music which does not rely solely on contingency to shape or form itself. Is this partly due to a change in conditions, and times, and do the musicians for whom you are writing govern your approach in any way? I'm thinking partly about how you approach a solo or small group piece in contrast to a large ensemble, or orchestra.

The mid-60s pieces like *Quartet* (1965) and the *Electric Spring* series (1966–70) are different from my usual contingent process pieces. They were pieces for particular and unusual instrumental combinations that happened to be available (and at the time I couldn't imagine they'd be played more than the one time). Aside from some piano pieces, the usual contingent pieces didn't specify instruments (e.g. *For 1, 2 or 3 People* (1964)) – and, incidentally, they still get played a lot more. Here the musicians available and their instruments caused a shift in approach. I think differently when writing for unspecified instruments. More abstractly, or some kind of generically, with regard to colour, for instance, while there might be a sharper focus on, say, the patterning of hocketed lines.

I've long been interested in a variety of degrees of indeterminacy or contingency, from almost none (the performer has to do exactly what's specified) to various extremes, say, an indication for the player to do whatever she wishes, though only somewhere within a time-space of two seconds, or to do something quite specified at any time at all. Sometimes this variety happens within one piece, sometimes from piece to piece. For instance, the openness of *Edges* (1968) – which is really just a guide for free improvisation, on the one hand, and the always recognizable tune in *Burdocks* (1970–71) (though there the instrument(s)'s not specified, nor dynamics nor tempo and you can read the notes in treble or bass, make spaces of free duration between phrases of the melody, play at any time and repeat as often as you like, or not).

More generally when I make a piece that's pretty much through-composed and specified – that looks like regular music (though I rarely indicate dynamics or articulation) – I don't have in mind one, single possible way of performing it. I evade performers' questions after playing: is this the way you wanted it? Partly because I don't know (though I might know a wrong-headed or wrong-eared way of playing) and partly because I'd like the performance to be as much an expression of the performers' sense of the music as of mine. I've always thought that's what's distinctive about music: even with the most elaborately detailed notation the music can't possibly ever be played exactly the same way twice (you only get exact repetition when you play a recording). I've taken that 'given', you could say, and composed with it.

By the 70s, to be sure, there was a noticeable shift towards making a music more like what I supposed most people regarded as music. I included pre-existing melodic material (from folk music mostly, and politically related), I notated conventionally pulsed rhythms, specified the pitches (except for the occasional call for a noise of the player's devising) and used recognizable counterpoint. This had less to do with the musicians for whom I was writing – though it might also in the case of musicians, say, like Frederic Rzewski, be because of shared political sympathies – than with changes in the times. The politically charged times of the late 60s and after – civil rights in the US, the Vietnam War, renewed awareness of social-economic justice issues, the women's movement – though I've come realize that all times are politically charged. Along with other friends, Frederic, Cornelius Cardew, Yuji Takahashi, Erhardt Grosskopf, Garrett List, John Tilbury among others, I thought that our music work should be politically awake.

At this time too the minimalism of Terry Riley, Philip Glass and Steve Reich emerged and made a great and refreshing impression, especially after what seemed an ever-deepening morass of hyper-complex music, and also after a sense of increasing introversion in experimental music. Suddenly it was ok to think about non-chromatic pitch arrangements and regularly pulsed music, and outgoingness. It was also at this time that John Cage started doing his 'cheap imitations' – using the pre-existing rhythms and pitch materials from pieces of Western classical music. And other composers, some previously very dodecaphonic, took up writing a nostalgic pastiche tonal music.

As for adjusting to what groupings of players I'm writing for – solo, ensemble, orchestra: sure, though a secondary consideration after the above. Apart from giving individual players ranges of choice in what and how to play, my main interest has been the mutual effects players have on each other in the real time of performance. That makes solo a special case. If there's to be some kind of performance interaction at the actual time of performance, it has to be with unpredictable features of the sound that the performer himself produces. I've tried to do a bit with that, but it's limited. So solo usually has me using less of compositionally arranged contingency. Smaller ensembles are ideal for interactive stuff. A larger ensemble or orchestra is a big challenge, not so much because of the numbers (pieces like *Burdocks* or *Changing the System* (1972–73) have been done by up to 50 or 60 players), but because of 'cultural' or social conditions.

Actually this applies to chamber groups too. If I'm to write for a 'professional' new music group with whom I've not had direct experience, I tend to write more conventionally or explicitly. At least in part, partly as an 'introduction' to the music. But there are likely to be more explicitly indeterminate patches as well (I've been working very much in patches for a long time now, starting, I guess, with *Bread and Roses* (1976) in the mid-70s). I'm always drifting, or pulled, in that direction, mixing in contingent procedures – some old, some new for me. I still like a range from quite determinate to a lot less determinate, and now also combinations of the two simultaneously. When I do know an ensemble, have a sense of them and know of their also doing indeterminate music, like, say, Apartment House, then I'll tend to start out from a more contingent centre.

Another thing to keep in mind is that the contingent pieces were so made in large part so they could be played by non-professionals. Professionals were certainly welcome to play, though they often – in the past, perhaps less so now – were put off by encountering material that didn't primarily address itself to their virtuosity or the special skills they'd been taught. Because the contingent music involved new notations, you could say that everyone, pros and amateurs, sometimes even non-musicians, started off from the same place, at the same level. What was required of everyone was a certain kind of musicality, inventiveness and general alertness.

When I finally got to orchestras as such – and that took a long time – it was something else again. The 'culture' of a standard orchestra doesn't sit well with contingency. It's all about hierarchical control. My first try, for the orchestra at Donaueschingen, had me writing cautiously and almost altogether explicitly, except, in a sense, for the percussion soloist, whom I knew well and who knew my work well – not that her part had explicitly indeterminate notation, but the general situation of percussion seems to me inherently contingent – you simply can't control fully all that material (all that skin, wood, metal and so on). 'Interpretation' is everything (organ music – every organ is different – I think is like this too). It was, in the end, passable, but not a very happy experience – partial indifference of many of the players, a feeling of uninvolvement, the stresses of too little rehearsal time, etc.

Actually my very first orchestra piece written for a performance, *Spring* (1995), did include parts that were indeterminate and not conductable, going on simultaneously with conducted material. That had been originally intended for an amateur, community orchestra.

Since then I've done two orchestra pieces for orchestras conducted by Petr Kotik and that's been fine. Petr is completely sympathetic while appreciating how to manage in the orchestral context. It helps that much of the music he programmes includes such composers as Cage, Feldman and Alvin Lucier, so that a certain musical climate is created – not necessarily involving contingency (in fact, hardly at all), but opening up possibilities for the kinds of music, however in particular different, that (my) contingent music might produce.

Technically I've tried a number of procedures, ranging, once again, from the fully, explicitly notated and conducted, to various kinds and degrees of freedom for individual players. The trick is to maintain a degree of clarity (but not necessarily all the time!) when a larger number of players play independently. They need to listen, which I've found is possible. You have to get past a sense individual players may have of their being swallowed up in a sort of mob of sound. One thing that can work (I did it some in *Spring* and fundamentally in *Changing the System*) is having smaller subgroups (duos, trios, quartets), internally dependent and supportive, but independent of, or dependent contingently on whatever else is going on, that is, chamber musics co-existing.

Well, I've a way to go in this direction.

Could you explain your working process, particularly with regard to your recent music? I'm interested in how you move from an initial idea (and what sparks those ideas) to the finished piece.

Working process? I wish I knew! I keep hoping to find one of those grooves, like late Cage or Feldman, so it wouldn't be such hard work. For each piece it feels different, or starts by feeling that I'm starting from scratch – though I have accumulated some experience and something of it (or a lot – I only hope not too much) may simply pop up. So it looks like more stories.

One piece this year (2004) started with a proposal-commission from Swedish Radio that I do something with the poet John Ashbery for broadcast (their idea, we didn't know each other, but knew something of each other's work). Neither of us to start with had any idea about what to do (Ashbery's poetry's been set quite a lot but mostly by rather different sorts of composers, Elliott Carter, for instance – *Syringa*). In the event Ashbery gave me a recent unpublished poem and said I could do anything I liked with it – break it up, use its sound elements, etc. (actually the poem was quite fragmented and disjunct, even for him). Then practical considerations entered in. The end product would be a recording – repeatable for several broadcastings. They wanted something about ten minutes long (not really worth a trip to Stockholm to work there). I got Ashbery recorded reading the poem. Then for me to organize a recording of music turned out to be logistically difficult and costly. As it happens, though, I know three wonderful musicians in Stockholm, who could record right there at the radio. They happened to represent the somewhat odd combination of a violin and two pianos – which I thought I could work with in this situation. As for the poem, I liked it so much just as it was that I didn't want to mess it about and decided to just make some music that would run concurrently with the recorded reading of it. So, before writing a note, all that's given.

At the moment I work by grasping at anything to start with, a little bit of this or that, maybe from a pre-existing tune (though rarely enough in a form that's recognizable), or maybe just a short first move of my own, simple, a bit of scale, a gesture, usually linear (melody). Then I move on with various possible procedures – for pitch, for instance, a kind of 12-tone transposition: say of a grouping of five initial pitches, transposed so: first pitch zero (untransposed) or transposed up or down a minor second; next pitch up or down a major second, third pitch a minor third up or down, etc. after the tritone it goes to fourth (or fifth – seconds are interchangeable with sevenths, thirds with sixths, etc.), etc. Since there were only five initial pitches the transposition continues with a sixth pitch which is already the transposition of the first of the five, and so on. I could have continued by cycling the original five pitches, which I sometimes do, but usually prefer to, so to speak, move forward.

Rhythms are often just intuitive. They're also generated by loops on grids. Say the grid has 20 divisions (spaces). Initially a rhythm is, say, sound, two spaces, sound, five spaces, sound, sound (zero space), one space (so cycle describable as 2-5-0-1). This cycle is then repeated. If a cycle doesn't finish at the end of the grid of 20 spaces, I might break it off or swing it back to the start of the grid. So here the cycle starts repeating at space 16, then to continue with five spaces you count the last four at the end of the 20 and one more back at the start of the 20, giving you a sound in the second space, and so on. If on cycling back through this way, a sound lands in a space already occupied by another sound (from a previous cycling), I make a choice: either considering that one sound in the space is enough (so the new one is absorbed in it, so to speak), or, if the instrumentation allows, two simultaneous sounds result (a chord), or there will be two successive sounds each at twice the speed of one (if the space represents a quarter note duration, you've now got two eighths). Variations and complications (say, two or more differently speeded grids simultaneously – as in three spaces of one taking up the same time as five in another).

This is all tedious to describe, but two kinds of ideas are involved: focusing choice, more or less binary (up or down) and setting up a pattern which produces results I can't quite foresee, at least in detail – what happens when those rhythmic cycles double back and overlap themselves or when the transposition cycle applies to fewer than 12 notes. I both do and don't want to know what I'm doing. The music needs to take over, take on a life of its own. Of course I'm implicated, and responsible if it doesn't work out – doesn't make a viable music, and the decision about whether or not it's viable is, at least initially, mine.

With the Ashbery piece (it's called *For John Ashbery's Hoelderlin Marginalia*), because I've got three musicians, and pianos too, there are decisions to be made about vertical relations (apart from what's solo, unison or hocketed). I decided to take a chance and just let the players play (and record) while the recording of the poem's reading was playing, without any specified coordination except for the very beginning which specifies that the reading starts (with the beginning of the title of the poem). The music was played with a lot of space in it – to let the voice be sometimes better heard and alone. And it turned out that because of this the music was about twice as long as the reading of the poem. So the reading was repeated as the music proceeded – which meant that parts of the reading that might have been obscured by the music the first time might at the second reading find themselves in a clearer place vis-à-vis the music. Similarly the music would be variously coloured by the same bits of text. The music is both scored with fixed co-ordinations for the players and has stretches where the performers proceed independently (but always listening to each other). So there are results that I both can and cannot foresee. Also rhythms, both in detail and in the feel of the form, that couldn't come about in any other way I could think of.

Among the givens for the piece, the inspirations or what sets things off, there is of course Ashbery's poem, which was there from the start. I don't really know what it's 'about', except that it shifts a lot, is highly fragmented, has bits that I half recognize (from life and reading), can be disconcerting, puzzling, surprising and beautiful. I don't try to connect the music in any particular way (wouldn't know what I'm connecting to). I just make the music knowing that if the poem weren't there the music wouldn't be the way it is. At the same time each, music and poem, go their own ways.

Another recent piece, without text but with its story, is *Another Possibility* (2004) for solo electric guitar. The Dutch electric guitar player Wiek Hijmans is looking for repertoire. He knows that Morton Feldman once wrote an electric guitar solo for me and that the piece got irretrievably lost (this was in 1967). He wanted me to make up this loss. My very approximate recollection of Feldman's piece came into what I wrote (e.g. there were mostly chords, as usual with Feldman beautifully voiced, occasional gestures of two or three notes and sometimes a longer sliding sound – using vibrato bar). I took that, and the instrument, as given. But I also just went ahead and made my own piece, with things that I do in it – something coming out of a tune, with counterpoint ('counterpoint sucks' – allegedly said by M.F.), a stretch of tablature which fixed rhythms but not pitches except those on open strings, rhythmic cycling on grids, etc. And I tried to make a piece that I thought Feldman would have liked.

How do I 'move from an initial idea to the finished piece'? I don't really, insofar as I have no notion of the finished piece when I start, nor, from the viewpoint of performance, even when the writing is finished. I proceed by fits and starts (I'm now working on a piano piece that I was asked to make very long – it's provisionally called *Stabs in the Dark*[1]). Trial and error – with quite a bit of the latter (lots of what's written gets thrown out). This is the part – how the overall form is constituted – that's really hard to account for. Where unreasonable hope (that it will work) comes in. Though it's also here, I think, that real experiment is still possible. A request or commission often suggests an overall timing – the approximate total space. With that I think about the instruments available and their players (I usually know who they'll be the first time), and possibly the performing situation if I know about it. Also practical matters: how much time do I have before the deadline? These are points of reference. I might misjudge them – pieces can take on a life of their own.

In general, and I know this isn't a very satisfactory answer, I proceed with some intuition and some judgement, not really knowing where one starts and the other leaves off. Other points of reference: inventiveness, and surprise (for myself to start with), at least the illusion that I'm not just repeating myself. Problems are useful too – something you've never had to do before (the long piano piece) and difficult situations, possibly produced by some system (fugues and canons have played this

---

1   This became the hour-long *Long Piano (Peace March 11)* (2004–2005).

role), requiring ingenuity to deal with, possibly to take you somewhere you hadn't thought of going.

In a way the old Marxists had the best notion of art: it should serve the people. But the art also has to be for real at its point of origin and production. Intuition and judgement have to be individual, for everybody. Also at the moment I'm better able to think of 'people' than 'the people'.

There's an openness to a lot of your work which is inviting to performers who might not have been musically trained (or at least are not members of a 'professional' ensemble), and you commented on your own involvement in your music with 'limited playing skills'. Is the involvement of non-specialist performers still something which is important to you, and how has your work as a performer informed your work as a composer? How do you approach pieces where this might be a factor (whether explicitly from the outset, or as a potential resultant)?

Yes, the involvement with 'alternative' musicians, non-specialists, student musicians and the like is still welcome – I'm doing a workshop at the Ecole des Beaux Arts in Paris next week for just such people, which I'm looking forward to. It's true that the material for that workshop will be mostly older – the late 60s and early 70s produced a lot of pieces for use by such musicians and non-musicians. But material does get added on – composers from the Wandelweiser group which started up I think in the later 80s (Beuger, Frey and Heuben are the ones whose work I know) make pieces that often don't require professionals to play them. I make the occasional such piece for particular occasions. That kind of activity seems to me to be happening now more in the context of improvisation. I see performers, who are not composers, taking up improvisation, and groups which may include non-professionals or non-musicians, alongside what are now really professional improvising musicians.

Working as a performer, both straight – from scores (albeit only such as are playable by me and (or) indeterminate ones) – and improvising, mostly affects my composing negatively, that is, when I write I try to do things that I wouldn't do as a performer. Or I should say that I couldn't do as a performer (I'm thinking primarily of improvisation). Of course doing the contingent scores I find out first-hand some of what's practical or not. I get a clearer sense of what's easier and harder to do. Which may affect how at some later time I might write something, not necessarily to the exclusion of quite difficult things. Mostly I think of playing and writing as quite different and separate. Of course writing for myself – keyboard music or melodica – I have to keep in mind my (considerable) technical limits as player.

Looking back at the first question, on 'contingent processes', I realize that I assumed by that term you meant contingent with respect to the relation of score to performer(s). Which you may well have. If, though, you also meant having to do with chance procedures in the process of composition, I thought I'd just add something. Cage of course did this, in a highly systematic way, first with *Music of Changes* (1951). I did it, about the same time, more casually and occasionally – in *For Prepared Piano* (1951), for instance, by laying out a piece as a square of measures (five by five I think) and writing, freely, the music down the first row of measures, then up the next and then down and so forth. The music was presented to be played in the usual way across from left to right, but that continuity was not the one I composed, or was at one remove, somewhat out of my immediate control. In connection with working procedures I mentioned working in such a way that I couldn't quite foresee results, or both could and could not. That's where that started. Another notion about contingent procedures, both in the process of composing and in the relation of score to performer(s): I believe they allow the possibility of a salutary kind of detachment, or a focus on each moment and sound without too much anxiety about being expressive (or making continuities along straight lines, or narrative – beginning, middle and end, climaxes, etc.). Another way to put it: avoiding a feeling of wilfulness, of self-assertion. This is by no means to exclude the possibility of expressiveness in the music or forceful and striking moments in it, but I'd like these to be a kind of surprising resultant of going about one's musical business. I'd like the music be free of rhetorical pressure. The listeners shouldn't be pushed around. They should be allowed to find their own ways.

The interview was conducted by email between 22 November 2004 and 15 April 2005.

Bibliography

Adams, John D.S. and Gray, D'Arcy Philip (eds), *The David Tudor Pages*, http://www.emf.org/tudor.

Atkinson, Simon and Landy, Leigh, *EARS: ElectroAcoustic Resources Site*, http://www.mti.dmu.ac.uk/EARS/.

Attali, Jacques, *Noise: The Political Economy of Music* (Minneapolis: University of Minnesota Press, 1985).

Aufermann, Knut, 'Feedback and Music: You Provide the Noise, the Order Comes By Itself', *Kybernetes: The International Journal of Systems and Cybernetics*, 34/3–4 (2005): 490-96.

Augoyard, Jean-François, *Step by Step: Everyday Walks in a French Urban Housing Project*, trans. D.A. Curtis (Minneapolis: University of Minnesota Press, 2007).

Augoyard, Jean-François and Torgue, Henry (eds), *Sonic Experience: A Guide to Everyday Sounds*, (Montreal: McGill-Queen's University Press, 2005).

Austin, Larry, 'David Tudor and Larry Austin: A Conversation (April 3, 1989, Denton, Texas)', *The David Tudor Pages*, http://www.emf.org/tudor/Articles/austin.html.

Badiou, Alain, *Being and Event*, trans. Oliver Feltham (London: Continuum, 2006).

Bailey, Derek, *Improvisation: Its Nature and Practice in Music* (Ashbourne, Derbyshire: Moorland Publishing, 1980; 2nd edn, New York and London: Da Capo, 1992).

Batchelor, David, *Minimalism* (London: Tate Gallery Publishing, 2001).

Benjamin, Walter, *The Arcades Project*, trans. Howard Eiland and Kevin McLaughlin, prepared on the basis of the German volume ed. Roy Tiedemann (Cambridge, Mass. and London: The Belknap Press of Harvard University Press, 2002).

Benjamin, Walter, *Charles Baudelaire* (New York and London: Verso, 1997).

Bentos, Pentos Fray, 'Feedback at the limits of precise control', *Resonance Magazine*, 9/2 (2002): 30–32.

Berio, Luciano, *Two Interviews with Rossana Dalmonte and Bálint András Varga*, trans. and ed. David Osmond-Smith (New York: Marion Boyars, 1985).

Beuger, Antoine, 'Grundsätzliche Entscheidungen', *Edition Wandelweiser*, http://www.wandelweiser.de/beuger/ABTexte.html.

Blesser, Barry, and Salter, Linda-Ruth, *Spaces Speak, Are You Listening? Experiencing Aural Architecture* (Cambridge, Mass.: MIT Press, 2007).

Blom, Ina, 'Boredom and Oblivion', in K. Friedman (ed.), *The Fluxus Reader* (New York: Academy Editions, 1998).

Böhme, Gernot, 'Acoustic Atmospheres: A Contribution to the Study of Ecological Aesthetics', trans. Norbert Ruebsaat, *Soundscape* 1/1 (Spring 2000): 14–18.

Bonito Oliva, Achille (ed.), *Ubi fluxus ibi motus 1990–1962* (Milan: Mazzotta, 1990).

Boulez, Pierre, *Boulez on Music Today*, trans. Susan Bradshaw and Richard Rodney Bennett (London: Faber and Faber, 1971).

Boulez, Pierre, *Orientations*, ed. Jean-Jacques Nattiez, trans. Martin Cooper (London: Faber and Faber, 1986).

Bourriaud, Nicolas, *Relational Aesthetics* (Paris, 2002).

Boros, James and Toop, Richard, *Brian Ferneyhough: Collected Writings* (Amsterdam: Harwood Academic Press, 1995).

Bowers, John and Archer, Phil, 'Not Hyper, not Meta, not Cyber but Infra-instruments', *NIME 2005 Proceedings* (Vancouver, 2005), pp. 5–10.

Bowers, John and Villar, Nicolas, 'Creating Ad Hoc Instruments with Pin&Play&Perform', *NIME 2006 Proceedings* (Paris, 2006), pp. 234–9.

Brecht, George, 'The Origins of Events', in Julia Robinson and Alfred M. Fischer (eds), *George Brecht – Events – A Heterospective* (Köln: Walther König, 2006), p. 236.

Bruggen, Coosje van, *Bruce Nauman* (New York: Rizzoli International Publications, 1988).

Bryars, Gavin, '"Vexations" and its Performers', *Contact*, 25 (Autumn 1983): 12–20.

Buck-Morss, Susan, 'The Flaneur, the Sandwichman and the Whore: The Politics of Loitering', *New German Critique*, No. 39, Second Special Issue on Walter Benjamin (Autumn, 1986): 99–140.

Bull, Michael and Back, Les (eds), *The Auditory Culture Reader* (Oxford: Berg, 2003).

Burns, Christopher and Burtner, Matthew, 'Recursive Audio Systems: Acoustic Feedback in Composition', *Leonardo Music Journal*, 13 (2003), Leonardo Electronic Almanac, http://www.mitpressjournals.org/doi/pdfplus/10.1162/096112104322750827 (accessed 10 January 2004).

Busoni, Ferruccio, *Entwurf einer neuen Ästhetik der Tonkunst* (Leipzig, 1911).

Caesar, Rodolfo, *The Composition of Electroacoustic Music*, PhD Thesis (University of East Anglia, 1992).

Cage, John, *For the Birds* (London: Marion Boyars, 1995).

Cage, John, *M: Writings '67–'72* (Middleton, Conn: Wesleyan University Press, 1973).

Cage, John, *Silence: Lectures & Writings* (Middleton, Conn.: Wesleyan University Press, 1961; London: Marion Boyars, 1978, 1980).

Cage, John, *A Year from Monday: Lectures & Writings* (London: Marion Boyars, 1968).

Cage, John and Feldman, Morton, 'John Cage and Morton Feldman in Conversation, pt 2, at 9.50, available at http://www.radiom.org.

Cage, John and Feldman, Morton, *Radio Happenings I–V*, trans. Gisela Gronemeyer (Köln: MusikTexte, 1993).

Cage, John and Knowles, Alison (eds), *Notations* (New York: Something Else Press, 1969).

Cage, John, Shattuck, Roger and Gillmor, Alan, 'Erik Satie: A Conversation' in *Contact*, 25 (Autumn 1982): 21–6.

Cardew, Cornelius, 'Report on Stockhausen's "Carré"', *The Musical Times*, 102/1424 (October 1961): 619–22. Reprinted in Edwin Prévost (ed.), *Cornelius Cardew (1936–1981): A Reader* (Matching Tye, Essex: Copula, 2006).

Cardew, Cornelius (ed.), *Scratch Music* (London: Latimer New Dimensions, 1972).

Cardew, Cornelius, *Stockhausen Serves Imperialism* (Latimer, London, 1974).

Cardew, Cornelius, 'Towards an Ethic of Improvisation', in *Treatise Handbook* (London, 1971). Reprinted in Edwin Prévost (ed.), *Cornelius Cardew (1936-1981): A Reader* (Matching Tye, Essex: Copula, 2006).

Cardew, Corneilus, *Treatise Handbook* (London, 1971), reprinted in Edwin Prévost (ed.), *Cornelius Cardew (1936–1981): A Reader* (Matching Tye, Essex: Copula, 2006).

Cardiff, Janet, *The Walk Book* (Vienna: Thyssen-Bornemisza Art Company and Cologne, 2005).

Chadabe, Joel, *Electric Sound: The Past and Promise of Electronic Music* (Englewood Cliffs, NJ: Prentice Hall, 1997).

Charles, Xavier, 'What Are You Doing With Your Music?', in Brian Marley and Mark Wastell (eds), *Blocks of Consciousness and the Unbroken Continuum* (London: Sound 323 Press, 2005), pp. 88–9.

Chion, Michel, *Audio-Vision: Sound on Screen* (New York: Columbia University Press, 1994).

Clark, Philip, 'Between Thought and Expression', *The Wire*, 289 (2008): 28–32.

Clarke, Eric, Cook, Nicholas, Harrison, Bryn and Thomas, Philip, 'Interpretation and Performance in Bryn Harrison's *être temps*', *Musicae Scienitae*, 9 (2005): 31–74.

Collins, Nicholas (ed.), 'My Favorite Things: The Joy of the Gizmo', *Leonardo Music Journal*, 17 (2007).

Cook, Nicholas, *A Guide to Musical Analysis* (Oxford: Oxford University Press, 1994).

Coomaraswamy, Ananda, *The Transformation of Nature in Art* (New York: Dover, 1956).

Corner, Philip, *I Can Walk Through the World as Music (first walk)* (New York: Printed Editions, 1980).

Coupe, Laurence (ed.), *The Green Studies Reader: From Romanticism to Ecocriticism* (London and New York: Routledge, 2000).

Cox, Christoph and Warner, David (eds), *Audio Culture: Readings in Modern Music* (New York: Continuum, 2006).

Crimp, Douglas, *On the Museum's Ruins* (Cambridge, Mass.: MIT Press, 1993).

Cross, Lowell, 'The Stirrer', *Source: music of the avant garde*, No. 4 (1968): 25–8.

Cutler, Chris, 'Thoughts on Music and the Avant Garde', in Chris Culter, Hanns-Werner Heister, Wolfgang Martin Stroh and Peter Wicke (eds), *Musik-Avantgarde. Zur Dialetik von Vorhut und Nachhut* (Oldenburg: BIS Verlag, 2006), pp. 52–73.

Davies, Hugh, 'Electronic instruments, IV, 6, iii: Electronic oscillators', *Grove Music Online*, http://www.grovemusic.com/shared/views/article.html?section=music.08694.4.6.

Davies, Hugh, *Sounds Heard* (Chelmsford: Soundworld, 2002).

De Certeau, Michel, *The Practice of Everyday Life* (Berkeley: University of California Press, 1988).

Deflem, Mathieu, 'Ritual, Anti-Structure, and Religion: A Discussion of Victor Turner's Processual Symbolic Analysis', *Journal for the Scientific Study of Religion*, 30/1 (1991): 1–25.

Deleuze, Gilles, *Essays Critical and Clinical*, trans. Daniel W. Smith and Michael A. Greco (Minneapolis: University of Minnesota Press, 1997).

Deleuze, Gilles, *Spinoza: Practical Philosophy*, trans. Robert Hurley (San Francisco: City Lights Books, 1988).

DeNora, Tia, *Music in Everyday Life* (Cambridge: Cambridge University Press, 2000).

Derrida, Jacques, *The Truth in Painting*, trans. G. Bennington and I. McLeod (Chicago: University of Chicago Press, 1987).

Dickinson, Peter (ed.), *Cage Talk: Dialogues with and about John Cage* (New York: University of Rochester Press, 2006).

Di Scipio, Agostino, 'Compositional Models in Xenakis's Electroacoustic Music', *Perspectives of New Music*, 36/2 (Summer, 1998): 201–43.

Eco, Umberto, *The Open Work*, trans. Anna Cancogni (London: Hutchison Radius, 1989).

Feldman, Morton, *Essays*, ed. Walter Zimmermann (Cologne: Beginner Press, 1985).

Feldman, Morton, *Give My Regards to Eighth Street: Collected Writings of Morton Feldman*, ed. B.H. Friedman (Cambridge, Mass.: Exact Change, 2000).

Fetterman, William, *John Cage's Theatre Pieces: Notations and Performances* (Amsterdam: Harwood Academic Publishers, 1996).

Fischer, Tobias, 'Gradual Changes: The Gruenrekorder Label', in Angus Carlyle (ed.), *Autumn Leaves: Sound and the Environment in Artistic Practice* (Paris: Double Entendre, 2007), pp. 115–16.

Flynt, Henry, 'Cage and Fluxus', in Richard Kostelanetz (ed.), *Writings about John Cage* (Ann Arbor: University of Michigan Press, 1993).

Ford, Andrew, *Composer to Composer: Conversations About Contemporary Music* (London: Quartet, 1993).

Fox, Christopher, 'Après Einstein: la succession minimaliste', *Contrechamps*, 6 (1986): 172–85.

Fox, Christopher, 'Cage – Eckhardt – Zimmermann', *Tempo*, 159 (1986): 9–15.

Fox, Christopher, 'Music as a Social Process: Some Aspects of the Work of Christian Wolff', *Contact*, 30 (1987): 6–14.

Fox, Christopher, 'Walter Zimmermann's Local Experiments', *Contact*, 27 (1983): 4-9.

Fried, Michael, *Art and Objecthood* (Chicago: University of Chicago Press, 1998).

Friedman, Ken (ed.), *The Fluxus Reader* (Chichester: Academy Editions, 1998).

Friedman, Ken, Smith, Owen and Sawchyn, Lauren, *Fluxus Performance Workbook*, supplement to *Performance Research*, 7/3 'On Fluxus' (2002).

Fulleman, John, 'An Interview with David Tudor, Stockholm May 31 1984', *The David Tudor Pages*, http://www.emf.org/tudor/Articles/fullemann.html.

Furlong, William, *Audio Arts: Discourse and Practice in Contemporary Art* (London: Academy Editions, 1994).

Gablik, Suzi, 'Minimalism', in Nikos Stangos (ed.), *Concepts of Modern Art* (London: Thames & Hudson, 1991), pp. 244–55.

Gagne, Cole and Caras, Tracy, *Soundpieces: Interviews with American Composers* (Metuchen, NJ: Scarecrow Press, 1982).

Gillespie, Brent, 'Haptics', in Perry Cook (ed.), *Music Cognition and Computerized Sound: An Introduction to Psychoacoustics* (Cambridge, Mass.: MIT Press, 1999).

Gorbman, Claudia, 'Narrative Film Music', in Rick Altman (ed.), *Cinema/Sound*, Yale French Studies, No. 60 (1980): 183–203.

Gray, D'Arcy Philip, 'David Tudor in the Late 1980's: Understanding a Secret Voice', *Leonardo Music Journal*, 14 (2004): 41–7.

Greenberg, Clement, 'Counter Avant-garde', in Robert C. Morgan (ed.), *Clement Greenberg: Late Writings* (Minneapolis: University of Minnesota Press, 2003), pp. 5–18.

Greenberg, Clement, 'Intermedia', in Robert C. Morgan (ed.), *Clement Greenberg: Late Writings* (Minneapolis: University of Minnesota Press, 2003), pp. 93–8.

Greenberg, Clement, 'Toward a Newer Laocoon' in Francis Frascina (ed.), *After Pollock* (London: Harpers and Row, 1985), pp. 35–46.

Griffiths, Paul, *Modern Music and After* (Oxford: Oxford University Press, 1995).

Halbreich, Harry, 'Müde Helden, neue Hoffnung', *Algorithmus, Klang, Natur: Abkehr von Materialdenken? Darmstädter Beiträge zur neue Musik*, 19 (1984): 56–9.

Halliwell, Graham, 'What Are You Doing With Your Music?', in Brian Marley and Mark Wastell (eds), *Blocks of Consciousness and the Unbroken Continuum* (London: Sound 323 Press, 2005): 52–3.

Hamilton, Andy, *Aesthetics and Music* (London: Continuum, 2007).

Harvey, Jonathan, *The Music of Stockhausen: An Introduction* (Berkeley: University of California Press, 1974)

Hendricks, Geoffrey, *Critical Mass: Happenings, Fluxus, Performance, Intermedia, and Rutgers University, 1958–1972* (Piscataway, NJ: Rutgers University Press, 2003).

Hendricks, Jon, *Fluxus Codex* (New York: Harry N. Abrams, 1988).

Henze, Hans Werne, *Music and Politics: Collected Writngs 1953–81* (London: Faber and Faber; Ithaca: Cornell University Press, 1982).

Hollier, Denis, 'The Death of Paper, Part Two: Artaud's Sound System', *October*, 80 (Spring 1997): 27–37.

Holzaepfel, John, *David Tudor and the Performance of American Experimental Music, 1950–1959* (CUNY Graduate Center, 1994).

Howes, David (ed.), *The Empire of the Senses: The Sensual Cultural Reader* (Oxford: Berg, 2005).

Hultberg, Teddy, '"I smile when the sound is singing through the space": An Interview with David Tudor by Teddy Hultberg in Düsseldorf May 17, 18 1988, available at http://www.emf.org/tudor/Articles/hultberg.html.

Hutcheon, Linda, *The Politics of Postmodernism* (London: Routledge, 1989).

Ihde, Don, *Listening and Voice: A Phenomenology of Sound* (Athens, OH: Ohio University Press, 1976).

Johnston, Jill, 'John Cage: Music for Museums', *Art in America* (January 1994).

Jordà, Sergi, 'Digital Instruments and Players: Part 1 – Diversity, Freedom and Control', *NIME 2004 Proceedings* (Hamamatsu, 2004), pp. 59–63.

Joseph, Branden W., *Beyond the Dream Syndicate: Tony Conrad and the Arts After Cage* (Cambridge Mass.: MIT Press, 2008).

Jung, Carl G. *Memories, Dreams, Reflections*, ed. Aniela Jaffe (London: Vintage 1963).

Kahn, Douglas, 'Audio Art in the Deaf Century', in Dan Lander and Micah Lexier (eds), *Sound by Artists* (Toronto: Art Metropole/Walter Phillips Gallery 1990), pp. 301–24.

Kahn, Douglas, 'John Cage: Silence and Silencing', *The Musical Quarterly*, 81/4 (Winter 1997): 556–98.

Kahn, Douglas, *Noise, Water, Meat: A History of Sound in the Arts* (Cambridge, Mass.: MIT Press, 1999).

Kanno, Mieko, 'Prescriptive Notation: Limits and Challenges', *Contemporary Music Review*, 26/2 (2007): 231–54.

Kaprow, Allan, *Essays on the Blurring of Art and Life* (Berkeley: University of California Press, 2003).

Kaye, Nick, *Site-Specific Art: Performance, Place and Documentation* (London: Routledge, 2000).

Kostelanetz, Richard, *Conversing with Cage* (London: Omnibus Press, 1989).

Kostelanetz, Richard (ed.), *Writings on Glass* (New York, 1997).

Kotz, Liz, 'Post-Cagean Aesthetics and the "Event" Score', *October*, 95 (Winter 2001): 55–89.

Kramer, Jonathan D., *The Time of Music* (New York: Schirmer Books, 1988).

Kraynak, Janet (ed.), *Please Pay Attention: Bruce Nauman's Words: Writings and Interviews* (Cambridge, Mass.: MIT Press, 2003).

LaBelle, Brandon, *Background Noise: Perspective on Sound Art* (London: Continuum, 2006).

Lazar, Julie, 'Nothingtoseeness', in *John Cage Rolywholyover, A Circus* (New York, 1994), unpaginated.

Lefebvre, Henri, *Critique of Everyday Life: Volume 1*, trans. John Moore (London: Verso, 1991).

Leibniz, Gottfried Wilhelm, *The Monadology and Other Philosophical Writings*, trans. Robert Latta (London: Oxford University Press, 1971).

Licht, Alan, *Sound Art: Beyond Music, Between Categories* (New York: Rizzoli, 2007).

Lockwood, Annea, *A Sound Map of the Hudson River* (New York: Lovely Music, 1989).

Lucier, Alvin, *Reflections* (Cologne: MusikTexte, 1995).

Lyotard, Jean-François, 'Critical Reflections', *Artforum* (April 1991): 92–3.

Lyotard, Jean-François, *Postmodern Fables*, trans. Georges van den Abbeele (Minneapolis: University of Minnesota Press, 1997).

Maconie, Robin (ed.), *Stockhausen on Music: Lectures & Interviews* (London: Marion Boyars, 2000).

Maconie, Robin, *The Works of Karlheinz Stockhausen* (Oxford: Oxford University Press, 1976).

Mahnkopf, Claus-Steffen and Veale, Peter, *The Techniques of Oboe Playing: A Compendium with Additional Remarks on the Whole Oboe Family* (Kassel: Barenreiter, 1998).

Mallarmé, Stephane, *Un coup de dés* (Paris: Gallimard, 2003).

Marcuse, Herbert, *One-Dimensional Man* (London: Beacon Press, 1991).

Marley, Brian and Wastell, Mark (eds), *Blocks of Consciousness and the Unbroken Continuum* (London: Sound 323 Press, 2005).

Matossian, Nouritza, *Xenakis* (London: Kahn & Averill, 1985).

Mertens, Wim, *American Minimal Music*, trans. Jan Hautekiet (London: Kahn & Averill, 1983).

Moholy-Nagy, Laszlo, *Visions in Motion* (Chicago: Institute of Design, 1947).

Möller, Torsten, Stäbler, Gerhard and Shim, Kunsu (eds), *SoundVisions* (Saarbrücken: PFAU, 2005).

Moore, Jerrold Northrop, *Spirit of England: Edward Elgar in his World* (London: Heinemann, 1984).

Morris, Adalaide (ed.) *Sound States: Innovative Poetics and Acoustical Technologies* (Chapel Hill: University of North Carolina Press, 1997).

Morris, Robert, 'Size Matters', *Critical Inquiry*, 26 (2000): 474–87.

Nauman, Bruce, *Image/Text 1966–1996* (Wolfsburg: Kunstmuseum Wolfsburg; Ostfildern: Hatje Cantz Verlag, 1997).

Neuhaus, Max, 'Listen', in Dan Lander and Micah Lexier (eds), *Sound by Artists* (Toronto: Art Metropole/Walter Philips Gallery 1990).

Neuhaus, Max, *Max Neuhaus: Inscription, Sound Works Volume 1* (Ostfildern: Hatje Cantz Verlag, 1994).

Neuhoff, John G., *Ecological Psychoacoustics* (London: Elsevier Academic Press, 2004).

Nevile, Ben, 'An interview with Kim Cascone', *Cycling '74*, http://www.cycling74.com/community/cascone.html (accessed 12 December 2007).

Nicolaus, Christoph and Inderhees, Carlo, *garonne (24) für sich*, documentation (Berlin, 1998).

Norman, Katherine, *Sounding Art: Eight Literacy Excursions through Electronic Music* (Aldershot: Ashgate, 2004).

Nyman, Michael, *Experimental Music: Cage and Beyond* (Cambridge: Cambridge University Press, 1999; first published London, 1974).

Oliveros, Pauline, *Deep Listening: A Composer's Sound Practice* (Lincoln, Nebr.: iUniverse, 2005).

Ono, Yoko, *Grapefruit* (New York: Simon & Schuster, 2000).

Orledge, Robert, *Satie the Composer* (Cambridge: Cambridge University Press, 1990).

Orledge, Robert, *Satie Remembered* (London: Faber and Faber, 1995).

Pace, Ian, 'Northern Light', *The Musical Times*, 139/1863 (Summer 1998): 33–44.

Paetzhold, Heinz, 'Adorno's Notion of Natural Beauty: A Reconsideration', in Tom Huhn and Lambert Zuidervaart (eds), *The Semblance of Subjectivity: Essays in Adorno's Aesthetic Theory* (Cambridge, Mass.: MIT Press, 1997), pp. 213–35.

Parsons, Michael, 'The Scratch Orchestra and Visual Arts', *Leonardo Music Journal*, 11 (2001): 5–11.

Parsons, Michael and Tilbury, John, 'The Contemporary Pianist', *The Musical Times*, 110/1512 (1969): 150–52.

Patterson, Lee, 'What Are You Doing With Your Music?', in Brian Marley and Mark Wastell (eds), *Blocks of Consciousness and the Unbroken Continuum* (London: Sound 323 Press, 2005), pp. 120–35.

Potter, Keith, 'Experimental Music: Cage and Beyond', *Contact*, 10 (1975): 39.

Pressing, Jeff, 'Cybernetic Issues in Interactive Performance Systems, *Computer Music Journal*, 14/1 (1990): 12–25.

Pressing, Jeff, 'Improvisation: Methods and Models', in John Sloboda (ed.), *Generative Processes in Music* (Oxford: Oxford University Press, 1987), pp. 129–78.

Pressing, Jeff, 'Psychological Constraints on Improvisational Expertise and Communication', in Bruno Nettl and Melinda Russell (eds), *In the Course of Performance: Studies in the World of Musical Improvisation* (Chicago: University of Chicago Press, 1998), pp. 47–67.

Prévost, Edwin, *Minute Particulars* (Matching Tye, Essex: Copula, 2004).

Prévost, Edwin, *No Sound is Innocent* (Matching Tye, Essex: Copula, 1995).

Pritchett, James, *David Tudor's Realization of John Cage's Variations II*, http://www.rosewhitemusic.com/cage/texts/Var2.html.

Pritchett, James, *The Music of John Cage* (Cambridge: Cambridge University Press, 1993).

Rainer, Yvonne, 'A Quasi Survey of Some "Minimalist" Tendencies in the Quantitatively Minimal Dance Activity Midst the Plethora, or an Analysis of Trio A', in Michael Huxley and Noel Witts (eds), *The Twentieth-Century Performance Reader*, 2nd edn (London: Routledge, 2002), pp. 327–34.

Raschèr, Sigurd M., *Top Tones for Saxophone*, 3rd edn (New York: Carl Fischer Music, 1994).

Rée, Jonathan, *I See a Voice: A Philosophical History* (London: Flamingo, 1999).

Revill, David, *The Roaring Silence: John Cage: A Life* (London: Bloomsbury, 1992).

Richards, John, '32Kg: Performance Systems for a Post-digital Age', *NIME 2006 Proceedings* (Paris, 2006), pp. 283–7.

Riley, Bridget, *The Eye's Mind* (London: Thames & Hudson, 1999).

Robert Morris, 'Size Matters', *Critical Inquiry*, 26 (2000): 474–87.

Rosenberg, Harold, 'The American Action Painters' (1952), reprinted in David and Cecile Shapiro (eds), *Abstract Expressionism – A Critical Record* (New York: Cambridge University Press, 1990).

Russell, Bertrand, *History of Western Philosophy* (London: Routledge, 1991).

Ryan, David, 'Y a-t-il une "école new-yorkaise"? – Entretien avec Earle Brown', *Dissonanz*, 52 (May 1997): 14–19.

Ryan, David 'ZEITMASCHINEN: Die englischen Komponisten Bryn Harrison, Tim Parkinson und James Saunders', *Dissonanz*, #82 (August 2003).

Sacks, Oliver, *Musicophilia: Tales of Music and the Brain* (London: Picador, 2007).

Sandler, Irving, 'The Club', in David and Cecile Shapiro (eds), *Abstract Expressionism – A Critical Record* (New York: Cambridge University Press, 1990).

Sandler, Irving, *The New York School* (New York: Harper and Row 1978).

Sarraute, Nathalie, *Tropismes* (Paris, 1957).

Sauer, Theresa (ed.) *Notations 21* (New York: Mark Batty, 2009).

Schaeffer, Pierre 'Typo-morphology' (1998, originally 1967).

Schaeffer, Pierre, 'Acousmatics', in Christoph Cox and Daniel Warner (eds), *Audio Culture: Readings in Modern Music* (New York: Continnum, 2004), pp. 76–81.

Schaeffer, Pierre, *Solfege' de l'objet sonore* (Paris, 1998).

Schafer, R. Murray (ed.), *European Sound Diary* (Vancouver: ARC Publications, 1977).

Schafer, R. Murray (ed.), *Five Village Soundscapes* (Vancouver: ARC Publications, 1977).

Schafer, R. Murray, 'The Music of the Environment', in Christoph Cox and Daniel Warner (eds), *Audio Culture: Readings in Modern Music* (London: Continuum, 2004), pp. 29–39.

Schafer, R. Murray (ed.), *The Vancouver Soundscape* (Vancouver: ARC Publications, 1978).

Schafer, R. Murray, *The Soundscape: Our Sonic Environment and the Tuning of the World* (Rochester, Vt.: Destiny Books, 1994; first published as *The Tuning of the World*, 1977).

Schonfeld, Victor and Tudor, David, 'From Piano to Electronics', *Music and Musicians*, xx/12 (1971): 24–6.

Schrader, Barry, *Introduction to Electro-acoustic Music* (Englewood Cliffs, NJ: Prentice Hall, 1982).

Seckerson, Edward, *Mahler* (London: Omnibus Press, 1984).

Serres, Michel, *Genesis*, trans. Geneviève James and James Nielson (Ann Arbor: University of Michigan Press, 1995).

Serres, Michel, *The Parasite*, trans. Lawrence R. Schehr (Minneapolis: University of Minnesota Press, 2007).

Small, Christopher, *Musicking: The Meanings of Performing and Listening* (Middletown, Conn.: Wesleyan University Press, 1998).

Smalley, Dennis, 'Spectro-morphology and Structuring Processes', in Simon Emmerson (ed.), *The Language of Electroacoustic Music* (London: Palgrave Macmillan, 1986).

Smalley, Dennis, 'Spectromorphology: Explaining Sound Shapes', *Organized Sound*, 2/2 (1997): 107–26.

Smith, Geoff and Smith, Nicola Walker, *American Originals: Interviews with 25 Contemporary Composers* (London: Faber and Faber, 1994).

Smith, Hazel and Dean, Roger, *Improvisation, Hypermedia and the Arts since 1945* (Amsterdam: Harwood Academic Press, 1997).

Smithson, Robert, 'Frederick Law Olmsted and the Dialectical Landscape', in Jack Flam (ed.), *Robert Smithson: Collected Writings* (Berkeley: University of California Press, 1996), pp. 157–71.

Solnit, Rebecca, *Wanderlust: A History of Walking* (New York, 2002).
Sterne, Jonathan, *The Audible Past: Cultural Origins of Sound Reproduction* (London: Duke University Press, 2003).
Süskind, Patrick, *Perfume: The Story of a Murderer* (London: Penguin, 1987).
Suzuki, Daisetz Teitaro, *An Introduction to Zen Buddhism* (London: Rider Books, 1991).
Szlavnics, Chiyoko, 'Opening Ears – the Intimacy of the Detail of Sound', *Filigrane*, #4, 'New Sensibilities' (2006).
Tenney, James, 'Postal Pieces', in *Soundings 13* (Soundings Press, Santa Fe, 1984).
Théberge, Paul, *Any Sound You Can Imagine: Making Music/Consuming Technology* (Hanover, NH: Wesleyan University Press, 1997).
Thibaud, Jean-Paul, *La Méthode des parcours commentés*, in Michèle Grosjean and Jean-Paul Thibaud (eds), *L'espace urbain en méthodes* (Marseilles: Parenthèses, 2001).
Thomas, Philip, 'Determining the Indeterminate', *Contemporary Music Review*, 26/2 (2007): 129–40.
Thompson, Emily, *The Soundscape of Modernity: Architectural Acoustics and the Culture of Listening in America, 1900–1933* (Cambridge, Mass.: MIT Press, 2002).
Thoreau, Henry David, *Walden* (Oxford: Oxford University Press, 1924).
Thoreau, Henry David, 'Walking', in Jeffrey Kastner and Brian Wallis (eds), *Land and Environmental Art* (London: Phaidon Press, 1998).
Tomkins, Calvin, *Ahead of the Game: Four versions of Avant-garde* (London: Weidenfeld and Nicolson, 1965).
Toop, David, *Haunted Weather: Music, Silence, and Memory* (London: Serpent's Tail, 2004).
Toop, Richard, 'Four Facets of "The New Complexity"', *Contact*, 32 (1988): 4–50.
Truax, Barry, *Acoustic Communication* (Stamford, Conn.: Ablex Publishing, 2001).
Truax, Barry, *Handbook for Acoustic Ecology* (Vancouver: Cambridge Street Publishing, 1999).
Tsunoda, Toshiya, 'Toshiya Tsunoda', in *Extract: Portraits of Sound Artists* (Vienna: Non Visual Objects, 2007).
Tuan, Yi-Fu, *Space and Place: The Perspective of Experience* (Minneapolis: University of Minnesota Press, 1977).
Tudor, David, Programme note for *Bandoneon!*, David Tudor Papers, Box 16, Folder 2, Getty Research Institute Archive.
Turetzky, Bertram, *The Contemporary Contrabass: The New Instrumentation* (Berkeley: University of California Press, 1974).
Turner, Victor, 'Liminal to Liminoid, in Play, Flow and Ritual', in Edward Norbeck (ed.), *The Anthropological Study of Human Play* (Houston: Rice University Studies, 1974), pp. 53–92.
Volans, Kevin, *Summer Gardeners: Conversations with Composers* (Durban: Newer Music Edition, 1985).
Webber, Mark, 'Looking for Mr Goodbear', *Resonance*, 7/1 (1998): 26–30.
Weinberger, Eliot (ed.), *American Poetry since 1950: Innovators and Outsiders* (New York: Marsilio, 1993).

Westerkamp, Hildegard, 'The Soundscape on Radio', in Daina Augaitis and Dan Lander (eds), *Radio Rethink: Art, Sound and Transmission* (Banff, Alberta: Walter Phillips Gallery, 1994), pp. 87–94.

Westerkamp, Hildegard, 'Soundwalking', in Angus Carlyle (ed.), *Autumn Leaves: Sound and the Environment in Artistic Practice* (Paris: Double Entendre, 2007), pp. 49–54.

Westling, Louise, 'Thoreau's Ambivalence Toward Mother Nature', in Laurence Coupe (ed.), *The Green Studies Reader: From Romanticism to Ecocriticism* (London and New York: Routledge, 2000), pp. 262–6.

White, Robin, 'Interview with John Cage', *View*, 1/1 (1978).

Wishart, Trevor, *On Sonic Art* (Amsterdam: Harwood Academic Press, 1996).

Wolff, Christian, *Cues: Writings and Conversations* (Cologne: MusikTexte, 1998).

Wörner, Karl H., *Stockhausen: Life and Work* (London: Faber and Faber, 1973).

Young, John, 'Sound Morphology and the Articulation of Structure in Electroacoustic Music', *Organized Sound*, 9/1 (2004): 7–14.

Zimmermann, Walter, *Insel Musik* (Cologne: Beginner Press, 1981).

Recordings

AMM, *AMMMUSIC*, Elektra EUK 256 (1966). Later re-released as AMM, *AMMMUSIC*, ReR AMMCD (1989).

Ashley, Robert, *Dust* (Lovely Music, New York) (2000).

Ashley, Robert, *Private Parts (The Record)* (Lovely Music, New York) (1977).

Behrman, David, *Electronic Sound*, Mainstream, MS/5010 (1972).

Berry, Chuck, *Johnny B. Goode*, Chess, 1691 (1958).

Cage, John, *Roaratorio: An Irish Circus on Finnegans Wake*, Mode Records 28/29 (1992).

Cage, John, *Roaratorio*, Wergo WER 6303-2 (1994).

Corner, Philip, *Pieces of (Acoustic) Reality and Ideality*, Alga Marghen, C 2NMN.013 (1997).

Cusack, Peter, *Baikal Ice (Spring 2003)*, ReR Megacorp, ReRPC2 (2004).

Flynn, George, *Wound/Winter Music* (Finnadar Records, New York) (1974).

Fox, Christopher, *You, Us, Me*, Metier, MSV CD92031 (1999).

Kirkegaard, Jacob, *4 Rooms*, Touch, Tone 26 (2006).

Kirkegaard, Jacob, *Eldfjall*, Touch, T33.20 (2005).

Mizutani, Kyoshi, *Bird Songs*, Ground Fault, GF010 (2000).

Mizutani, Kyoshi, *Scenery of The Border: Environment and Folklore of the Tanzawa Mountains*, And/OAR, and22 (2006).

Mizutani, Kyoshi, *Transcend Sideways*, Artware Production, Artware 19 (1997).

Mizutani, Kyoshi, *Waterscape*, e(r)ostate, ErosCD 001 (1997).

Prévost, Edwin, *Entelchy*, Matchless Recordings, MRCD67 (2006).

Thomas, Philip, *Comprovisation*, Bruce's Fingers, 66 (2007).

Tsunoda, Toshiya, *Low Frequency Observed at Maguchi Bay*, Hibari, Hibari 11 (2007).

Tsunoda, Toshiya, *O Respirar Da Paisagem*, Sirr, sirr012 (2003).
Tsunoda, Toshiya, *Pieces of Air*, Lucky Kitchen, LK016 (2001).
Vitiello, Stephen, *Listening to Donald Judd*, Sub Rosa, SR245 (2007).
Watson, Chris, *Weather Report*, Touch, TO:47 (2003).
Westerkamp, Hildegaard, *Transformations*, empreintes DIGITALes, IMED 9631 (1996).

Index

(References to musical examples and illustrations are in **bold**)